# CEYLON
## IN THE
# JUBILEE YEAR

WITH AN ACCOUNT OF THE PROGRESS MADE SINCE 1803,
AND OF THE PRESENT CONDITION OF ITS
AGRICULTURAL AND COMMERCIAL ENTERPRISES;

THE RIGHT HONOURABLE SIR WILLIAM H. GREGORY, K.C.M.G., GOVERNOR OF CEYLON:

ERECTED BY THE INHABITANTS OF THE ISLAND IN COMMEMORATION OF THE MANY BENEFITS CONFERRED BY HIM UPON THE COLONY DURING HIS ADMINISTRATION OF THE GOVERNMENT FROM 1872 TO 1877.

(*See page* 406).

# CEYLON
## IN THE
# JUBILEE YEAR

WITH AN ACCOUNT OF THE PROGRESS MADE SINCE 1803,
AND OF THE PRESENT CONDITION OF ITS
AGRICULTURAL AND COMMERCIAL ENTERPRISES;

**JOHN FERGUSON**

THIRD EDITION

ISBN : 978-93-5324-561-0 (HB)

First Published, London, 1887

Published, 2020

*Published by*

Facsimile Publisher
12 Pragati Market
Ashok Vihar, Ph-2
Delhi-110052
E-mail: books@facsimilepublisher.com

*Printed at:* G. Print Process, Delhi.

**Ceylon in the Juilee Year**

Author: John Ferguson

# CEYLON

## IN THE

# "JUBILEE YEAR."

*WITH AN ACCOUNT OF THE PROGRESS MADE SINCE* 1803, *AND OF THE PRESENT CONDITION OF ITS AGRICULTURAL AND COMMERCIAL ENTERPRISES;*

THE RESOURCES AWAITING DEVELOPMENT BY CAPITALISTS;

AND THE UNEQUALLED ATTRACTIONS OFFERED TO VISITORS.

**WITH MUCH USEFUL STATISTICAL INFORMATION, SPECIALLY PREPARED MAPS, AND NUMEROUS ILLUSTRATIONS.**

BY

JOHN FERGUSON,

*Co-Editor of "Ceylon Observer," "Tropical Agriculturist," "Ceylon Handbook," &c.*
*Life Member of the Ceylon Branch of the Royal Asiatic Society;*
*Honorary Corresponding Secretary of the Royal Colonial Institute.*

"Embassies from regions far remote:
* * * *
From India and the Golden Chersonese,
And utmost Indian Isle TAPROBANE."—MILTON.

THIRD EDITION: REVISED, ENLARGED, AND BROUGHT DOWN TO DATE.

London:
JOHN HADDON AND CO., 3, BOUVERIE STREET.
Colombo:
A. M. & J. FERGUSON.
1887.

TO

THE RIGHT HONOURABLE

SIR WILLIAM H. GREGORY, K.C.M.G.,

WHO WAS GOVERNOR OF THE ISLAND OF CEYLON AND THE

DEPENDENCIES THEREOF FROM 1872 TO 1877;

THIS LITTLE VOLUME IS RESPECTFULLY

**Dedicated,**

IN THIS HER MOST GRACIOUS MAJESTY'S

JUBILEE YEAR;

AS A SLIGHT TESTIMONY TO THE BENEFICENCE

OF HIS ADMINISTRATION IN CONDUCING TO THE

ADVANCEMENT OF CEYLON AND

THE WELL-BEING OF THE COMMUNITY, AND MORE ESPECIALLY IN

PROMOTING GOOD FEELING AND MUTUAL RESPECT

AMONG THE

DIFFERENT CLASSES AND RACES

REPRESENTED IN ITS VARIED POPULATION;

BY HIS OBEDIENT AND HUMBLE SERVANT,

THE AUTHOR.

# PREFACE TO THE THIRD EDITION.

It is necessary to explain that the basis of the following Volume was an account of Ceylon (with accompanying Map) prepared in April, 1883, as a Paper to be read before the members of the Royal Colonial Institute. It was, however, received too late for the day fixed, and accordingly was published in book form, under the title of "Ceylon in 1883," by Messrs. Sampson Low, Marston, Searle, and Rivington. A second edition, under the auspices of the same firm, was issued within a few months of the first, entitled, "Ceylon in 1884."

This latter work has now been out of print for some time, and the author has been frequently urged to arrange for a third issue.

It is appropriate that this revised and considerably enlarged edition should appear in the year of the "Queen's Jubilee," as giving some account of what is the most important, whether in population or wealth, of Her Majesty's Crown Colonies, and bringing the information, so far as it goes, down to the present date. Besides large additions to nearly all the chapters—more especially to those on Social and Legislative Progress, on Agricultural and Planting Industries, and on the future Government of Ceylon—a new chapter has been introduced dealing with the Life, Customs, Caste, and Occupations of the natives. Additions have also been made to the Appendix, more especially in reference to Missions, Caste, the Tea Industry, Statistical Information, and the re-publication of recent letters of Mr. A. M. Ferguson, describing the Pearl Fisheries and ancient Ruins of Ceylon. This edition also includes a second Map, prepared to show the Railway system of the Island, and it contains over a score of additional Illustrations.

Apart from this being a Jubilee volume, it affords gratification to the author that he is enabled to dedicate the present edition to one whom he considers to have been in many respects a model administrator for a Crown Colony—a gentleman who, as Her Majesty's representative, did more to smooth away the angularities peculiar to colonial life in the tropics, and to promote good understanding between the governing and the various ranks, classes, and castes of the governed, than any other living Governor of Ceylon. The author refers to the Right Honourable Sir William H. Gregory, K.C.M.G., who, when he left its shores, did not, like nearly all previous Governors, remove his interests and practically forget the existence of Ceylon, but who, as a private individual, has since devoted capital and time to the development of its resources, while he still retains the deepest personal interest in all that concerns the welfare of the Island and its people.

A full index, which will be found sufficient for ready reference, has been added to the present edition.

In conclusion, the author bespeaks the forbearance of Ceylon readers, considering that he has had no opportunity of seeing the main portion of the proof-sheets in the short time available for the printing and publication of the book many thousands of miles away from his adopted home.

COLOMBO, CEYLON.
*June* 17, 1887.

## CORRIGENDA.

[The fact that the author was unable to see the greater portion of the pages when passing through the press will account for the number of corrections noted here.]

*Page* 2, *last line but one*, for "C.E.I." after Mr. Burrows' name, substitute "C.C.S." (Ceylon Civil Service).

*Page* 3, *sixth line from bottom*, for "all was" at end of line, substitute "everything was."

*Page* 4, *at end of second paragraph*, after "Tyre," read "of Eastern and Southern Asia."

*Page* 5, *fourth line from top*, for "Kopok" read "Kapok."

*Page* 10, *in table, opposite "Military-Imperial Share*," substitute "£160,000" for "£80,000." The word "nil" should appear under "1796–1815," opposite "Post Office Savings Banks," "Exchange and Deposit Bank Offices," "Volume of business," "Government note issue," "No. of newspapers despatched."

*Page* 12, *under engraving*, for "Mahavelligang*e*, at Gangaru*n*a," read "Mahavelligang*a*, at Gangaru*w*a."

*Page* 24, *under engraving*, for "Topa*v*i" read "Topa*r*i."

*Page* 34, *seventh line from top*, for "Stuart" read "Ste*w*art" Mackenzie.

*Page* 45, *last line after* "60,000 Sinhalese" add "and Tamils."

*Page* 46, *eleventh line from top*, for "*Z*odi-ella" read "*Y*odi-ella."

*Page* 49, *sixteenth line from top*, for "villages" substitute "districts."

*Page* 51, the paper, referred to in the first note to this page, on the "coconut" has not yet been read before the Asiatic Society.

*Page* 54, *fifth line from top*, for "umbracolifera" read "umbrac*u*lifera."

*Page* 55, *first line*, for "pap*ua*s" read "papa*w*s."

*Page* 59, *second paragraph*. It has been shown by Dr. Trimen, of the Royal Botanic Garden, since this was written, that there is no reliable evidence of the Arabs having introduced coffee into India and Ceylon, and it is more probable that the seed was first brought to the island by the Dutch towards the end of the seventeenth century.

*Page* 68, *in sub-heading*, read "cacao" for "cocoa."

*Page* 72, *ninth line*, for "directed" read "diverted."

*Page* 82, *fourth line*, for "no attentive aid," read "no attention."

*Page* 94, *nineteenth line*, for "forming," read "and have formed."

*Page* 121, *last line*, for "Trime*r*" read "Trime*n*."

*Page* 123, *first line*, delete comma after "Cycas"; delete "a" in "cocoanut" in seventh, ninth, and eleventh lines.

*Page* 129, *note*, see Mr. A. M. Ferguson's "Letters from Anurádhapura" in appendix.

*Page* 130, *second note*, see Letters by A. M. Ferguson from "Pearl Fishery of 1887" in appendix.

*Page* 132, *eleventh line from bottom*, for "Ca*r*ropus" read "Ca*n*opus."

*Page* 169, *last line*, for Appendix "VII." read "VIII."

*Page* 257. *Add to the List of Benefactors*—T. E. B. Skinner, Ceylon Civil Service, for his work in improving the Postal and Telegraphic Service of the Colony.

# CONTENTS.

## CHAPTER I.

### PAST HISTORY.



## CHAPTER II.

### THE ISLAND IN 1796–1815, AND SEVENTY YEARS LATER.



## CHAPTER III.

### SOCIAL PROGRESS IN NINETY YEARS.

## CHAPTER IV.



## CHAPTER V.



## CHAPTER VI.



## CHAPTER VII.



## CHAPTER VIII.

## CHAPTER IX.



## CHAPTER X.



## CHAPTER XI.



## CHAPTER XII.

## CHAPTER XIII.



## CHAPTER XIV.



## CHAPTER XV.



## CHAPTER XVI.

## APPENDICES.

---

FOR GENERAL INDEX SEE PAGE 417.

# LIST OF ILLUSTRATIONS.

## NOTE.

Most of the Ceylon photographs from which the engravings were made for this volume were taken by Messrs. W. L. H. Skeen and Co., Colombo; but those of the Ceara rubber-tree (page 83) and of the Liberian coffee (page 104) were by Mr. C. T. Scowen, photographer, Kandy and Colombo, Ceylon. For the engraving of Cinchona on page 71 the author is indebted to Messrs. Howard and Sons. A few of the engravings added in this edition are from the "Souvenirs of Ceylon," by A. M. Ferguson, 1870. Acknowledgment is made on page 62 to the Rev. S. Langdon and his publisher for the use of four engravings. And we have further to express our obligation to Messrs. Taylor and Francis for the loan of the engravings illustrative of the Paper on the Shadow of Adam's Peak, page 315.

Hon. F. North, Earl of Guilford.

General Sir Robert Brownrigg.

Lieut.-General Sir Edward Barnes

Sir Robert Wilmot Horton.

Right Hon. J. A. Stewart Mackenzie.

Sir James Emerson Tennent.

Sir Henry George Ward.

Major-General Henry Lockyer.

Sir Charles J. MacCarthy.

Major-General T. O'Brien.

Sir Hercules G. R. Robinson.

Lieut.-General S. J. Hodgson.

Rt. Hon. Sir W. H. Gregory.

Sir J. R. Longden.

Sir Arthur H. Gordon.

**SOME OF THE BRITISH GOVERNORS OF CEYLON.**

(*For complete list see Appendix V., page* 252.)

# Ceylon in the Jubilee Year.

## CHAPTER I.

### PAST HISTORY.

The Ophir and Tarshish of Solomon—Northern and Southern Indian dynasties—Chinese invasion and connection with the Island in ancient and modern times—Portuguese and Dutch rule—British annexation.

I TAKE it for granted that the readers of this work will have some general acquaintance with the position, history, and condition of Ceylon. It is the largest, most populous, and most important of her Britannic Majesty's Crown Colonies, which are so called because the administration of their affairs is under the direct control of the Colonial Office.

Ceylon has long been

> "Confess'd the best and brightest gem
> In Britain's orient diadem."

There can be no danger now-a-days of a member of Parliament getting up in his place to protest against British troops being stationed in Ceylon on account of the deadly climate of "this part of West Africa," the "utmost Indian isle" being then confounded with *Sierra Leone!*

Known to ancient voyagers as far back as the time of King Solomon (of whose Ophir and Tarshish many believe Ceylon to have formed a part), the story of its beauty, its jewels, and its spices was familiar to the Greeks and Romans, who called it *Taprobane,* and to the Arab traders who first introduced the coffee plant into this island, and who placed in *Serendib* the scene of many of Sindbad's adventures. It was also known to the Mohammedan world at large, who to this day regard the island as the elysium provided for Adam and Eve to console them for the loss of Paradise, a tradition used as a solatium by Arabi and his co-Egyptian exiles a few years ago, when deported from their native land. To the people of India, to the Burmese, Siamese, and Chinese, Lanká, "the resplendent," was equally an object of interest and admiration, so that it has been well said that no island in the world, Great Britain itself not excepted, has attracted the attention of authors in so many different countries as has Ceylon.

There is no land, either, which can tell so much of its past history, not merely in songs and legends, but in records which have been verified by monuments, inscriptions, and coins; some of the structures in and around the ancient capitals of the Sinhalese are more than 2,000 years old, and only second to those of Egypt in vastness of extent and architectural interest.* Between 543 B.C., when Wijaya, a prince from Northern India, is said to have invaded Ceylon, conquered its native rulers, and made himself king, and the end of the year 1815, when the last king of Kandy, a cruel monster, was deposed and banished

* *See* "Buried Cities of Ceylon," by S. M. Burrows, C.E.I., published by A. M. and J. Ferguson.

by the British, the Sinhalese chronicles present us with a list of well-nigh 170 kings and queens, the history of whose administrations is of the most varied and interesting character, indicating the attainment of a degree of civilization and material progress very unusual in the East at that remote age. Long, peaceful, and prosperous reigns were interspersed with others chiefly distinguished by civil dissensions and foreign invasions. The kings of Ceylon, however, had given sufficient provocation to foreign rulers when in the zenith of their power. In the twelfth century the celebrated king Prákrama Báhú not only defeated the rulers of Southern Indian states, but sent an army against the king of Cambodia, which, proving victorious, made that distant land tributary to Ceylon.* On the other hand, in retaliation for the plundering of a Chinese vessel in a Sinhalese port, a Chinese army, early in the fifteenth century, penetrated to the heart of the hill-country,

* The king of Cambodia (Siam) in these days is a tribute-offerer to Lanká, as the following paragraph from a Sinhalese paper last year will show:—

"PRESENTS FROM THE KING OF CAMBODIA TO THE BUDDHIST COLLEGE, MALIGAKANDA, COLOMBO.—Several gold images, an excellent umbrella, ornamented with precious stones, and a brush made of the king's hair, to be kept for use (sweeping) in the place where Buddha's image is placed, have been sent by the king of Cambodia to the high priest in charge of the college. Two or three priests have also come down to receive instruction in Pali, &c., &c.—*Kirana*, April 19."

During a visit to China in 1884 nothing struck the author more than the exact resemblance between a Buddhist temple in Canton and one in Ceylon; the appearance of the priests, their worship and ceremonies, all were alike. *Outside*, in that Mongolian world, all was so different; the country, the towns, the customs, and the people with their pigtails, their oval eyes, and dress, all were strange and novel; but *inside* this Canton temple, before the shaven, yellow-robed monks, one felt for a moment carried back to "Lanká," and its numerous Buddhist temples.

and, defeating the Sinhalese forces at the then royal capital, Gampola, captured the king, and took him away to China; and the island had for some time to pay an annual tribute to that country. At that time the Chinese exported from Ceylon a large quantity of the *kaolin* for pottery, which still abounds in the island. The close connection in early times between the island and the great Eastern Empire constitutes a very interesting episode. Fa-hien, the Chinese monk-traveller, visited Ceylon in search of Buddhist books about 400 A.D., and abode two years in the island.

Ceylon was, however, exposed chiefly to incursions of Malabar princes and adventurers with their followers from Southern India, who waged a constant and generally successful contest with the Sinhalese. The northern and eastern portions of the island at length became permanently occupied by the Tamils, who placed a prince of their own on the Kandyan throne, and so far had the ancient power of the kingdom declined, that when the Portuguese first appeared in Ceylon, in 1505, the island was divided under no less than seven separate rulers. Ceylon, in the Middle Ages, was "the Tyre of Asia."

For 150 years the Portuguese occupied and controlled the maritime districts of Ceylon, but it was more of a military occupation than a regular government, and martial law chiefly prevailed. The army of Roman Catholic ecclesiastics introduced under Portuguese auspices alone made any permanent impression on a people who were only too ready to embrace a religion which gave them high-sounding honorific baptismal names, and interfered seldom, if at all, with their continued observance of Buddhistic feasts and ceremonies. The Portuguese established royal monopolies in cinnamon, pepper, and musk; exporting besides cardamoms, sapan-wood, areca nuts, ebony, elephants, ivory, gems, pearls, and small quantities of tobacco, silk, and tree cotton ("kopok" of modern times).

The Dutch, who by 1656 had finally expelled the Portuguese rulers from the island, which the Lisbon authorities had said "they had rather lose all India than imperil," pursued a far more progressive administrative policy; though, as regards commerce, it was selfish and oppressive. Still confined to the low country (the king of Kandy defying the new as he had done the previous European invaders), the Dutch did much to develop cultivation and to improve the means of communication—more especially by canals in their own maritime territory—while establishing a lucrative trade with the interior. The education of the people occupied a good deal of official attention, as also their Christianization through a staff of Dutch chaplains; but the system of requiring a profession of the Protestant religion before giving employment to any natives speedily confirmed the native love of dissimulation, and created a nation of hypocrites, so that the term "Government Christian," or "Buddhist Christian," is common in some districts of Ceylon to this day.

The first care of the Dutch, however, was to establish a lucrative commerce with Holland, and their vessels were sent not only to Europe, but also to Persia, India, and the Far East ports. *Cinnamon* was the great staple of export,* next came *pearls* (in

* The peeling of cinnamon, the selling or exporting of a single stick, save by the appointed officers, or even the wilful injury of a cinnamon plant, were made crimes punishable by death by the Dutch.

the years which gave successful pearl-oyster fisheries in the Gulf of Mannár); then followed elephants, pepper, areca or betel nuts, jaggery-sugar, sapan-wood and timber generally, arrack spirit, choya-roots (a substitute for madder), cardamoms, cinnamon oil, &c. The cultivation of coffee, indigo, and even some tea was begun, but not carried on to such an extent as to benefit the exports.

Agriculture was promoted by the Dutch for an essentially selfish purpose, but nevertheless good resulted to the people from the system of forced labour, as in the case of the planting of coco-nut palms along the western coast, from Colombo southwards, which, so late as 1740, was described by Governor Van Imhoff as waste-land to be surveyed and divided among the people, who were bound to plant it up. At the end of last century, when the British superseded the Dutch in the possession of the maritime provinces of Ceylon, the whole of the south-western shore, for nearly 100 miles, presented the unbroken grove of palms which is seen to this day.

From 1797 to 1802 Ceylon was placed under the East India Company, who administered it from Fort St. George, Madras; but in the latter year it was made a Crown colony, and it soon became evident there could be no settled peace until the tyrant king on the Kandyan throne—hated by his own chiefs and people—was deposed, and the whole island brought into subjection to the British Crown. This was accomplished in 1815, when, at the instigation of the Kandyan chiefs and people themselves, Wikkrama Sinha, the last king, was captured, deposed, and exiled by the British to Southern India.

So great was the value attached to Ceylon as the

"*key* of India," as well as on account of the supposed fabulous wealth, in precious stones and valuable produce, available in the interior, that, at the general peace, Britain chose to give up Java to the Dutch, and retain this little island, so inferior in area, population, and natural resources.

## CHAPTER II.

### THE ISLAND IN 1796, 1815, AND SEVENTY YEARS LATER.

Extent and topographical features—Condition of the island, previous to, and after seventy years of British rule, contrasted.

HAVING now arrived at the British period, it may be well to give some idea of the condition of Ceylon and its people in the early part of this century, and to compare the same with what is realized after British government has been established for seventy-two years throughout the whole island.

The position of Ceylon as a "pearl-drop on the brow of India," with which continent it is almost connected by the island of Ramisseram and the coral reef called Adam's Bridge, is familiar to all who have ever glanced at a map of Asia. To that great continent it may be said to be related as Great Britain is to Europe, or Madagascar to Africa. In extent it comprises nearly sixteen million acres, or 24,702 square miles, apart from certain dependent islands, such as the Maldives. The total area is about five-sixths of that of Ireland, but is equal to nearly thirty-seven times the superficial extent of the island of Mauritius, which sometimes contests with Ceylon the title of the "Gem of the Indian Ocean." One-sixth of this area, or about 4,000 square miles, is comprised in the hilly and mountainous zone which is

NEW HARBOUR OF COLOMBO

To face p. 8

situated about the centre of the south of the island, while the maritime districts are generally level, and the northern end of the island is broken up into a flat, narrow peninsula and small islets. Within the central zone there are 150 mountains or ranges between 3,000 and 7,000 feet in altitude, with ten peaks rising over the latter limit. The highest mountain is Pídurutalágala, 8,296 feet, or nearly 1,000 feet higher than Adam's Peak (7,353 feet), which was long considered the highest, because to voyagers approaching the coast it was always the most conspicuous, mountain of Ceylon.

The longest river, the Mahaveliganga (the Ganges of Ptolemy's maps), has a course of nearly 150 miles, draining about one-sixth of the area of the island before it reaches the sea at Trincomalee on the east coast. There are five other large rivers running to the west and south, besides numerous tributaries and smaller streams. The rivers are not favourable for navigation, save near the sea, where they expand into backwaters, which were taken advantage of by the Dutch for the construction of their system of canals all round the western and southern coasts.

There are no natural inland lakes, save what remain of magnificent artificial tanks in the north and east of the island, and the backwaters referred to on the coast. The lakes which add to the beauty of Colombo, Kandy, and the Sanatarium, Nuwara Eḷiya, are artificial or partly so.

Most of the above description was true of Ceylon at the beginning of the century even as it is now; but in other respects how altered! It is impossible to get full and exact information as to the condition in which the British found the island and its people in the early years, and up to the subjugation of the Kandyan division in 1815. But from the best authorities at our command we have compiled the following tabular statement to show at a glance a few of the salient points in which the change is most striking, by far the greater part of the change having taken place within the reign of Queen Victoria :—

CEYLON.

| | In 1796—1815. | In 1887. |
|---|---|---|
| Population . . . . | From $\frac{3}{4}$ to 1 million | 2,950,000 |
| No. of houses . . . | 20,000 (tiled) | 500,000 |
| Population of the capital, Colombo | 28,000 | 120,000 |
| Military force . . . | 6,000 | 1,150 |
| Cost of ditto . . . | £160,000 | £100,000 |
| Imperial Share . . | £80,000 | £40,000 |
| Volunteer Corps . . | nil | 680 efficients |
| Cost . . . . . | — | £4,000 |
| Police . . . . . . | nil | 1,650 |
| Cost . . . . . | — | £60,000 |
| Revenue . . . . . | £226,000 | £1,300,000 |
| Expenditure . . . . | £820,000 | £1,280,000 |
| Trade :— | | |
| Imports—value . | £266,790 | £4,700,000 |
| Exports ,, . | £206,588 | £3,700,000 (local Customs' value, really worth much more) |
| Roads . . . . . . . | Sand and gravel tracks | Metalled, 1,350 miles<br>Gravelled, 900 miles<br>Natural, 700 miles |
| Bridges . . . . . | none | Too numerous to mention |
| Railways . . . . . | none | 181 miles |
| Canals . . . . . . | 120 miles | 170 miles |
| Tonnage of shipping entered and cleared . | 75,000 tons | 4,000,000 tons |
| Government Savings Bank :— | | |
| Deposits . . . . | nil | £210,000 |
| No. of Depositors | nil | 11,000 |
| Post Office Savings Banks | — | 73 |
| | — | Depositors 5087 |

| | In 1796—1815. | In 1887. |
|---|---|---|
| Exchange and Deposit Bank Offices . . . | — | 12 |
| Annual volume of business in Colombo Banks' Clearing-house . . . . . | — | about R60,000,000 |
| Government note issue | — | R4750,000 |
| Educational expenditure | £3,000 (for schools and clergy) | £70,000 |
| No. of schools . | 170 | 2,200 |
| No. of scholars . | 2,000 | 120,000 |
| The Press . . . . | Govt. Gazette only | 35 newspapers and periodicals |
| Medical expenditure . | £1,000 | £60,000 |
| No. of civil hospitals and dispensaries . | nil | 120 |
| Covenanted Civil servants: Revenue officers | 6 | 48 |
| Covenanted Civil servants: judges, magistrates, &c. . . | 6 | 40 |
| Charitable allowances from general revenue | £3,000 No Poor Law | £8,000 Friend in Need Society for Voluntary Relief, £2,000 No Poor Law |
| Post offices . . . . | 4 | 130 |
| Total No. of letters . | — | 15,000,000 |
| Money order offices . | — | 115 |
| Telegraph wires . . . | nil | 1,200 miles |
| No. of newspapers despatched . . . . | | 70,000 |
| Area cultivated (exclusive of natural pasture) | 400,000 acres | 3,100,000 acres |
| Live stock:— Horses,[1] cattle, sheep, goats, swine, &c. | 250,000 | 1,500,000 |
| Carts and carriages . | 50 | 20,000 |

[For a fuller statistical statement, see the "Summary of Information respecting Ceylon," published as Appendix; and for more detailed information still, see the latest edition of Ferguson's "Ceylon Handbook and Directory."]

* Of 13,000 horses imported between 1862 and 1887, the greater portion have been bought by native gentlemen, traders, coach-owners, &c.

There is of course an immense amount of improvement which cannot be tabulated, even if we extended our comparison in this form to much greater length.

VIEW ON THE MAHAVELLIGANGE, AT GANGARUNA, NEAR KANDY.

The greatest material change from the Ceylon of pre-British days to the Ceylon of the present time is most certainly in respect of means of internal communication. If, according to Sir Arthur Gordon (as quoted by Charles Kingsley in "At Last"), the first and most potent means of extending civilization is found in roads—the second in roads—the third again in roads, Sir Edward Barnes, when Governor of Ceylon (1824 to 1831), was a ruler who well understood his duty to the people, and he was followed at intervals by worthy successors.

When the English landed in Ceylon in 1796, there was not in the whole island a single practicable road, and troops in their toilsome marches between the fortresses on the coast dragged their cannon through deep sand along the shore. Before Sir Edward Barnes resigned his government in 1831, every town of importance was approached by a carriage-road. He had carried a first-class macadamized road from Colombo to Kandy, throwing a "bridge of boats," which exists to this day, over the Kelani river near Colombo, erecting other bridges and culverts too numerous to mention *en route*, and constructing, through the genius of General Fraser, a beautiful satin-wood bridge of a single span across the Mahaveliganga (the largest river in Ceylon) at Peradeniya, near Kandy. On this road (72 miles in length) on the 1st of February, 1832, the Colombo and Kandy mail-coach—the first mail-coach in Asia—was started; and it continued to run successfully till the road was superseded by the railway in 1867.

There can be no doubt that the permanent conquest of the Kandyan country and people, which had baffled the Portugese and Dutch for 300 years, was effected through Sir Edward Barnes's military roads. A Kandyan tradition, that their conquerors were to be a people who should make a road through a rocky hill, was shrewdly turned to account, and tunnels formed features on two of the cart-routes into the previously almost impenetrable hill-country. The

BRIDGE OF BOATS, COLOMBO.

spirit of the Highland chiefs of Ceylon, as of Scotland seventy years earlier, was effectually broken by means of military roads into their districts; and although the military garrison of Ceylon has gone down from about 6,000 troops to 1,000, and, indeed, although for months together the island has been left with not more than a couple of hundred of artillerymen, no serious trouble has been given for nearly seventy years by the previously warlike Kandyans or the Ceylonese generally.

So much for the value of opening up the country from a military point of view. Governor Barnes, however, left an immense deal to do in bridging the rivers in the interior, and in extending district roads, of which not much was attempted until the arrival of his worthiest successor, Sir Henry Ward. This governor, with but limited means, did a great deal to open up remote districts, and to bridge the Mahaveliganga at Gampola and Katugastotte, as well as many other rivers which in the wet season were well-nigh impassable. He thus gave an immense impetus to the planting enterprize, which may be said practically to have taken its rise from the year of the Queen's accession, 1837. For the restoration and construction of irrigation works to benefit the rice cultivation of the Sinhalese and Tamils, Sir Henry Ward did more than any of his predecessors. He also began the railway to Kandy, which was successfully completed in the time of his successors, Sir Charles MacCarthy and Sir Hercules Robinson. In the latter, Ceylon was fortunate enough to secure one of the most active and energetic governors that ever ruled a Crown colony.

Sir Hercules Robinson left his mark in every province and nearly every district of the country, in new roads, bridges, public buildings, and especially in the repair of irrigation tanks and channels, and the provision of sluices. He extended the railway some seventeen miles, and he laid the foundation of the scheme through which, under his successor, Sir William Gregory, the Colombo Breakwater was begun; and through the engineering skill of Sir John Coode, and his local representative, Mr. John Kyle, this latter work has ensured for the capital of Ceylon one of the safest, most convenient, and commodious artificial harbours in the world.

To Sir William Gregory belongs the distinction of having spent more revenue on reproductive public works than any other governor of Ceylon. The roads in the north and east of the island, which were chiefly gravel and sand tracks, were completed in a permanent form, and nearly every river was bridged. The North-Central Province, a purely Sinhalese rice-growing division of the country, was called into existence, and large amounts were invested in tanks and roads; planting roads were extended; about fifty miles added to the railway system, and preliminary arrangements made for a further extension of some sixty-seven miles, forty-two of which have since been undertaken and completed. When Governor Gregory left in 1877, there were few rivers of any importance left unbridged, a large extent of previously unoccupied country had been opened up for cultivation, and an impetus given to both natives and the European colonists in the extension of cultivation, especially of new products, which alone has saved the island from a serious collapse in the years of commercial depression and blight on coffee which have followed. Since 1877 not many miles of new road have been added, although Governor Gordon has improved existing roads, and constructed some important bridges, especially in the new and rising Kelani Valley tea district; but it is something to say that, whereas the Rev. James Cordiner, chaplain to the Governor of Ceylon in 1807, could write, "Strictly speaking there are no roads in Ceylon," now, after about ninety years of British rule, some 1,300 miles of first-class metalled roads, equal to any in the world, have been constructed, besides about 900 miles of gravelled roads for light traffic, supplemented by 600 miles of natural tracks available in dry weather to traverse districts where as yet there is little or no traffic. The main roads are those from Colombo to Batticoloa *viâ* Ratnapura, Haputalé, and Badulla, right across the island; from Colombo to Trincomalee *viâ* Kandy, and another branch *viâ* Kurunégala, also right across the breadth of the island, but north instead of south of the Central Province; from Jaffna southwards through the centre of the island to Kandy, and thence to Nuwara Eliya and Badulla, and by a less frequented route to Hambantota on the south coast; from Kandy to Mannár on the north-west coast—the great immigration route; and the main roads on the coast, Colombo to Galle and Hambantota, and north to Mannár and almost to Jaffna. Subsidiary first-class roads, especially in the Central Province, are too numerous to mention.

The benefit which this network of roads has conferred on the people, it is impossible to over-estimate. Secluded districts have been opened up, and markets afforded for produce which previously was too often left to waste; settlements, villages, and even large towns, have sprung up within the last fifty years (during our good Queen's reign) alongside roads where, previously, all was jungle and desolation, and means of employment have been afforded to a people who had scarcely ever seen a coin.

As in India, so on a smaller scale in Ceylon, it is a recognized fact that there is no more effectual preventive of famine than internal means of communication, whether by road, rail, canal, or navigable river. There has probably never been a year in which India, within its widely-extended borders, did not produce enough food to supply all its population; but unfortunately there has been no means of getting the superabundance of one district transferred to the famine area in another part of the continent. So in Ceylon, in years gone by, there has been great scarcity and mortality in remote districts without the central Government at Colombo being made properly aware of the fact, or being able to supply prompt relief. The mortality from fever and food scarcity in some parts of the country must thus have been very great before British times.

Roads, again, are great educators, but in this they are surpassed by railways in an Oriental land. The railways in India and Ceylon are doing more in these modern days to level caste and destroy superstition than all the force of missionaries and schoolmasters, much as these latter aid in this good work.

The railway between Colombo and Kandy, projected originally about forty years ago, was not seriously taken in hand till the time of Sir Henry Ward. After many mistakes and alterations of plans, it was successfully completed under the skilful engineering guidance of Mr. G. L. Molesworth, C.I.E. (now consulting engineer to the Government of India), Mr. W. F. Faviell being the successful contractor. The total length is 74¼ miles, and, including a good deal of money unavoidably wasted in dissolving and paying off a company, it cost the colony, from first to last, as much as £1,738,413; but the line (on the broad Indian gauge of 5 ft. 6 in.) is most substantially constructed, including iron-girder bridges, viaducts, a series of tunnels, and an incline rising 1 in 45 for 12 miles into the mountain zone, which gives this railway a prominent place among the remarkable lines of the world.

Since 1867 the railway has been extended by Sir Hercules Robinson, on the same gauge, for 17 miles from Péradeniya to Gampola and Náwalapitiya, rising towns in the Central Province; and by Sir William Gregory, for 17½ miles from Kandy to Mátalé, a town on the borders of the Central Province: while in the low country the same governor constructed a seaside line from Colombo, through a very populous district, to Kalutara, 27½ miles, and also some 3½ miles of Wharf and Breakwater branches.

To Governor Gregory's time also belongs the inception and practical commencement of the extension from Náwalapitiya to the principality of Uva, 67 miles, of which 41½ were commenced in 1880, and finished in 1885. This line includes two long inclines, with gradients of 1 in 44, a tunnel 614 yards long, and the present terminus at Nánu-oya is 5,600 feet above sea-level, within four miles of the sanatarium and town of Nuwara Eliya (6,200 feet above sea-level), and on the borders of Uva, which rich country, however, cannot properly be served until a further extension of 25½ miles to Haputalé is carried out, as it is earnestly hoped that it may be very shortly. Governor Gordon, after some doubt and delay at first, has been thoroughly convinced of the importance of this work.

In all there are 184 miles of railway open in Ceylon, but only 91 may be said to have been working long enough to afford a fair test of the traffic and the benefit to colonists, natives, and the country generally. The seaside line, however, has a wonderfully large passenger traffic, and if only extended to Bentota, and still more to Galle, would also secure profitable freight. With the revival of planting prosperity through tea, the Nánu-oya and Mátalé lines are also certain to be fully employed, although the first-named must be extended into Uva before a full return can be got for the outlay.

The main line to Kandy has more than repaid its cost in direct profit, apart from the immense benefits it has conferred. It is sometimes said that this railway and other lines in Ceylon, constructed as they were mainly for the planting enterprise and with the planters' money, confer far more benefit on the Europeans than on the native population. An answer to this statement, and an evidence of the immense educating power of our railways, is found in the fact that during the past twenty years well nigh twenty-six millions of passengers have been carried over the lines, of whom all but an infinitesimal proportion were natives (Sinhalese and Tamils chiefly). On the Kandy line alone it would have taken the old coach, travelling both ways twice daily, and filled each time, several hundred years to carry the passengers who have passed between the ancient capitals and provinces in the past twenty years. There was scarcely a Kandyan chief or priest who had ever seen, or, at any rate, stood by the sea until the railway into the hill country was opened in 1867, whereas, for some time after the opening, the interesting sight was often presented to Colombo residents of groups of Kandyans standing by the sea-shore in silent awe and admiration of the vast ocean stretched out before them, and the wonderful vessels of all descriptions in Colombo harbour.

In pointing out that the Dutch (equally with the Portuguese) constructed no roads, we must not forget that the former, true to their home experience, constructed and utilized a system of canals through the maritime provinces along the western and south-western coast. In this they were greatly aided by the back-waters, or lagoons, which are a feature on the Ceylon coast, formed through the mouths of the rivers becoming blocked up, and the waters finding an outlet to the sea at different points, often miles away from the line of the main stream. The canals handed over by the Dutch at first fell into comparative disuse, but within the last thirty years they have been fully repaired and utilized, and there are now about 170 miles of canal in the island.

With the construction of roads wheeled traffic became possible, and a large number of the Sinhalese speedily found very profitable employment, in connection with the planting industry mainly, as owners and drivers of bullock carts, of which there must be from 15,000 to 20,000 in the island, besides single bullock-hackeries for passenger traffic. In nothing is the increase of wealth among the natives more seen, in the Western, Central, and Southern Provinces, than in the number of horses and carriages now owned by them. Thirty or forty years ago, to see a Ceylonese with a horse and conveyance of his own was rare indeed; *now* the number of Burghers, Sinhalese, and Tamils driving their own carriages, in the towns especially, is very remarkable. The greater number of the horses imported during the past twenty-five years—the imports during that time numbering 13,000—have certainly passed to the people of the country.

## CHAPTER III.

### SOCIAL PROGRESS IN NINETY YEARS.

**Population—Buildings—Postal and Telegraphic services—Savings banks—Banking and Currency—Police and Military defence —Medical and Educational achievements—Laws and Crime.**

HAVING thus described more particularly the vast change effected in British times by the construction of communications all over the island, we must touch briefly on the evidences of social progress given in our table (pages 10, 11).

The increase in population speaks for itself. It is very difficult, however, to arrive at a correct estimate of what the population was at the beginning of the century, as the Dutch could have no complete returns, not having any control over the Kandyan provinces. The first attempt at accurate numbering was in 1824, by Governor Barnes, and the result was a total of 851,440, or, making allowance for omissions due to the hiding of people through fear of taxation, &c., say about a million of both sexes and all ages. As regards the large estimate of the ancient population of Ceylon located in the northern, north-central, and eastern districts, now almost entirely deserted, we are by no means inclined, with the recollection of the

TOPAVI TANK, NEAR THE RUINS OF POLONARUWA.

famous essay on the "Populousness of Ancient Nations before us, to accept the estimates published by Sir Emerson Tennent and other enthusiastic writers. There can be no doubt, however, that a very considerable population found means of existence in and around the ancient capitals of Ceylon, and the great Tank region of the north and east, a region which affords scope for a great, though gradual, extension in the settlement of both Sinhalese and Tamils in the future. At present it must be remembered that fully two-thirds of the population are found in the Western, Southern, and Central Provinces, occupying a good deal less than half the area of the island, and that there are large districts, once the best-cultivated with rice, with *now* perhaps only half a dozen souls to the square mile.

As regards the number of inhabited houses, in 1824 there were not more than 20,000 with tiled roofs in the island; that number has multiplied manifold, but the half-million now given refer to all descriptions of inhabited houses, most of these being huts roofed with coconut leaves. The improvement in the residences of a large proportion of the people is, however, very marked: among one class the contrast between the old and modern homes has been well described as being as great as that between a begrimed native chatty (clay vessel) and a bright English tea-kettle.

In the town of Kandy, which has now about 4,000 dwelling-houses—the large majority substantially built, many of two stories—eighty years ago no one but the tyrant-king was allowed to have a tiled roof, or any residence better than a hut. In all the towns, and many of the villages of the island, substantial public buildings have been erected: revenue offices, court-houses, hospitals and dispensaries, prisons, schools, and post and telegraph offices. A great change for the better in respect of these institutions was effected by Governors Robinson and Gregory.

Further evidences of the good done through a liberal and enlightened administration we find in an admirable internal postal service, made possible by the roads through which every town and village of any consequence is served, the total number of post-offices being 111, supplemented by 16 telegraph stations, there being 1,100 miles of telegraph wire in the island; while, in addition, the Postal-Telegraph Department has opened Postal savings-banks in all the towns and important villages. This is apart from a long-existing Government savings-bank, with about 10,000 depositors, owning deposits to the amount of perhaps two million rupees.

With the rise of local trade and foreign commerce, chiefly through the export of planting products, came the need of banking and exchange facilities, and the call for these led to the establishment of a local Bank over forty years ago. This was superseded, however, soon after by the Oriental Bank Corporation, which gradually controlled by far the larger share of local business, so that the Ceylon branches became among the most important and profitable of this well-known Eastern bank. This gradually tempted its managers to depart from legitimate business by lending its capital too freely on planting, produce, and estates, and when this bank closed its doors in March, 1880, nowhere was the shock felt more widely or acutely than throughout Ceylon. The effect and distrust among the natives would have been greatly aggravated were it not for the bold step taken by Sir Arthur Gordon in extending an official guarantee to the bank's note issue, which eventuated in a Government note issue soon after, much to the advantage of the people and the exchequer, as will yet be seen. So far, the circulation of Government notes is rapidly approximating to five millions of rupees. Nor is any loss likely to be sustained from taking up the notes of the Oriental Bank, which, in fact, ought never to have closed its doors. The New Oriental Bank Corporation founded upon it, is already prospering, and the plantations have been mainly taken over by a Limited Company, and are likely to be worked at a good profit. Ceylon has suffered a good deal at times from plantation companies, chiefly through the "Ceylon Company, Limited," which, though so named, was really founded to take up bad business in Mauritius, where its heaviest losses were sustained. Other banks and agencies prospering in Ceylon are those of the Chartered Mercantile Bank of London, India, and China, the Bank of Madras, and the National Bank of India, besides mercantile agencies of other Eastern banks. It may be mentioned that Sir Hercules Robinson gave Ceylon the benefit of a decimal currency in rupees and cents of a rupee, thus placing it in advance of India, where the cumbrous subdivisions of the rupee into annas, pice, and pies still prevail; in this respect Ceylon is indeed in advance of the mother-country.

We need scarcely say that, at the beginning of British rule, there was no post-office, and for many years after, the service was of the most primitive, although expensive, kind; nor were there police or volunteer corps in those days; but there was an army corps (infantry, artillery, and even cavalry, altogether

5,000 to 6,000 men) kept up for many years, out of all proportion to the necessities of the case. The Home Government had the idea seventy years ago that the hidden wealth of Ceylon would enable a handsome annual subsidy to be paid to the treasury of the mother-country after all local expenses of government were defrayed. In place of that, so long as the government remained a mere military dependency, it was a dead loss to, and drain on, the imperial treasury. By degrees, however, it was seen that four British and as many native (Malay, Tamil, and Kaffir) regiments were not required, and, the force being cut down, it was decided by a commission appointed by the Secretary of State in 1865, that Ceylon should bear all the military expenditure within its bounds, the local force being fixed at one regiment of British infantry, one of native (the Ceylon Rifles), and one brigade of artillery, with a major-general and staff. The Ceylon Rifles again were disbanded a few years later, in 1873.

The island, therefore, has cost the Home Government nothing for the last twenty years: on the other hand, the force in Ceylon has been utilized very frequently for imperial and inter-colonial purposes. This will be alluded to later on, but we may mention here that Governor Gordon was instrumental, in view of the recent depression of the revenue, in getting the military contribution reduced to 600,000 rupees in place of about a million. The former amount is now counted as a naval, as well as military, contribution, and is a very fair appraisement of the responsibility of Ceylon, considering that no internal trouble beyond the capacity of police and volunteers can be feared.

In no direction has more satisfactory work been done in Ceylon by the British Government than through its Medical and Educational Departments. Here are branches which give the natives a vivid idea of the superiority of English over Portuguese or Dutch rule, and, to judge by the way in which hospitals, dispensaries, and schools are made use of, it is evident that the Sinhalese and Tamils value their privileges.

Of civil, lying-in, contagious diseases, and other hospitals, with lunatic and leper asylums, and out-door dispensaries, there are now 120 in the island, in or at which some 175,000 persons are treated annually, more than two-thirds being, of course, for trifling ailments at the dispensaries.

In this connection, the Ceylon Medical College, founded by Sir Hercules Robinson in 1870, most heartily supported by his successor, Governor Gregory, and liberally endowed and extended by two wealthy Sinhalese gentlemen, Messrs. De Soyza and Rajepakse, is worthy of mention. Out of some 240 Ceylonese students entered, about sixty have qualified and obtained licences to practise medicine and surgery; about as many more are hospital assistants and dispensers; some have taken service under the Straits' Government; while others have gone home to qualify for degrees at British Universities. The college has a principal and seven lecturers; and the Ceylonese have already shown a peculiar aptitude for the profession, surgeons of special, even of European eminence, having come from their ranks. We should mention here the good work done by Dr. Green, M.D., of the American Mission, in his medical classes for native students long before the Government College was founded. (See Appendix for reference to medical benefactors.)

In education, generally, although there is still an immense deal to do, Ceylon is far in advance as compared with India. This has been chiefly through the agency of the several Christian Missions at work in the island, which have done a noble work, more especially in female education; but Sir Hercules Robinson gave an immense impetus to education by the establishment of an admirable grant-in-aid system, while Sir W. Gregory extended the work, multiplying especially Government vernacular schools. Latterly, special attention has been given to practical, and even technical, education: an Agricultural Training School has been started, and in connection with Experimental Gardens (under the auspices of the separate Botanic Gardens' Departments) in different parts of the country, much good is likely to be effected. Industrial schools for other branches are also encouraged. The great improvements in the educational, as well as in some other special, departments of recent years, is very much owing to the employment, as their heads, of public servants with local experience, in place of importing "fresh blood," a penchant which cost the colony a great deal previously. Under that system a half-pay naval officer was sent out as Director of Prisons, and an impracticable theorist as Director of Public Instruction, while other departments have similarly suffered. At present the proportion in Ceylon is one pupil to every twenty-eight of population; in India it is about one to every 150, while in Great Britain it is, we suppose, one to every six or seven. In other words, while practically all children of school-going age are being served educationally in Great

Britain, only 10 per cent. of those in Ceylon go to school, while not much more than 1 per cent. in India are being instructed.

Visitors always remark on the large number of the people in Ceylon, the domestic servants especially, who understand and speak English, as compared with servants in India. In ancient times each Buddhist temple had its pansala or school; but although such pansalas are still kept up in some low-country districts, in the Kandyan country for many years the priests have neglected their duty in teaching and other respects, being entirely independent of the people through the endowments in land left them by the Kandyan kings, which have in this case proved a curse instead of a blessing to the priests themselves, as well as to the people. These "Buddhist Temporalities," now being worse than wasted, will, it is hoped, ere long be utilized by express ordinance for the benefit of the mass of the people in promoting vernacular and perhaps technical education. In the low-country there are no endowments.

Educated Ceylonese are now, in many cases, finding it difficult to secure openings in life suited to their taste: the legal profession has hitherto been the most popular, it being occupied almost entirely by them as notaries, attorneys or solicitors, advocates, barristers, and even judges. In this way Sir Richard Morgan, born and educated in Ceylon, rose to be attorney-general, chief justice, and knight. At this moment a Sinhalese gentleman is judge of the Supreme Court; and other Ceylonese fill the important offices of attorney-general, and solicitor-general, while others are county judges, leading barristers, and solicitors.

The Sinhalese fondness for litigation is proverbial; their cases in court abound, even to disputing about the fractional part of a coconut-tree. Crime generally is represented by a daily average of about 2,000 convicted prisoners in the gaols of the island, a large number being for petty thefts and assaults. The cost of the administration of justice for the criminal class—police, courts, gaols, &c.—cannot be less than R1,000,000, or about £80,000, per annum. A penal code after the fashion of that of India was arranged for by Sir Bruce Burnside, the present Chief Justice of the island, and successfully introduced in 1885; and codification of the civil laws—an urgent want—is expected shortly to be brought forward by Government.

## CHAPTER IV.

### LEGISLATIVE AND GENERAL IMPROVEMENTS UNDER THE RULE OF SUCCESSIVE BRITISH GOVERNORS,* THE NEED OF PROMOTING CO-OPERATION AND GOOD FEELING BETWEEN DIVERSE CLASSES AND RACES.

AMONG the political and social reforms introduced into Ceylon by the British during the present century may be mentioned the abolition by the first governor, the Hon. F. North, of torture and other barbarous punishments abhorrent to English feeling, and the relaxation during the time of his successor of the severe laws against Romanists, twenty years before Catholic emancipation was granted in England. Trial by jury was first introduced by a new charter of justice in 1811; but it was not till 1844 that all caste and clan distinctions in the jury-box and all slavery were finally abolished.

A new and much improved charter of justice, the establishment of a Legislative Council with unofficial members, an order in Council abolishing compulsory

* Lists of the British governors of the island, chief justices, commanders of the troops, and executive councillors, together with the names of other official and non-official residents, who deserve to be specially mentioned as public benefactors, are given in Appendix IV.

labour, the establishment of a free press, the relinquishment of the cinnamon monopoly, the institution of a Government savings-bank and the Colombo Academy, all served to mark the years between 1830 and 1840, when such enlightened governors as Sir Robert Wilmot-Horton, and the Right Hon. J. H. Stuart-Mackenzie, administered Ceylon affairs.

During the next decade a tax on fishermen of one-tithe of all the fish taken was abolished; the bonds of slavery were finally removed; great efforts were made to extend education and medical relief to the masses, and the important planting industry took its first start; a wise and most useful law for the improvement of roads, exacting six days' labour per annum, or its value, from all able-bodied males between eighteen and fifty-five years of age, was passed; the last national disturbance of the Kandyans was quickly suppressed without the loss of a single life; the colony passed through a commercial and financial crisis, and on the ruins of the Bank of Ceylon the Oriental Bank Corporation arose.

In 1850 there was commenced in Ceylon the most successful service with carrier-pigeons ever known in connection with the press. The *Ceylon Observer* carrier-pigeons travelled regularly between Galle (the mail port) and Colombo with budgets of news, including Crimean and Indian Mutiny war news, for over seven years, till 1857, when they were superseded by the telegraph. All official connection between the British Government and Buddhism was closed in 1855, the year in which Sir Henry Ward commenced to rule, and a new impetus was given to Native and European industry by useful legislation. The restoration of irrigation works, the construction of roads, the commencement of a railway, the reorganization of the public service, the introduction of penny postage (with a halfpenny rate for newspapers), the establishment of steam navigation round the island and of telegraph communication between the principal towns, the reform of the Kandyan marriage laws, and the abolition of polyandry, also marked this period.

The following decade, 1860–1870, is chiefly distinguished for Governor Sir Hercules Robinson's energetic and most useful administration, with measures for the civil registration of marriages, births, and deaths, and of titles to land; the opening of the railway to Kandy; the publication by the people of Sinhalese and Tamil newspapers; the formation of the towns of Colombo, Kandy, and Galle into municipalities, with Boards composed of elected and official members; the revival of gansabháwa, or village councils; the adoption of a grant-in-aid scheme for promoting the education of the people; the abolition of export duties; the founding of the Ceylon Medical School; and the visit in 1870 of H.R.H. the Duke of Edinburgh.

The next decade in the history of Ceylon has its interest in the very prosperous, busy, and successful government of Sir William Gregory. The first systematic census of the population was taken in 1871. Measures were adopted for the conservation of forests and for preventing the extinction of elk, deer, elephants, &c.; the registration of titles was provided for; Colombo, Kandy, and Galle were much improved, arrangements for a good water-supply to each town being made; while for the sanatarium (Nuwara Eliya) and seven other minor towns a bill was passed establishing Local Boards on the elective principle; the gansabháwa, or village councils, were improved and encouraged; an immense impetus was given to rice cultivation, 100 village tanks being repaired every year, besides larger works; the North-Central Province, in purely native interests, was formed, and the great lines of communication between the north and east were permanently opened; Anurádhapura, the ancient capital, was cleared of jungle, and rendered a healthy revenue station; gaols, hospitals, and schools were greatly improved, gaol discipline being put on a new footing; pilgrimages on a large scale injuriously affecting public health were discouraged and practically stopped; scientific education was provided for; temperance was promoted by the reduction of the number of licences granted to grog-shops; gas lighting was introduced into Colombo; the stoppage of all payments from the revenue in aid of religion ("Disestablishment") was arranged for; the industry in the growth of new products—tea, cinchona, and cacao—took its first systematic start; an enactment dealing with service tenures in connection with temples was passed; road and railway extension were actively taken in hand; a public museum was erected and well filled at Colombo; and in 1875 H.R.H. the Prince of Wales visited the island, and laid the first stone of the Colombo Breakwater, designed and constructed by Sir John Coode, and since successfully completed (in 1886) by the resident engineer, Mr. Kyle. A Northern Arm and Graving-dock for the Imperial Navy (in supersession partly of Trincomalee), as well as for commercial purposes, though fully supported by the Admiralty, has yet (1887) to be commenced.

Since 1880 the colony has suffered from financial

TRINCOMALEE HARBOUR.

depression, due chiefly to the falling off in the coffee crops. A volunteer corps was established under Governor Longden's patronage; but almost the only work of importance during his rule of six years was an extensive lunatic asylum, costing R600,000 (to finish) which is deemed much beyond the wants of the colony, being built on a scale likely rather to astonish than benefit poor rural Sinhalese lunatics, taken from jungle huts to be lodged in brick and mortar palaces. An increase to the fixed expenditure of the Colony made in 1878 in Governor Longden's time, including an addition of R10,000 to his own salary,* was to say the least injudicious, although sanctioned by the Legislature, and this was shown by the revenue depression which set in from the following year onwards.

Sir Arthur Gordon assumed the Government of Ceylon at the end of 1883, and a period of renewed activity in useful legislation and material improvement was eagerly anticipated; but the result up to date has not quite answered expectations. The important laws dealing with "Buddhist Temporalities," a Civil Code, Excise and General Revenue Reform, have yet to appear. The railway extension, opened as far as Nánu-oya in 1885, has not yet been sanctioned into the important division of Uva (Uva was created a new province in February, 1886), notwithstanding the Governor's urgent and repeated requests, backed by his Executive Council and by reliable public opinion. A step in revision of taxation undertaken in 1885 has

* Making the salary of the Governor of Ceylon R80,000 per annum. Rather a contrast to that of the Dutch Governors, which was £30 per month (besides rations and allowances), but then they were expected to make a fortune in other and secret ways.

not been well received or proved successful; but a reduction in the military contribution, the issue of Government Currency Notes after the Governor's bold guarantee of the Oriental Bank Notes, and a measure of municipal reform, have naturally found acceptance.

The great failure of Sir Arthur Gordon has been in not promoting and cementing that good feeling between the governing and governed classes, and especially between the different races and ranks, embraced in the very varied community of Ceylon, which Sir William Gregory, above all his predecessors, was successful in fostering. In the time of the latter Governor, Europeans, Burghers (European descendants), and natives, co-operated more cordially, and supported the Government more trustfully, than at any period before or since. His successor, (Sir James Longden) was too antiquated and sleepy in his ideas to promote this desirable state of feeling, or any other movement beyond the bounds of red-tape official routine; while Governor Gordon, by arbitrary, inquisitorial proceedings early in his term of government, by his favour of ceremonial supported by high-caste natives, and by ill-judged special patronage of Buddhist priests at his levees, &c., has created distrust, and we fear has undone much of the good effected during 1872–1877. A frank, genial, straightforward administrator, free of all official prejudice or predilection for outward ("caste") show, recognizing merit wherever it is to be found, and good work for the benefit of the body-politic, no matter by whom promoted, has nowhere a more encouraging or fruitful field to work in than Ceylon, and this is why, as has often been said, a governor, straight from "the free air of the British House of Commons," has often proved a bright success in this first and most important of Crown Colonies. It may not be known to people in England interested in our tropical dependencies, how much evil, cliques—official and otherwise—promoted to some extent by "club" life, are working, and are likely still further to work, in India and Ceylon. The Englishman carries his "club" with him—it has been said—wherever he goes, and has the undoubted right to do so; but it is a question whether in Crown Dependencies "public servants," not excluding the Queen's Representative, drawing their salaries and pensions from taxes paid by the people at large, have the right to patronize clubs which practically exclude all Her Majesty's native-born subjects, without exception, no matter what their merit or degree; and still more whether occult influences should dictate (through aide-de-camps and private secretaries), who are to be honoured, if not received, at "Queen's House." It was to the credit of Sir William Gregory that he never allowed himself to be restricted by the sneers of would-be colonial "society" dictators, but sought out and marked by his attentions merit and good work, wherever he found them. In this way Sinhalese, Tamils, and Burghers (and not merely a few "high caste" families favoured by narrow-minded officials), found their industry and integrity noticed by the Governor, who again had at his table, as honoured guests, the heads and chief workers in the various Missions and principal Educational Institutions, whether Christian or secular, Hindu or Buddhist, showing his personal interest in every thing or person calculated to advance the colony and people committed to his care by Her Most Gracious Majesty the Queen.

In a short time after these pages appear, a new Governor for Ceylon will have to be selected, and it is to be hoped he may be one of the high-minded, liberal, progressive type, we have attempted to indicate.

# CHAPTER V.

## NATIVE AGRICULTURAL AND MANUFACTURING INTERESTS.

Paddy (rice) cultivation — Cinnamon — Coconut, Palmyra, Kitul, Arecanut, and other Palms—Essential oils—Tobacco—Cotton—Sugar-cane—Other Fruit-trees and Vegetables—Natural pasture —Local Manufactures.

WHETHER or not Ceylon was in ancient times the granary of South-Eastern Asia, certain it is that long before the Portuguese or Dutch, not to speak of the British, era, that condition had lapsed, and so far from the island having a surplus of food products, the British, like their European predecessors, had to import a certain quantity of rice from Southern India to feed their troops and the population of the capital and other chief towns.* There can be no doubt as to the large quantity of rice which could be grown around the network of tanks in the north and east, which have been lying for centuries broken and unused in the midst of unoccupied territory.

Driven from the northern plains by the conquering Tamils, the Sinhalese, taking refuge in the mountain zone more to the south and west, found a country in many respects less suited for rice than for fruit and root culture; but yet, under British, as under native,

* Old Sinhalese records show that rice was imported into Ceylon from the Coromandel Coast in the second century before Christ.

A COCONUT PLANTATION.

rule, *rice* or *paddy-growing* continues to be the one most general and favourite occupation of the Sinhalese people, as indeed it is of the Ceylon Tamils in the north and east of the island. Agriculture, in their opinion, is the most honourable of callings, and although in many districts fruit and root—that is, garden—culture would prove more profitable, yet the paddy field is more generally popular.

Nowhere in Ceylon are there tracts of alluvial lands so extensive as those which mark the banks and deltas of rivers in India, and the average return of rice per acre in Ceylon, under the most favourable circumstances, is considerably below the Indian average. It was the opinion of one of the most experienced of Ceylon civil servants—Sir Charles P. Layard, who served in the island from 1829 to 1879—that the "cultivation of paddy is now the least profitable pursuit to which a native can apply himself; it is persevered in from habit, and because the value of time and labour never enters into his calculations." This view has been contested more recently (in 1885) by an experienced revenue officer, Mr. E. Elliott, who shows that rice cultivation is fairly profitable; but his calculations refer chiefly to select districts, rather than to the island generally. On the principle of buying in the cheapest and selling in the dearest market, it would certainly appear that the people of Ceylon (with but few exceptions in the Matara, Batticaloa, and Jaffna districts) could more profitably turn their attention to plantation and garden products, such as coconuts, areca or betel nuts, pepper, cinnamon, nutmeg, cacao, tea, cardamoms, and fruits of all tropical kinds (even putting tea on one side for the present); then selling the produce to advantage, they could buy rice from southern and northern India and Burmah more cheaply than they can produce it. But it is impossible, even if it were politic—which we doubt—to revolutionize the habits of a very conservative people in this way; and therefore, so soon as the sale of forest land to planters, and the introduction of capital for the planting enterprise, put the Government in possession of surplus revenue, Sir Henry Ward acted wisely in turning his attention to the restoration and repair of such irrigation works in the neighbourhood of population, as he felt would at once be utilized for the increased production of grain. In this way he changed a large extent of waste land into an expanse of perennial rice culture, for the benefit of the industrious Mohammedans and Hindus of the Batticaloa district in the Eastern Province. Similarly, he spent large sums for the benefit of the Sinhalese rice cultivators in the southern districts.

Sir Hercules Robinson conceived a statesmanlike law by which expenditure on irrigation works, chiefly village tanks, on terms far more liberal to the people than any offered in India, formed a part of the annual budget. Most cordially was this policy supported by his successor, Sir William Gregory, who, moreover, entered on an undertaking of greater magnitude than any previously recorded in British times: namely, the formation of a new province around the ancient capital of Ceylon, and the restoration of tanks and completion of roads and bridges within its bounds, sufficient to give the sparse Sinhalese population every advantage in making a start in the race of prosperity. At a considerable expenditure, spread over four or five years, this was accomplished, and a population of some 60,000 Sinhalese were thereby more directly benefited than they had been by any of their rulers, native or European, for several centuries back. Curiously enough not the Sinhalese but the Tamils—who have been called "the Scotchmen of the East," from their enterprise in migrating and colonising—are likely to take chief advantage of the expenditure in this north-central region—an expenditure continued by Governor Longden, and to a still more marked degree by Governor Gordon, who has entered on large and important works in restoring the Kalawewa and Zodi-ella Irrigation tanks and channels. The formation of a permanent Irrigation Board for the colony, with a settled income in a proportion of the land revenue, is another step of the present governor in the interests of rice culture, more commendable for its motive, perhaps, than for the soundness of the political economy by which the arrangement can be defended. Special encouragement to other branches of agriculture in certain districts would do much good; but as yet Government and its revenue officers have not even established district Agricultural Shows for products and stock with suitable prizes.

Governor Gregory also introduced a measure for substituting compulsory commutation for the renting of the grain-tithes on a scale so liberal as to amount to a considerable lessening of taxation on locally-grown grain, which may be said now to be "protected" when compared with the tax on the imported article. The effect of the liberal policy to the local farmer, above described, on the part of successive governors, from Sir Henry Ward's time on to that of Sir Arthur Gordon, has undoubtedly been to bring a far larger area under grain cultivation now than was the case at the beginning of the century;

but it is impossible, in the absence of a cadastral survey, to give the exact extent.

The accepted estimate is that there are now 660,000 acres under rice or paddy, and about 150,000 under dry grain, Indian corn, and other cereals. And the striking fact is that, so far from the import of grain decreasing as the local production has extended, the reverse has been the case. In this, however, is seen the influence of the expanding planting enterprise: fifty years ago, when coffee-planting was just beginning in Ceylon, the total quantity of grain required from India was an import of 650,000 bushels; now, it is as high as five and six million bushels. The import in 1877, the year of the Madras famine, when Ceylon planters had to provide for 170,000 fugitives from Southern India, besides their usual coolie labour force, amounted to no less than 6,800,000 bushels.

The disposal of the increasing local production simultaneously with these imports is explained by the rapidly increasing population in the rural districts, and the much larger quantity of food consumed in a time of prosperity. In the early part of the century the average Sinhalese countryman consumed, probably, only half the quantity of rice (supplemented by fruit and vegetables) which he is now able to afford. Our calculation is that more than three-fifths of the grain consumed is locally produced against less than two-fifths imported.*

Turning from the main staple of native agriculture

* For further information see paper on "Food Supply of Ceylon," by the author, in "Ferguson's Ceylon Handbook and Directory," and also papers on "Grain Taxation in Ceylon," quoted by Sir William Gregory in despatches to Earl Carnarvon.

to garden produce, we have to note that, while the Dutch monopolies in cinnamon, pepper, &c., were probably worked at a loss to the Government, even with forced labour at their command, the export of the cinnamon spice was insignificant as compared with what it has become under the free British system. There can be no doubt that Ceylon *cinnamon* is the finest in the world, celebrated from the middle of the fourteenth century according to authentic records, and one of the few products of importance indigenous to the island. It was known through Arab caravans to the Romans, who paid in Rome the equivalent of £8 sterling per pound for the fragrant spice. Ceylon (called by De Barras the "mother of cinnamon") has, therefore, well earned the name "Cinnamon Isle," whatever may be said of its "spicy breezes," a term originally applied by Bishop Heber, in his well-known hymn, to Java rather than to Ceylon. The maximum export attained by the Dutch was in 1738, when 600,000 lb., valued at from 8s. 4d. to 17s. 8d. per lb., was sent to India, Persia, and Europe, from Ceylon. In the commercial season, 1881–82, Ceylon sent into the markets of the world, almost entirely through London, as much as 1,600,000 lb. of cinnamon quill bark, and nearly 400,000 lb. of chips, the finest bark being purchasable at the London sales for from 2s. 6d. to 3s. per lb.; while in season 1885–86 the export was 1,630,000 quill and 550,000 lb. of chips, and the price has fallen almost 50 per cent. in six years. The above quantity is yielded by an area of about 35,000 acres, cultivated entirely, and almost entirely owned, by the people of Ceylon.

Of far greater importance now to the people, as well as to the export trade of the island, is its *Palm cultivation*, which has enormously extended since the time of the Dutch, especially in the maritime districts. European capital has done much in turning waste land into coconut plantations; but there is, also, no more favourite mode of investment for the native mercantile, trading, and industrial classes of the people (Sinhalese and Tamils), who have greatly increased in wealth during the past fifty years, than in gardens and estates of coconuts, arecas, palmyras, and other palms and fruit trees. Within the Dutch and British periods a great portion of the coast-line of Ceylon (on the west, south, and east), for a breadth varying from a quarter of a mile to several miles, and extending to a length of 150 miles, has been planted with coconut palms. More recently, inland villages, such as the delta of the Maha-oya (river), have been planted with coconuts as far as thirty miles from the coast. In the Jaffna peninsula, again, the natives have chiefly planted the equally useful palmyra. The palms, together with a little rice and a piece of cotton cloth, are capable of supplying most of the wants of the people.

It has been commonly remarked that the uses of the coconut palm * are as numerous as the days of the year. Percival, early in this century, relates that a small ship from the Maldive islands arrived at Galle which was entirely built, rigged, provisioned, and laden with the produce of the coco-palm.† Food,

* See "All about the Coconut Palm," published by A. M. and J. Ferguson, Colombo.

† The food value of the coconut is not generally understood; a short time ago the crew of a wrecked vessel cast away on a South Sea island subsisted for several months on no other food than coconuts and broiled fish, and added to their weight in that time.

drink, domestic utensils, materials for building and thatching, wine, sugar, and oil are amongst the many gifts to man of these munificent trees. Unlike the other trade staples, tea, coffee, cinchona bark, and cinnamon, by far the largest proportion of the products of the coconut palm—nuts, oil, arrack (intoxicating spirit), leaves for thatch, fences, mats and baskets, timber, &c., are locally utilized.

Arrack (in varying quantities, according to the demand in the Madras Presidency) is exported, but the export is not to be compared with the large local consumption, which unfortunately increases with the increasing wealth of the people. The British are blamed for regulating and protecting the arrack and liquor traffic, but the consumption was pretty general before the British came to Ceylon. It may be a question whether taverns have not been too widely multiplied, and whether we should not take a leaf out of the Dutch policy in Java, where the consumption of intoxicating liquors among natives is very rigidly restricted. Our calculation is that seven millions of rupees are spent by the people of Ceylon on intoxicants, against not much more than a tenth of this amount devoted to education by the people, missions, and the government.

A good many millions of coconuts are annually exported, but the chief trade is in coir fibre from the husk, and still more in the oil expressed from the kernel of the nut, used in Europe as a lubricator, for soap-making, and dressing cloths, and (partially) for candle-making and lighting purposes; African palm oil and petroleum are its great rivals. The average value of the products of the coconut-palm exported may be taken at about the following figures: oil,

£400,000; coir, £60,000; arrack, £20,000; "koppara" (the dried kernel sent to India for native food, and latterly to France to be expressed), £100,000; "punac" (the refuse of the oil, or oil-cake, used for cattle food), £10,000; nuts, £10,000; miscellaneous products, £5,000; making a total of over £600,000; while the value of the produce locally consumed must be nearly one and a half million sterling per annum, and the market value of the area covered with coconuts rather over than under twelve millions sterling. The local use of coconuts is sure to increase with railway extension and the development of the interior of the island. There are perhaps thirty millions of coconut palms cultivated in Ceylon, covering about 500,000 acres, all but about 30,000 acres being owned by natives themselves. The annual yield of nuts cannot be much under 100 millions. There are nearly 2,000 native oil-crushers driven by bullocks, apart from steam establishments in Colombo, Negombo, &c., owned by natives as well as Europeans, while the preparation of the fibre affords occupation to a large number of the people.*

After the coconut tree, the palmyra has been regarded as the richest plant in the East. Both require from eight to twelve years to come into bearing, but they are supposed to live from 150 to 300 years.† By many the palmyra is thought a richer tree than the coconut, and it is especially adapted to the drier regions of the north and east of

* For an account of the introduction and spread of coconut cultivation in Ceylon, from the earliest period to the present day, see a Paper read before the Royal Asiatic Society, Ceylon Branch, in 1886, by the author, John Ferguson.

† See William Ferguson's Monograph on "The Palmyra Palm."

the island. It is estimated there are eight millions of palmyras owned by the people in the Jaffna peninsula, the edible products of which supply one-fourth of the food of 280,000 inhabitants. The Tamil poets describe 800 different purposes to which the palmyra can be applied, and their proverb says "it lives for a lac of years after planting, and lasts for a lac of years when felled." The timber is prized for house-building purposes, especially for rafters, being hard and durable. Besides there being a large local consumption, as much as £10,000 worth is still annually exported from Ceylon, while of jaggery sugar about 20,000 cwt. are made from this palm, the cultivation of which covers 40,000 acres, yielding perhaps seventy millions of nuts annually; this nut is much smaller than the coconut.

A COCONUT CLIMBER.

The kitul or jaggery palm (*Caryota urens*), known also as the bastard sago, is another very valuable tree common in Ceylon. Jaggery sugar and toddy wine are prepared from the sap, the best trees yielding 100 pints of sap in twenty-four hours. Sago is manufactured from the pith, and fibre from the leaves for fishing-lines and bowstrings, the fibre from the leaf-stalks being made into rope for tying wild elephants. Of the fibre, from £3,000 to £7,000 value is exported annually; of the jaggery sugar, £2,000 worth. The quantity used in the country is very great. This palm is found round every Kandyan's hut; indeed it has been said by Emerson Tennent that a single tree in Ambegamua district afforded the support of a Kandyan, his wife, and children. The area covered is, perhaps, equal to 30,000 acres. The trunk timber is used for rafters, being hard and durable.

The cultivation of the *Areca catechu* (which is compared to "an arrow shot from heaven" by the Hindu poets) was always one of the chief sources of the Ceylon trade in ante-British times. In the Portuguese era great quantities of the nuts were exported, and these formed the chief medium of exchange for the proportion of grain which the natives of Ceylon have for centuries drawn from Southern India. The Dutch esteemed the areca-nut as a very great source of revenue, and they made an exclusive trade of it. They exported yearly about 35,000 cwt. About the same quantity was annually shipped between 1806 and 1813. Of recent years as many as 160,000 cwt. of nuts have been shipped in one year. The export is almost entirely to Southern India. An areca-nut tree requires five years to come into bearing. It grows all over the low country and in the hills up to an elevation above sea-level of between 2,000 and 3,000 feet. Some coffee estate proprietors around Kandy in the early days planted areca-nuts along their boundaries, thereby forming a capital division line, and the cultivation has anew attracted the attention of colonists in recent years, especially in the Matale and Udagama districts. The chief areca gardens owned by natives are, however, to be found in the Kegala district. The home consumption is very large, and the area covered by the palm must be equal to 50,000 acres. The annual value of the exports of areca-nut produce is from £60,000 to £100,000.

There are numerous other palms, more especially the magnificent talipot (*Corypha umbracolifera*), which flowers once (a grand crown of cream-coloured blossom twenty feet high) after sixty or eighty years, and then

TALIPOT PALM IN FLOWER.

dies, and which is freely used for native huts, umbrellas, books, &c.; the heart also being, like that of the sago palm, good for human food.

The bread-fruit tree, the jak, orange, and mango, as well as gardens of plantains and pine-apples, melons, guavas, papuas, &c., might be mentioned among products cultivated and of great use to the people of Ceylon; in fact, there is scarcely a native land-owner or cultivator in the country who does not possess a garden of palms or other fruit trees, besides paddy fields. The total area cultivated with palms and fruit trees cannot be less than from 700,000 to 750,000 acres (in addition to 100,000 acres under garden vegetables, yams, sweet and ordinary potatoes, roots, cassava, &c.); and although by far the major portion, perhaps four-fifths, of the produce is consumed by the people, yet the annual value of the export trade in its various forms, from this source, approximates to three quarters of a million sterling, against less than £90,000 at the beginning of the century. Among food products recently added to the list of easily grown fruits and vegetables (by Mr. Nock of the Hakgalla Gardens) are the tree-tomato, chocho, a parsnip, and a small yam, all introduced from the West Indies, and already very popular with the Sinhalese, especially of the Uva province.

Besides coconut oil, there is an export of essential oils expressed from citronella and lemon-grass, from cinnamon and cinnamon leaf, which, valued at £25,000 to £30,000, is of some importance to a section of the community.

Of more importance to the people is their tobacco, of which about 25,000 acres are cultivated, the greater part of the crop being consumed locally, though as much as 48,000 cwt. of unmanufactured leaf, valued at £100,000, are exported to India.

The natives have always grown a little cotton in certain districts, and at one time a good deal of cotton cloth was manufactured at Batticaloa, but the industry has almost entirely ceased, being driven out by the cheapness of Manchester goods. An industry which has sprung up of recent years, however, is the collection of the short-stapled cotton from the pods of the silk-cotton tree (*Bombax Malabaricum*), exported under the name of "Kapok" (a Malay term) to Australia and Europe, to stuff chairs, mattresses, &c. A small quantity of this tree cotton was annually exported from Ceylon so far back as the time of the Portuguese.

Sugar-cane is largely grown in native gardens for use as a vegetable, the cane being sold in the bazaars, and the pith eaten as the stalk of a cabbage would be. At one time the eastern and southern districts of the island were thought to be admirably adapted for systematic sugar cultivation, but after plantations on an extensive scale had been opened by experienced colonists, and a large amount of capital sunk, it was found that, while the cane grew luxuriantly, the moist climate and soil did not permit of the sap crystallizing or yielding a sufficiency of crystallizable material. There is, however, still one plantation and manufactory of sugar and molasses in European hands, near Galle.

Before leaving the branches of agriculture more particularly in native hands, we may refer to the large expanse of patana grass and natural pasturage, especially in the Uva and eastern districts, which is utilized by the Sinhalese for their cattle, a certain number of which supply the meat consumed in the Central Province. By far the greater portion, however, of the beef and mutton required in the large towns of the island is (like rice, flour, potatoes, and other food requisites) imported in the shape of cattle and sheep, to the value of £80,000, from India. In some years the return has been over £120,000, but that was chiefly through the demand for Indian bullocks for draught purposes. There is no doubt much scope for the people of Ceylon to do more to meet the local demand for such food supplies, although the natural pasturage is, as a rule, rather poor. In Guinea and Mauritius grass (as also, for the high elevations, in the "prairie grass" of Australia), which grow freely with a little attention, some of the best fodder grasses in the world are easily cultivated in Ceylon.

---

### *Native Manufactures.*

Of *Manufacturing Industries* Ceylon has a very poor show. The Sinhalese are good carpenters, and supply furniture and carved work in abundance; both they and the Tamils make good artizans; witness the roll of workmen in the Government factory, Colombo, and the Colombo Ironworks, where ocean-going steamers are repaired, as well as a great variety of machinery is turned out, such as steam-engines, water-motors, and coffee, tea, and oil-preparing machines. The Sinhalese were distinguished as ironworkers in very ancient days; they knew nothing about firearms until the Portuguese era, and yet they soon excelled European gunmakers in the beautifully-worked muskets they turned out for their king. They were early workers in brass and glass, as their ancient ruins show, and they must have known a little about electricity, for it is related in the *Mahawansa* that King Sanghatissa, A.D. 234, placed a glass pinnacle on the Ruanwelli Dagoba, to serve as a protection against lightning. In these days the natives have watched with interest the introduction of the electric telegraph, telephone, and light, and when a suitable electric motor is made available, the numerous and splendid streams and waterfalls of the hill-country ought to afford ready force for utilization. Native cotton spinners and weavers were at one time common, but the industry is dying out; very little tobacco is manufactured; the making of mats, baskets, and coir-rope gives some employment. The masons of the country are now chiefly Moormen; though the Sinhalese must have done much in the building of tanks and other huge erections in ancient times. Fishing and mining plumbago and search for precious gems, as well as hunting, afford a good deal of employment. Workers in ebony, tortoise-shell, and porcupine quills, and in primitive pottery, are also numerous among the Sinhalese.

## CHAPTER VI.

### THE ORIGIN AND RISE OF THE PLANTING INDUSTRY.

**Coffee introduced by Arabs—First systematically cultivated by the Dutch in 1740—Extensive development in 1837—Highest level of prosperity reached in 1868-70—Appearance of Leaf Disease in 1869—Its disastrous effects.**

We now turn to the great planting industry in coffee, and the later additions in tea (now the rising and most important staple), cacao, the chocolate or cocoa plant, not to be confounded with the coconut palm: cinchona, rubber trees, cardamoms, &c.; to these the past rapid development and prosperity of the island are mainly due, and on them its future position as a leading colony must still chiefly depend.

The Arabs first introduced coffee into India and Ceylon, and the shrub was grown here before the arrival of the Portuguese or Dutch; but the preparation of a beverage from its berries was totally unknown to the Sinhalese, who only used the young coffee leaves for their curries, and the delicate jasmine-like coffee flowers for ornamenting their shrines of Buddha.

The first attempt at systematic cultivation was made by the Dutch in 1740, but, being confined to the low country, it did not succeed, and they seem never to have exported more than 1,000 cwt. in a

GENERAL VIEW OF A YOUNG DIMBULA PLANTATION (ABBOTSFORD).

**Tea and Cinchona Nurseries in foreground; rows of Coffee around buildings in centre; felled and standing Forest beyond.**

***From a Photograph by Messrs. W. L. H. Skeen & Co., of Colombo.***

year. The Moormen (Arab) traders and Sinhalese, having once discovered the use of coffee, kept up the cultivation and trade, but when the British took Ceylon and up to 1812, the annual export had never exceeded 3,000 cwt. So it continued until the master-mind of Sir Edward Barnes opened road communication between the hill country and the coast, and began to consider how the planting industry could be extended, and the revenues of the country developed. The Governor himself led the way, in opening a coffee plantation near Kandy, in 1825, just one year after the first systematic coffee estate was formed by Mr. George Bird, near Gampola. These examples were speedily followed, but still the progress was slow, for in 1837, twelve years after, the total export of coffee did not exceed 30,000 cwt.

It is usual to date the rise of the coffee planting enterprise from this year, which witnessed a great rush of investments, and the introduction of the West India system of cultivation by Robert Boyd Tytler, usually regarded as the "father" of Ceylon planters. An immense extension of cultivation took place up to 1845, by which time the trade had developed to an export of close on 200,000 cwt. Then came a financial explosion in Great Britain, which speedily extended its destructive influence to Ceylon, and led to a stoppage of the supplies required to plant and cultivate young plantations. Much land opened was abandoned, and for three years the enterprise was paralyzed; but nevertheless the export continued to increase, and by the time Governor Sir Henry Ward appeared, in 1855, confidence had been restored, and all was ready for the great impetus his energetic administration gave to an enterprise which, in twenty years, had come to be regarded as the backbone of the agricultural industry of the island, and the mainstay of the revenue. The Sinhalese soon followed the example set them by the European planters, and so widely and rapidly developed their coffee gardens throughout the hill-country, that between 1849 and 1869, from one-half to one-fourth of the total quantity of coffee shipped year by year was "native coffee."

LIBERIAN COFFEE.*

The highest level of prosperity was reached in 1868, 1869, and 1870, in each of which years the

* For the use of this illustration, as also fcr the plates of the "Coconut Climber," the "Talipot Palm," and the "Coffee Tree," we are indebted to the Rev. S. Langdon, the author of a charming account of the missionary's home and its rich surroundings of animal and vegetable life in a tropical land. This volume, "My Mission

exports slightly exceeded a million cwt., of a value in European markets of not less than four millions sterling, against 34,000 cwt., valued at £120,000, exported in 1837: a marvellous development in thirty years of a tropical industry!

In 1869 the total extent cultivated on plantations (apart from native gardens) was 176,000 acres, and the return from the land in full bearing averaged over 5 cwt. an acre, a return which should, under favourable circumstances, give a profit of from £7 to £10 an acre, or from twenty to twenty-five per cent. on the capital invested. Nothing could be brighter than the prospects of the colony and its main enterprise in 1869: Sir Hercules Robinson's administration, then in mid-course, was most beneficial; the railway between Colombo and Kandy, two years open, was a grand success; and, with an unfailing supply of cheap free labour from Southern India, remarkable facilities for transport, and a splendid climate, the stability of the great coffee enterprise seemed to be assured.

Its importance was fully realized through the statistics of the actual extent cultivated which were for the first time compiled, in full detail (by the author), and although it began to be felt that the good land at the most suitable altitude had all been taken up, and most of it brought under cultivation, yet no one doubted the comparative permanency of such plantations under a liberal, scientific system of

Garden," and another by the same author, "Punchi Nona, a story of Female Education and Village Life in Ceylon," both give vivid, entertaining, and truthful pictures of Ceylon life and mission work, and they show what good is being done to the people of the country by patient teaching. Published by T. Woolmer, 2, Castle Street, City Road, E.C.; and at 66, Paternoster Row, E.C.

cultivation. But in this same year there first appeared an enemy, most insignificant in appearance, which in less than a dozen years was fated to bring down the export of the great staple to one-fifth of its then dimensions, and that notwithstanding a wide extension of new cultivation. This enemy was a minute fungus on the leaf, new to science, and named by the greatest fungoid authorities *Hemileia vastatrix*, from its destructive powers, now popularly known as "coffee-leaf disease."

First appearing in one of the youngest districts, at a remote corner, it rapidly spread all over the coffee zone, being easily distinguished by the appearance of bright orange spots on the leaves, which subsequently wither and drop off. At first it was treated as a matter of little moment by all but the late Dr. Thwaites, F.R.S., the Director of the Ceylon Botanic Gardens, and for several years it apparently did little harm, crops being only slightly affected, and any decrease being attributed to seasonal influences rather than to a minute pest, which, it was supposed, only served to remind the planter of the necessity of more liberal cultivation. Another cause, moreover, served most effectually to blind the eyes of all concerned to the insidious progress of the pest, and the gradual but sure falling-off of crops, namely, a sudden and unprecedented rise in the value of coffee in Europe and America—a rise equivalent, in a few years, to more than fifty per cent. This great access of value to his returns more than sufficed to compensate the Ceylon planter for any diminution of crop. It did more: it stimulated a vast extension of cultivation into the largest remaining reserve, known as the Wilderness of the Peak, extending from Nuwara

Eliya through a succession of upland valleys in Dimbula, Dikoya, and Maskeliya, to the Adam's Peak range, an area of forest covering some 400 square miles, having the most delightful climate in the world, but until this time (1868–69) regarded as too high and wet for coffee. This region had been previously utilized as a hunting-ground by an occasional party of Europeans or Kandyans, the pilgrims' paths to Adam's Peak, winding their way through the dense jungle, and intercepted by a succession of large unbridged rivers, being the only lines of communication. The rush into this El Dorado had begun in the time of Sir Hercules Robinson, who energetically aided the development by extending roads and bridging rivers, thus utilizing some of the large surpluses which the sale of the lands and the increased customs and railway revenues afforded him.

A cycle of favourable—that is, comparatively dry—seasons still further contributed to the success of the young high districts, so that coffee (which had previously been supposed to find its suitable limit at 4,000 or 4,500 feet) was planted and cultivated profitably up to 5,000 and even 5,500 feet. All through Governor Gregory's administration the high price of coffee and the active extension of the cultivated area continued, the competition becoming so keen that forest-land, which ten or twenty years before would not fetch as much as £2 an acre, was sold as high as £15, £20, and even £28 an acre. Even at this price planters calculated on profitable results; but there can be no doubt that speculation, rather than the teachings of experience, guided their calculations.

Between 1869 and 1879 over 400,000 acres of

Crown land were sold by the Ceylon Government, bringing in more than a million sterling to the revenue, and of this 100,000 acres were brought into cultivation with coffee, at an outlay of not less than from two to two and a-half millions sterling, almost entirely in the upland districts referred to.

Meantime the insidious leaf-fungus pest had been working deadly mischief. High cultivation, with manure of various descriptions, failing to arrest its progress, the aid of science was called in, special investigations took place, its life-history was written; but the practical result was no more satisfactory to the coffee planter than have similar investigations proved to the potato cultivator, the wheat farmer fighting with rust, or the vine-grower who is baffled by the fatal *phylloxera.* Less deadly than the *phylloxera,* the leaf-fungus had nevertheless so affected the Ceylon coffee enterprise that in the ten years during which cultivation had extended more than fifty per cent., the annual export had fallen to three-fourths of the million cwt. The same fungus had extended to the coffee districts of India and Java, with similar results in devastated crops, but in the greatest coffee country of all—Brazil—the impetus to an extension of cultivation which the high prices from 1873 onwards had given, was not checked by the presence of this fungoid, or other coffee diseases, and from thence soon began to pour into the markets of the world such crops as speedily brought prices to their old level, reacting disastrously on the Ceylon enterprise, which had at the same time to encounter the monetary depression caused by the collapse of the City of Glasgow Bank and other financial failures in Britain. Misfortunes never come singly, and accordingly a series of wet seasons crowned the evils befalling the planters in the young high districts, while the older coffee lower down began to be neglected, so enfeebled had it become in many places under the repeated visits of the fungus. This so disheartened the coffee planter that he turned his attention to new products, more especially cinchona, and, later, tea, planted among and in supercession of the coffee, as well as in new land. Tea especially succeeded so well, as will be fully related further on, that coffee over a large area has been entirely taken out, and the area cultivated has been reduced from the maximum of 275,000 acres in 1878 to not much more than 100,000 acres in 1887. The result is that in the present season (1886–7) in place of the million cwt. exported sixteen years ago, the total shipments of coffee from Ceylon will not exceed one-fifth of that quantity, and although with a more favourable blossoming time this year it may be increased in the succeeding season, yet there is no escape from the drawbacks which still beset the coffee planter in Ceylon. The leaf-fungus still hovers about, though in a much milder, and, as some think, a diseased form; but another enemy has appeared in the shape of a *coccus* (called "green bug"), which has done much harm. Nevertheless, in certain favoured coffee districts, such as the Uva divisions, Bopatalava, Maturatta, Agras division of Dimbula, and Middle and Upper Dikoya, coffee still looks vigorous, and may continue to repay careful cultivation, more especially as prices have again improved, and a scarcity of the product is anticipated. The mitigations of the disaster—the silver lining to the dark cloud which came over the prospects of the majority of Ceylon coffee planters—will be alluded to later on.

At an early stage in the history of coffee leaf disease in Ceylon one cause, and that perhaps the chief, of the visitation had become apparent in the limitation of cultivation to one plant, and one only, over hundreds of square miles of country which had previously been covered with the most varied vegetation. Nature had revenged herself, just as she had done on Ireland when potatoes threatened to become the universal crop, as well as on extensive wheat fields elsewhere, and on the French vineyards. The *hemileia vastatrix* was described by Dr. Thwaites as peculiar to a jungle plant, and finding coffee leaves a suitable food in 1869 it multiplied and spread indefinitely. It could not be said that the fungus thus burst out in Ceylon because of coffee being worn out or badly cultivated, for it first appeared in a young district upon vigorous coffee, and it afterwards attacked old and young, vigorous and weak trees, with absolute impartiality. The true remedy, then, for the loss occasioned by this pest—apart from the wisdom of the old adage not to have all one's eggs in one basket—lay in the introduction of *New Products.*

## CHAPTER VII.

### NEW PRODUCTS.

Tea—Cinchona—Cocoa—India-rubber—Cardamoms—Liberian Coffee, &c.

TEA cultivation was tried in Ceylon in the time of the Dutch, but was not persevered with; and although there is a wild plant (*cassia ariculata*), called the Matara tea plant, from which the Sinhalese in the south of the island are accustomed to make an infusion, yet nothing was done with the true tea plant till long after coffee was established. Forty-five years ago the Messrs. Worms (cousins of the Rothschilds, who did an immense deal in developing Ceylon) introduced the China plant, and, planting up a field on the Rambode Pass, proved that tea would grow well in the island. Mr. Llewellyn about the same time introduced the Assam plant into Dolosbagie district, but no commercial result came from these ventures. Attention was, however, frequently called to this product, and in 1867 a Ceylon planter was commissioned to report on the tea-planting industry in India. In that same year the attention of planters was also first turned to the cinchona plant, which had been introduced six years earlier to India and Ceylon by Mr. Clements Markham. The Director of the Botanic Garden, Dr. Thwaites, however, found great difficulty in getting any planter to care about cultivating a "medicine plant," and when the great rise in prices for coffee came, all thought of tea and cinchona was cast to the winds, and the one old profitable product, which everybody—planters and coolies alike—understood, was alone planted.

Very early in his administration Sir William

THE TEA PLANT.

Gregory, to his special credit be it said, saw the necessity for new products, and he used all his personal and official influence to secure their development, introducing a new feature into the Governor's annual speech to the Legislative Council in special notices of the progress of tea, cinchona, cacao, Liberian coffee, and rubber cultivation. The influence of the principal journal in the colony (the *Ceylon Observer*) was cast into the same scale, and practical information to aid the planter of new products was collected for it from all quarters, more especially from the tropical belt of the earth's surface.*

When Governor Gregory arrived in 1872 only 500 acres of cinchona had been planted, but before he left in 1877 not only had these increased to 6,000 acres, but the planters had begun thoroughly to appreciate the value of the new product, its suitable-

CINCHONA SUCCIRUBRA † (*Genuine Red Bark*).

ness for the hill-country and climate of Ceylon, and the profits to be made from judicious cultivation. The great rush, however, took place on the failure of

* In June, 1881, the monthly periodical, *The Tropical Agriculturist*, was started by the author from the *Observer* press for the special purpose of meeting the requirements of planters. It circulates all round the tropical world, and has received high encomiums in Britain, United States, and Australia.

† The original drawing of this illustration has been kindly supplied by Messrs. Howards and Sons, of Stratford, E.

coffee in 1879 and the next three years, so that by 1883 the area covered by this plant could not be less than 60,000 acres. The enormous bark exports which followed from Ceylon so lowered the price (involving the great blessing of cheap quinine) that it became no longer profitable to cut bark in the native South American cinchona groves, or to plant further in Ceylon, India, or Java. Attention has, therefore, since 1884 been directed from cinchona; nevertheless the exports from the existing area continue high, and the area still under cinchona, making allowance for what is planted throughout the tea and coffee plantations, cannot be less than 30,000 acres, with several (perhaps forty) million trees above two or three years, of all descriptions of cinchona growing thereon. The export of bark, which was 11,547 lb. in 1872, rose to nearly 14,000,000 lb. the last season (1885–6), and it will not be less during 1886–7, while, with a fair price, it could be maintained at from eight to ten million pounds per annum. Very great mistakes were made at first in cinchona-planting in the use of immature seed and by the choice of unsuitable species and unsuitable soil, but the Ceylon planters rapidly qualified themselves to be successful cinchona growers, and many still find how much may be done to supplement their staples (tea and coffee) through this product.

It has long been the conviction of many who have studied the climate and the character of Ceylon soils that the country is far more fitted to become a great tea producer than ever it was to grow coffee. It is now realized, too, that a large proportion of the area opened with the latter product—apart from the appearance of leaf-fungus altogether—would have done much better under tea. Unlike India, there is never in the low country, western and south-western,

THE COFFEE TREE.

or in the central (the hilly) portions of Ceylon, a month of the year without rain, the annual fall in this region ranging from 80 to 200 inches, while the alternate tropical sunshine and moisture form the perfection of climate for the leaf-yielding tea-shrub. Untimely downpours, which so often wrecked the blossoms and the hopes of the coffee-planter, do no harm to the leaf crop of the tea-planter. Not only so, but the harvesting of tea-leaf is spread over six, or even nine, months of the year. If a fresh flush of young leaf fails from any cause this month, the planter has generally only a few weeks to wait for another chance, and, save for the "pruning" and the very wet season in Ceylon, the tea-planter can look for some returns nearly all the year round. Very different was the case with coffee, the crop of which for a whole year was often dependent on the weather during a single month; or even a week's (or a day's) untimely rain or drought might destroy the chance of a return for a whole year's labour. Even in the favoured Uva districts there were only two periods of harvesting coffee in the year. Again, while the zone suitable for the growth of coffee ranged from 1,500 or 2,000 to 4,500 or 5,500 feet above sea-level, tea seems to flourish equally well (the Assam indigenous kind, or good hybrid) at sea-level, and (a hardy hybrid or China kind) at 6,000 and even to close on 7,000 feet above sea-level. The tea shrub is found to be altogether hardier and generally far more suitable to the comparatively poor soil of Ceylon than ever coffee was. Nevertheless it took many years to convince Ceylon planters of the wisdom of looking to tea; and for some years even after it was gone into in earnest, much less progress was made than in the case of cinchona. There were good reasons for this in the greater cost of tea seed, and the much greater

ASSAM TEA TREE.

trouble entailed in the preparation of the produce for the market. Beginning from 1873 with an extent planted of 250 acres, in ten years this area increased to about 35,000 acres, while in the succeeding year, 1884, this was doubled, as much being also added in 1885, and a large extent in 1886, so that before the Jubilee Year of Queen Victoria's reign is closed, there will not be less than 150,000 acres covered with the tea plant in Ceylon. Tea seed is now cheap enough, and the manufacture of the leaf is no longer a mystery, and Ceylon is on the highway to become a rival to the most important of the Indian districts in the production of tea. The tea export from Ceylon of 23 lb. in 1876 has risen to 7,849,886 lb. in 1886, and it is expected to go on for some time almost at a geometrical rate of progression, so that, when the 150,000 acres are in bearing, the total export will not be less than forty million lb., say in 1890–91. There are large reserves of Crown land suitable for tea, for, as already said, it is found to produce profitable crops on land a few hundred feet above sea-level, as well as at all altitudes up to the neighbourhood of Nuwara Eliya, approximating to 7,000 feet.

The rapid development of the tea-planting industry in Ceylon during the past four or five years constitutes the most interesting and important fact in the recent history of the island. The future of the colony depends upon this staple now far more than on any other branch of agriculture, and so far the promise is that the industry will be a comparatively permanent and steadily profitable one. On favoured plantations, with comparatively flat land and good soil (tea loves a flat as coffee did a sloping hill-side), tea crops have already been gathered in Ceylon for some years in succession in excess almost of anything known in India. With unequalled means of communication by railway and first-class roads—Uva districts still want their railway—with well-trained, easily-managed, and fairly intelligent labourers in the Tamil coolie, with a suitable climate and soil, and, above all, with a planting community of exceptional intelligence and energy in pushing a product that is once shown to be profitable for cultivation, the rapid development of our tea enterprise from the infant of 1876–80 to the giant of 1883–7 may be more easily understood. Ceylon teas have been received with exceptional favour in the London market, and the demand already exceeds the supply. The teas are of a high character and fine flavour, perfectly pure, which is more than can be said of a large proportion of China and Japan teas. It is therefore expected by competent authorities that as the taste for the good teas of Ceylon and India spreads—one never enjoys a common adulterated tea after getting accustomed to one of good flavour—the China teas, to a great extent, may fall out of use. Whether this be the case or not, there is no doubt that the Ceylon tea-planter can hold his own. The consumption of his staple is spreading every year, and if the English-speaking people of the United States only did equal justice to the tea with their brethren elsewhere, the demand would there also exceed the supply. Moreover, tea can be delivered more cheaply from Ceylon, allowing for quality, than from either India or China. As was the case with coffee, the preparation of the new staple in Ceylon is in a fair way to be brought to perfection. Improved machinery has already been invented by local planters and others to save labour, counteract the effect of unsuitable weather (for withering the leaf, &c.), or to turn out teas with better flavour; and yet the industry cannot be said properly to be seven years old in the island! Already its beneficial influence on local business, export trade, and revenue is widely felt. The Sinhalese, in many districts, are volunteering to work for the tea-planters, and native tea-gardens are also being planted up on many low-country road-sides. This process is bound to go on until there is a wide area covered with tea under native auspices. The cultivators will probably, as a rule, sell their leaf to central factories owned by colonists; but there is no reason why, as time runs on, they should not manufacture for themselves. The atmosphere of planting, business, and even official circles in Ceylon just now is highly charged with "tea," and the number of Tea Patents (for preparing machines), of Tea publications,* Tea Brokers, Tea selling and Tea planting companies would greatly astonish a Ceylon coffee planter of the "fifties," "sixties," or even "seventies," if he "revisited the glimpses of the moon" in the Central or Western province of the island. Tea deserves a special chapter in this "Jubilee" book on Ceylon, and we could not say less about it. We call attention to our several engravings of the tea tree, and more especially to the pictures at the end of our volume (with letterpress), supplied by the Planters' Association of Ceylon in connection with the "Colonial and Indian Exhibition of 1886" (Appendix XI.).

---

A minor product as compared with tea, but still a very

* *See* the "Ceylon Tea Planters' Manual," "Tea and other New Products," "Planters' Note Book," "Tea Tables," and "Tropical Agriculturist," published by A. M. and J. Ferguson, Colombo

promising one in its own place, is Theobroma Cacao ("food for gods") of Linnæus, producing the "cocoa"

PODS OF THE CACAO TREE,
Each containing twenty-four seeds in pulp, which, when prepared, give the chocolate of commerce.

and chocolate of commerce. This plant can never

be cultivated in Ceylon to the same extent as coffee, tea, or cinchona, for it requires a considerable depth of good soil, in a favourable situation, at a medium elevation, with complete shelter from wind, and these requisites are only to be found in very limited areas in this island. Nevertheless, where these conditions exist, cacao promises to be a most lasting and profitable cultivation. To the late R. B. Tytler belongs the credit of introducing this cultivation in the Dumbara valley, and in his hands Ceylon cocoa speedily realized the highest price in the London market, experienced brokers remarking that there must be something in the soil and climate of the districts where it is cultivated in Ceylon peculiarly suited to cacao. The Mátalé, Kurunugala, and Uva districts also show fine cacao "walks," and the export of "cacao" has risen from 10 cwt. in 1878 to 13,056 cwt. in 1886. There are several thousand (14,000) acres now planted, which ought to give an export of 50,000 cwt. (or 5,600,000 lb., as counted in the West Indies) a few years hence. From experience in the West Indies, as well as Ceylon, it is found that up to ten years of age cacao is an uncertain, even delicate, plant, but after that it is credited in British Guiana with going on for 100 years yielding fairly remunerative crops without much trouble. Ceylon cacao planters have already improved on the means of preparing the bean for the London market, and further improvements are under consideration. It is possible that ultimately an area exceeding 30,000 acres under this plant will enable Ceylon to send 120,000 to 150,000 cwt. of its product into European markets.*

* *See* pamphlets on "Cacao Cultivation," published by A. M. and J. Ferguson, Colombo.

*Cardamoms* spice (called "grains of paradise") is another minor product, the cultivation of which has

THE CACAO TREE.

benefited a good many Ceylon planters, the export rising from 14,000 lb. in 1878 to 239,000 lb. in 1886;

the latter a quantity sufficient to seriously affect the price in the London market. It is, indeed, a significant fact that in respect of two products, practically receiving no attentive aid from our planters ten, or, at any rate, fifteen years ago, Ceylon now rules the markets of the world. We refer to cinchona bark and cardamoms, for the supply of which, as of cinnamon, coconut oil, and plumbago, this colony is pre-eminent.*

The *Caoutchouc*, or India-rubber trees of commerce, from South America and Eastern Africa, are of recent introduction, but their cultivation and growth in the planting districts of Ceylon have so far not given very satisfactory results. The growth of the trees has been generally satisfactory, indeed wonderful, equalling in some cases forty-eight feet in height, and forty-five inches in circumference in five years, and when more is known about the mode of harvesting the rubber the industry may prove very profitable.†

Among minor new products Liberian coffee was introduced from the West African Republic of that name (in 1875–79 chiefly), in the hope that its large size and strong habit would enable it at the low elevation in which it grows to resist the leaf-fungus; but this hope has not been realized, and although the acreage planted is giving fair crops, there is no attempt to extend this area for the present.‡

Pepper, African palm-oil nut, nutmegs, croton oil seeds, and annotto dye plant are among the other

* Pamphlet on "Cardamoms Cultivation, &c.," has been published by A. M. and J. Ferguson, Colombo.

† *See* "All about Rubber," second edition, published by A. M. and J. Ferguson, Colombo.

‡ *See* "Liberian Coffee," illustrated, published by A. M. and J. Ferguson, Colombo.

products to which, by reason of the reverse in coffee, planters in the hill and low country of Ceylon have been turning their attention in isolated cases, with results more or less satisfactory. In the variety of all the industries detailed in the foregoing pages it is

THE CEARA RUBBER TREE.

A specimen of rapid growth in Ceylon (Sembawattie Estate); 17 ft. high, 10 in. in circumference, and only nine months old.

felt there is sufficient guarantee to warrant the belief that the coffee leaf fungus will prove eventually, if it has not already proved, a blessing in disguise to the island, its colonists, and native people. The latter suffered with their European brethren, not only through the disease affecting their coffee gardens, but much more through the absence of employment in so many branches which the prosperous coffee enterprise opened out to them. Tea plantations are now rapidly filling up the blank left by coffee, while many of the natives, led by their chiefs and intelligent headmen and villagers, are themselves planting new products —tea, cinchona, and cacao—and so following the example of the European planters. In this way the Planting enterprise in all its ramifications in Ceylon is fraught with the promise of a greater and more reliable prosperity than ever appertained to coffee alone in its palmiest days.

# CHAPTER VIII.

## PRESENT POSITION OF AGRICULTURAL ENTERPRISE, LOCAL INDUSTRIES, AND FOREIGN TRADE.

Exports of last decade—The plumbago trade—Gold and Iron—Native industries generally flourishing—Tea especially and Cinchona will make up for the deficiency in Coffee.

To sum up and show at a glance the present position of the trade arising from our agricultural enterprise and local industry, we here insert a statement of the *staple exports* for the past fourteen commercial seasons. [See Table on next page.]

These figures differ slightly from those already quoted for the calendar years; the *commercial* season closes on 30th September, having been fixed by the Colombo merchants many years ago, so as to separate as fairly as possible each coffee crop.

There are a few headings in this table that we have not touched on yet, and the principal one of these is *plumbago*, or graphite. This is the only mineral of commercial importance exported from Ceylon. The mining industry is entirely in the hands of the Sinhalese; mines of from 100 to 200 and even 300 ft. depth are worked in a primitive fashion, and the finest plumbago in the world for

# STAPLE EXPORTS OF CEYLON, 1873–1886.

*Total Quantities of the following Articles exported from Colombo and Galle annually during the past Fourteen Years.*

| Total Exports from | Coffee. | | | Cinchona. | Tea. | Cocoa. | Cardamoms. | Cinnamon. | | Coconut. | | |
|---|---|---|---|---|---|---|---|---|---|---|---|---|
| | Plantation. | Native. | Total. | Branch & Trunk. | | | | Bales. | Chips. | Oil. | Copra. | Poonac. |
| | cwt. | cwt. | cwt. | lb. | lb. | cwt. | lb. | lb. | lb. | cwt. | cwt. | cwt. |
| 1st Oct. 1885 to 30th Sept. 1886 | 215,576 | 8,117 | 223,693 | 15,364,912 | 7,170,329 | 13,347 | 236,056 | 1,629,548 | 548,037 | 234,308 | 127,899 | 42,484 |
| do. 1884 do. 1885 | 294,506 | 20,305 | 314,811 | 11,678,360 | 3,796,684 | 6,758 | 152,405 | 1,574,022 | 628,914 | 274,998 | 178,361 | 54,245 |
| do. 1883 do. 1884 | 312,458 | 11,483 | 323,941 | 11,492,947 | 2,262,539 | 9,863 | 66,319 | 1,796,372 | 538,577 | 423,830 | 177,347 | .. |
| do. 1882 do. 1883 | 245,631 | 14,422 | 260,053 | 6,925,595 | 1,522,882 | 3,588 | 21,655 | 1,402,429 | 336,872 | 306,299 | 122,825 | .. |
| do. 1881 do. 1882 | 522,949 | 41,897 | 564,846 | 3,099,895 | 623,292 | 1,018 | 28,127 | 1,599,327 | 394,731 | 183,768 | 54,004 | .. |
| do. 1880 do. 1881 | 415,456 | 38,302 | 453,758 | 1,207,720 | 277,590 | 479 | 16,069 | 1,319,406 | 321,772 | 247,113 | 43,337 | .. |
| do. 1879 do. 1880 | 622,306 | 47,308 | 669,614 | 1,208,518 | 103,624 | 122 | * | 1,395,534 | 474,484 | 316,508 | * | .. |
| do. 1878 do. 1879 | 767,293 | 57,216 | 824,509 | 373,511 | 81,595 | .. | .. | 1,219,208 | 188,518 | 213,622 | .. | .. |
| do. 1877 do. 1878 | 551,046 | 69,246 | 620,292 | 173,497 | 3,515 | .. | .. | 1,298,304 | 259,174 | 112,825 | .. | .. |
| do. 1876 do. 1877 | 851,201 | 91,846 | 943,047 | 56,589 | 1,775 | .. | .. | 1,063,107 | 284,664 | 152,416 | .. | .. |
| do. 1875 do. 1876 | 626,636 | 93,791 | 720,427 | 16,842 | 282 | .. | .. | 1,262,250 | 258,381 | 194,306 | .. | .. |
| do. 1874 do. 1875 | 855,661 | 113,033 | 968,694 | 18,731 | .. | .. | .. | 902,733 | 200,607 | 121,214 | .. | .. |
| do. 1873 do. 1874 | 521,193 | 96,149 | 617,342 | .. | .. | .. | .. | 1,082,541 | 183,303 | 116,199 | .. | .. |
| do. 1872 do. 1873 | 861,575 | 133,918 | 995,493 | .. | .. | .. | .. | 1,023,210 | 242,547 | 163,274 | .. | .. |

| Total Exports from | Plumbago. | Coir. | | | Ebony. | Deer Horns. | Sapanwood. | Orchella weed. | Kitul Fibre. | Citronella Oil. | Cinnamon Oil. |
|---|---|---|---|---|---|---|---|---|---|---|---|
| | | Rope. | Yarn. | Fibre. | | | | | | | |
| | cwt. | cwt. | cwt. | cwt. | cwt. | cwt. | cwt. | cwt. | cwt. | oz. | oz. |
| 1st Oct. 1885 to 30th Sept. 1886 | 190,153 | 7,816 | 74,146 | 17,219 | 26,590 | 1,080 | 1,848 | 665 | 2,906 | 6,461,278 | 139,094 |
| do. 1884 do. 1885 | 197,221 | 10,419 | 84,057 | 12,732 | 10,013 | 2,125 | 2,834 | 430 | 1,631 | 5,721,112 | 117,023 |
| do. 1883 do. 1884 | 213,514 | 14,473 | 85,195 | 13,672 | 16,724 | 937 | 2,413 | 827 | 1,466 | 4,827,020 | 104,185 |
| do. 1882 do. 1883 | 279,057 | 11,792 | 68,896 | 18,009 | 18,273 | 2,552 | 11,404 | 1,057 | 1,762 | 3,335,780 | 76,224 |
| do. 1881 do. 1882 | 240,714 | 7,479 | 65,885 | 6,199 | 17,532 | 2,503 | 10,561 | 1,157 | 1,073 | 2,666,917 | 118,762 |
| do. 1880 do. 1881 | 206,723 | 11,640 | 43,747 | 6,117 | 34,057 | 1,007 | 9,756 | 880 | 880 | 1,760,677 | 41,719 |
| do. 1879 do. 1880 | 209,096 | 7,290 | 56,838 | 5,862 | 42,616 | 1,677 | * | * | * | * | * |
| do. 1878 do. 1879 | 160,302 | 8,201 | 51,915 | 9,676 | 24,399 | 4,367 | .. | .. | .. | .. | .. |
| do. 1877 do. 1878 | 74,535 | 7,810 | 57,671 | 5,347 | 21,919 | 1,505 | .. | .. | .. | .. | .. |
| do. 1876 do. 1877 | 108,824 | 3,641 | 55,590 | 3,624 | 20,797 | 1,429 | .. | .. | .. | .. | .. |
| do. 1875 do. 1876 | 129,801 | 4,242 | 48,974 | 6,769 | 9,607 | 1,180 | .. | .. | .. | .. | .. |
| do. 1874 do. 1875 | 91,472 | 7,507 | 46,026 | 10,265 | 15,750 | 1,668 | .. | .. | .. | ... | ... |
| do. 1873 do. 1874 | 157,359 | 10,638 | 44,855 | 11,276 | 29,176 | 1,260 | .. | .. | .. | .. | .. |
| do. 1872 do. 1873 | 168,627 | 8,782 | 43,917 | 9,222 | 46,635 | 1,278 | .. | .. | ... | .. | .. |

**N.B.—A Table of the Staple Imports for the calendar years 1887 to 1886, inclusive, will be found in Appendix VI.** *** No records previous to 1880–81.**

crucible purposes is obtained. The industry has taken a great start of recent years, the average export increasing about 50 per cent. within the decade; the value of the trade averages about £350,000 per annum, and this mining industry has sprung up entirely within the last forty years.*

Of other minerals mention may be made of the precious stones found and exported in certain quantities, the chief being rubies and sapphires and cat's eyes. "Pearls" are included in the Customs returns with "precious stones," and the total value of all recorded in any one year for exports has never exceeded £9,000; but the large proportion of both pearls and precious stones taken out of the island on the persons of natives or others leaving would not be entered at all in the Customs returns.

Gold is freely distributed in the primary rocks of Ceylon, but it has not been found in paying quantities. Rich iron ore is very abundant, but there is no coal.

Of other minor exports affording some trade to native huntsmen are deer-horns, the trade in which indicates a considerable destruction of deer, so that a law has been passed to protect them as well as other game and elephants. The export of "hides and skins" is considerable, and might be more important were it not for the Sinhalese habits of cutting and marking the hides of their cattle. The local industry in tanning is very limited, though the materials are at hand to extend it considerably. There is also much scope for the export of dyeing (as well as tanning) substances. The export trade in timber—apart from ebony—is considerable, such as satin-

* See Monograph on "Plumbago," by A. M. Ferguson, contributed to the Royal Asiatic Society's Journal (Ceylon), in 1885.

wood, palmyra, tamarind, &c., to a total average value of £20,000 per annum.

It will be observed that the branches of trade more particularly in the hands of the natives—coconut oil, cinnamon, and minor exports—are in a sound, flourishing, and progressive condition. The case is very different with coffee, and the significance of the figures in our table will be understood when it is remembered that between 1865 and 1878 the average export of coffee shipped was equal in value to more than double of all the other exports put together. But instead of four or five millions of pounds' worth of coffee, we are now reduced to a value of from one to one and a quarter million sterling. Now, however, come in the new headings in our export table of tea, cinchona, and cacao, the latter two of which henceforth divide attention with coffee, while to tea will belong the honour of representing our planting enterprise *par excellence.*

As to the future of coffee, we think that an average export of a million pounds' sterling worth (200,000 to 250,000 cwt.) may still be counted on; and to make up the deficiency of three millions we may look to a steady export of cinchona bark, worth from three to five hundred thousand pounds per annum; while cacao, cardamoms, &c., should make a further considerable addition. But the main dependence must be on *tea;* and, considering the rapid way in which this has been planted, we see no reason to doubt that the area cultivated will suffice a few years hence to produce a quantity, of say thirty to forty million pounds' weight, worth a sum approximating to two million pounds sterling. Some authorities indeed calculate that there is no reason why Ceylon, with 200,000 acres planted with tea, should not by and by supply between sixty and

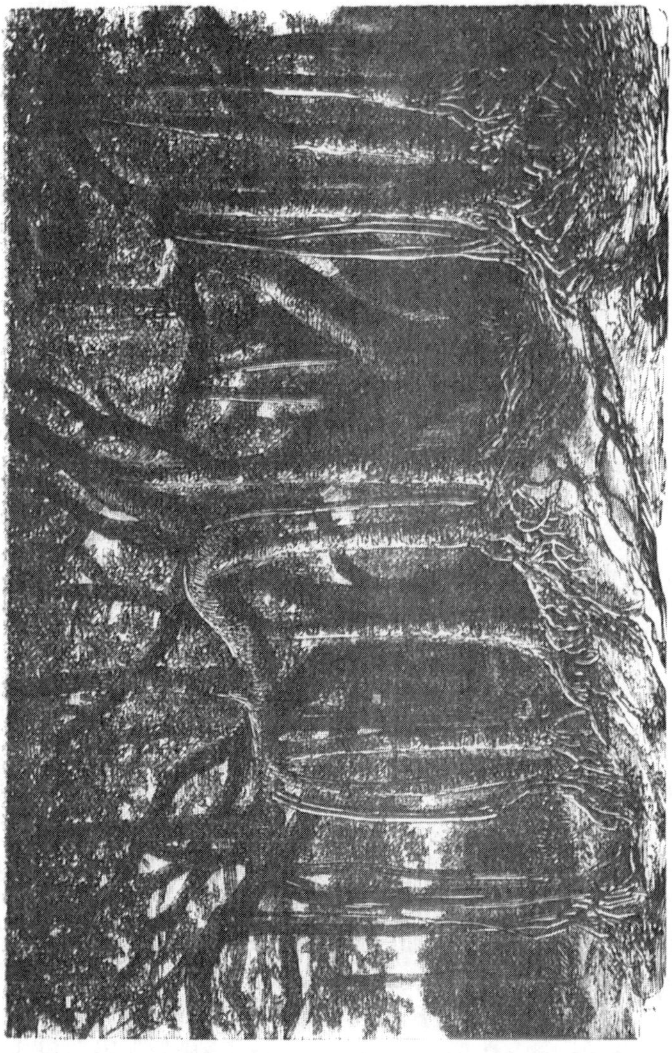

THE BANYAN TREE (*Ficus Indica*).

seventy million pounds of tea of the best qualities for the markets of the world.

## CHAPTER IX.

### WHAT THE PLANTING INDUSTRY HAS DONE FOR THE MOTHER-COUNTRY.

Recent years of depression considered—Planting profits absorbed IN THE PAST by Home capitalists—Absence of reserves of local wealth—The accumulated profits of past years estimated.

THE recent financial depression and scarcity of capital in Ceylon can readily be understood when a succession of bad coffee seasons, involving a deficiency in the planters' harvests of that product equal to many millions of pounds sterling, is taken into consideration. There have been periods of depression before in the history of the Ceylon planting enterprise, and these, curiously enough, have been noted to come round in cycles of eleven years. Thus, in 1845, wild speculation in opening plantations, followed by a great fall in the price of coffee and a collapse of credit, arrested progress for a time; in 1856-7, a sharp financial shock affected the course of prosperity which had set in; and again, in 1866-7, the fortunes of coffee fell to so low an ebb that a London capitalist, who visited the island, said the most striking picture of woe-begone misery he saw was the typical "man who owned a coffee estate."

Yet this was followed by good seasons and bounteous coffee harvests.

The depression which set in during 1879, was, however, the most prolonged and trying. True, agriculture nearly all over the world has been suffering from a succession of bad harvests, more particularly in the mother-country; but there are certain grave distinctions between the conditions of a tropical colony and lands in a temperate zone. In Ceylon a generation among European colonists has usually been considered not to exceed ten years—not at all on account of mortality, for the hills of Ceylon have the perfection of a healthy climate, but from the constant changes in the elements of the European community—the coming and going which in the past made such a distinct change in the broad elements of society every ten or certainly every fifteen years.

Those colonists who made fortunes in coffee in the island—only 10 per cent. of the whole body of planters, however—did not think of making it their permanent home. The capitalist who sent out his money for investment got it back as soon as possible. The "accumulated profits" made during the time of prosperity, which at home form a reserve fund of local wealth to enable the sufferer from present adversity to benefit by past earnings, were utterly wanting in Ceylon. We had no reserve fund of past profits to fall back upon, no class of wealthy Europeans enriched by former times of prosperity living amongst us and circulating the liquidated products of former industry, when the period of adversity and depression arrived.

Ceylon, in fact, in the best coffee days, used to be a sort of "incubator" to which capitalists sent their eggs to be hatched, and whence they received from time to time an abundant brood, leaving sometimes but the shells for our local portion. Money was sent out to Ceylon to fell its forests and plant them with coffee, and it was returned in the shape of copious harvests to the home capitalist, leaving in some cases the bare hill-sides from whence these rich harvests were drawn. Had the profits from the abundant coffee crops in those past days been located here and invested in the country and its soil, a fund of local wealth might have existed when the lean years came, manufactures might now have been flourishing, a number of wealthy citizens of European origin might have been living in affluence, and we should have possessed resources to help us over the time of adversity and depression!

The total amount of coffee raised on the plantations of Ceylon since 1849 is about 19,000,000 cwt., and there were produced previously (excluding native coffee in both cases) about 1,000,000 cwt. at the least, making a grand total of coffee of 20,000,000 cwt. as the produce of imported capital. Including interest and all items of local cost, we may safely say that this coffee has been produced for £2 2s. per cwt., and has realized at the least £3 net on an average; it has therefore earned a net profit of £18,000,000. The coffee so produced has been yielded by plantations of not more than 320,000 acres in the aggregate, after including a due allowance for lands abandoned; and the average cost of the estates, including the purchase of the land, has certainly not exceeded £25 per acre, involving a total capital of £8,000,000. There should therefore have been a sum of £10,000,000 of liquidated profit returned to the capitalist, besides the refund of his principal, and there would still remain the existing plant of say 200,000 acres of land under cultivation by means of the said capital, worth at least £10 per acre, or altogether £2,000,000—thus showing a total profit of £12,000,000. Looking at some tracts of land which have been relegated to weeds and waste—tracts which for long years poured forth rich harvests for their owners—the question will force itself upon us: What would now have been the condition of these lands if their owners had been settled on them, and their families, homesteads, and accumulated profits had remained to enrich the island?

Possibly the lands now waste would have been flourishing farms, whose natural fertility would have been maintained, or probably increased, by fostering care and scientific treatment, and they might long ago have been covered with other tropical products wherever the old "King Coffee" had been dethroned by age or sickness.

Where, so far as the planters are concerned, is now the fruit of these wasted lands? Is it not, we may ask, absorbed in the wealth of the mother-country, swelling its plethora of resources and luxury? Hence comes it that, though Ceylon can show many outward and visible signs of material wealth since the establishment of the planting enterprise, in a greatly-increased revenue, great public works, railways, roads, harbour works, tanks, irrigation canals, and public buildings, and in a native population greatly raised in the scale of civilization and in personal and home comforts, yet there is scarcely a wealthy European in the island. Riches have been heaped up elsewhere —that is, in the mother-country—out of Ceylon;

while there are no large local incomes (save among a limited number of natives) to meet the era of short crops and financial disasters which began in 1879.

Of course, we are now looking at the Ceylon planting enterprise from the colonial point of view. When a financial crisis comes, and home capitalists find they cannot realize and sell their property through the absence of local purchasers, they are apt to speak disparagingly of the colony which has done so much for their brethren, if not for themselves, in years gone by, and which will yet give a good return on capital invested in the future.

Fortunately, within the past generation, a considerable change has taken place in the conditions of planting in Ceylon. An unusually large number of younger sons, and others with a certain amount of capital of their own, have settled in the higher and healthier districts—possessing in fact one of the finest climates in the world—forming comparatively permanent homes, in the midst of their tea as well as coffee and cinchona fields. The number of resident proprietary and of married planters has largely increased within the past twenty years, notwithstanding depression and difficulty, and with the return of prosperity, further settlement in this way may be anticipated.

As regards the native cultivation of exportable articles, the profits from six or seven million cwt. of native-grown coffee shipped, and from cinnamon, coir, coconut oil, plumbago, &c., have of course come back and enriched the people in a way which is visible on all sides, and is more particularly striking to old colonists. There is a very large number of wealthy native gentlemen enriched by trade and agriculture within British times, and nearly all the property in the large towns, as well as extensive planted areas, belong to them; while, as regards the labouring classes, the artizans and carters, the benefit conferred by planting expenditure will be more particularly referred to in our next chapter.

## CHAPTER X.

### WHAT THE PLANTING INDUSTRY HAS DONE FOR CEYLON.

Population nearly doubled—Revenue quadrupled—Trade expanded sixteen to twenty fold—Employment afforded to natives—An El Dorado for the Indian immigrant—Coffee in the past, as tea in the future, the mainstay of the island—The material progress in the Planting districts.

WHAT British capital and the planting enterprise have done for Ceylon would require an essay in itself to describe adequately. In 1837, when the pioneer coffee planters began work, Ceylon was a mere military dependency, with a revenue amounting to £372,000, or less than the expenditure, costing the mother-country a good round sum every year, the total population not exceeding one and a half million, but requiring well-nigh 6,000 British and native troops to keep the peace.

Now we have the population increased to very nearly the three millions, with only about 1,000 troops, largely paid for out of a revenue averaging £1,300,000, and a people far better housed, clothed, and fed, better educated and cared for in every way. The total import and export trade since planting began has expanded from half a million sterling in value to from eight to ten millions sterling, according to the harvests. During the forty-five years referred to some thirty to forty millions sterling have been paid away in wages earned in connection with plantations to Kandyan axemen, Tamil coolies, Sinhalese carpenters, domestic servants, and carters. A great proportion of this has gone to benefit Southern India, the home of the Tamil coolies, of whom close on 200,000 over and above the usual labour supply were saved from starvation in Ceylon during the Madras famine of 1877-8. In fact, Ceylon at that time, mainly through its planters, contributed nearly as much aid to her big neighbour as the total of the "Mansion House Fund" subscribed in the United Kingdom.

According to official papers there are sixteen millions of people in Southern India whose annual earnings, taking grain, &c., at its full value, do not average per family of five more than £3 12*s*., or 1*s*. 6*d*. per month —equal to ½*d*. per head per day. Incredible as this may appear, it is true, although with better times now perhaps 1*d*. would be a safe rate *per caput*. No wonder that to such a people the planting country of Ceylon, when all was prosperous, was an El Dorado, for each family could there earn from 9*s*. to 12*s*. per week, and save from half to three-quarters the amount. The immigrant coolie labourers have suffered of late years from the short crops and depression like their masters, but now, with the revival of profitable industry through tea, with medical care provided, cheap food, comfortable huts, and vegetable gardens, few labouring classes in the world are better off. Nor ought we to forget the Tamil Coolie Mission which is doing a good work in educating and Christianizing many amongst the Tamil coolies, mainly supported as it is by the planters.

Our calculation is that from each acre of coffee or tea land kept in full cultivation in Ceylon five natives (men, women, and children) directly or indirectly derive their means of subsistence. It is no wonder then that, with a population increased in the planting era by seventy to eighty per cent., four to five times the quantity of cotton cloth is consumed, and ten times the quantity of food-stuffs imported. As a contrast must be mentioned a calculation made respecting the British pioneers of planting—the men who worked say from 1837 to 1870—which showed that only one-tenth of these benefited themselves materially by coming to Ceylon. Ninety per cent. lost their money, health, or even life itself. Latterly the experience is not so sad, especially in respect of health.

The British governors of Ceylon have repeatedly acknowledged that the planting enterprise is the mainstay of the island. None have more forcibly shown this than Governor Sir William Gregory, who, in answer to the remark that the general revenue of the colony was being burdened with charges for railway extension and harbour works, benefiting chiefly the planting industry, said: "What, I would ask, is the basis of the whole prosperity of Ceylon but the planting enterprise? What gave me the surplus revenues, by which I was able to make roads and bridges all over the island, causeways at Mannár and Jaffna, to make grants for education and to take measures to educate the masses—in short, to promote the general industry and enterprise of the island from Jaffna to Galle—but the results of the capital and energy engaged in the cultivation of coffee? It follows, therefore, that, in encouraging the great planting enterprise, I shall be furthering the general interests of the colony." Sir William Gregory was able to create a new province in Ceylon, entirely occupied by the poorest and previously most neglected class of natives—namely, the North-Central Province—with roads, bridges, buildings, forest clearings, and irrigation works, solely by the surplus revenues obtained from the planting enterprise.

The pioneer planter introduces into regions all but unknown to man a host of contractors, who in their turn bring in a train of pedlars, tavern-keepers, and others, eager to profit by the expenditure about to take place. To the contractors succeed the Malabar coolies, the working bees of the colony, who plant and cultivate the coffee, and at a subsequent period reap the crop. Each of these coolies consumes monthly a bushel of rice, a quantity of salt and other condiments, and occasionally cloth, arrack, &c., the import, transport, and purchase of which find employment for the merchant, the retail dealer, the carrier, and their servants; and, again, the wants of these functionaries raise around them a race of shopkeepers, domestics, and others, who, but for the success of coffee planting, would have been unable to find equally profitable employment.

Nor are the results bounded by the limits of the colony. The import of articles consumed gives employment to hundreds of seamen and to thousands of tons of shipping that, but for this increased trade, would never have been built. The larger demand for rice stimulates and cheers the toil of the Indian ryot; the extended use of clothing stimulates the Manchester spinners and weavers and all dependent on them; and the increased demand for the implements of labour tells on Birmingham and Sheffield, which also benefit, as regards the tea industry, by the demand for varied machinery, for sheet lead, hoop iron, and a host of other requisites. Who shall say where the links of the chain terminate, affecting as they do indirectly all the great branches of the human family?

Then again, when the estate becomes productive, how many of the foregoing agencies are again called into operation. On arrival in Colombo the parchment coffee is usually peeled, winnowed, and sized by powerful steam machinery; cinchona bark is packed by hydraulic machines, while it is often re-bulked and re-fired, agencies which provide employment for engineers, smiths, stokers, wood-cutters, &c.

Colombo "stores" in their best days (mainly through the drying, picking, and sorting of coffee) gave occupation to thousands of the industrious poor natives, and enabled them to support an expenditure for food, clothing, and other necessaries, the supply of which further furnished profitable employment to the shopkeeper, merchant, seaman, &c. This is of course still true to a large extent. In fact, it is impossible to pursue in all their ramifications the benefits derived from the cultivation of the fragrant berry which has become the staple product of Ceylon. Other results, too, there are—moral ones—such as must sooner or later arise from the infusion of Anglo-Saxon energy and spirit into an Eastern people, from the spread of the English language, and, what is of more importance still, the extension of civilization and Christianity.

The material change in the planting districts and the Central Province of Ceylon within the last fifty years has been marvellous. Villages and towns have appeared where all was barren waste or thick jungle;

roads have been cut in all directions; and prosperous villages have sprung up like magic in "The Wilderness of the Peak." Gampola, Badulla, and Mátalé, which each consisted of a rest-house and a few huts, and Náwalapitiya, which had no existence at all in 1837, are now populous towns; while Panwila, Tel-deniya, Madulkelle, Deltota, Haldummulla, Lunu-gulla, Passera, Wellimadde, Balangoda, Ratotte, Rakwána, Yatiantotte, &c., are more than villages.

Some of the planting grant-in-aid roads, carried through what was dense forest or waste land, are lined for miles with native houses and boutiques, as also with native cultivation in gardens or fields. The change cannot be better described than in the words of the Rev. Spence Hardy, of the Wesleyan Mission, who, after spending twenty-two years in Ceylon, between 1825 and 1847, returned to England, and re-visited the island in 1862. Mr. Hardy was accustomed to travel through nearly all the Sinhalese districts.

Writing in 1864, he says:—"Were some Sinhalese *appuhami* to arise, who had gone down to the grave fifty years ago, and from that time remained unconscious, he would not know his own land or people; and when told where he was he would scarcely believe his eyes, and would have some difficulty with his ears; for though there would be the old language, even that would be mixed with many words that to him would be utterly unintelligible. Looking at his own country-men, he would say that in his time both the head and the feet were uncovered, but that now they cover both; or perhaps he would think that the youths whom he saw with stockings and shoes and caps were of some other nation. He would be shocked at the heedlessness with which *appus* and *naidas* and everybody else roll along in their bullock-bandies; passing even the carriage of the white man whenever they are able by dint of tail-pulling or hard blows; and when he saw the horsekeepers riding by the side of their masters and sitting on the same seat, there would be some expression of strong indignation. He would listen in vain for the ho-he-voh of the palanquin-bearers and their loud shouts, and would look in vain for the tomjohns and doolies, and for the old lascoreens with their talipots and formal dress. He would be surprised at seeing so many women walking in the road and laughing and talking together like men, but with no burdens on their heads and nothing in their hands, and their clothes not clean enough for them to be going to the temple. He would perhaps complain of the hard road, as we have heard a native gentleman from Kalpitiya do, and say that soft sand was much better. He would wonder where all the tiles come from for so many houses, and would think that the high-caste families must have multiplied amazingly for them to require so many stately mansions; and the porticoes, and the round white pillars, and the trees growing in the compound, bearing nothing but long thin thorns, or with pale yellow leaves instead of green ones, would be objects of great attraction. He would fancy that the Moormen must have increased at a great rate, as he would take the tall chimneys of the coffee stores to be the minarets of mosques, until he saw the smoke proceeding from them, and then he would be puzzled to know what they could be. In the bazaar he would stare at the policemen and the potatoes and the loaves of bread, and a hundred other things that no bazaar ever saw in his day. And the talk about planters and barbacues, coolie immigration, and the overland and penny postage, and bishops and agents of Government, and the legislative council and banks, newspapers and mail-coaches, would confuse him by the strangeness of the terms. He would listen incredulously when told that there is no rájakáriya, or forced labour, and no fish tax; and that there are no slaves, and that you can cut down a cinnamon tree in your own garden without having to pay a heavy fine. Remembering that when Governor North made the tour of the island, he was accompanied by 160 palanquin-bearers, 400 coolies, 2 elephants, and 50 lascoreens, and that when the adigar Æhælapola visited Colombo he had with him a retinue of a thousand retainers, and several elephants, he would think it impossible that the governor could go on a tour of inspection, or a judge on circuit, without white olas lining the roadside, and triumphal arches, and javelin men, and tomtoms, and a vast array of attendants. He would ask, perhaps, what king now reigns in Kandy, and whether he had mutilated any more of the subjects of Britain. From these supposed surprises, we may learn something of the changes that have taken place in the island, but we cannot tell a tithe of the whole."

If this was true when the veteran missionary wrote in 1862, the picture might well be heightened and intensified by the experiences of 1887, for the progress in the second half of our good Queen's reign among the people of Ceylon is not less remarkable than it was between 1837 and 1862.

As to the comparative freedom from poverty and suffering which distinguishes the lower classes, the vast masses of the natives of Ceylon, it must be remembered that they live as a rule in the most genial of climates, where suffering from cold is impossible, and the pangs of hunger are almost unknown, little more than a few plantains a day being sufficient to support life in idleness, if so chosen. Sir Edward

A B

COFFEE.

A. The ARABIAN, or East African; B. The LIBERIAN, or West African; with Coolie attendant employed to shoot squirrels, rats, or hares on plantation.

Creasy, in his "History of England," says: "I have seen more human misery in a single winter's day in London than I have seen during my nine years' stay in Ceylon."

## CHAPTER XI.

### PRESENT PROSPECTS FOR CAPITALISTS IN CEYLON.

Ceylon still a good field for investment—Its freedom from atmospheric disturbances—Shipping conveniences at the new harbour of Colombo—Low freights—Cheap and unrivalled means of transport—Large tracts available for Tea and other tropical culture—Openings for young men with capital—High position taken by the Ceylon planter—Facilities for personal inspection of investments.

WHAT we have said in the previous chapter will show the value of the planting enterprise to the settled inhabitants and to the government of Ceylon. We have also pointed out the immense advantages gained in commerce and profits by the mother-country. Let us endeavour to show the British Capitalist, who, during the period of deficient coffee crops, grievously lost confidence in Ceylon, how many reasons there are for him to forbear condemnation, and to look still on this colony as one of the best of British dependencies for the judicious investment of capital. It may be unnecessary now, in 1887, to do so, because tea has already begun to receive a liberal measure of support; but still in many home circles Ceylon is decried.

The situation of Ceylon in the Eastern World is

peculiarly favoured in certain respects. The atmospheric disturbances which periodically agitate the Bay of Bengal, and carry, in hurricanes and cyclones, destruction to the shipping in the exposed Madras roadstead and the devoted Hooghly, seldom or never approach the north-eastern shores of this island. If Java and the rest of the Eastern Archipelago boast of a far richer soil than is to be found in Ceylon, it is owing to the volcanic agency which makes itself known at frequent intervals by eruptions and earthquakes, the utmost verge of whose waves just touches the eastern coast of the island at Batticaloa and Trincomalee in scarcely perceptible undulations. On the west, again, Ceylon is equally beyond the region of the hurricanes which, extending from the Mozambique Channel, visit so often and so disastrously the coasts of Madagascar, Mauritius, and Zanzibar. The wind and rain-storms which usher in periodically the south-west and north-east monsoons, sometimes inflict slight damage on the coffee and rice crops, but there is no comparison between the risks attaching to cultivation in Ceylon and those experienced by planters in Java and Mauritius.

The same absence of risk holds good with reference to the formerly open roadstead of Colombo, and the island shipping trade, which has for years been nearly all centred there.

Except for an occasional gale from the south-west, there was no special danger to be guarded against, and the risks to vessels lying at Colombo were much less than to those at Calcutta, Madras, or Bombay. But the delay in the transaction of shipping business, owing to the prevalence of a heavy surf and a stiff breeze during monsoon months, was more than sufficient to justify the very substantial breakwater and allied harbour works which, under the direction of Sir John Coode and his representative, Mr. Kyle, have just been successfully completed at Colombo. The capital of Ceylon is now the great central mail and commercial steamer port of the East. All the large steamers of the P. and O. Company, the British India, Star, Ducal, and most of the Messageries, Nord-Deutscher Lloyds, Austro-Hungarian Lloyds, Rubattino, the Clan, Glen, City, Ocean, Anchor, Holts, and other lines for Europe, India, China, the Straits, and Australia, call at Colombo regularly. One consequence of this, valuable to the merchant and planter, is the regular and cheap freight offered to the world's markets. Freights now do not average one-half of the rates prevalent some years ago.

There is no tropical land—indeed there are few countries anywhere—so thoroughly served by railways and roads, canals and navigable streams, as are the principal districts of Ceylon at the present day. The means of cheap transport between the interior and the coast (a few remote districts only excepted) are unequalled in the tropics. Indian tea-planters confess that their Ceylon brethren have a great advantage over them in this respect, and still more so in the abundant supply of good, steady, cheap labour, trained by long experience to plantation work. A more forcing climate, too, than that of Ceylon does not exist under the sun; while now that the country is fully opened, the risks to health are infinitesimal compared with those of pioneers in new countries or of the tea-planters in the Terai of India. Whatever may be said of the inimical effects of bad seasons on coffee—too much rain at blossoming time—there can be no doubt of the advantage of abundance of moisture and heat for *tea*, and it is in respect of the fitness of large tracts of undeveloped country for tea production that we would especially ask for the attention of British capitalists.

Indian tea-planters, who have come to see how tea is growing in Ceylon, confess that we are bound to beat Northern India. Tea, of as good quality as that from Assam, can be placed on board ship at Colombo for a good deal less per pound than Indian tea on board ship at Calcutta. This has been proved, although Ceylon planters have not long begun the systematic cultivation and preparation of tea. But tea (although the principal) is only one among a list of valuable tropical products which Ceylon is well fitted to grow.

As a body, Ceylon planters are among the most intelligent, gentlemanly, and hospitable of any colonists in British dependencies. The rough work of pioneering in the early days before there were district roads, villages, supplies, doctors, or other comforts of civilization, was chiefly done by hard-headed Scots: men bivouacked in the trackless jungle with the scantiest accommodation under tropical rains lasting for weeks together, with rivers swollen to flood-level and impassable, while food supplies often ran short, as none could be got across the wide torrents. All these and many other similar experiences are of the past in the settled planting districts of Ceylon, although there are outlying parts where pioneers can still rough it to their hearts' content. In the hill-country the pioneers about twenty years ago began to be succeeded by quite a different class of men. Younger sons with a capital, present or prospective, of a few thousand pounds, educated at public schools, and many of them University men, found an opening in life on Ceylon plantations far more congenial than that of the Australian bush or the backwoods of Canada. Of course some of these did not succeed as planters, as they probably would not succeed at anything in the colonies; but for well-inclined young men of the right stamp, not afraid of hard work, Ceylon still presents an opening as planters of tea, cinchona, cacao, &c., provided the indispensable capital is available.

The usual mode, and the safe one, is to send the young man fresh from home, through the introduction of some London or Colombo firm, to study his business as a planter, and to learn the colloquial Tamil spoken by the coolies, under an experienced planter for two or three years. In prosperous times such young assistants were taught and boarded free in return for their help, and began to earn a salary after a year or so. Now, a fee for board and teaching (£50, or at most £100 for a year) may be needful. Nowhere in the whole wide world can young men learn so thoroughly the mysteries of coffee, tea, cinchona planting, &c., or be so well equipped as *tropical* agriculturists as in Ceylon. Ceylon planters and machinists have taught the rest of the tropics how to grow and prepare coffee properly; more is known in it about the mysteries of cinchona bark culture than anywhere else; the Ceylon tea-planter is likely, ere long, to beat both India and China in the race for fine teas. Ceylon cacao beans have already sold highest in the London market, just as she sends thither the finest cinnamon, coconut-oil, coir, &c. It may truly be said that the *Press* of Ceylon has greatly aided the planters in acquiring this pre-eminence. *The Ceylon Observer* has sent special correspondents to report on the tea regions of Assam and Darjeeling, on the cinchona gardens of the Nilgeries, and of Java; to West Africa to learn all about Liberian coffee, and to South and Central America to ascertain the progress of coffee; while its manuals on coffee, tea, cinchona, cacao, india-rubber, coconut and areca palms, cardamoms and cinnamon planting, on gold and gems, are known throughout the tropics. Of late years, since 1881, a monthly periodical, *The Tropical Agriculturist*, published at the same office, has been effectually bringing together all the information and experience available in reference to everything that concerns agriculture in tropical and sub-tropical regions. This is merely mentioned, *en passant*, in part explanation of the high position taken by the Ceylon-trained planter, wherever he goes.

After the depression of 1879 many Ceylon plantation managers and assistant superintendents had to seek their fortunes elsewhere; and, indeed, the planting districts of Southern India may be said to be offshoot settlements from Ceylon, while in Fiji, Northern Australia, the Straits Settlements, Burmah, and North Borneo, there are Ceylon planters now pioneering and building up a planting enterprise.

But with the success of tea, many of our wandering colonists have been returning, and there is still ample scope for the capitalist and for the young man who can, after he has learned planting, command capital in Ceylon. There is a wide extent of forest land well suited for tea, and, when sold by Government, it may be had for £2 or £3, sometimes for £1 an acre, crown title freehold. Owing to the depression, property in plantations already formed fell greatly in value, and, even now, old coffee estates may be bought cheaply, very suitable for tea; but discrimination should certainly be exercised. One beneficial result of the scarcity of capital has been to secure the utmost economy in doing work, and land is now opened and cultivated for far less than was the case some years ago.

The convenience afforded by quick passages in large steamers *viâ* the Suez Canal, and by railways and roads in Ceylon, is such that capitalists can now inspect their property in Ceylon with as much ease and pleasure as they would have in a two months' trip to the Highlands of Scotland or to the South of Europe; and it is becoming quite a common thing for the retired proprietor or business man to run out to Ceylon for the winter months. How different the case was twenty years ago! We remember a Glasgow capitalist, owning a property worth £100,000 in Ceylon, coming out to see it, and after getting to Nuwara Eliya, within forty miles of the property, refusing to go further, so bad were the roads; and he, a man of sixty-eight or seventy, returned home without ever having seen the plantation, and ultimately sold his interests to a Limited Company at a considerable profit!

The carriage of produce from the estates to Colombo, from 100 to 200 miles, used often to take as much time and cost as much as the freight 15,000 miles round the Cape. From the Uva districts to Colombo carriage still costs in time and money more than freight to London *viâ* the Canal; but, as a whole, Ceylon is magnificently roaded, with an ample supply of cheap labour, and a particularly favourable climate.

Finally, let the capitalist know that obnoxious *laws* connected with the Roman-Dutch system are to be

LOW-COUNTRY SINHALESE MAN AND WOMAN.

reformed. Codes are being framed, and antiquated laws have either been, or are likely soon to be, superseded.

## CHAPTER XII.

### ATTRACTIONS FOR THE TRAVELLER AND VISITOR.

The voyage a pleasure trip—Historical monuments, vegetation, &c.—Variety of climate—Colombo, the capital—Kandy, the Highland capital—Nuwara Eliya, the sanitarium—The Horton Plains—Adam's Peak—Uva and its long-delayed railway—Ancient cities of Anuradhapura and Polonnaruwa—Occasional Pearl fisheries—Probable expense of a visit to Ceylon—The alleged inconveniences of tropical life.

To the traveller and visitor Ceylon offers more attractions even than to the capitalist and would-be planter. It is a joke with disappointed men that the stranger can see on the hills of Ceylon the graves of more British sovereigns than of Kandyan kings! But the latter are not wanting, and no dependency of Britain—India not excepted—presents more attractions than Ceylon to the intelligent traveller, to the botanist, the antiquarian or the man of science, the orientalist, or even to the politician and the sociologist. Visitors from America and North India have said that Ceylon, for natural beauty, historical and social interest, is the "show-place of the universe," and that, as such, it might well, in these days of travelling sight-seers, be leased by either a Barnum or Cook! The voyage of twenty-four to twenty-eight days from London to Colombo (of eighteen to twenty-one from Brindisi or

Marseilles) on a first-class steamer of any of half a dozen lines competing at from £40 to £65 for the single, or less than double for the return passage, is, at the proper season of the year—September to March or April—a pleasure trip of the most enjoyable and instructive kind. The calling by some steamers at Gibraltar, Malta, Port Said, Suez, and Aden affords instruction and pleasure of a high order; while the beauty of Ceylon vegetation and scenery, the interest attaching to her people, towns, and ancient cities and monuments, amply reward even the worst sea-traveller for the unpleasantness of a voyage. Tennent well says that Ceylon, from whatever direction it may be approached, unfolds a scene of loveliness and grandeur unsurpassed, if it be rivalled, by any land in the universe. Its names—"Lanká, the resplendent," of the Brahmins; the "pearl-drop on the brow of Ind," of the Buddhists; "the island of jewels" of the Chinese; "the land of the hyacinth and ruby" of the Greeks; and "the home of Adam and Eve after losing Paradise," according to the Mohammedans—as Arabi and his fellow exiles said soon after their arrival—will show the high esteem in which it has been held both in the East and the West.

As for its history, as already mentioned, no region between Chaldea and China can tell so much of its past deeds as Ceylon, while the ruins of its ancient capitals in palaces, temples, dágobas, and tanks are only second to those of Egypt. These ruins are all now rendered accessible in a few days' trip by railway and carriage from Colombo, without risk or inconvenience, and at very little expense to the traveller.*

* *See* Burrows' "Guide to the Buried Cities of Ceylon," published by A. M. and J. Ferguson.

As to vegetation and natural history generally, Ceylon is one huge tropical garden, presenting objects of intense interest to the botanist and zoologist, from the coral reef and pearl oyster banks around its coasts, and the palms and creepers bending down to meet "the leaguelong rollers thundering on its shores," to the grassy pathways running up to hills clothed to their summit with the most varied forest trees, or to the plateaux of Nuwara Eliya and the surrounding plains—"the Elysium of Ceylon"—where, at an elevation of over 6,000 feet, in grass, and flowers, and trees, a bit of

"Europe amid Asia smiles."

There, in snug cottages, wood fires and blankets are often required to keep away the cold. In one day the visitor can pass from Colombo with its average temperature of 81° to the sanatarium, with its wintry comforts, and temperature falling to freezing-point occasionally, but averaging 57°. During March, April, and May—"the season" at the sanatarium—the weather is very equable, comparatively dry, and delightful. September and part of August and October, are very pleasant, and often January and February, as well as December sometimes, though thin ice on the water, and hoar frost on the herbage, are then not uncommon. The very wet months are June, July, and December. Sir Samuel Baker lived eight years continuously at Nuwara Eliya, and speaks very highly of its healthfulness.* Indian civilians and other residents declare that Nuwara Eliya is

* *See* Sir Samuel Baker's "Eight Years" and "Rifle and Hound in Ceylon."

more pleasantly accessible to them than most of their own sanitaria, the short sea-voyage from Calcutta or Bombay being an additional benefit to many who come from the hot dry plains of Central India. For invalids, the marine boarding-house at Mount Lavinia, as well as the Colombo marine hotels, are very safe and suitable places of resort.

The perfection of climate, in an average of 65° all the year round, is found at 5,000 feet, among the bungalows of Dimbula, Dikoya, Maskeliya, or of Uva, with its dryer and at times more pleasant climate. It is no wonder then that parents and others, with their sons, daughters, or other relatives settled in Ceylon, should have begun to visit it in order to escape the trying winter and spring months in England. Not a few who used to winter in Egypt find it nearly as convenient and more interesting to come on to Ceylon. The late Mr. C. A. Cameron and his wife, Mrs. Julia Cameron (the well-known artist and friend of Tennyson), even when in advanced years (approaching to or over fourscore), made the voyage across several times to visit and stay for considerable periods with their sons settled in the island. Of late years winter visitors from Europe and hot-weather refugees from India have been numerous, apart from "globe-trotters" calling in.

Colombo, the capital, a city of close on 120,000 inhabitants, with its fine artificial harbour (projected by Sir Hercules Robinson), has much to interest the visitor in its beautiful drives over the smoothest of roads through the "Cinnamon Gardens;" its lake, and the Kelani river, with Sir Edward Barnes's bridge of boats; its public museum, erected by Sir William Gregory, and containing objects of interest from all parts of the island; the old Dutch church, containing the tombs and monuments of Dutch governors; the bungalows and gardens of the Europeans; still more unique are the crowded native parts of the town, teeming with every variety of oriental race and costume—the effeminate light brown Sinhalese, the men as well as women wearing their hair tied behind in knots (the former patronizing combs, the latter elaborate hairpins), the darker and more manly Tamils, Hindus of every caste and dress, Moormen or Arab descendants, Afghan traders, Malay policemen, a few Parsees and Chinese, Kaffir descendants,* besides the Eurasians of Dutch, or Portuguese, or English and native descent.

Colombo has two first-class, besides minor hotels, and the stranger is soon surrounded by native pedlars, especially jewellers with their supply of gems, from rare cat's-eyes, rubies, sapphires, and pearls, to first-class Birmingham imitations.

The scene to the new-comer is bewilderingly interesting, visions of the "Arabian Nights" are conjured up, for, as Miss Jewsbury sang after her visit some forty years ago:—

> "Ceylon! Ceylon! 'tis nought to me
> How thou wert known or named of old,
> As Ophir, or Taprobanè,
> By Hebrew king, or Grecian bold:—
>
> To me thy spicy-wooded vales,
> Thy dusky sons, and jewels bright,
> But image forth the far-famed tales—
> But seem a new Arabian night.

* Kaffirs first arrived in Ceylon as a company of soldiers sent from Goa to help the Portuguese against the Sinhalese in 1636–40.

And when engirdled figures crave
 Heed to thy bosom's glittering store—
I see Aladdin in his cave;
 I follow Sinbad on the shore."

Although the mean temperature of Colombo is nearly as high as that of any station in the world as yet recorded, yet the climate is one of the healthiest and safest for Europeans, because of the slight range between night and day, and between the so-called "seasons," of which, however, nothing is known there, it being one perpetual summer varied only by the heavy rains of the monsoon months, May, June, October, and November. But in the wettest months it rarely happens that it rains continuously even for two whole days and nights; as a rule, it clears up for some hours each day.

Waterworks have been constructed, at a heavy cost, to convey water from mountain streams, distant thirty miles, to serve Colombo, some parts of which are badly off for a good supply. When the works and distribution over the city are completed—the city reservoir, costing R600,000, has been a *fiasco*, cracking again and again in 1886–7, through a bad foundation—and when the drainage is thus improved, Colombo will more than ever be entitled to its reputation of being one of the healthiest (as well as most beautiful) cities in the tropics, or indeed in the world. A convenient system of tramways is also being projected, while at present, besides the railway through one side of the town, there are numerous conveyances of different descriptions for hire, and many "jinirickshaws" (man-power carriages), peculiar to Japan and the Far East.*

* "Jinirickshaws," which have become very popular in Ceylon towns, in Colombo, Kandy, and Nuwara Eliya especially, were first

There are several places of interest in the neighbourhood of Colombo that are well worth a visit.

A seaside railway line runs for twenty-seven miles as far as Kalutara (the Richmond of Ceylon), the border inland being one continuous avenue of coconut trees. The enjoyment of the scene to a lover of natural beauty is indescribable: the cool shade of the palm groves, the fresh verdure of the grass, the bright tints of the flowering trees, with occasional glimpses through openings in the dense wood of the mountains of the interior, the purple zone of hills above which the sacred mountain of Adam's Peak is sometimes seen, all combine to form a landscape which in novelty and beauty is unsurpassed:

> "So fair a scene, so green a sod,
> Our English fairies never trod."

As Miss Martineau wrote, fifty years ago, in her political romance, "Cinnamon and Pearls"—"The Blue Lake of Colombo, whether gleaming in the sunrise or darkening in the storms of the monsoon, never loses its charm. The mountain range in the distance is an object for the eye to rest lovingly upon, whether clearly outlined against the glowing sky, or dressed in soft clouds, from which Adam's Peak alone stands aloft, like a dark island in the waters above the firmament."

The mildness of the climate of Colombo, the murmur of cricket and insect life at night, and the brilliancy of the moonlight, strike the stranger, although the closeness of the atmosphere then is sometimes

introduced in 1884, on the suggestion of the author, after a visit to China and Japan, where he thought the "rickshaws" peculiarly fitted for Colombo roads.

felt to be oppressive, and the attention of mosquitoes at certain seasons is far from pleasant. But the low country can easily be exchanged for the hills. In four hours one passes from Colombo by a splendid

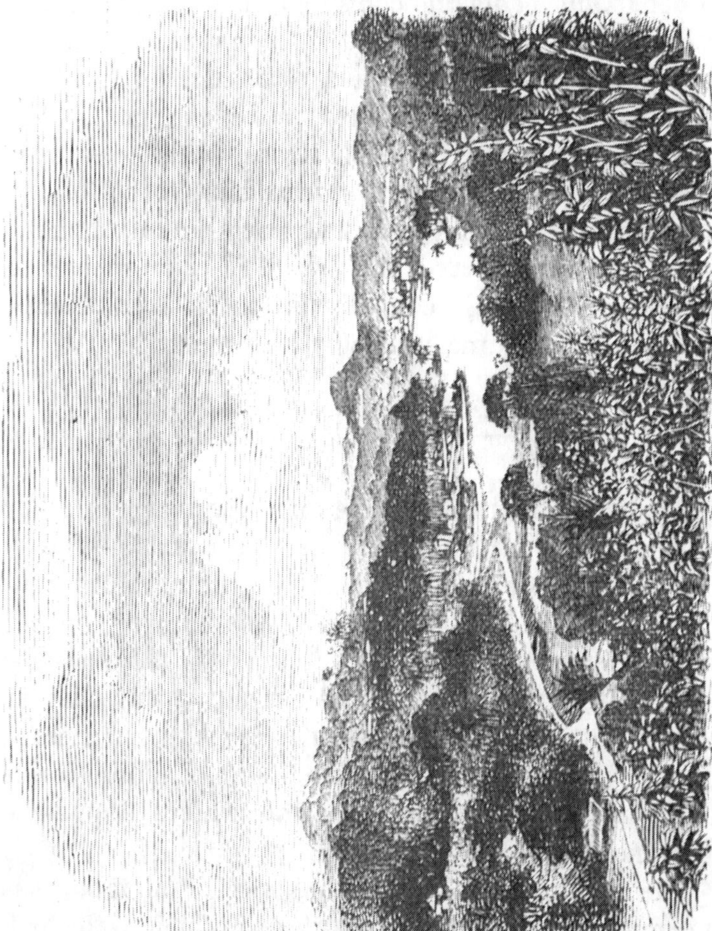

KANDY LAKE.

railway running through interesting country, surmounting an incline which is one of the greatest railway ascents in the (at least, tropical) world, 1,600 feet above sea-level, to the last capital of the native kings of the island—Kandy—a town of 22,000 people. Kandy is uniquely beautiful: the most charming little town in the world, travellers usually describe it. It is situated in a valley surrounded by hills, and boasts an artificial lake, Buddhist and Hindu temples, including the Maligáwa, the most sacred Buddhist temple in the world; this contains the so-called relic of Buddha's tooth, to which the kings and priests of Burmah, Siam, and Cambodia send occasional offerings, and which is had in reverence in portions of India, Thibet, and even China and Japan. "The Pavilion," one of the three official residences of the governor in the island, with its gardens and grounds, surmounted by the public "Lady Horton's Walk" on a hill-range overlooking the Dumbara valley, will attract attention. The view of the town from any of the hill-sides surrounding it is surpassingly interesting.*

The Botanical gardens at Péradeniya, three miles from Kandy, "beautiful for situation exceedingly," as well as full of interest in the vegetation, are well worth a visit.†

The group of palms at the entrance has always been an object of admiration to strangers, and it shows how well adapted Ceylon is to be the home of this family. We reprint an engraving of this group, and append here the—

NAMES OF PALMS, &c., IN GROUP.

(*See Engraving, page* 122.)

1. Corypha umbraculifera (Talipot)—highest plant, in the centre.
2. Phytelephas macrocarpa (Ivory-nut Palm)—in front of foregoing, and behind native servant.

---

* *See* Burrows' "Guide to Kandy, &c.," published by A. M. and J. Ferguson.

† An interesting little guide-book and list of plants, &c., have been prepared by the director, Dr. Trimer, and are available.

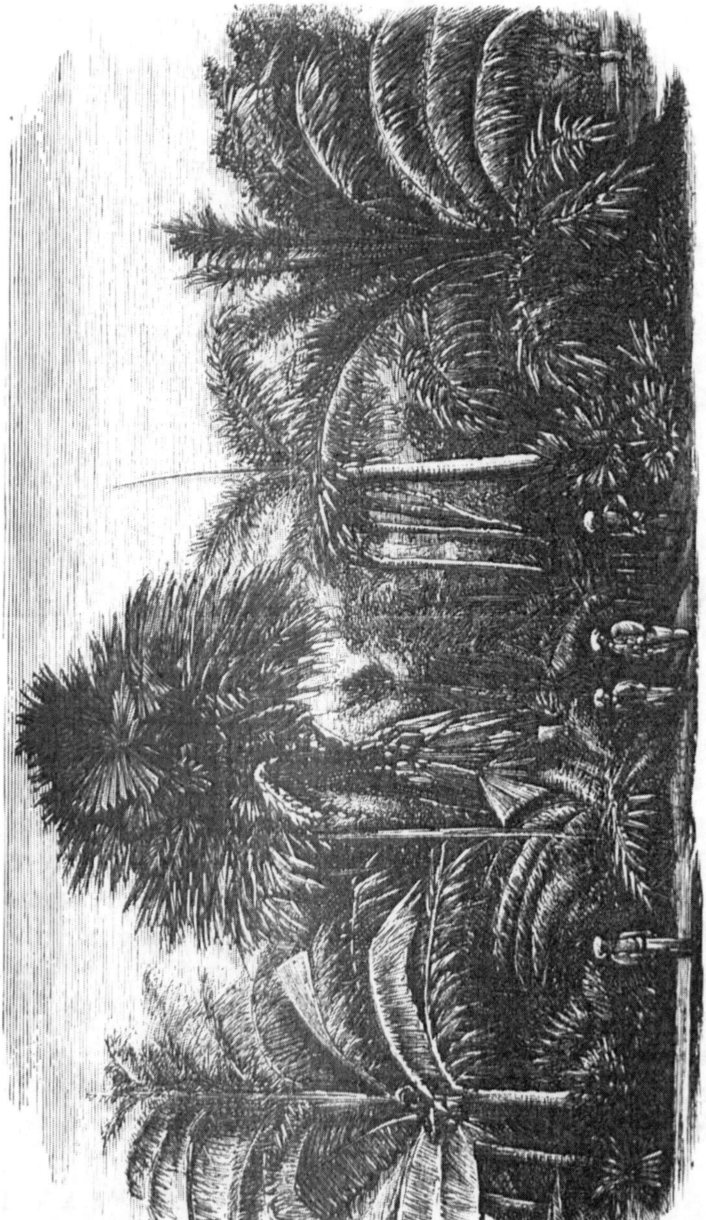

GROUP OF PALMS, &C., BOTANIC GARDENS, PERADENIYA.

3. Cycas, circinalis (called erroneously "Sago Palm")—immediately to the left of preceding, in front.
4. Areca Catechu—directly behind the Cycas, and with its head of leaves amongst those of the Talipot.
5. Yucca gloriosa—a cluster of shoots of this in front; to the left of the Cycas.
6. Cocos nucifera (Cocoa-nut)—immediately behind the Yucca.
7. Oncosperma fasciculata ("Kattoo Kittool")—behind, between the Talipot and Cocoa-nut.
8. Acrocomia sclerocarpa—behind the Yucca, and with its trunk a little to the left of that of the Cocoa-nut.
9. Livistona sp.—at the extreme left of the group.
10. Livistona Chinensis ("Mauritius Palm")—behind and directly to the right of the Talipot.
11. Livistona sp.—immediately to the right of the coolie, in front.
12. Oreodoxa regia (Cabbage Palm)—directly behind No. 11; trunk large, smooth, bulged above the middle.
13. Sabal Palmetto ("Palmetto" of the Southern States of America)—to the right of the group, in front.
14. Eloesis Guineensis ("Palm Oil Palm" of Africa)—with numerous long spreading leaves; behind and overtopping No. 13, and to the extreme right of the group.

Between Colombo and Kandy extensive paddy or rice cultivation can be seen in the low country; while higher up the Kandyans' terraced rice-fields and fields of tea, with some Liberian coffee and chocolate trees, may be noted.

From Kandy a visit to the Dumbara valley, five or six miles by road, or to Mátalé, twenty miles by railway, will show some of the finest cacao (chocolate) plantations; while southward, the railway journey to Gampola and Náwalapitiya, for seventeen miles, and then on for forty-two miles, rising by successive inclines nearly 4,000 feet, to Nánu-oya, near Nuwara Eliya, will carry the visitor through long stretches of tea and cinchona, with some coffee, plantations, amidst enchanting mountain scenery, with rivers, forests, waterfalls, and gorges that nothing can

NUWARA ELIYA, THE MOUNTAIN SANATARIUM,
(6200 feet above sea-level, and within four miles of Nanu-oya railway terminus).
*From a Photograph by Messrs. W. L. H. Skeen & Co., of Colombo.*

surpass. Altogether, the railway ride from Colombo to Nánu-oya for 130 miles, rising from sea-level to 5,300 feet (over one mile up in the air), is one of the most varied and interesting in the world.* The

FALLS OF RAMBODA.

journey is made by a first-class broad-gauge railway,

* *See* "Guide to Ceylon Railways and Railway Extensions, with Notice of the Sanitarium," compiled and published by A. M. and J. Ferguson.

with a refreshment car attached, for two-thirds of the way, in seven to eight hours, without any change of train or carriage.

Nánu-oya is only about four miles from Nuwara Eliya, the sanatarium, by a fine road, on which coaches or other conveyances run for the convenience of railway travellers. There is good hotel and boarding-house accommodation; the "Gregory Lake," due to Sir William Gregory, is a fine feature; plantations of tea and cinchona, and the finely situated and admirably kept Hakgalla experimental gardens, are in the neighbourhood. The summit of the highest mountain in Ceylon, Pídurutalágala, 8,296 feet, or 2,000 feet above the Plains, can be easily attained in a walk before breakfast; while a trip to the top of the far more interesting Adam's Peak (sacred alike to Buddhists, Hindus, Mohammedans, and even Roman Catholics) can be readily arranged, the railway and a good road running for forty miles to a point on the mountain breast about 3,000 feet from the summit, which is 7,353 feet high. The climb up Adam's Peak is a stiff one, particularly the last portion, where steps are cut out, and even chains fixed in the rock, to prevent the climber from slipping or being blown down the side of the precipice in stormy seasons. The view from the top in clear weather is ample reward for all trouble, and the projection of the shadow across the low country to the sea as the sun rises is a sight, once seen, never to be forgotten.*

From Nuwara Eliya a day's ride suffices to reach the Horton Plains, 1,000 feet higher; and there, as well as between these two points, is a large extent of

* *See* Appendix X. for paper on "The Shadow of the Peak," by Hon. Ralph Abercromby.

upland in a delightful climate, well suited for comparative settlement by Europeans. At any rate their children could be kept here in rude health until twelve to fourteen years of age; and the soil is well fitted for small farms and vegetable gardens, as well as for growing cinchona and the finer qualities of tea. As a sanatarium for British troops, this site is unequalled, both for climate and accessibility.

Already the surrounding districts, served by road and railway, and having villages, stores, churches, clergymen, and doctors, are beginning to be regarded as the comparatively permanent homes of many of the planters. Nuwara Eliya and the Horton Plains border on the Uva Principality, with its comparatively dry upland climate, where so deliciously pleasant and health-giving is the air that to breathe it has been compared to a draught of the pure juice of the grape. A waterfall in Eastern Haputale, one of the divisions of Uva, is the highest in Ceylon (page 131), while the Ella Pass and the view of the low country and sea coast from the hill range is very striking.* As we write, the

* Perhaps there is not a scene in the world which combines sublimity and beauty in a more extraordinary degree than that which is presented at the Pass of Ella, where, through an opening in the chain of mountains, the road from Badulla descends rapidly to the lowlands, over which it is carried for upwards of seventy miles, to Hambantotte, on the south coast of the island. The ride to Ella passes for ten or twelve miles along the base of hills thickly wooded, except in those spots where the forest has been cleared for planting coffee. The view is therefore obstructed, and at one point appears to terminate in an impassable glen; but on reaching this the traveller is startled on discovering a ravine through which a torrent has forced its way, disclosing a passage to the plains below, over which, for more than sixty miles, the prospect extends, unbroken by a single eminence, till, far in the distance, the eye discerns a line of light, which marks where the sunbeams are flashing on the waters of the Indian Ocean. —*Emerson Tennent.*

whole colony is eagerly awaiting the sanction of the Secretary of State to another section of Railway extension from Nanu-oya for 25½ miles to Haputale. This line will rise to nearly 6,300 feet, summit level, and then descend to 4,400 feet near the Haputale Pass. The journey over the dividing range and the burst into the grand Uva amphitheatre of mountain range, embracing rolling pastures (grassy plains), rich, cultivated valleys with sparkling streams and glistening irrigation channels, will be full of an interest of its own to travellers. The Uva province too, perhaps more than any other in Ceylon, will offer attractions and opportunities to the planting settler and capitalist for investment, its soil and climate being generally considered the best in the island for the staple products of the colonist as well as for the fruits and vegetables cultivated by the natives. In the Park country division of the province, there is also rich pasturage for feeding cattle, while opportunities for sport, from snipe to elephants, are presented on all sides. As already stated, civil and military officers, merchants and others, from India, are now beginning to regard Ceylon, with its seaside boarding-establishments, and its comfortable accommodation at Nuwara Eliya sanatarium, as more desirable than Indian hill-stations during the hot season.

From Kandy the trip to the ancient capitals of Anurádhapura and Polonnáruwa, from ninety to sixty miles to the north and east, can easily be arranged for the visitor; and from amid the ruins of Anuràdhapura (2,000 years old) one can despatch a telegram to friends at home in England, or post a budget of news.*

* With the permission of Mr. Richard Bentley, the publisher, extracts from Major Forbes's "Eleven Years in Ceylon" (published in 1840),

For sportsmen there is elephant shooting in the far South in the Hambantota district, elk hunting round

DAGOBA.

Nuwara Eliya, or wild buffalo, bear, boar, or wild

bearing on the ruins of Anurâdhapura and the Buddhist religion, are given as Appendix II., but for the best modern description we refer to "The Buried Cities of Ceylon," by Mr. Burrows, C.C.S., published by A. M. & J. Ferguson, Colombo.

hog, and cheetah hunting in the forests of the north and east.*

In 1888–9, and probably in further successive years, the opportunity may be afforded of being present at a pearl-oyster fishery off the north-west coast, for which Ceylon has been famous from time immemorial. The primitive mode of diving for and gathering the oysters by a particular caste of native divers, their sale by Government auction, and the business in pearls with thousands of dealers and their followers, who collect from all parts of India in the hope of a good fishery taking place,—all this is full of novelty.†

The cost of living in Ceylon at hotels ranges from 10s. per day upwards, board and comfortable accommodation by the month being available at from £7 to £10 per month for each adult. A lady and gentleman leaving England on the 15th of November, and returning by the 15th of May, spending four clear months in a comfortably-furnished bungalow in the hill-country of Ceylon, could do so for a total cost of from £250 to £300, including cost of trips to the points of interest in the island; the greater portion of this amount being for passage-money to and fro, which now ranges from £70 to £100 for return tickets. With further competition there can be no doubt, as the steamer's margin of profit allows of a considerable

* Elephant kraals—a system of capturing elephants peculiar to Ceylon — are now of rare occurrence, being organized only on special occasions. A description by the author of the kraal arranged for the entertainment of the Princes Albert Victor and George of Wales on their visit to the colony, which, though not very successful in its primary object, was characterized by some stirring incidents, will be found in Appendix I. Herds of as many as 200 elephants and 100 wild hogs have been seen at one time in Ceylon.

† For particulars of the "Pearl Fisheries" see Ferguson's "Ceylon Handbook and Directory," for successive years.

reduction, that the day is not far distant when £35 should secure a first-class passage between Ceylon and

FALLS ON THE DIYALUMAOYA, NEAR NAULA, EASTERN HAPUTALE, 535 FEET HIGH.
*From a Photograph by the late E. F. Grigson.*

England, and £50 a return ticket extending over six months. Before the Suez Canal opened £100 was the single rate for the overland route.

It may be averred that little has been said about the *drawbacks* to life in, or even to a visit to, Ceylon. The tropical heat in the low country must be endured; but, if found trying, a single day's journey will carry the visitor to a cool region. As to the detestable leeches described by Tennent as infesting every country pathway, and the poisonous snakes, the visitor may be months, or even years, in Ceylon without ever seeing the one or the other, being no more troubled by them than by the enormous crocodiles in the river or the voracious sharks round the coast. Repulsive insects, such as centipedes, scorpions, and large spiders, are also most rare in any well-ordered bungalow; while mosquitoes are only occasionally troublesome, and that chiefly in the low country. The brilliancy of the light, under a full moon, in the tropics is generally a great treat to strangers; so also are the stars and constellations of the Southern Hemisphere, including the bright fixed star Carropus and the interesting as well as brilliant constellation of the Southern Cross. The hum of insect life, as soon as day closes, in the moist, warm, low country at once arrests the ears of new comers, though local residents become so accustomed to it as not to hear it until their attention is specially directed. The monotony of perpetual summer, and of days and nights of about the same length all the year round, affords one point of strong contrast to England, but is pleasing, rather than otherwise, to the visitor.

# CHAPTER XIII.

## THE REVENUE AND EXPENDITURE OF CEYLON.

**Chief sources of Revenue:—Grain and Customs dues, sales of Crown Land, and Railway profits.**

Until 1828 there was an annual excess of expenditure over revenue in Ceylon; but between 1829 and 1836 the balance was on the right side, owing chiefly to a series of successful pearl fisheries. From 1837 to 1842, and again from 1846 to 1849, expenditure once more exceeded revenue; but from that time there was a surplus, and the amount of revenue quadrupled within twenty-five years, owing to the rapid development of the planting enterprise—the sale of Crown forest lands largely contributing—until in 1877 it attained a maximum of £1,702,619. Since then, owing to the falling off of the crops, the revenue has gone down, until it now may be said to stand about £1,300,000.

The main sources of this revenue are found in import duties on the rice imported from India for feeding the coolies and others directly or indirectly connected with the great planting enterprise of Ceylon, including a large proportion of the urban population. The Sinhalese and Tamil rice cultivators barely grow enough grain to support themselves and their dependents; on locally-grown grain there is also a Government levy, the remains of the old tithe or rent paid to the native kings, but this has been greatly reduced of late years by the application of commutation, so

KANDYAN (HIGHLAND) SUBORDINATE CHIEFTAIN.

that the import duty on grain is now decidedly protective of local industry.* The other most productive import duties are those on wines, spirits, hardware,

* For a full table of imports, during the last fifty years, of rice, cotton goods, fish, cattle, &c., see Appendix VI.

and cotton goods. Altogether the customs bring in between a quarter and a fifth of the entire revenue. The annual income from the railways all held by the Government (and 122 out of 185 miles the free property of the colony) makes up nearly as much of the general revenue as the Customs duties. Sales of Crown lands chiefly to planters have in some years also been as productive as the customs, but latterly the extent of land offered for sale, and the consequent revenue have greatly fallen off. Among the rules guiding the Forest Department formed of recent years is one prohibiting the sale of Crown forest above 5000 feet or on the ridges of mountains or banks of rivers below that height.

It is felt now that a great mistake was made fifty years ago in not keeping the proceeds of land sales in a separate fund as capital to be expended in reproductive public works, apart from the general revenue. The same may be said of the large railway receipts, in some years equal to a fifth of the revenue. Had this been done, the expenditure on fixed establishments would not have been allowed to increase year by year as if the general revenue from land sales and railway profits were a permanent source of income. The railway profits were for many years almost entirely due to the carriage of coffee from the interior to Colombo, and of rice, general goods, and manure for the plantations. Now tea (and tea requisites), with cinchona bark, cocoa, and other new products, take the place of coffee, to a great extent. Apart from the customs, the grain tax, land sales, and railway profits, the excise on the sale of spirits, stamp duties, and the monopoly or tax on salt, are the main sources of revenue, with an occasional contribution of from £10,000 to £50,000 from a pearl fishery. The latter is one of the most acceptable, but one of the most uncertain, sources of Ceylon wealth.

**ESTIMATE OF THE REVENUE AND EXPENDITURE OF THE COLONY OF CEYLON, FOR THE YEAR 1887.**

**[In rupees and cents of a rupee: the silver rupee being at present equal to about 1s. 5d. to 1s. 6d. English.]**

| Revenue. | Rs. | c. |
|---|---|---|
| Arrears of Revenue of former years | 155,000 | 0 |
| Customs | 3,000,000 | 0 |
| Port and Harbour dues | 485,000 | 0 |
| Land Sales | 410,000 | 0 |
| Land Revenue | 1,050,000 | 0 |
| Rents, exclusive of Land | 350,000 | 0 |
| Licenses | 1,440,000 | 0 |
| Stamps | 1,060,000 | 0 |
| Taxes | 36,000 | 0 |
| Postal, and Commission on Money Orders | 35,000 | 0 |
| Fines, Forfeitures, and Fees of Court | 50,000 | 0 |
| Government Vessels | 50,000 | 0 |
| Sale of Government Property | 1,060,000 | 0 |
| Reimbursements in aid of Expenses incurred by Government (including local refunds for Education) | 540,000 | 0 |
| Electric Telegraph | 56,400 | 0 |
| Miscellaneous Receipts | 210,000 | 0 |
| Interest (including interest on Cash Balances) | 160,000 | 0 |
| Pearl Fishery | 3,530 | 0 |
| Special Receipts | 10,000 | 0 |
| Railway Receipts | 3,000,000 | 0 |
| Total Rs. | 13,160,930 | 0 |

| Expenditure. | Rs. | c. |
|---|---|---|
| Establishments | 4,678,543 | 75 |
| Pensions, Retired Allowances, and Gratuities | 729,218 | 61 |
| Revenue Services, exclusive of Establishments | 347,090 | 0 |
| Administration of Justice, ditto | 130,672 | 0 |
| Charitable Allowances | 50,462 | 0 |
| Education, exclusive of Establishments | 245,684 | 0 |
| Hospitals and Sanitation, ditto | 442,142 | 0 |
| Police Services, ditto | 109,610 | 0 |
| Prison Services, ditto | 363,578 | 0 |
| Rent | 4,785 | 0 |
| Transport | 113,700 | 0 |
| Conveyance of Mails and Postal-Telegraph Services, exclusive of Establishments | 285,983 | 0 |
| Works and Buildings | 207,191 | 0 |
| Roads, Streets, Bridges, and Canals | 1,420,871 | 0 |
| Miscellaneous Services | 122,151 | 0 |
| Interest | 753,497 | 0 |
| Colonial Store | 22,400 | 0 |
| Military Expenditure | 631,500 | 0 |
| Government Vessels, exclusive of Establishments | 54,500 | 0 |
| Refund of Duties, Drawbacks, &c. | 40,000 | 0 |
| Lands taken for Government Purposes | 5,620 | 0 |
| Immigration | 82,908 | 0 |
| Railway Services { Interest & Sinking Fund | 900,001 | 0 |
| Railway Services { Other Services | 1,042,239 | 0 |
| Exchange | 127,060 | 0 |
| Forest Services, exclusive of Establishment | 137,000 | 0 |
| Total Rs. | 13,048,406 | 36 |

Colonial Secretary's Office, Colombo, December 30, 1886.

CECIL C. SMITH, Colonial Secretary.

## CHAPTER XIV.

### WHAT ITS GOVERNMENT CAN DO FOR CEYLON.

Active and independent Administrators required—The obstruction to progress offered in Downing Street—Railway extension, and Graving Dock at Colombo, urgently called for—Law reform needed—Technical, industrial, and agricultural education needs encouraging—The Buddhist Temporalities question—Fiscal reform of Road, Excise laws, Salt monopoly, Food taxes and Customs duties—The Duke of Buckingham's Ceylon and Southern India railway project—Ceylon and India—Waste Crown lands.

As regards the wants of Ceylon, its government is a paternal despotism; and the Governor and Secretary of State (with his Colonial Office advisers) being to a great extent irresponsible rulers, much depends on their treatment of the island. There can be no doubt that in the past, progress has been made in spite of, rather than with, the prompt, zealous co-operation of Downing Street. In support of this view we would quote from a review in the London *Spectator* (January 1, 1887) of Mr. Salmon's "Crown Colonies of Great Britain":—

"The system of Crown Colonies is supposed to be that of a benevolent despotism, a paternal autocracy. It is in many cases that of a narrow and selfish oligarchy. It is supposed that the Colonial Office exercises a beneficial supervision, and is everywhere the guardian angel of the bulk of the population in all the British Colonies. The supposition that a few Civil Servants, most of whom have never lived out of England, or engaged in any trade or business but that of clerks in the Colonial Office, could really exercise any such power, is extravagant on the face of it. There are more than thirty Crown Colonies, as various and widely scattered as Hong Kong, Fiji, Cyprus, Malta, Heligoland, Jamaica, Honduras, Ceylon, and Sierra Leone. How could any body of officials in London, however large, highly educated, and capable, adequately exercise any form of real control or intelligent supervision over such a mixed lot of *disjecta membra?* As for the Secretary of State, who is changed, on the average, once a year, it is impossible that he can be more than a figure-head, or have any real voice in the determination of anything except large questions of policy when there is Colonial trouble. Parliament is, however, supposed to exercise a control." But this control is limited, as Mr. Salmon points out, to questions put from time to time in the House of Commons, the answers to which are supplied in the first instance by the same Colonial Office clerks, and in the last resort by the people who are to be controlled, the actual administrators of the various Colonies.

We do not approve of much in Mr. Salmon's volume, especially in reference to Ceylon, which he has never visited, we believe, and of the circumstances of which he is necessarily to a great extent, ignorant. But we have had sad experience in Ceylon of the terrible loss of time, money and patience (equivalent to loyalty), increased through the obstructions offered to well-considered local schemes of progress, by the permanent officials of the Colonial Office speaking through the nominal and temporary Secretary of State.

An active, energetic, independent Governor, however, exercises an immense influence, especially if he is at the same time frank, free from any weakness for inquisitorial, underhand proceedings, and is inflexibly just. Every department of the public service, indeed almost every individual officer, feels the effect of such a ruler's presence, just as the whole administrative machinery goes to rest and rust in this tropical isle when the fountain-head of authority and honour is found to be somnolent and indifferent himself.

Statesmen bred in the free air of the House of Commons, as a rule, make the best governors of Crown Colonies; at least three or four in the Ceylon list—Governors Wilmot Horton, Stewart Mackenzie, Sir Henry Ward, and Sir William Gregory—had such a training, and stand out pre-eminently as among her best administrators, although equally able and useful were two others—Governors Sir Edward Barnes and Sir Hercules Robinson—who had not home parliamentary experience.

Ceylon wants a governor like Sir Henry Ward or Sir William Gregory, who has his whole heart in his work, is ready to sympathize with all classes and races, to see provinces, districts, and public works for himself—by journeys on horseback where necessary—open to receive counsel as to proposed legislation from the most diverse quarters, while deciding for himself after giving it due consideration; a Governor, moreover, not easily led away in his councils or provinces by officers, it may be of long experience but with special "hobbies," nor by oriental gossip and suspicion, which if once listened to leads into one quagmire after another. He should also apply as far as possible the commercial principle "Will it pay?" to all proposed expenditure of any considerable amount, whether on roads, irrigation works, or railways. Such an administrator will always be the best gift that Britain can offer to the natives and colonists of Ceylon, provided that his hands are not tied by the Colonial Office in Downing Street.

The only large public works at present under construction in Ceylon may be said to be the restoration of the Kalewewa Irrigation tank and channels in the North-Central province, the Colombo Waterworks being completed all but an abortive Service Reservoir, the bursting of which reflects little credit on the engineers concerned. But the Extension of the Dimbula-Uva railway for twenty-five miles to Haputalé, to serve the populous and rich Uva principality, with its numerous native gardens and European plantations, urgently calls for construction; for, without this Extension, the forty-two miles constructed to Nànu-oya cannot soon be profitable, the *additional new* traffic of Uva being required to make it so. This is a case in which the Colonial Office has baffled the wishes of the local public for so many years that at last divisions among the natives and colonists themselves arose on the subject, although no impartial, intelligent person can doubt that much loss to both the districts concerned and the public revenue has resulted from the delay. An ordinance to provide for this Extension passed by the Legislative Council in January, 1886, has not yet been sanctioned by the Secretary of State, and a variety of excuses—chiefly the state of the revenue—being offered for the delay, although a sure way to depress the revenue is to deny and delay this all-profitable section of Railway Extension. Sir Arthur Gordon has, as some people think, written almost too strongly on the subject; but as yet without avail. Such is government from Downing Street. Another very profitable and equally delayed Railway Extension is that from Kalutara to Galle or even Motara; and very promising proposals include a branch line from Veyangode towards Ruwanwela; a line from Heneratgoda to Negombo and thence to Chilau, and Extension from Polgahawela to Kurunegala and on *viâ* Anuradhapura to Jaffna. A more immediately urgent public work is the construction of a Graving Dock for Colombo Harbour, which has the express favour of the Lords of the Admiralty and of the Colombo Chamber of Commerce, and would be certain to prove a most useful and remunerative work. Nearly all these proposals in fact come under the head of reproductive undertakings. A public loan for the the more pressing of these works—the Uva and Galle Railway Extensions and the Graving Dock—may well be voted urgent, and we trust to see all these undertakings under construction very shortly.

Remembering that the colony within twenty-five years has paid, almost entirely through its planting enterprise, the whole cost of the grand Colombo and Kandy railway, with the seaside and Náwalapitiya branches—in all 120 miles, amounting to two and a half millions sterling, now the free property of the Ceylon Government; also that the harbour and waterworks (costing over a million sterling) are likely to pay their own way; that the splendid network of roads and series of restored irrigation tanks and public buildings (costing six million pounds sterling) have all been paid for from general revenue, there should be little hesitation in adding another three-quarters of, or a million pounds sterling to the debt of Ceylon —the whole debt even then not being much more than two years' revenue—in order to enable the above undertakings to be carried out.

We may here call attention to the railway map of the island, illustrating the system existing and projected, with needful statistics.* It shows at a glance the Ceylon Government Railways completed; the Extensions surveyed, estimated, and, we may add, officially promised; other Extensions projected but not finally surveyed; also possible lines which may be made eventually; together with lines projected but abandoned. Among the lines projected, next to the Haputalé and Badulla Extension in importance are the Extension of the seaside line from Kalutara to Bentotta, nine miles ready for construction, and thence a distance of about thirty-four miles to Galle on almost a dead level, for which there can be little doubt of the existence of a profitable passenger and goods traffic; secondly, the construction of a light line from a point at or near Veyangode towards Ruwanwela to serve the new and rapidly developing tea districts in that neighbourhood — and a branch which would prove a useful feeder to the main line, while it relieved one of the most expensively kept up roads in the country—namely, that *viâ* Hanwela and Avisawela, of a good deal of heavy traffic; thirdly, a branch from Heneratgoda to Negombo, and possibly on to Chilau for the salt traffic; fourthly, a branch from Polagahawela to Kurunegala, the capital of the North-Western province, which was proposed so far

* *See* Appendix XVI.

back as the time of Sir Hercules Robinson, and for which we believe there would also be a remunerative traffic; to be extended eventually *viâ* Dambula and Anuradhapura to Jaffna, Manaar, and perhaps by and by to Trincomalee.

We would further call attention to the table of railway statistics given with the map, showing that notwithstanding last year being a time of a specially short coffee crop and depression, the total profit from all the Government lines, including that to Mátalé, was no less than R1,139,621 (after covering the year's working expenses and certain permanent improvements to the lines, or the equivalent of nearly 4 per cent. on the capital cost of the 181 miles of railway open; and this, be it remembered, although the full return on the large cost of the Nanu oya railway can never be obtained until the new Uva traffic is brought into it by the extension to Haputalé.

We would merely add that all but the Mátalé and Nánu-oya branches, or 121¾ miles, are the free property of the colony; and the fact that the cost of this length has mainly been defrayed through the planting enterprise is another and forcible argument for urging the extension of relief to one of the most important provinces of the island and by far the richest of the planting districts. Indeed a progressive policy in Railway Extension generally is urgently called for.

In legislative and social improvements there is much to do: law reform in improved Mortgage, Bankruptcy, and other measures—in fact, the codification of our Civil Laws—is urgently wanted; while education, especially in the vernacular, has to be promoted.

Still more needful is a system of technical, industrial, and agricultural education. Something has been done towards a beginning in agricultural teaching by the present Director of Public Instruction with the limited means at his disposal; but we can only speak of this as "a beginning." It is felt by many that Ceylon junior civil servants, like those of Java, should pass at an agricultural college and spend one or two years on arrival in the island at Government experimental gardens or plantations. The influence of the personal example and precept of the revenue officers of Government over the head men and people in getting them to try new products or extend cultivation is immense; experimental gardens to supply the natives with plants and seeds and to show them how to cultivate the same, ought to be multiplied and bonuses offered for the growth of certain qualities of new products in different districts. Another beneficial reform would be the establishment of an agri-horticultural exhibition, with holidays and sports for the people, in connexion with each Kachchéri (district station) in the island.

The people of Ceylon are perhaps the least warlike of any nation under British rule: not a soldier has sustained a scratch here since 1817, when the Kandyan kingdom was finally subdued. Street riots in Colombo through religious feuds or dearness of rice, at rare intervals, only require the sight of a red-coat to subside; a few artillerymen (a picked company of the local volunteers would do) with a light field-gun would be sufficient to cope with the most formidable gathering that could possibly take place as a breach of the peace.

Nevertheless, it is important to note that for imperial purposes Ceylon is a most central and useful station for even more than one regiment of infantry with a good staff. This will be readily seen from what has happened during the past twenty-five years. Sir Henry Ward sent the 37th Regiment at a day's notice to Calcutta in 1857 to the aid of Lord Canning against the mutineers, those troops being the first to arrive; in 1863 the troopship *Himalaya* took the 50th Regiment from Ceylon to New Zealand to aid in suppressing the Maoris; later on, part of the Ceylon garrison did good service in China, the Straits, and Labuan; in 1879 the 57th Regiment was despatched at short notice to Natal; and, with equal expedition, the 102nd was sent thither in 1881, when the colony was practically denuded of infantry without the slightest inconvenience.

Ceylon is by far the most central British military garrison in the East; its first-class port, Colombo, is distant 900 miles from Bombay, 600 from Madras, 1,400 from Calcutta, 1,200 from Rangoon (Burmah), 1,600 from Singapore, 2,500 from Mauritius, a little more from Madagascar, about 4,000 from Natal, 3,000 from Hong-Kong, 3,000 from Freemantle or Western Australia, and about 2,500 from Aden. Its value, therefore, as a station from whence troops can, at the shortest notice, be transferred to any one of these points, should make it the Malta of the Eastern Seas; indeed its hill station, served by railway, as already mentioned, might be made the sanatarium for all the troops in Southern India.

Ceylon tax-payers would also fain see the head-quarters of the East India naval station removed from Trincomalee to Colombo, for the good of the port, now that first-class harbour works have been constructed; and this would probably be done if only the construction of a Graving Dock were taken in hand.

There are legislative reforms urgently needed in connection with the wide area of valuable lands with which the Kandyan Buddhist temples are endowed, and the revenues of which are now utterly wasted by priests and headmen without any benefit to the people, the majority of whom would gladly vote for their appropriation to the promotion of vernacular and technical, especially agricultural, education in each district. It is recorded that King Wijayo Bahu III., who reigned in Ceylon in 1240 A.D., established a school in every village, and charged the priests who superintended them, to take nothing from the pupils, promising that he himself would reward them for their trouble. This was probably done by temple endowments now wasted. In the more distant future the intelligent public of Ceylon hopefully look forward to the time when a reconstruction if not mitigation of taxation may take place, the *road tax*, some *stamp duties*, and the *salt* monopoly being the first to be modified or abolished. The small annual levy under the Roads or Thoroughfares Ordinance on every able-bodied man between eighteen and fifty-five in the island (the Governor, Buddhist priests, and a few more, alone excepted) has been productive of much good—in providing a network of district roads—since it was drafted by the late Sir Philip Wodehouse over forty years ago. But in some districts, the tax, small as it is, leads to a good deal of trouble and expense through defaulters; and its collection is everywhere, even in the towns, attended with an immense amount of corruption and oppression. This is the case with all direct taxes in an

Oriental land, and therefore an indirect levy in any form would undoubtedly be an unmitigated blessing to the people. Certain Stamp Duties were raised by Sir Arthur Gordon in 1885, and experience has shown that mischief rather than good has resulted. A liberal revision and reform of local Postal and Telegraphic rates and rules is much required, and a modification, if not abolition, of the Salt tax would be a great boon. This tax, though scarcely felt by the mass, debars agricultural improvement in certain directions, and occasionally affects the health of the people in the remoter districts.

In the estimation of the reformers of the Cobden Club, as put forth in Mr. Salmon's book already referred to, there is a financial reform of greater importance than any of these, namely, the abolition of the "Food-taxes of Ceylon," or the levy made on locally-grown grain crops, and the Customs duty imposed on imported rice. But while the internal tax has been inherited from the Sinhalese rulers as a *rent,* the only substitute possible for both this and the Customs duty is a general land-tax, and against this the whole body of the natives would cry out. One of the most intelligent Sinhalese, the late Hon. James Alwis, M.L.C., opposing this proposal, said, "it would be equivalent to taxing the curry, as well as the rice of the people." The lands held by colonists could, of course, be taxed, though, having bought their properties in freehold, their position is rather different from that of planters in India. But the natives would resist any change in every way they possibly could, and even the Dutch, as well as the English, were baffled in trying to make a small levy on the coconut gardens of the Sinhalese, and had to abandon it.* Of late years, the rent or tax on rice lands has been greatly lowered, and opportunities for oppression by headmen removed, by Sir Wm. Gregory's system of commutation; and Sir Arthur Gordon has gone to the verge of imprudence by legislating for a certain portion of this rent being annually appropriated by an Irrigation Board for the special benefit of the grain-growers. The section of the community paying the import duty, as indeed all consumers of taxed grain, may fairly complain and ask that something should be done for them from the import levy, which, as it now stands, is really protective of the local farmers. In principle, the rice taxes are fair—Stuart Mill being witness—and the heaviest portion of the tax is borne by the planters and their coolie labourers, who depend almost entirely on imported rice, while untaxed fruits, vegetables, and roots, enter largely into the food of the Sinhalese and Ceylon Tamils.

Fiscal reformers for Ceylon would do well to study the history of the fish-tax established by the Portuguese, continued by the Dutch, superseded by the British by a license for boats, which nearly stopped fishing altogether. The old form had to be resumed, but the tax was reduced again and again, without in the least benefiting the industry, for the fishermen simply caught less, having no longer duty to pay, and when the tax was finally abolished by Government, the Roman Catholic priests stepped in, and continued it.

* "The most precious inheritance of a Sinhalese is his ancestral garden of coconuts; the attempt to impose a tax on them in 1797, roused the populace to rebellion, and it is curiously illustrative of that minute subdivision of property, that a case decided in the District Court of Galle, referred to the 2,520th part of 10 *coconut trees.*"—*Emerson Tennent.*

without demur from the fishermen, who are mostly of that Church. In the same way, grain cultivators who have had their tax or rent remitted, have been known to allow a portion of their fields to go out of cultivation in view of no rent to pay—so much less work to do was their idea of the benefit of remission of taxation.

Of course the removal of all Customs' duties and the inauguration of Colombo as a free port would add immensely to the importance of Colombo and the colony. But the time for that is still afar off, even if it were desirable in the interests of the native population. On the contrary, if all the revenues raised in such dependencies as India and Ceylon could be levied through the customs, the railway, or even stamps—by indirect means—the blessing to the mass of the people for some generations yet, would be one of the greatest that could be bestowed. When the grand scheme which the Duke of Buckingham, as Governor of Madras, propounded to Sir William Gregory, of connecting the railway systems of Ceylon and Southern India, is carried out, in order to serve the very large passenger traffic in coolies and traders, as well as to carry the produce of Southern India to the safe and commodious Colombo harbour—the Madras harbour works being, at all events for the present, a great failure;—then may we look for a closer approximation between the fiscal systems of the two countries. At present India has no import tax on cotton goods—a very dubious reform in the interest of her people—but an export tax is levied on the rice shipped from Calcutta and Madras to Ceylon.

One great difference between the two countries is the much larger Covenanted Civil Service, and number of European officials generally, in Ceylon, in proportion to population and area, than in India.* Of course the individual salaries are much lower here, but it is a question whether the island has not too many public servants of the higher ranks, and whether there is not room for reform in the system of administration such as was referred to by Sir Emerson Tennent in his Financial Reports over forty years ago. The pension list of Ceylon is becoming a serious burden to the colony, and some steps are urgently called for to prevent a continuance of growth such as has been experienced of recent years. On the other hand the cry is getting up here, as in India, on behalf of the educated Ceylonese (natives and Burghers), that room should be found for a greater number of them in the public service. Schemes for a subordinate uncovenanted service have been propounded, both in their interest and in that of economy, as saving the need for many principal appointments, and some step in this direction may be necessary before long. At the same time, in a country situated like Ceylon, agriculture in one of its

* Ceylon for its three millions of people and 24,000 square miles has more than half as many Civil Servants as the Presidency of Madras with six times its area and ten times its population. The following may be of general interest:—

| | Area: Sq. miles. | Population. | No. of Covenanted Civil Servants. |
|---|---|---|---|
| Bengal and Assam .. | 202,905 .. | 72,000,000 .. | 266 |
| N.-W. Province .. | 106,111 .. | 44,107,000 .. | 348 |
| Punjaub .. .. | 106,632 .. | 18,850,000 .. | |
| Bombay .. .. | 124,122 .. | 16,500,000 .. | 162 |
| Madras .. .. .. | 139,900 .. | 31,000,000 .. | 157 |
| Burmah (Upper and Lower) .. .. | 278,000 .. | 6,736,000 .. | — |
| CEYLON .. .. | 25,000 .. | 2,900,000 .. | 81 |

many forms ought to be kept steadily before educated Burghers and natives alike, as the one sure means of affording a livelihood. Tea planting, we are glad to think, is likely to do much for young men of these classes; in the tea factories there should be room for a large number of intelligent young men of the country, as tea makers, clerks, &c., and very many of the natives ought to cultivate tea-gardens of their own, besides trying other new and profitable products.

A reform tending to extend local industry would be the throwing open, for a merely nominal price, of Crown waste lands, at present unsaleable (at the upset price of R10 per acre), to cultivators who would spend money and labour on them. This applies to both low and high lands. A "stock farm" is a great want in Ceylon, yet an offer made by a responsible colonist to lease waste Crown lands near Nawara Eliya, and introduce good stock in cattle and horses from Australia, was rejected some years ago, because the fiat of the Secretary of State had decided that nothing should be done with Crown lands over 5,000 feet altitude.

# CHAPTER XV.

## SOCIAL LIFE AND CUSTOMS.

Social life and customs of the natives of Ceylon—How little colonists may know of village life—Domestic servants—Caste restrictions—Curious occupations among the people—Sinhalese philanthropists, Messrs. De Soyza and Rajapakse.

The variety of race, colour, physiognomy, and costume among the people in the busy streets of Colombo—especially the Pettah, or native market-place—at once arrests the attention of the stranger. But, save what he sees in the public highways, and may learn from his servants, the ordinary colonist may live many years in the island without learning much of the every-day life and habits of the people of the land, whether Sinhalese or Tamils, in their own villages and homes. There is a beaten track now for the European to follow, be he merchant or planter, and there is so much of western civilization and education on the surface that the new comer is apt to forget very soon that he is in the midst of a people with an ancient civilization and authentic history of their own, extending far beyond that of the majority of European nations; and with social customs and modes of life, when separate from foreign influences, entirely distinct from anything to which he has been accustomed. The foreigners who see somewhat of this inner life of the people, especially in the rural districts, are the civil servants and other public officers of Government, and the missionaries. Now, as regards the work of the latter, the average European planter or merchant returning home after six, ten, aye, or even twenty years in Ceylon, too often declares that the missionaries are making no way in Ceylon, that they live comfortably in the towns, and content themselves with ordinary pastoral duties in their immediate neighbourhood, and in fact, that they (the colonists), never saw any evidence of mission work or progress among the natives, unless it were through the catechists and other agents of the Tamil Coolie Mission visiting the plantations. Now, the way to meet such a negative statement would be by an inquiry as to whether the colonist had ever interviewed a missionary to the Tamils or Sinhalese, whether in Colombo, Kandy, or Galle, to go no further, and had asked to accompany him to his stations. Had he done so, he could have been taken to village after village, with its little church and good, if not full, attendance of members, presided over in many cases by pastors of their own people, and in some instances supported by themselves. He would have seen schools of all grades—mission boarding-schools for native girls and lads, and training institutions for the ministry. Now, just as this branch of work in the rural districts of Ceylon is unknown to many scores, if not hundreds, of European colonists who never trouble their heads about anything beyond their own round of immediate duties or pleasures; so it is, for an even wider circle, in reference to the social life and customs of the natives.

Education has made such strides that in the towns,

English is rapidly becoming the predominant language among all classes. In India all foreigners learn a native language, and domestic servants never think of speaking English, even if some few of them under-

MOORMAN "TAMBY" (PEDLAR).

stand it. Here, in Ceylon, English is almost universally in domestic use, and there is scarcely a roadside village in Ceylon now where the traveller could not find some persons to speak English, or interpret for him. The coolies on the plantations are different; with few exceptions they only know Tamil, and the planters have to learn that language colloquially. Civil servants pass examinations in the languages. Very amusing are some of the servants, occasionally, who are only beginning to acquire English, or who try to show a command beyond their depth; like the Sinhalese appoo (butler) who, one day, on being remonstrated with by his Christian mistress for attending some tomfooleries of ceremonies at a temple, replied, Yes, he knew better, but he only did it "to please the womens" (his wife and daughters!), the hold of superstition and heathenism in Ceylon, as elsewhere, being strongest on the female portion of the household. On another occasion a horsekeeper (Tamil groom), coming to report to his master that his horse had gone lame, expressed himself thus, holding up his fingers in illustration, "Sar, three legs very good; one leg very bad!" Some of the letters and petitions in English of budding clerks, or warehousemen, or other applicants for situations, are often comical in the extreme. Both Sinhalese and Tamils make the most docile and industrious of domestic servants. Of course there are exceptions, but ladies who have been for some years in Ceylon, after visiting "home" again, or especially after going to Australasia or America, are usually glad to get back to their native servants.

Caste in Ceylon has not one tithe the hold on the people that it has in India, and in respect of domestic service, only one-half to one-third the number of men-servants is required here, in consequence of one man making no objection to different kinds of work. Sinhalese "appoos" and "boys," with their often smooth cheeks, and hair done up in a knot, surmounted by a comb, and with white jackets and long "comboys" (long petticoats), are frequently taken for female servants, the latter having no comb, but a silver or other pin in their hair, and only taking service as ayah (nurse), or lady's attendant. In the hotels passengers frequently make the mistake of supposing they are attended by maid, instead of men, servants. The Sinhalese have, indeed, been called the women of the human race, and the story is that in trying to make soldiers of them, the British instructors in the early days never could get them not to fire away their ramrods !

Of course there are some bad native servants, but they are the exceptions ; at any rate a good master and mistress generally get good service. But sometimes robberies do occur in households, and usually then some one or other of the servants has been conspiring with outside thieves. A few colonists prefer Malay servants.

The demand for holidays is often a nuisance, and the saying is that native servants must have half a dozen grandfathers each from the number of funerals of grandfathers they have to attend. The fact is that the western habit of constant work does not suit the Oriental taste at all, the proverbial saying of the Buddhist Sinhalese being, "Better to walk than to run, to sit down than walk, and best of all to go to sleep."

We have said that caste has not a great hold in Ceylon ; but in one point of social life, it is still almost universally observed, there can be no marriage between persons of different castes. Your servant may be a man of higher caste than your wealthy native neighbour driving his carriage, and yet the appoo would probably never consent to allow his daughter to marry the son of the rich but lower caste man.

Christianity is working against caste, and among native Christians there are many cases of caste being disregarded; but, on the other hand, when the Duke of Edinburgh was entertained by a Sinhalese gentleman of medium caste, it was stated that Sinhalese

THE DHOBY.

officials (including a Christian chaplain) of the Vellale (agricultural) caste absented themselves from the entertainment where all were expected to be, because they could not enter the grounds or house of a man of the Fisher caste. The most striking case in recent times in Ceylon was that of a young girl of good family in a Kandyan village, who fell in love with the son of a trader in the same village, of greater wealth but lower caste than her father, who was a decayed Chief. The lad and girl had seen each other in school days, and acquaintance had ripened into more than friendship, and they were bent on defying caste, family opposition, and any other obstacle to their marriage. But a young brother of the girl haughtily forbade the courtship, threatening his sister if ever he saw her with the young trader. The lovers planned a clandestine match, so far that (being both Buddhists) they should get married by civil registration before the magistrate. They stole away one morning and were mixing in the crowd usually awaiting the opening of the magistrate's court in county towns, when the young chief, finding out what had happened, rushed up and peremptorily ordered his sister home. She refused and clung to her lover, when the brother suddenly drew a knife from his girdle and stabbed her to the heart. She fell dead on the spot; the murderer holding the knife aloft and shouting, in Sinhalese, "Thus I defend the honour of my family," and going to the scaffold a few weeks after, exulting in his deed. Education and the railway are, however, aiding Christianity to weaken the hold of caste, and the people of Ceylon will, before many generations go by, learn that—

> "Honour and shame from no condition rise,
> Act well your part, there all the honour lies";

And that—

> "From yon blue heavens above us bent,
> The grand old gardener and his wife,
> Smile at the claims of long (or caste) descent."

It is a striking evidence of the slight influence of Buddhism that here, in its sacred or holy land, where it has prevailed for over two thousand years, caste, which is utterly condemned by its founder and its tenets, still exercises a baneful influence over the Sinhalese people. All castes, however low, were declared to be eligible to Buddha's priesthood; but in Ceylon ordination gradually became the privilege of the Vellale caste alone, until a Sinhalese of a lower caste went to Burmah and got ordained, so making two castes of priests in the island. In other Buddhist countries, Burmah, Siam, and Thibet, caste does not exist in any similar form. A stanza from a Ceylon Buddhist work runs as follows—

> " A man does not become low caste by birth,
> Nor by birth does one become high caste;
> High caste is the result of high actions—
> And by actions does a man degrade himself to a caste that is low." *

Native weddings, with the peculiarities of each race—Sinhalese, Tamil, or Moormen (Mahomedan)—are sometimes very curious, and, as the parties are generally rather proud than otherwise of Europeans being present, there is no difficulty about getting an invitation. The youthfulness of the bride—perhaps thirteen to fifteen years—and the quantity of jewellery, literally weighing her down (collected and borrowed from all the family circle of relatives for the occasion), are two peculiarities. There are scarcely any unmarried native women, and, as is always the case in a naturally ordered community, the males exceed the females in number. The Sinhalese have no army or navy or flow of emigration to supply, and no artificial customs to interfere with or delay the marriage of

* *See* Appendix with extracts on " Caste."

their daughters. Of the influence of the Buddhist and Hindu religions upon the people, enough is said elsewhere, but we may just refer here to the fact that a people bred under the influence of tenets (Buddhist), for-

DEVIL DANCER, WITH ATTENDANT TOM-TOM BEATER.

bidding the taking of life, have developed some of the most cruel and exquisite forms of torture known to history in reference to the lower animals. A law had to be passed forbidding the roasting of tortoises alive, in order to get the tortoise-shell of a finer lustre than if taken from the dead animal; and only the other day a military officer discovered in Colombo that native cooks were in the habit of cutting out the tongues of the living turkeys, in order that the flesh, when cooked, might be the more tender. But a long list of such instances might be given, as well as illustrations of the hypocrisy which makes Buddhist fishermen say: "We do not kill the fish, we take them out of the water and they die of themselves!" Householders put out the old dog or cat on the highway for the wheel of a passing vehicle to go over and kill, so that they may have no sin; or shut up the deadly snake in wicker-work on the river to be carried to the sea; while early in the present century it was the custom to expose old and helpless human beings in the jungle, each with a bowl of rice and chatty of water, to die without troubling their relatives, or to be devoured, as was often the case, by beasts of prey. And all this in one of the most bigoted of Buddhist districts—Matara—in the south of the island. It was in the same district a veteran missionary demonstrated the hypocrisy of a catechist, of whom he had authentic accounts that, while professing to be doing certain work as a Christian teacher for the sake of a salary, he was in heart a Buddhist, attending all the temple ceremonies. In a remote village there was no check, and on being questioned by the missionary, while sitting in a room together, he utterly denied that he had any belief in Buddhism. Taking a small brass image of Buddha from his pocket, the missionary placed it on the table, when immediately (as all Buddhists should do) the would-be catechist sprang to his feet, placed his hands before his forehead with a low obeisance towards the image, and then slunk from the room discomfited!

Among the more curious occupations of the people, as related in the census, are such novelties as 1,532 devil-dancers (see page 160), 36 jugglers and monkey-dancers, 121 snake charmers, 240 astrologers and fortune-tellers, 32 actors and puppet-showmen, 640 tom-tom beaters, 160 comedians and nautch dancers, 16,357 dhobies or washermen (see page 157), nearly 2,000 barbers, 50 elephant-keepers and huntsmen, about 5,000 fakirs and devotee-beggars, 1,500 grave-diggers, 200 lapidaries, 400 workers in ivory and tortoise-shell, and 3,000 in jewellery, &c.*

European civilization and Christianity are both taking a firm hold of the people. Education is desired by the natives, perhaps not yet for its own sake, but as a means of advancement, as very few good posts are to be obtained in which English is not needed.

Once in our mission schools (and education, especially in the villages, is mainly in the hands of the missionaries) children acquire new habits of industry and perseverance, and in time come to regard truthfulness as desirable, and care for others, whether of their own blood or not, as a duty. Though Buddha led a most self-denying life, and taught others to do the same, yet his example had made small impression on his followers, and philanthropy was not regarded as a duty by the Sinhalese or their priests. Now it is different. Each of our missions can quote many instances of noble generosity and hearty zeal for the welfare of the people.

* The main results of the census will be found tabulated in Appendix VI.

The de Soysa family, especially C. H. de Soysa, Esq., J.P., Mudliyar of the Governor's Gate—whose engraving we give, and who is expected by the people of Ceylon to be knighted by Her Most Gracious Majesty in this Jubilee year—are well known as the

C. H. DE SOYSA, ESQ., J.P.

leading native philanthropists in Ceylon. That the present representative of the family has made a good use of his wealth may be seen from the by no means complete list of his benefactions which will be found in Appendix XII.

No less worthy of record are the benefactions and good works of Sampson de Rajapakse, Esq., J.P., Mudliyar of the Governor's Gate, of an ancient and honourable family. We give his portrait in full

SAMPSON DE RAJAPAKSE, ESQ., J.P.

official dress as Mudliyar, and also his genealogical tree as a curiosity (*see* Appendix XIII.).

*Pour encourager les autres.* If the notice of two of our philanthropists and the publication of their benefactions should prove an incentive to other wealthy Oriental British subjects to follow the example of

Messrs. de Soysa and Rajapakse, there will be perhaps sufficient excuse for this memorial of their liberality to the Ceylon community.

We have merely touched the skirts of topics in this chapter, which might well require for their treatment a volume in themselves. Those interested in the subject may be referred to good old Robert Knox's veracious account of his sojourn, as a prisoner, among the Kandyan people for twenty years—1659 to 1680—or to more modern books, in Cordiner's, Percival's, Davy's, Forbes's, Pridham's, or Emerson Tennent's histories, with Spence Hardy's "Eastern Monachism," "Jubilee Memorials," and "Legends of the Buddhists."

# CHAPTER XVI.

## CONCLUSION.

Relation and importance of Ceylon to India—Progress of Christianity and Education—Statistics of Population—Need of Reform in the Legislative Council, and sketch of a scheme for the Election of Unofficial Members—Loyalty of People to British Rule, as evinced during Royal visits, and in connection with the Jubilee of Her Majesty the Queen-Empress—Jubilee Celebration.

CEYLON, in a social and political way, bears the same relation to India and the Far East that England has done to the European continent. Mr. Laing, when Finance Minister for India, confessed it was most valuable to law-makers and administrators in the Indian Presidencies, to have Ceylon under a separate form of government, and to have experiments in administrative and legislative reforms tried here, which served as an example or a warning to the big neighbouring continent, the peoples being allied in so many respects. There is, for instance, no distinction made between native and European judges and magistrates in Ceylon; and the acting Chief Justice, lately, was a Eurasian, while at present a Sinhalese barrister is Judge of the Supreme Court; and other Ceylonese fill the responsible offices of Attorney-General and

Solicitor-General of the Colony. Again, in Ceylon, we have a decimal system of currency, a great step in advance of the cumbrous Indian system, and we have entire freedom of all religions (including Christianity) from State patronage and control.

The progress of Christianity and education among the people is greater than in any other Eastern State, and should Buddhism, the religion of one and three-

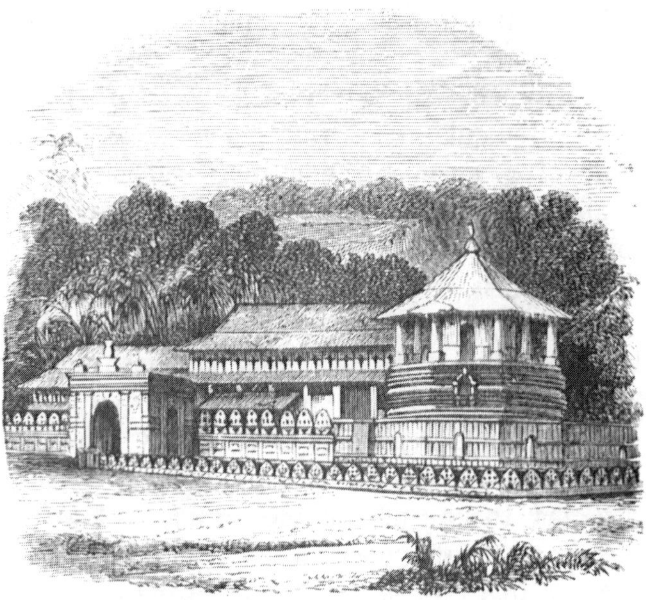

KANDY MALIGAWA, OR TEMPLE OF THE TOOTH.

quarters of a million of Sinhalese, fall here, it would have a great effect on the millions of Burmah, Siam, and even China, who look to Ceylon as the sacred home of Buddhism. The kings of Burmah and Siam especially, continue to take an interest in, and make offerings to, the Buddhist "temple of the tooth" at Kandy. Roman Catholicism has been propagated since the arrival of the Portuguese in the sixteenth century; while English Protestant missions have worked in Ceylon since 1811.* The Roman Catholics number about 220,000, the Protestants 60,000, against 1,700,000 Buddhists and demon worshippers, 600,000 Hindus, and nearly 200,000 Mohammedans. The population at the census of 1881 included 6,300 Buddhist. 1,250 Hindu, and 574 Mohammedan priests, 465 Christian ministers and missionaries, 2,210 schoolmasters, 759 lawyers and notaries public, and 3,321 physicians and medical practitioners of all grades.

Some allusion should be made to more than one local movement in Ceylon for a reform in the system of government, and more especially in the liberalizing of the Legislative Council. Sir Hercules Robinson, while opposing this claim, originated municipal institutions in the three principal towns, as a means of training the people in the art of self-government. The working of these has, however, unfortunately, not been so successful as was hoped, and one reason is a curiously oriental one, namely, that respectable Ceylonese consider it derogatory to go and ask the people below them—often ignorant and poor franchise-holders—for "the honour of their votes." "Honour comes from above, not from below," they say; and so the better classes of natives abstained from the Municipal Boards, and left many disreputable men to get in. A reformed and restrictive municipal constitution law just passed, may work better. But as regards the Legislature, the occupation of one of three seats allotted to the Ceylonese by nomination of the Governor has always

* For illustrations of the progress of modern Protestant Christian Missions, *see* Appendix III.

been greatly coveted, and an object of ambition to every rising man in the country.* A reform in the present practice of according what are practically life seats, would be to change the unofficial members every three years, so educating and testing an increasing number of Ceylonese for public life. There is no reason, however, why a few more unofficial seats should not be added to the Legislative Board. Indeed, the elective principle might, under due safeguards, be applied in the eight provinces of the island,—under a severely restricted franchise to begin with,—so giving eight elected unofficial members, to whom might be added two to four nominees of the Governor, from among the merchants or other classes not adequately served by the elections. Elections and nominations could take place every six years, or on the advent of each new Governor, and a few more privileges might be accorded to the members, such as the right of initiating proposals, even where such involved the expenditure of public money up to a certain moderate limit. The Governor, for the time being, could always command a majority against any unwise scheme, and his own veto, as well as that of the Secretary of State, would continue operative. Some such improvement of the Legislative Council—which has continued without change for over fifty years, or since the days of Governor Sir Robert Wilmot Horton in 1833—cannot long be delayed, and if asked for on broad grounds by a united community, it might well be granted in honour of the Queen's Jubilee year.

Another practical reform of importance would be the ensuring that four out of the six members of the

* For further information about the government, *see* Summary of Information concerning Ceylon (Appendix VIII.).

Executive Council—that is, the Colonial Secretary, Attorney-General, Auditor-General, and Treasurer—should always be trained public servants of the colony, with local experience. The farce has been seen even in recent years of a Governor and his five Executive advisers in Ceylon, not counting half a dozen years of local experience between them.

Ceylon was honoured with a visit from H.R.H. the Duke of Edinburgh in 1870, from H.R.H. the Prince of Wales in 1875, and from the young Princes Albert and George of Wales in 1881. On each occasion the loyalty and devotion of the people to the British Crown, and their warm personal interest in the happiness and welfare of their sovereign, were very conspicuous. This has been still more shown during the present year, in connection with the Jubilee of Her Most Gracious Majesty the Queen-Empress Victoria, when all classes and races have vied with each other in the endeavour to do honour to the occasion. Liberal support has been given to the Imperial Institute, dear to the Queen; as a local memento of the occasion, a Home for Incurables is to be erected in Colombo, and loyal addresses, as well as a Women's Offering, have been sent to Windsor.

The Jubilee was celebrated throughout Ceylon with great enthusiasm. In Colombo was the chief demonstration, that being the head-quarters of the representative of the Queen; but the whole of the island towns may be said to have been decorated and *en fête*. The Military Review on Galle Face Esplanade at 7 a.m., was the event of the morning of the twenty-eighth, in the capital, and the Volunteers shared with the regulars the duties of the occasion. The *feu de joie* and three ringing cheers were the soldiers' expression of loyalty at its close. This was followed at 10.30 by services in all the places of worship. In the Mission Churches the interesting feature was the union of English, Sinhalese, Tamils, and even Portuguese descendants, at the same service, addresses being given in all four languages in succession. The Queen's letter, requesting that prayer and thanksgiving be offered up, had been sent from Queen's House to the different pastors, and was duly read at the services, while at the close a collection was made in many churches for the "Ceylon Victoria Home for Incurables."

Then came the feeding of large numbers of the poor in all the towns and chief villages, each applicant getting either a measure of rice and five cents (one penny), or a piece of calico.

A good dinner was given by the citizens of Colombo (led by Mr. J. J. Grinlinton) to the soldiers in garrison and their wives and children, numbering 951 persons.

In the afternoon came the great celebration on Galle Face Esplanade, Colombo, where from fifteen to twenty graceful pandals had been erected for the accommodation of the many who could not stand exposure to a tropical sun. Nothing can exceed the graceful beauty of such erections, when the Sinhalese and Tamils set themselves to do their best; loops of plaintain and young coco-nut leaf, green moss and fern, and yellow olas, and clusters of coco-nuts, oranges, or other fruits, offer the best possible material for covering the bamboo framework that may be put together in a night.

It is computed that about 25,000 human beings of all classes and races, the vast majority clad in bright garments, varying from white to the richest and most brilliant hues, were assembled round the centre where the Governor read the Record of the Chief Events of the Fifty Years, received the Address from the inhabitants of Ceylon to their Gracious and Beloved Monarch, and made proclamation of the Queen's desire (in conjunction with her God-fearing subjects everywhere) to return thanks to Almighty God for the blessings of the fifty years; to see the Royal Standard hoisted and to hear the salute of fifty guns fired in honour of the Royal Lady who had reigned so long and so well. High festival as it was, the quiet and orderly conduct of the crowd was the subject of emphatic and approving remark. Amongst the most interesting incidents of the day was the singing of the Royal Anthem by the Sunday-school children, and the procession of these and other young people, scholars in the various schools and colleges to the number of about 2,000. There were numerous processions of various races and religionists, including some seventy-seven Buddhist priests in bright yellow robes, men who must be better than their creed, if they sincerely joined in the thanksgiving to Almighty God. Salutes consisting of the cracking of long Kandyan whips were sources of curiosity to newcomers, while the chanting of both Malay and Sinhalese processions to well-known popular tunes produced much amusement. One of the most striking incidents of the day was the appearance of Arabi and three of his fellow-exiles—Mahmood Samy, Toulba, and Abdulal, at the head of the Muhammadan procession. Their appearance imparted an element of romance to the proceedings, reminding one of those "Arabian Nights Tales," in which the isle of Serendib figures so prominently. The most fertile of imaginations could not, some years ago, have anticipated that a contingent of Egyptian officers, exiled to Ceylon for rebellion against their own sovereign, should take a voluntary part in celebrating the Jubilee of a Queen whose army had defeated the forces which they had led in insurrection, and so rendered abortive their ambitious (or patriotic ?) designs.

The other three Egyptian exiles, Ally Fehmy, Mahamood Fehmy, and Yacoob Samy, preferred presenting an address at Queen's House, which the Governor received and promised to forward to Her Majesty. The following is a literal translation of their address written in Arabic :—

"May it please your Excellency,—With heartfelt loyalty, we the undersigned Egyptian exiles in this country, though few our number, have reason to approach your Excellency on this auspicious day set apart by your Excellency for the celebration, by the general public of this island, of the Jubilee of Her Gracious Majesty Victoria, Queen of England, and Empress of India, whom your Excellency as Ruler of this country represents, and we beg to address the following :—

"No one would deny that for the period of fifty years during which Her Majesty has uninterruptedly occupied the throne, Her Majesty has been just and merciful, and the brightness of her reign has reflected all over the world, and been a source of gratitude which we always feel in our hearts, and of which we are full.

"We pray for all those gracious and liberal gifts to us that Almighty God may bless Her Majesty and give her grace, prolong her glorious and beneficent reign, and give her health, happiness, and honour.

"We must confess that, in our position which is

known to all, the pain in the centre of our hearts, as strangers from our country, felt, has been removed since our stay in this country, by the prompt extension to us of relief and justice, by the many acts of kindness, humanity, and generosity done to us. All these acted as a remedy which cured the pain which we felt in our hearts, making room for our peace and comfort.

"We have indeed, therefore, special reason to be most sincerely loyal and faithful, and to humbly yield to the feelings and inclinations of our hearts. We beg, therefore, to lay at the foot of Her Majesty's throne our unbounded heartfelt thanks, and to offer the same to your Excellency, as Her Majesty's great Representative in this country, in which we enjoy favours and overflowing justice.

"We feel infinite happiness and pleasure that we are accorded the privilege of taking a part ourselves in the enjoyments of this joyful, happy, and auspicious day, set apart for the honour and praise of Her Majesty the Queen."

Other addresses were presented to the Governor for transmission to Her Majesty by the people of Ceylon, the Legislative Council, the Planters' Association, which represents the backbone of the prosperity of the island, and the small Malay community. From the latter we quote a part:—

"We desire to offer your Excellency, as the representative of her Majesty Queen Victoria, our sincerest and dutiful thanks for the manifold advantages we have received during the beneficent reign of Her Majesty, through her many noble representatives who ruled this island. It is with the proudest satisfaction we say, and in saying it we are but expressing the feeling of the entire Malay community, that no community has proved more loyal and faithful; and its loyalty and fidelity have stood the very best tests. Fifty years ago, when Her Majesty ascended the throne, the Malays constituted a Military Corps, they rendered valuable service abroad and in this island, which, although it has been only the land of their adoption, has, in consequence of the disbandment of the corps in 1873, become their home. A mere military corps has during the last fifty years made rapid strides towards material advancement, and what had been a mere corps of a few hundred fighting men has developed into a large, free, and independent community. This happy realization is due to the beneficent rule of Her Majesty Queen Victoria. It nevertheless still retains its martial spirit, and we may assure your Excellency, should there ever be occasion for it, the Malays to a man would joyfully rally round the British Standard and fight to the death like good soldiers."

The different colleges of Colombo each had their own pandal, and a visitor would be very much interested in the Ceylonese lads trained in the Royal, St. Thomas's and Wesley Colleges, in the Medical College; and also in the pandal headed, "Widyodaya College," inside of which were ranged in rows, some seventy-five Buddhist students, clad in their yellow robes, these being with a few exceptions made of silk; while in front, in a *sanctum* all by himself, sat Sumangala, the high priest of Adam's Peak, and president of the College. These young celibates, though they had their fans in their hands, did not make much use of them, but stared about and enjoyed the fun as much as any one else. What would the Buddha have said if he had seen them thus gathered to do honour to a *woman* (according to his dictum woman is—not sinful—but *sin* itself!); and to hear later on, when the school children were singing "God save the Queen," a young monk chant a number of Pali stanzas, composed by the learned Sumangala himself, in honour of this same woman. In these pandals the official record was read in English, Sinhalese, or Tamil, by the leaders of the classes represented. Sir Arthur Gordon also read the Record through, and then proclaimed in Her Majesty's name that the lands sold for default of payment of commutation rates, since the introduction of the Grain Commutation Ordinance into any province, which shall remain in the hands of the Crown, should be restored to their former possessors. He also announced that the following classes of prisoners—173 in number—had been released on that day as an example of Her Majesty's mercy and clemency:—(1st) all prisoners in prison for debt due to the Crown; (2nd) all women not undergoing imprisonment for very serious offences; (3rd) all prisoners whose sentences of imprisonment were shortly to expire.

From the official record of British progress in fifty years, prepared by the Governor, we quote the few items referring to Ceylon:—

In 1838 the Legislative Council of the Colony, created but not completed in 1833, received its full complement of members.

In 1844 the last remains of Slavery were wholly abolished.

In 1848 a slight insurrectionary movement took place in a part of the Kandyan districts, which is only worthy of mention in order to contrast it with the loyalty of all classes ten years later, on which the Governor of Ceylon was able safely to rely, when in 1857 he sent all the available troops in this Island to assist in the suppression of the Indian Mutiny.

In 1856 Sir Henry Ward commenced the restoration of the long-neglected Irrigation System of the Island; and in 1857 the ancient Village Councils were revived, chiefly with a view to the promotion and enforcement of Irrigation Works.

In the same year the first sod was cut of the first Railway in Ceylon.

In 1858 Ceylon was united with India by the Electric Telegraph.

In 1865 the Municipalities of Colombo and Kandy were established.

In 1868 the general scheme of Public Education now in force was adopted by the Legislature.

In 1870 legislative measures enabling the tenants of Temple Lands to commute their services were adopted, and in the same year the Ceylon Medical School was established.

In 1871 the powers of Village Councils were largely extended, and Village Tribunals instituted.

In 1875 the first stone of the Colombo Breakwater was laid by His Royal Highness the Prince of Wales.

In 1881 an Ordinance, which however did not come fully into effect until 1886, was passed, withdrawing pecuniary aid, saving in the case of vested life-interests, from all Ecclesiastical Bodies.

In 1883 a Code of Criminal Law and Procedure was passed, which came into operation at the beginning of 1885.

In 1885 Currency Notes were first issued by the Government.

In 1886 the Colombo Breakwater was completed.

The Population of Ceylon, which in 1837 was estimated at 1,243,066, and on the first census taken in 1871 was found to be 2,405,287, now amounts to about 3,000,000.

The Revenue, which in 1837 was £371,993, amounted in 1867 to £969,936, and in 1886 to R12,682,549.

The number of miles of Main Roads open in 1837 was about 450; in 1887 it was 3,343.

The number of Estates in the hands of European Settlers in 1837 probably did not exceed 50; in 1887 it was over 1,500. The development of Agricultural Industry which these figures denote is, in itself, the most remarkable feature in the History of Ceylon during Her Majesty's reign. It is a development which has changed the physical appearance of the country, and profoundly modified its social condition, and which is due to the energy and perseverance of men who have shown that they can bear adversity with fortitude as they sustained prosperity with credit.

The Royal Standard was then hoisted, and a royal salute of fifty guns was fired. Next the Volunteer Band, led by Mr. Lüschwitz, played "The National Anthem," while the children, led by the Rev. S. Coles, C.M.S., sang the same.

Processions closed the afternoon's proceedings, and effective displays of fireworks, with less effective illuminations, entertained a large concourse till midnight.

The chief permanent Memorial of the Jubilee is to be the Ceylon "Victoria Home for Incurables."

Nowhere in the British Empire are there more loyal or contented subjects of her Most Gracious Majesty than in "Lanká," "the pearl-drop on the brow of India."

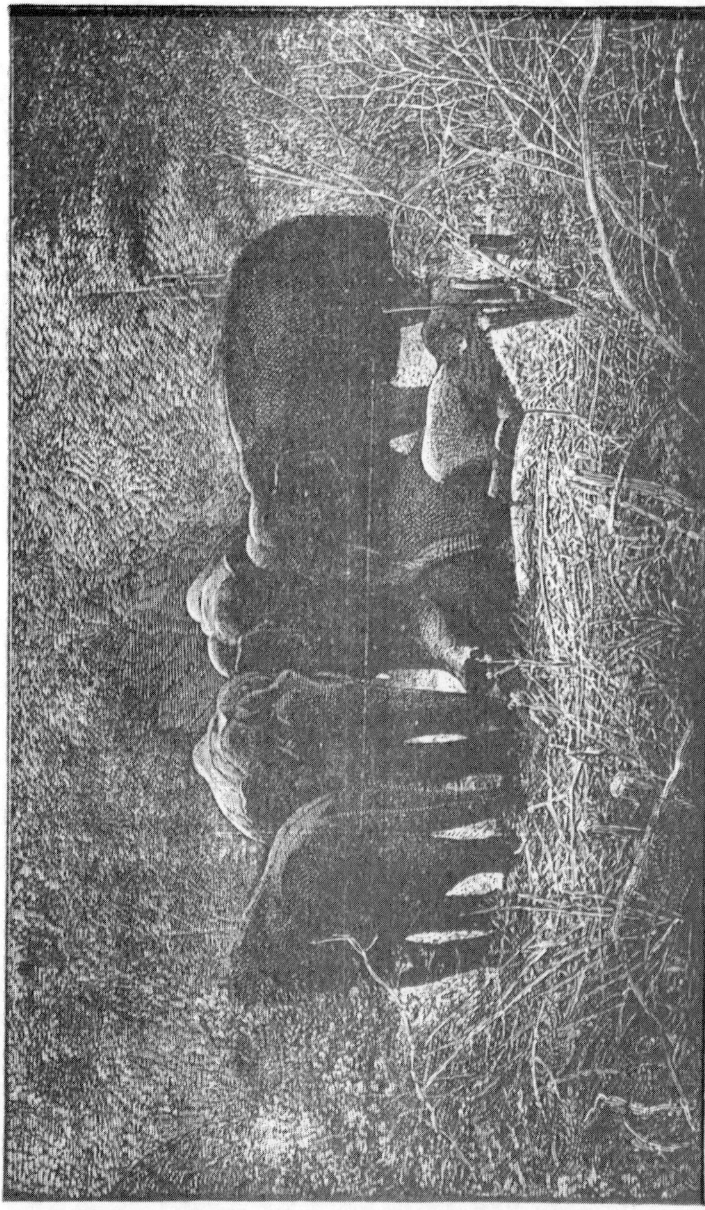

WILD ELEPHANTS IN THE LABUGAMA (YOUNG PRINCES') KRAAL, OF 1882, MOURNING OVER THEIR DEAD COMPANION.
*From a Photograph by Messrs. W. L. H. Skeen & Co., of Colombo.*

# APPENDICES.

## APPENDIX I.

### SHOOTING TRIPS IN CEYLON.*

GOOD CENTRES FOR SPORT, AND HOW TO REACH THEM FROM COLOMBO.

No. 1.—The Park Country and Batticaloa Tanks :—*Game:* elephants, deer, cheetahs, bears, pigs, teal, snipe, peafowl, &c., &c. To Nanuoya by rail; to Badulla, hired carriage, 40 miles; to Bibile, hired carriage, 37 miles; to Nilgala, good bridle road, 15 miles. This is a good centre for the Park country. To Ambari Tank, 31 miles.

[Excellent country for all the above game, Erikamam, Devilane, and other large tanks in the vicinity.]

No. 2.—The Horton Plains :—*Game:* elk, deer, elephants, spur fowl, &c., &c. To Nanuoya by rail; to the Horton Plains, turning off at Blackpool 2 miles from the Nanuoya station on the road to Nuwara Eliya, 18 miles.

No. 3.—Trincomalee District :—*Game:* elephants, bears, cheetahs, deer, teal, snipe, &c., &c. To Trincomalee, by steamer, or by road through Kandy and Matale, rail to Matale, thence by road to Trincomalee, 97 miles. Trincomalee to Kottiar by boat, Kottiar to Toppur (Allai-Tank), 7 miles. Good centre for sport of all sorts. Kanthalai Tank, 24 miles from Trincomalee on Kandy road, good centre for sport.

No. 4.—Puttalam District :—*Game:* elephants, bears, cheetahs, deer, partridge, &c., &c. To Puttalam by canal or road, 84 miles. Puttalam to Pomparipo by lake or

* The best available book on Sport is still Sir Samuel Baker's "Rifle and Hound in Ceylon," though published nearly thirty years ago: a new edition was published a few years ago.

road, 25 miles. Good centre for sport. Pomparipo to Marichikaddi, 18 miles bridle road. Excellent country for game of all sorts.

No. 5.—Hambantota District:—To Kalutara by rail; coach to Galle and Matara; thence a hired trap to Hambantota. By steamer to Galle and Hambantota and cart to Yalé.

No. 6.—Minery and Polonaruwa:—To Matale by rail. Matale to Habaranne by road, 44 miles, good carriage road. Habaranne to Minnery, bridle road, 15 miles; Minnery to Topari (Polonnaruwa) 12 miles.

---

## THE ELEPHANT KRAAL OF 1882.

A DESCRIPTION OF THE ELEPHANT KRAAL HELD AT LABUGAMA (CEYLON) FOR THE ENTERTAINMENT OF THE PRINCES ALBERT VICTOR AND GEORGE OF WALES IN 1882.

(From an account by Mr. J. Ferguson in the *Ceylon Observer*).

### AT THE KRAAL.

Kraaltown, Monday Evening, January 30, 1882.

#### ARRIVAL OF THE PRINCES.

The Princes arrived at the kraal at 5 p.m. Prince George was mounted on a spirited steed and cleared the stream which runs between the official and unofficial portions of Kraaltown in magnificent style, showing that he knows how to ride. Large crowds of planters and others cheered him vociferously. Prince Albert Victor arrived on foot, walking with his Excellency the Governor alongside of Lady Longden, who was carried in a chair. There are two herds of elephants within a mile of the kraal, seven in one herd and fifteen in the other. A successful drive is expected early to-morrow morning.

Tuesday Forenoon, January 31, 1882.

#### THE ELEPHANTS INDISPOSED TO CARRY OUT THE OFFICIAL PROGRAMME.

The little programme sketched out by the Government Agent, and which the energetic Dawson hoped to put into execution, ran somewhat as follows:—The driving from the outer into the inner beat to commence last night, to be followed this morning by the drive into the kraal, which, it was hoped, would be effected before noon; the noosing and tying-up to be at once begun and continued on Wednesday. This would have enabled the princes to see all the operations connected with a kraal and to start back so as to reach Colombo in good time on Wednesday.

But, so far, we have only an illustration of the well-worn aphorism that—

> "The best-laid plans of mice and men
> Gang aft agley;"

and we all know how often, especially in the case of elephants, are the plans of men at fault. An old chief last evening gave me the opinion, based on his experience of a good many kraals, that while a herd of elephants were difficult to compass and drive from their native jungle in the first instance, once start them and get the beat fairly established, and by the time they come within driving distance of the kraal they are all fairly cowed and very easy of management. No doubt comparatively this is the case; but in the history of kraals we have too many instances of successful charges and escapes to feel that the final drive is such an easy matter as the old chief would have us believe. Last night's experience is no exception. The herd that it was proposed first to capture, after being driven into the inner beat, broke through into the wider range, and the evening's labour went for nothing. No doubt the wet evening—rain extinguishing fire and torches—had a good deal to do with the breach effected. Of nothing is the elephant so much afraid as of fire, and with nothing will a Kandyan approach a wild elephant so readily. You will remember Major Skinner's experience on the Anurádhapura road as an illustration. How he found the road to his camp wilfully, if not deliberately (and of malice aforethought), blocked up one evening by a herd of elephants which had been prowling in the neighbourhood; how all the efforts of himself and his men to clear the road of the intruders proved unavailing—the leader, an old tusker, charging furiously when any attempt was made at dislodgment; and how this went on for some hours until finally a Kandyan arrived with a huge torch, with which he marched right up to the tusker, who stood his ground until the fire almost touched his trunk, and then turned tail and fled with all his belongings. In the hands of a man of Mr. Saunders's nerve, no doubt an umbrella alternately opened and shut would prove as effectual as a torch, and very probably the Government Agent found occasion to use it last night, for he and Mr. Dawson are reported to have spent most of the night with the beaters.

Very early astir this morning, probably the first from the official encampment, was Captain Foot (of H.M.S. *Ruby*), and a long walk round the kraal and on along the line of beaters failed to afford a sight of waving forest tree-tops, or the sound of crashing through "batali" (small bambu), much less the sight of an elephant. The hope now is that one herd may be driven in this afternoon, but there are doubts about it, and the headmen are more than usually susceptible to the presence of strangers, insisting that their beaters should not be visited, and that no bugle should be sounded for the benefit of "Kraaltown" until the barrier-gate shall be closed and the herd secured. There is, as usual, too, some little jealousy among the chiefs, the one insisting on his herd being first disposed of and by no means mingled with the others.

Meantime the princes are enjoying themselves under "the merrie greenwood." Their quarters have been most delightfully chosen—for situation beautiful exceedingly—and much care and taste have been displayed in fitting them up. A "crow's-nest" for four has been established at a good point for a sight of the drive-in, while the principal grand stand is, as usual, erected partly inside the kraal to secure a good sight of the final and really interesting operations.

TUESDAY EVENING.

THE ELEPHANTS STILL OBSTINATE—A VISIT TO THE BEATERS' LINES—A FALSE ALARM—THE CHIEF EKNELIGODA.

This has been a day of disappointment for all concerned. The drive-in, which was expected to take place last night was considered certain for this morning, and in hurrying up from a distance of ten miles (where I had taken up my quarters last night) I feared the risk of missing an exciting portion of the proceedings, but was consoled to find everybody still waiting for the elephants. The afternoon was now considered certain for the drive, and in preparation thousands of natives wended their way kraalwards, from which, however, they were kept off at respectable distance.

I started off to find the outer line of beaters, and at about two miles from Kraaltown I came upon their small jungle huts, or rather nests and camp-fires. Very picturesque was the scene and wonderful the interest of the people in their work, from the old grey-headed Kandyan sire with his flowing white beard, who had probably passed through more kraals than he could recall, to the young stripling by his side who was on the "corral" beat for the first time. From the far-distant jungle came the signal of their chief, Ekneligoda, or his henchman, and immediately the cry was taken up,

> "Hari—hari—hari—hari,
> Hari—hari—ho-ho!"

winding up with a prolonged cheer. Passing from the bridle-road, the outer cordon line led through the small bambu jungle up hill and down dale; camp-fires, huts, and beaters with their long forks were passed, or here and there an old musket, and again at regular intervals a crow's-nest with an agile, keen-eyed watchman swung up in a tree. Suddenly a wild "halloo!" is raised by the Sinhalese on the river bank; there is crashing of jungle, firing of guns, and flinging of stones; two or three indefatigable appuhámis literally throw themselves into the stream across which the cordon line now runs, to pick up rocks and fling them into the jungle. The elephants are surely coming, and right down upon us in the river, is the first thought. Three beaters at our side look out for trees, and the thought of shelter becomes a leading consideration. Suddenly the assistant agent, Mr. Dawson, accompanied by the indefatigable Captain Foot and a few other officers, break from the cordon line into the river-bed. Their presence has a wonderful effect; the beaters redouble their furious attack on the supposed advancing "aliyas," shouts and yells, shots and shells in the form of pieces of rock, crashing and trampling, form a proper accompaniment, and it seems more than ever needful to look out for danger. As a Colombo wallah I could not help thinking discretion the better part of valour, and my friends looked, if they did not speak it—

"He who ascends into a tree
May next day climb again with me;
But he by elephant that's gored
May see at once that he is floor'd."

But, before we moved a step, the clamour and shindy subsided as suddenly as it was commenced, and it did not require the "knowing" look of a friend up to "the ways that are dark" of the beater folk to see that all was got up as a "plant" (excuse slang) in honour of the visitors, to afford them a little sensation for their jungle trip. "The elephants are upon you," they said, in fact, in order to see how we should stand the test or show a clean pair of heels. But fortunately we stood it all, while we followed on in search of the elephants.

I was anxious to see the old chief, Ekneligoda, who at the head of 500 men directed this drive of fifteen elephants—his people having been out for nearly a month, while he has been half that period living and lodging as best he can in the jungle. "Here he comes," cries my companion, who knows the old man well: a little, dark, skinny old man, bearded like the wandura, with an ordinary comboy which he is holding up as he walks barefoot through jungle and water—the inevitable dilapidated billy-cock hat setting off a figure which a stranger would at once say belonged to a poor old Kandyan of no consequence. But a glance at his face revealed power and authority, set off by a keen eye and aquiline nose—a man of few words, yet his English is good. We met him later on coming back from one of his beats, when he frankly assured us he did not think we could see the elephants, penetrate and push on as we might. He complained, not loudly, but expressively, of the difficult task set to him: more troublesome elephants had probably never come under his care.

WEDNESDAY EVENING, Feb. 1st, 1882.

PARTIAL SUCCESS: SEVEN ELEPHANTS DRIVEN IN, BUT THE ATTEMPT TO NOOSE THEM UNSUCCESSFUL—ONE SHOT, AND THE TAIL PRESENTED TO PRINCE ALBERT VICTOR — A BEATER KILLED AND OTHERS WOUNDED — DEPARTURE OF THE GOVERNOR AND THE PRINCES.

Ekneligoda has his headquarters on the north side of the Peak in the Yatiyantota district, as his relative and superior, Iddamalgoda, holds sway over the richer and more popular south. He is a man of few words, but when I met him the second time in the bed of the expansive rocky ela, which feeds the Maha-oya, the chief, who looked disconcerted after his interview with his civilian superior, threw out his hands in the expressive oriental fashion and deprecated this English plan of fighting against time and nature, hurrying up the elephants, *nolens volens*, whether inclined to go on or not. "Now," said the chief, "the Sinhalese way is to wait on the elephants; don't allow them to go back; wait until they go, or only at proper times help them to go forward." In the light of last night's and to-day's experiences, there is much wisdom in the old chief's remark.

Tuesday passed, and no elephants approached, but the beaters had begun to work in earnest, the position of the herd had been noted by the waving of the jungle, and the chief was very sanguine of passing into the kraal valley and probably driving his herd in during the night. With this anticipation the princely and viceregal party, as well as Kraaltown, had to be content for Tuesday evening.

The princes were for part of this day entertained with the performances of the tame elephants, and they had several walks to the "crow's-nest" in front of the kraal.

### Wednesday's Experiences.

Day broke, and in the grey morning mist, from 5 to 7 a.m. (and a few hours afterwards), the denizens of Kraaltown might be seen climbing the hillside, and passing on to the kraal entrance in the hope of all being ready for business at last, but "No elephants; not likely to be any kraal," was all that one could learn. Later on, however, came better news, and we awaited patiently for hours the approach of elephants which, judging by the nearness and loudness of the cries of the beaters, might be expected at any moment, from 9 a.m. onwards, to burst from their final fastness along the drive into the kraal.

Wednesday Night.

### Capture of Iddamalgoda's Herd of Elephants.

About breakfast-time came the news that the two herds of from seventeen to twenty elephants were to be kraaled simultaneously. This was received as a welcome relief by the weary bystanders. Very patiently, though with eager expectation, did we all wait for the sudden rustling of the jungle and the burst inwards, which would afford ocular demonstration of a herd being kraaled. But hour after hour sped away, and, though numerous were the alarms, no approach to the entrance followed. It was a case of

> "How often we Prince Rupert kill'd,
> And bravely won the day,—
> The wicked Cavaliers do read
> The clean contrary way.'

ELEPHANT CHARGE: THE FINAL SHOT.

At one time the tame elephants were ordered down into the jungle to charge the wild herd upwards if possible, but the attempt failed: the work was one in which the tame ones had no practice, and the "cow" in the herd, already nearly driven desperate about her calf, threatened to undo all the labour of many weeks, if any weak point were left exposed. Fiercely, and again and again, did this gallant brute and faithful mother charge the beaters; she refused to be driven back, and after injuring, directly or indirectly, several of the beaters, she at last killed her man, and it was resolved she must perish. Mr. James Munro was requested to punish the offender, not by killing but by wounding her, which he did at forty paces by a shot in the forehead. This laid the cow prostrate for from five to ten minutes, during which blood poured out of the wound in a torrent, forming quite a pool; but after this interval the animal rose, much to the delight of its distracted calf, and trotted after the herd, thoroughly cured of further designs on the beaters, and in a few minutes more—unfortunately in the absence of the crow's-nest party at luncheon—the whole herd, four large and three small, dashed along the entrance drive into the kraal, trampling down the bambu jungle and passing at lightning speed and with the sound of rumbling thunder into the kraal.

"Caught at last!" was the cry, and the grand stand was speedily occupied, while the order went forth to old Iddamalgoda, who now appeared on the scene, that an attempt should at once be made to move and tie up one of the herd.

But, alas, the princes were timed to leave at 1.30; they lingered on till about 3 p.m., and so secured a passing sight of the herd in the kraal and were presented with the tail of the elephant shot. Then Prince Albert Victor, His Excellency the Governor, Lady Longden, Sir Edwin Johnson, Lieut. Adair, and Captain Hayne, A.D.C., started for Colombo; while Prince George, with his tutor, the Rev. J. Dalton, Captains Lord Charles Scott, Durrant, and Foot—as well as Admiral Gore-Jones—remained some hours longer in the hope of witnessing a noosing and tying up. Beaters were already hard at work with catties, and very soon two or three of the tame elephants lent their effective aid, butting down gently but effectually trees of no mean magnitude: everything in the shape of light jungle speedily disappeared from around the royal stand. The enormous government "tusker," fully roped and equipped for the noosing and tying business, now moved down in stately measure among the spectators to the eastern side of the kraal, where, at the word of command, he lightly and readily slipped aside the top beam and dropped the one end from his trunk to the ground. He crossed the lower beam, still over four feet high, without difficulty, and proceeded into the jungle. I passed on to the remoter end of the kraal, where a continuous trumpeting, varied by stentorian but painful cries of the bereaved baby-elephant, indicated the presence of the herd hidden in the dense bambu jungle. Nothing could be seen of them here, however—only the occasional waving of the bambus. Turning back, I found that the government tusker had got rid of his keeper inside the kraal for some reason, and was vainly trying by himself to slip back the upper beam again in order to get out of the kraal! Fortunately for the thousands of natives and some Europeans too (who could not well stampede through the close jungle) the beam had been firmly secured, and very soon the keeper once more resumed his work and authority, and the tusker went to work, although, apparently, he was not to be depended on so much as the remaining tuskers' trio. After a good view of this end of the kraal from Mr. Charles de Soysa's stand, I went on to the grand stand, inside the kraal, where Prince George and party were waiting for the exhibition which never came off. Although two or three encounters took place, and although a band of volunteer European parties undertook to drive from the lower end of the kraal, no favourable opportunity for noosing could be obtained, and the prince had to be contented with the several ineffectual attempts made.

The fact is that the attempt to noose on the same evening as the capture is unprecedented, and the civil officers scarcely expected success. The usual and proper course is to allow a night to intervene, during which the captives trample down all the "batali" and other jungle stuff, exhaust themselves in examining their prison, and finally lie down in whatever puddle may remain in the hollows. Noosing and tying can then proceed in a business-like way. Clearly, neither chief nor retainers could feel much enthusiasm in the after-proceedings of this afternoon. That the tame elephants and keepers did their duty well is vouched for by the experience of a planting friend who, occupying a prominent position in a high tree inside the western side of the kraal, witnessed a charge of three tame elephants on to the quartette of big ones in the herd, which fairly astonished him. The trio were arranged in line, facing the position in the bambu, where the herd gave evidence of their presence, and all at once in regular and most rapid motion, at the word of command, they charged, butting the herd fairly over or on before them. So rapid and regular was the run, that the three seemed as one, and to run like a racehorse.

As a finish to my day's work, I paid a visit to the dead elephant, which lay in the bambu jungle not far from the western entrance. The fatal shots on the forehead were examined, as well as one in the ear; the ears and feet as trophies or talismans had already been either cut off or hacked about. We were a party of twenty or thirty, including natives, around the prostrate animal, when suddenly a crash through the jungle near at hand was followed by the cry of "Here comes the herd!" and, sure enough, the wild elephants, closely followed by two of the tame ones, appeared to be making directly for us. There was screaming and shouting enough in good earnest, and although the only risk lay in a hurried stampede in one direction, the pursuers being behind, clearly discretion was the better part of valour, and a rush was made for the barrier.

THURSDAY EVENING, February 2nd, 1882.

A HARD DAY'S WORK, RESULTING FINALLY IN THE CAPTURE OF TWELVE ELEPHANTS, INCLUDING A SPLENDID TUSKER.

We were met at an early hour by an official intimation —probably written the night before—to the effect that the public were requested not to approach the stockade and kraal, as Ekneligoda's herd was within easy distance, and the attempt was to be made to open the barrier gate, drive them in and kraal all together. This was a disappointment, because it added to the risk of there being no noosing at all this day; but before we had fully realized the new "situation" created by the official "proclamation," came the authentic news, meeting us on the road up to the kraal, that the whole of the six elephants kraaled the night before had escaped during the night, and that the kraal was vacant!

This proved to be the fact, and the explanations rendered were most varied. One statement was that part of Ekneligoda's herd had broken in during the night, and the palisade being knocked down, all escaped scot-free again; another account made it appear that the gate must have been opened preparatory to the further kraaling, and so in being too greedy, crying "more, more," those already held were lost. The official report is that a "tusker" from Ekneligoda's herd—and it is supposed to be the same "tusker" as visited the kraal the night before—broke in again so effectually as to release his sisters and brethren, old and young, in distress. But where were the watchmen planted all round the kraal the night before with wands and spears immediately alongside the barricade? Well, there can be no doubt they were grievously to blame, and as evidence that they have not escaped punishment I may mention that the Government Agent visited them at an early hour this morning to give them "a bit of his mind," winding up, I believe, with a smash of "crockery" (!) in-including chatties—a great deprivation for Sinhalese "jungle-wallahs."

But, in defence of these poor fellows, let me say that their story has it that they were beset by wild elephants prowling round the kraal from the outside, and so, between two fires, they could not give their attention to their charge as they would have liked. There are further explanations however, namely, that their chief Iddamalgoda had to listen to some sharp words the night before on account of the slowness of his people to effect a noosing, the threat finally being that the Government would not allow them to have a single elephant from the herd, since they allowed Prince George to leave without tying up one. The old chief said nothing, merely shrugging his shoulders; but it is quite conceivable that his people cared little about keeping strict watch and ward over the herd that was to be taken from them. Another reason for discouragement was the shooting of the big "cow" elephant: the beaters did not like it a bit:—"Here we have been driving in the jungle for weeks, and after we have brought this elephant eighty miles or so to within as many feet of the gate of the kraal, you go and shoot it!" This is certainly not the native plan, and it is all attributable to the terrible haste made in the present proceedings in order "to catch the princes." Another six hours must undoubtedly have brought in the mother as well as calf in safety.

From an early hour Mr. Templer (who had so steadily accompanied Iddamalgoda's herd to the kraal) was out with Ekneligoda and the larger herd, now coming rapidly forward. Whether this chief's circle of beaters had intercepted and added to their herd the six escaped elephants is a matter of doubt; but they certainly brought on as many as twelve elephants of their own, and beating up from early morning, the most perfect stillness being maintained in and around the stockade—due very much to the great number of departures—shortly after noon the herd was reported well on in the kraal drive,* and at one o'clock Mr. Saunders's report was: "Drive-in probable in a quarter of an hour." From that time on to five o'clock, most trying, vexatious, disappointing, and yet most exciting was the experience. I question if ever before in the history of kraals there has been so strange and mixed an experience.

The following sketch will give an accurate idea of the

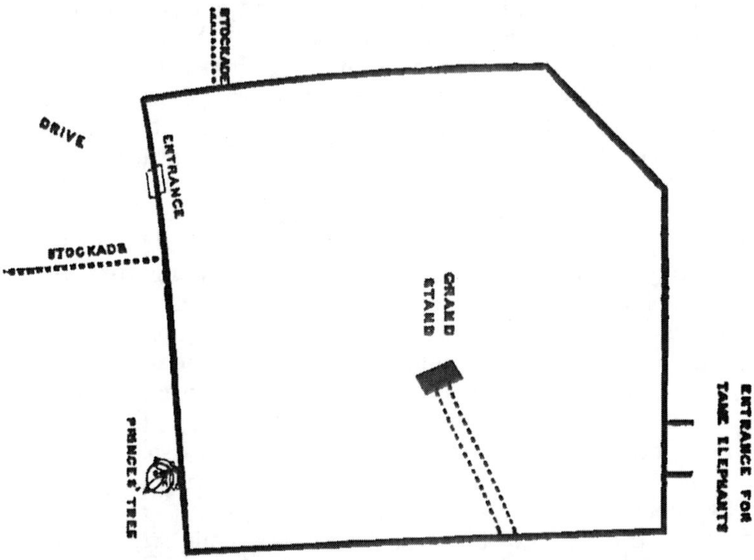


way in which Ekneligoda's herd had to approach the kraal. There is a ridge and valley behind the kraal valley.

The herd, after coming down the drive, had rounded the hill and faced the kraal about 1 p.m., as I have said. The cries of the beaters came steadily onwards so far, and

* The drive for a couple of miles round the range, down the gorge and on towards the kraal till the stockade was reached, was most finely carried on: the cries of the beaters ever came nearer and nearer; but when the elephants sighted and scented the stockade they stopped short at once.

progress, though a good deal slower, was made for an hour more. Most exciting was the scene then; the proximity of the elephants was evident, the tree-tops waved, the bambus cracked, and every now and then uplifted trunks rose over the bambus, and a rumbling of trumpeting—the simmering of baffled rage—swelled the excitement of the few hidden and silent onlookers, as well as that of the beaters. Between 2 and 3 p.m. the drive-in became so certain and imminent that Ekneligoda and his immediate bodyguard or attendants (five stalwart swarthy fellows) left "the beat" to see if all was right at the Government Agent's corner, whence the entrance could be commanded. This was below the princes' "crow's nest," to-day, alas! deserted. [I wish I had time to give you a proper idea of Ekneligoda, as he came up the path of watchers outside the drive, billycock hat and common cloth as usual, closely followed, however, by his umbrella-bearer in gorgeous costume of flowered comboy, big comb, &c. Evidently the Sinhalese chieftain when on the "corral" path likes to look like his work and to leave all outward show to his servants.] Sure enough, Ekneligoda had not been long at our end, when the elephants rushed as if for the entrance; but they stopped short, irresolute; then, getting into the open, some of them made a dash at the palisades of the drive facing us, and immediately we all—a dozen Europeans, backing the watchers led by Ekneligoda—shouted and screamed and struck trees and fences to our hearts' content. This drove them in a mob on the other side, where, at the palisade as well as far up the hillside were a number of planters, besides the usual stockade guard. They soon made it plain to the herd they could not break through there; and then was witnessed a sight probably never before paralleled — seven or eight goodly-sized elephants standing in a semicircle together, heads to the centre, immediately in front of the entrance to the kraal, and yet not making the slightest attempt to enter! The rest of the herd farther up the drive kept the beaters back by charging now and then; * but evidently there was now

* About 1.30 the tusker made a full charge; there were some visitors at the time with the beaters; later on, when a great many European volunteers had joined, a regular charge of the herd took place, and three elephants escaped up a ridge along the centre of the drive, being seen from the stockade to pass through the beaters. Altogether four charges were made on the volunteers.

an obstacle in the way, or such demoralization as made it most uncertain what to expect of the elephants. The most likely explanation became evident with the recollection of the "dead elephant," shot the night before inside the entrance, and the track of blood which no doubt ran along from the barrier. On smell elephants chiefly depend to warn them of danger. The scent of danger ahead was only too apparent. "Better perish where we are" seemed the thought of the seven companions in danger, as they stood rubbing each other sympathetically, than pass that truly bloody gateway and be shot behind it.

Baffled again and again, and worn out by their exertions, it became clear that Ekneligoda's men wanted help. This had been suggested to the chief already once or twice, and Mr. C. S. Agar, who had been summoned at an early hour by Mr. Dawson to aid with his trusty rifle, had been eager for some time to join the drive, and by discharging blank shot to inspire the beaters to urge the drive on.* Mr. W. S. Murray at last conveyed the pressing request to Ekneligoda (who had again rejoined his people) for Mr. Agar and twenty or thirty European volunteers to join the ring, and, after an interval, it was granted on condition that no shot should on any account be fired at the elephants.

Mr. Agar, rifle in hand, quickly followed Mr. Murray to the beat in the valley, and, Mr. Saunders sending the call round, I speedily saw pass on from our side Messrs. Thring, Talbot, and C. R. White, the admiral's flag-lieutenant (the admiral had all day attended closely on the proceedings with imperturbable good humour and encouragement), and three or four more whom, in their hasty descent through the scrub, I did not recognize. A still larger body, chiefly planters, passed into the drive round the opposite side of the kraal. Most unfortunately, the volunteers had barely reached the circle of advance when the rain, which had been threatening for some time, began to descend in torrents: black and hopeless rolled the clouds over the devoted valley and the apparently ill-fated drive; the thunder boomed and the rain poured, and

* Mr. A. J. Campbell had previously pressed to be allowed to lead twenty-five Europeans and fifty native beaters, guaranteeing success with the drive, but, Ekneligoda then protesting, this was considered unadvisable.

it seemed as if "hari-hari-hooi-ooi" was at an end. The cry was raised again and again, but was positively drowned in the greater noise of the elements. From many points of view this ill-timed rain seemed to doom the whole enterprise. It gave the thirsty elephants refreshment, a breathing space, and fresh courage; night was coming on; the drivers could not stand their ground so close up to the herd all night; their camp-fires must prove a failure;—and hope had sunk to zero! The dead elephant had, apparently, saved a score of living companions from being kraaled.

I had taken refuge from the rain in a watcher's hut; but about 4.30, finding the rain soaking through, and no appearance of a clearing up, hopeless of a kraal, and anxious to get on ten miles homewards after my boxes, which had, alas, gone on before me, I determined to start off. I made for Kraaltown in a woeful condition; the pathways were being swept by torrents, the road down the hill at some corners was a perfect rapid, and at its foot the "ela" in front of Kraaltown, which had hitherto been crossed at a low ebb, was becoming an impassable river. I arrived early enough, however, to be carried over with the help of two coolies and a Sinhalese servant, who rushed to our assistance when in a hole near the other side. I found Kraaltown pretty well deserted; and, with boxes gone, no "change" was available, though I was drenched to the skin. Eventually, however, I secured sufficient for a change by borrowing in four different quarters! I merely give these trivial personal details to show what kind of an evening had come on, and what the experience of many others was; and still more what was the state of the men at the post of honour and of danger in the jungle drive.

About six o'clock grand tidings came down with men who, drenched to the skin already, thought little of wading or swimming the river. Gathering up the reports of half a dozen of the eye-witnesses or partakers in the final charges and drives, I will endeavour hastily to present a consecutive trustworthy account. For the elephants now, it was clearly a case of

Officers to the right of them,
Planters on left of them,
Beaters behind them,
While all the herd wondered,—

or rather felt a much less pleasant sensation. Messrs. Agar, Thring, Talbot, and their party lost little time, rain or no rain, in beating to quarters: they urged the drive in again and again; shot succeeded shot; "hari-hari" became the rule; and the drive was one scene of excitement. Several minor charges to the line took place; but the rain and the advent of the Europeans sent the beaters to huddle under trees and clear out. It became evident that the Europeans could not work without a base line being cut out of the jungle, and the natives were brought back to cut down a semicircular path behind the elephants. Torches were also prepared, weapons improvised, and all made ready to force the herd on.

Mr. Saunders now appears to have, as a last effort, descended into the beat, and, while his volunteers were using every exertion to drive in, he climbed up a tree to catch the exact situation. I am guessing at this intention from what followed. On the stockade near the drive, at the angle joining the kraal, sat four planters watching the struggle, who had not yet joined in it. Mr. Saunders called on them to lend a hand, and they immediately passed in, led by Mr. Sandison. Arrived at the beat, and immediately behind the herd, Mr. Sandison, who carried a short spear, looking round for a torch, the most trustworthy of all weapons of defence in dealing with wild elephants, spied Mr. Unwin alongside with one, and arranged in a word that they should go on, shoulder to shoulder, together. But Mr. Sandison's former companions, not understanding the arrangement, pressed on between. Several others from the beating line followed. Sandison advanced right up to the elephant, and with a prod sent it—a huge mother with a little calf—right on the herd with a rush! Some of the main body of elephants thus charged sprang over the ravine towards the entrance, pressed on by Messrs. Wighton, Thring, Talbot, and others. Not so the wild mother and her calf, the tusker, and two or three more: they only rushed forward to wheel round and charge fairly back into the centre of the Europeans, who, much in advance of the natives, were left without any support. The rank broke, and the volunteers tried, but only tried, to get out of the way in all directions; for there was no room, and a bambu "batali" jungle is not the place to escape through. Down went the men as if shot; about twenty were in the scrimmage, and more or less "down"—very "down in their luck," it must be confessed, did a good many consider themselves to be. The "Laird of Logie," who had done yeoman service all along, went down as if felled, and this was by far the narrowest escape, I learn from the others, for the calf fairly vaulted over his prostrate form!

Intercepted by the native beaters farther out, it is said that the infuriated female and her calf once again returned in a rush through the adjoining ravine up to the entrance; but it is very doubtful if she went in.

A few minutes before the gate was closed—on, certainly, a dozen elephants—a part of the barrier near the princes' crow's-nest was the object of a fierce charge by a huge brute—perhaps the "tusker" which Mr. R. H. Morgan, from one of the stands, rightly declared he saw inside. For a hundred yards the barrier shook as if it were going to fall, and the charger got his forefeet through; but two or three Europeans, led by Mr. H. Whitham, rushed to the spot and drove him back.

### Friday Morning, February 3rd, 1882.

COMPENSATION FOR ALL THE DELAY—EXCITING DAY IN THE KRAAL—NOOSING AND TYING—SIX OUT OF TWELVE ELEPHANTS NOOSED—GREAT SPORT.

Yesterday morning, while waiting for the early drive we then expected, we spent some time with the four tame elephants belonging to Mr. Charles de Soysa, and by him, with commendable public spirit, ordered to the kraal in case their services should be required. One huge tusker, "Siriwala," is supposed to be over eighty years of age, and therefore too old to be of much service in "noosing" and "tying up" wild elephants. But he will be useful in beating up and blocking the way of retreat, since his stately presence is of itself sufficient to inspire a wholesome terror in the minds of his comparatively puny compeers, and as elephants have been described as "half-reasoning animals," they will no doubt keep at a safe distance from Siriwala's tusks. Much less attractive, though far more useful to his owner, is the small and tuskless "Rajah," for which Mr. de Soysa paid double the price of old Siriwala. Rajah cost £100. He goes through a number of performances to perfection. The 'cuteness with which he looks after the equivalent of "threepenny bits" in the mud—blowing away the latter, and at last, when baffled in his attempt to pick up the tiny coin by the edge with his sensitive trunk, drawing it in by suction, was very striking. Once caught, he held it safely until, with upturned trunk, he delivered it to the keeper on his back. Mr. de Soysa turns his elephants to account in carting, ploughing, road-making, and felling jungle in his Ratnapura and other extensive properties; and surely this last-mentioned is an occupation for which they are specially well adapted in the low-country, considering the way in which they knock down with their heads trees which would take some time for a Kandyan to cut through. Why should not a "felling" elephant, more especially for low-country planters, be hired out like a portable steam threshing-mill at home?

Many people, in speaking of last night's work, condemn the native beaters because they refused to do what the Europeans effected; but this is a very inaccurate and foolish mode of criticism. The natives knew the actual danger of the situation from long experience—the Europeans did not. The beaters, knowing that a charge or succession of charges would be the result so soon as the "durais," or "mahatmayás,"* went in with fire and spear, cleared out of the way as fast as possible: the more men in the way in such a case, the more havoc. Finally, we would ask how many of the volunteer beaters and of "the forlorn hope" would repeat their work under the same circumstances were the opportunity offered to them? We think the men who came out saying they had been taught a lesson which would last a lifetime, were those who took the right view, and instead of depreciating the work of the beaters, who had been driving for weeks together when the elephants were *fresh*—not half-starved and worn-out—the opinion of the volunteers respecting their endurance and pluck ought to be sustained.† No wonder that Mr. Dawson should say that he wished the visitors who ridiculed the slow work made on Tuesday and Wednesday

* *Durai* Tamil, *Mahatmayá* Sinh., for *master* or *gentleman*.

† There can be little doubt that, if the natives had been left to their own *time* and ways, the whole twenty-three elephants of the two herds would have been kraaled.

had come down to see the character of the jungle through which the work had to be done, or that the princes had been allowed to inspect it. The small cane-like bambu grows so closely together as to be impenetrable; the only paths are those made by the elephants, or which are cut out by the beaters. The bambu, when levelled by the elephants, is as slippery as ice, and the rain had rendered it, if possible, more so.

Let me now describe the spot. The last part of "the drive" between the stockades is about 150 yards across; it was covered with the densest bambu jungle; it consisted of two hollows or ravines with a ridge between, and all inclining towards the entrance to the kraal. From the entrance to where the European volunteers took up their position could not be more than 250 yards, the elephants being between. It will be readily seen, therefore, that the ground was as difficult a place to work in as ever an old campaigner or sportsman encountered.

Returning to the grand stand, now well filled, it was evident that the four safe, working, tame elephants, and the two or three of the reserve force, had commenced active operations. They were mounted by from two to three noosers each, while several assistants with spears and ropes followed behind at the sides of the elephants, under which they occasionally ran when there appeared to be any danger of a charge. The wild elephants were in a state of great perturbation, rushing from one side of the kraal to the other, occasionally resting under the few patches of jungle that still remained, going down into the hollows to throw water and mud over their backs—spurting each other with water seemed to be a favourite occupation. It was a most amusing as well as touching sight to see the little calves do this to the tame elephants when near them once or twice, as if to appease them and make friends. Clear views of all the herds were now had, and the elephants could be counted. The "tusker" is a huge fellow in bulk more than in height: he has lost half his tail, as if it had been shot off, and his tusks are most unusually far apart in the way they stick out, and they also seem to have had the points broken off. He never seems to lead the herd, but rather to follow after. Nevertheless, Mr. Unwin is sure it is the same animal that came to the kraal at midnight, and was shut in and afterwards let loose. This was in a manner proved by the frequency with which he made for the western gate to-day in his wanderings, in the hope, no doubt, of getting out once more. Once only did he try to charge the palisade, but, before he could get as far, the pointed sticks and spears of the watchers and the shouts of thousands of spectators drove him back. After the "tusker" came one large "cow" and five more medium-sized elephants; then three well-grown calves and two puny, diminutive little things whose dusty, tired appearance excited much pity, more especially from the ladies and a few children present.

The tame elephants and noosers were now at work, trying to break the herd into detachments, to segregate one or more, so as to get a chance of surrounding and noosing. Very troublesome and difficult is this operation: occasionally it is done by good luck in the minimum of time, while again hours may be spent over it. As it was, after what seemed a long time to the onlookers (relieved, however, by some exciting and still more amusing passages), two, or indeed three, got noosed almost instantaneously. Save with the little ones, there was no attempt by the herd at fraternizing with, or even recognizing the tame ones. The sight of men on their backs seemed to put an end to all thought of such a thing, and they steadily avoided a meeting as long as they could, dodging up and down, in and out and round about, until, once too often, they came across through a hollow, and the Philistines—in the shape of Ranhámi and Ellawala's man of "the breeches"—were among them. A slight attempt at a charge or fight was quickly repressed with a few blows from the spears, and a thump with the head of the tame elephant; the "tusker" sheering off, showing no inclination to interfere. But not so with the little calf, who, when two of the larger elephants were jammed up, and a noosed rope, cleverly placed on a leg of each, was tied about them, cried out, and would not be comforted or induced to leave. "Breeches" and Ranhámi were now in for serious work; their prizes struggled with elephantine strength; one especially—the mother of a calf—could not be moved from the spot, and in rage and despair at last fell prostrate, never to rise again! The struggle was a short but severe one, and the natives at once recognized it as a case of "broken heart." The poor brute lay panting for an hour or so afterwards, then heaved a deep sigh, and at last all was still, save that the little calf would not leave her side for a long time, and that once or twice the rest of the herd in passing the spot, attempted to heave up their companion. Far more touching, however, was the sight witnessed the night before by Mr. D. Mackay, when two elephants made a persistent endeavour to raise their fallen companion, the dead cow, while its little calf tried once more to obtain sustenance from its parent.*

To return, however, to the second large elephant noosed: he was a plump, vigorous, medium-sized fellow, and resisted most determinedly the moving, pushing, and dragging of him halfway across the kraal, and the final tying to the tree. This, in fact, was only accomplished when Ranhámi and "Breeches" jammed him between their elephants, who, evidently fully understanding what was wanted, pressed so hard and so guarded the ways of exit with their trunks, that their captive had perforce to remain perfectly still. All this was a most interesting, instructive sight, and then, when the tying was done—the hind legs only being securely clasped in several folds of strong rope, which again were drawn several times round a tree immediately alongside the grand stand—how the poor prisoner writhed and twisted, using all his prodigious strength to break away the rope, or pull the tree down, running round and round in despair of an outlet, pawing the earth, stretching himself with eel-like contortions, and then, in hopelessness of any release, and under the agony of his disgrace, like a true oriental, throwing up clouds of dust over his head and back with his trunk! Very soon, another of similar size and appearance was noosed and dragged up a long way to a tree facing Byrde's stand, and one of the active bull-calves being simultaneously caught, very quickly the fun became "fast and furious." This little calf gave more trouble than the two big ones; the noosers left him as soon as one leg was confined to a tree, and to less experienced hands was left the task of tying a rope round his neck and shoulders so as to keep him quiet and secure.

* Messrs. W. L. H. Skeen and Co.'s photograph of one of these pathetic incidents is reproduced in the illustration facing page 179.

But how the fellow resisted, struggled, twisted, and threw the rope off! The noose had to be passed over his head as well as trunk, but the latter was sent out at all impossible angles, so that no rope could be placed round it. At last, Messrs. C. Agar and Munro descended to the rescue, but they were baffled again and again; as soon as the rope was round it slipped off; they were charged and had to fly back; the little fellow bellowed like a bull; he blew at them, he would not be tied, and not until some one seized the trunk and held it, was the rope got round and a secure shoulder-knot made. This done, the calf set up a regular series of bellowings, making more ado than all the others put together. Great was the amusement afforded by this capture, and again and again was the wish expressed throughout the stand that the princes had stayed for this day's experiences, which well repaid all the trouble and delay.

But still greater fun was to follow; another calf, plump and strong, had been noosed, as well as a third big elephant, and as these were being pulled towards two suitable trees one of the noosers, getting an ugly shove from the calf, received a wound on his forehead which drew blood. Almost simultaneously Mr. Saunders sent orders to release these two captives at once, and noose the "tusker," as many had to leave and the day was now wearing on. No sooner was the calf released than he charged right and left, with trunk uplifted, bellowing as he went, and carrying all before him among rows of native beaters and a number of planters and others who had now descended into the kraal near the stands. The scene was comical in the extreme; there was just the least spice of danger to add zest to it, but the little fellow turned at the show of a pointed stick. It seemed as if he said, "You have given me a great fright; now I'll do my best to give you a taste of the same." White clothes especially seemed to provoke his anger; one or two gentlemen in white coats were followed again and again; one of them, Mr. E. Smyth, between laughing and dodging and keeping off his mad but 'cute little antagonist, had quite enough to do, and the spectators roared at the fun. Tired out at last, the little fellow with a loud grunt made for the tame elephants, and ranged himself alongside, as if with his friends. He did not seem to care about the wild herd now; he was a civilized elephant, and followed the tamers wherever they went. At last he found out Soysa's "tusker" standing on one side, and charging under him created a tremendous uproar, for the tusker didn't like it a bit, and trumpeted out what seemed to be: "You mind your own business, you young rascal, or I'll settle you." Nothing, however, could quiet this "irrepressible" altogether; at odd moments he would make a charge on his own account right across the kraal, and there can be no doubt that he greatly disturbed the rest of the noosing, so that it was a pity he was let loose, save for the amusement he gave to the company. The wild "tusker" would not be caught; he showed no fight, would shirk a broadside, slunk aside and dodged; and yet it became evident the tame elephants and the noosers did not care to get too near him. The fact is he is too old to be trained, and is of no service at all, save for his ivories, which can be got by shooting. ["Cured of sores" is the expression used to indicate a tamed elephant.] Enough had, however, been seen to warrant all who waited over Thursday, in pronouncing the kraal a success in showing the various operations connected with one; a notable success in affording a more than usual amount of sport and comical fun, as also in raising, at moments, feelings of sympathy and pity; an extraordinary success in the unprecedented work done by European volunteers—"the forlorn hope," the sudden charge, the marvellous escape, and the crowning victory in the forcing in of a dozen elephants into the kraal on Wednesday night.

How many more of the six or seven wild elephants I left running about the kraal were noosed to-day (Saturday), and whether the "tusker" was tied, I have yet to learn; but my part as narrator is over, and I can only say I am not likely ever to forget

THE LABUGAMKANDA KRAAL IN HONOUR OF PRINCES ALBERT VICTOR AND GEORGE IN 1882.

# APPENDIX II.

THE following interesting extracts from the first volume of Major Forbes's "Eleven Years in Ceylon" * are given with the permission of the publisher. The orthography of native names found in the original has been retained.

[No. 1.—CHAPTER X.]

## THE ANCIENT CAPITAL, ANURADHAPOORA.†

> "Remnants of things that have pass'd away,
> Fragments of stone rear'd by creatures of clay."—BYRON.

IN ages of impenetrable antiquity, the plain on which Anurádhapoora was afterwards built had acquired a sacred character; for it is recorded that when the first Buddha of the present era visited this place he found it already hallowed as a scene of the ancient religious rites of preceding generations, and consecrated by Buddhas of a former era. The position of Anurádhapoora has nothing to recommend it for the capital of Ceylon; and the site, if not chosen from caprice, was probably dictated by superstition. It would not, therefore, be difficult to account for its final desertion, consequent decay, and present desolation, even if history had not preserved a record of the feuds, famines, wars, and pestilence which at various times oppressed the country, and reduced the number of inhabitants, so as to render the remainder

* "Eleven Years in Ceylon; comprising Sketches of the Field Sports and Natural History of that Colony, and an Account of its History and Antiquities." By Major Forbes, 78th Highlanders. 2 vols. London: Richard Bentley.

† For the latest account of Anurádhapoora and the ancient ruins, see "The Buried Cities of Ceylon," by S. M. Burrows, C.C.S., published by A. M. and J. Ferguson.

A SCENE AMONG THE RUINS OF POLANNARUA, ONE OF THE ANCIENT CAPITALS OF CEYLON, *See page 206.*

incapable of maintaining the great embankments of their artificial lakes. These having burst, their waters spread over the country as their channels were neglected, and this made its unhealthiness permanent by forming noxious swamps and nourishing unwholesome forests. The warm and damp nature of the Ceylon climate excites an activity of vegetation, which the indolence and apathy of the native character are not calculated to struggle against; and the present population is inadequate either in number or energy to do more than resist the incessant effort of the vegetable kingdom, stimulated by an eternal spring, to extend its beautiful but baneful luxuriance over that portion of the surrounding districts which man still retains in precarious subjection.* Anurádhapoora is first mentioned by that name about 500 years before Christ; it was then a village, and the residence of a prince who took the name of Anurádha on his settling at this place, which the King Pánduwása had assigned to him when he came to visit his sister the Queen Bhadda-kacháne. They were grandchildren of Amitódama, the paternal uncle of Gautama Buddha. It was chosen for the capital by the King Pádukábhya, B.C. 437; and in the reign of Dewenipiatissa, which commenced B.C. 307, it received the collar-bone of Gautama Buddha, his begging-dish filled with relics, and a branch of the bo-tree under which he had reclined. Anurádhapoora had been sanctified by the presence of former Buddhas, and these memorials of Gautama increased its sacred character; additional relics were subsequently brought, for which temples were reared by successive sovereigns; and Wahapp, who commenced his reign A.D. 62, finished the walls of the city, which were sixty-four miles in extent, each side being sixteen miles, and thus enclosed a space of 256 square miles. Anurádhapoora is mentioned, or rather is laid down in

* Six years after the time of which I am now writing, Government formed a road to Aripo, and established a European officer at Anurádhapoora as revenue and judicial agent for the district, in order, if possible, to hasten the development of its resources. When I left the island it was considered an unhealthy station, but, by perseverance, there is little doubt that it will improve. Had this district been formerly unhealthy, Anurádhapoora would not so long have remained the capital of the island. [Anurádhapoora district and town have, we need scarcely say, been greatly improved of recent years.—J. F.]

the map of Ptolemy in its proper position, and by the name of Anurogrammum.*

For upwards of 1200 years Anurádhapoora remained as the capital of the island, with the exception of one reign, when a parricide and usurper transferred the insignia of royalty to the impregnable rock-fort of Sigiri. In the eighth century Polannarua was chosen as the capital in preference to Anurádhapoora; at which place the fame of wealth had survived its possession, and too often attracted the spoiler. The religious edifices were occasionally repaired by pious sovereigns until the time of Mágha, a successful invader, who held sway in Ceylon from A.D. 1219 until 1240, during which time he completed the destruction of many temples, and endeavoured to destroy the Cingalese records.

Knox, speaking of Anurádhapoora, which he passed in making his escape from captivity in A.D. 1679, says, "It is become a place of solemn worship, in consequence of the bo-tree under which Buddha sat." He adds, "They report ninety kings † have reigned there successively, where, by the ruins that still remain, it appears they spared not for pains and labour to build temples and high monuments to the honour of this god, as if they had been born only to hew rocks and great stones, and lay them up in heaps: these kings are now happy spirits, having merited it by these their labours." In making his escape along the bed of the Malwatte-oya,‡ Knox passed another part of the ruins, but does not seem to have been aware that they were part of Anurádhapoora. He says, "Here and there, by the side of this river, is a world of hewn stone pillars and other heaps of hewn stones, which I suppose formerly were buildings; and in three or four places are the ruins of bridges built of stone, some remains of them yet standing upon stone pillars."

The above extracts are taken from "An Historical Relation of the Island of Ceylon in the East Indies, by Robert Knox, a captive there for nearly twenty years."

* Gráma, or Gramya, is used for a town; so also is Poora, but the latter generally means city.

† It is the general belief of uneducated natives that the name of the city is derived from Anu-Rajah (ninety kings); but it was from the name of the constellation Anurádha, under which it was founded.

‡ Malwatte-oya, flower-garden river.

This is a work of great interest, and was originally published in London in 1681. Nothing can be more admirable than the extent of memory, acute observation, and inflexible veracity exhibited in his account of the country and people; nor can anything be more interesting than the simple narrative of his own sufferings. His perseverance, fortitude, and firm religious belief enabled him to overcome misfortunes, to rescue himself from a tedious captivity, and finally to regain his station as commander of a ship under the East India Company.

The father of Robert Knox was also named Robert: he commanded the *Ann* frigate in the service of the East India Company, and sailed on the 21st of January, 1657, from the Downs; the vessel was dismasted in a storm on the Coromandel coast on the 19th of November, 1659, and proceeded to the bay of Cotiar (opposite to Trinkomalee) to refit, and with permission to trade there. For about twenty days the crew of the ship were allowed to land and return without any interruption; but after that, a native chief, by order of the Kandian king, contrived by falsehood and treachery to seize the captain and seven of his men; then, by the same devices, he got hold of another boat and her crew of eleven men. He next attempted to gain possession of the ship, by inducing the captain to send an order to the officer on board, directing him to bring the vessel up the river; the captain sent his own son, but it was to warn the officer, and direct him to proceed without loss of time to Porto Novo. Young Knox, however, returned to share his father's captivity; and the whole of those taken prisoners were removed into the interior of the country. The captain and his son (Robert) were sent to the village of Bandar Koswatte, and there were soon attacked by severe fever and ague, which carried off the father, February the 9th, 1661. Young Knox was then very ill, and it was not without much difficulty that he managed to get his father's body buried; and for many months he suffered severely from the effects of the same disease. It was not long after the loss of his father that he accidentally had an opportunity of purchasing an English Bible at a price sufficiently moderate for his means. Never for a moment laying aside his design of escape, yet behaving with such discretion as never to incur suspicion from the jealous tyrant who then ruled in Kandy, Knox acquired a character for prudence, industry, and honesty, which is even yet preserved by tradition in the neighbourhood of the place where he resided, and where a spot is still known as the white man's garden.* After a captivity of nearly twenty years' duration he contrived to accomplish his escape, not without great danger from the numerous wild animals and crocodiles that are to be found near the course of the Malwatte-oya, which flows through a dense forest and a country void of population. Knox reached the Dutch fort of Aripo on the 18th of October, 1679; afterwards, having been sent to Batavia, he from thence returned to England in September, 1680, and was soon after made captain of the *Tarquin* in the East India Company's service.

All the ruins at Anurádhapoora, even the lofty monuments which contain the relics of the Buddha, are either entirely covered with jungle, or partly obscured by forests;† these the imagination of natives has peopled with unholy phantoms, spirits of the unrighteous, doomed to wander near the mouldering walls which were witnesses of their guilt, and are partakers of their desolation.

Although simplicity is the most distinguishing characteristic of the ancient architectural remains of the Cingalese, yet some of the carving in granite might compete with the best modern workmanship of Europe (in the same material) both as to depth and sharpness of cutting; and the sculptures at Anurádhapoora, and places built in remote ages, are distinguished from any attempts of modern natives, not less by the more animated action of the figures than by greater correctness of proportion.

The only place clear of jungle was in front of the Maha-wihare (great temple), where a shady tree occupied the centre of a square, and a stone pillar, fourteen feet high, stood beside the figure of a bull cut in granite, and revolving on a pivot. In the entrance from this square into the Maha-wihare are a few steps admirably carved with laborious devices, and still in perfect preservation. Ascending these, and passing through a mean building of modern construction, you enter an enclosure 345 feet in length by 216 in breadth, which surrounds the court of the Bo-tree, designated by Buddhists as Jaya-Sri-maha-

* Between Kandy and Gampola.

† Great clearings have taken place of late years.—J. F.

Bodinwahawai (the great, famous, and triumphant fig-tree).* Within the walls are perceived the remains of several small temples; and the centre is occupied by the sacred tree, and the building in which it is contained or supported. This tree is the principal object of veneration to the numerous pilgrims who annually visit Anurádhapoora: they believe what their teachers assert, and their histories record, that it is a branch of the tree under which Gautama sat the day he became a Buddha, and that it was sent from Patalipoora by the King Dharmasoka, who gave it in charge to his daughter Sanghamitta; this priestess had been preceded by her brother, Mihindoo, who, B.C. 307, was successful in re-establishing in Ceylon the purity of the Buddhist religion.

No one of the several stems or branches of the tree is more than two feet in diameter; and several of the largest project through the sides of the terraced building in which it is growing. This structure consists of four platforms, decreasing in size as you ascend, and giving room for a broad walk round each of them.† From the self-renovating properties of the bo-tree, it is not at all impossible that this one might possess the great antiquity claimed for it by the sacred guardians:‡ if so, the forbearance of Malabar conquerors must be accounted for by their considering this tree sacred to other gods; the profits derived from pilgrims may also have induced them to give full weight to the alleged partiality of Brahma for this beautiful tree.

One side of the square in front of the Maha-wihare is

* Ficus religiosa, generally called by natives Bo-gaha, bo-tree, the name generally used by Europeans.

† The spot on which the tree stands is believed to have at former periods been the position where the emblematic trees of former Buddhas grew, viz. Kakusanda Buddha's, the mahari tree; Konagamma Buddha's, the atika tree (ficus glomerata); and Kaseyapa's, the nigrodi (baniayan).

‡ Buddhists assert that the sacred tree at Buddha Gya in Bahar "was planted by Dugdha-Kamini, King of Singhal-Dwipa, 414 years before the birth of our Saviour."—*Hamilton's E.I. Gazetteer.* Dootoogaimoonoo, King of Ceylon, and a most zealous Buddhist, reigned from B.C. 164 until B.C. 140; and if the tree at Gya was planted by him, as above mentioned, not only the original one there, but also one planted by Dharmasoka, King of India, in the fourth century before Christ, at the same city, must have been destroyed by the votaries of an adverse faith.

occupied by the ruins of the Lowa-Maha-Paya, called also (from the materials with which it was covered) the Brazen Palace. The remains of this building consist of 1600 stone pillars placed in forty parallel lines, forty pillars in each, and occupying a square space, each side of which is 234 feet in length. The pillars in the middle of this ruin are still eleven and a half feet above the ground, and measure two feet in breadth by one foot and a half in thickness; the middle pillars are slightly ornamented, but those in the outer lines are plain, and only half their thickness, having been split by means of wedges, the marks of which operation they still retain. The Lowa-Maha-Paya was erected by the King Dootoogaimoonoo B.C. 142: its height was 270 feet; it contained 1000 apartments for priests, and was covered with one sheet of metal. This edifice seems soon to have fallen into decay; and was rebuilt by Dootoogaimoonoo's successor, who reduced its height, making it seven instead of nine storeys, which it was at its original formation. It underwent many repairs, and was varied in height by several different kings, until A.D. 286, at which time it was thrown down by Mahasen during the period of his temporary apostacy: so completely did this monarch execute his work of destruction on this and several other religious buildings, that their sites were ploughed up and sown with grain. Having returned to his former faith, Mahasen commenced rebuilding the Maha-Paya, but died before it was finished; and it was completed by his son and successor, Kitsiri Maiwan, soon after his accession in A.D. 302. It was then that the original pillars were split to supply the places of those which had been broken. Amongst the sacred occupants of this building, the priests most eminent for their piety were exalted to the uppermost storey, whilst those who had fewest claims to sanctity were lodged nearest to the earth. As native stairs only differ in name from ladders, the ascent of nine stories must have been a severe trial to the bodily infirmities of the elder priests; but one of the strongest prejudices of the natives, and about which they continue to be exceedingly jealous, was not allowing an equal or inferior to sit on any seat or remain in any place more elevated than themselves. From adherence to punctilio on this subject, there was a ludicrous scene at Colombo in 1802, when the

Kandian ambassadors remonstrated against entering the carriage sent to convey them to an audience with Governor North, because the coachman was placed on a more elevated seat than the one which they were to occupy. This weighty matter was happily adjusted to their satisfaction, and they entered the carriage; but positively refused to allow the doors to be shut, fearing they should appear as prisoners.

On the left of the road leading from the Maha-wiharé towards the dágoba of Ruwanwelli, and in thick jungle, six carved stones define the limits of a small mound. This is the spot where a grateful people and a zealous priesthood performed the last duties to the remains of Dootoogaimoonoo; a king whose valour and piety had restored the supremacy of the Cingalese race and Buddhist religion, and who had not only repaired the injuries which the capital had sustained from foreign invaders of an adverse faith, but had ornamented it with many of these buildings which even now attract attention and excite wonder after having endured for 2000 years.

The quantity of game in the immediate neighbourhood of the ruins was astonishing, and in no part of the island are elephants more numerous; for within the precincts of this hallowed city, at the time I speak of, 1828, no native would have ventured to transgress the first commandment of the Buddha, viz., "From the meanest insect up to man, thou shalt not kill." As if aware of their right of sanctuary, whole herds of spotted deer and flocks of pea-fowl allowed us to approach very near to them; and while employed in examining the ruins, in the presence and with the assistance of the priests, I deemed it advisable to commit no murder on the denizens of the forest; but on the last day of our stay we left the gentlemen of the long yellow robe behind, and proceeded to hunt deer with Mr. C——'s dogs in a plain about three miles from the place of our temporary residence.

When not employed in speaking, our followers seemed to be eternally occupied in chewing betel, a custom almost universal at this time with all ranks of natives; and although the name of the leaf of a creeping-plant resembling pepper is used as a general term, three component parts are necessary for this masticatory; viz. areka-nut, which is used in very thin slices; fine powdered lime, made into a paste; and a small portion of these two being rolled up in a betel-leaf, the whole is put in the mouth. This preparation tinges the saliva, the lips, and even the teeth of a dark-red colour; but I believe it to be perfectly wholesome, and to have some useful properties, such as soothing nervous excitement, and acting as a stimulant, without any of the evil effects produced by the use of spirits, which nevertheless is, I am afraid, too often superseding the use of betel. Those who could afford it mixed up cardamom-seeds and the leaves of various aromatic plants with the areka-nut, and the value of the instruments for preparing the betel gave one a pretty good idea of the wealth and rank of the possessor: a pair of nippers for slicing the areka-nut, a small box for holding the lime, and a straw case to contain betel-leaves, might, I believe, have been found tucked in the waist-cloth of every one of the several hundred natives who accompanied us. Night and day they were chewing betel, and when they were awake they seemed to talk of nothing else; exchanging leaves and the contents of their lime boxes seemed like the old Scotch custom of exchanging snuff-mulls.

Amongst the ruins of this city, the dágobas,* or monumental tombs of the relics of Buddha, the mode in which they are constructed, the object for which they are intended—above all, their magnitude—demand particular notice. The characteristic form of all monumental Buddhistical buildings is that of a bell-shaped tomb surmounted by a spire, and is the same in all countries which have had Buddha for their prophet, lawgiver, or god. Whether in the outline of the cumbrous mount, or in miniature within the laboured excavation, this peculiar shape (although variously modified) is general, and enables us to recognize the neglected and unhonoured shrines of Buddha in countries where his religion no longer exists, and his very name is unknown. The gaudy Shoemadoo of Pegu, the elegant Toopharama of Anurádhapoora, the more modern masonry of Boro Budor in Java, are but varieties of the same general form; and in the desolate caves of Carli, as in the gaudy excavations and busy scenes of Dambool, there is still extant the sign

* Dágoba, from Dhatu-garbe (womb, or receptacle of a relic): see engraving on page 129.

of Buddha—the tomb of his relics. Dágobas may be referred to the first stage of architectural adventure, although I cannot agree with those writers who assert that the character and form of Buddhist buildings betray evident marks of having been borrowed from the figure of a tent; for in my opinion their progress may clearly be traced from the humble heap of earth which covers the ashes or urn of the dead up to the stupendous mount of masonry which we see piled above some shrunken atom of mortality. These monuments in Ceylon are built around a small cell, or hollow stone, containing the relic; along with which a few ornaments and emblems of Buddhist worship were usually deposited, such as pearls, precious stones, and figures of Buddha: the number and value of these depended on the importance attached to the relic, or the wealth of the person who reared the monument.

The description given in Cingalese histories of the rich offerings and rare gems deposited with some of the relics is very splendid, but the existence of wealth and wonders which cannot be reached may well be doubted; the accounts of the external decorations and ornaments of these dágobas are also magnificent, and probably more correct. In a sohona, or Cingalese cemetery, may be perceived a variety of miniature dágobas: if the little earthen mound raised over the ashes of the dead be encircled with a row of stones, we see the origin of the projecting basement; if the tomb be that of a headman or high priest, we may find it cased with stone, and perhaps surrounded with a row of pillars: on all these we find an aewaria branch planted; which, after taking root and shooting out its cluster of leaves, gives the semblance of the spire and its spreading termination.* In short, the monumental tombs of Buddha's relics only differ in size, and in the durability of their materials, from the humble heap which covers the ashes of an obscure priest or village chief. The tomb of Alyattes, as described by Herodotus, and which he informs us as a monument of art was only second to the remains in Egypt and Babylon, appears to have been of the same form as the sepulchral mounds of the Buddhists. In material and construction

* Called Kot by the Cingalese, and Tee by the Siamese.

the dágobas of Anurádhapoora far exceed the tomb of Alyattes, and fully equal it in size. All the dágobas at Anurádhapoora were built of brick, and incrusted with a preparation of lime, coco-nut water, and the glutinous juice of a fruit which grows on a tree called by the natives Paragaha. This preparation is of a pure white; it receives a polish nearly equal to marble, and is extremely durable. The Ruwanwelli-saye, one of these monuments of peculiar sanctity, was built by the King Dootoogaimoonoo; but the spire being unfinished at the time of his death, B.C. 140, it was completed by his brother and successor, Saidatissa. It stands in the centre of an elevated square platform, which is paved with large stones of dressed granite, each side being about 500 feet in length, and surrounded by a fosse seventy feet in breadth; the scarp, or sides of the platform, is sculptured to represent the fore-parts and heads of elephants, projecting and appearing to support the massive superstructure to which they form so appropriate an ornament. In the embankment surrounding the fosse, a pillar, deep sunk in the earth, still projects sixteen feet above the surface, and is four feet in diameter; this stone is believed to have been removed from the spot where the dágoba now stands, and that it once bore an inscription and prophecy, which in a superstitious age no doubt caused its own fulfilment. The prediction ran, that at the place where this stone stood, a superb dágoba of 120 cubits* in height would be reared by a fortunate and pious monarch.

Dootoogaimoonoo, during his last illness, caused himself to be conveyed near to this monument of his piety; and when all hopes of completing the spire during his lifetime were at an end, his brother had the model of it made of light timber: this placed on the dome, and covered with cloth, satisfied the anxious wish of the expiring king. The place to which Dootoogaimoonoo was conveyed is a large granite slab surrounded with pillars; near this a stone, hollowed out in the shape of a man's body, is shown as the bath which he used when suffering from the bite of a venomous snake.

On the stone pavement which surrounds the Ruwan-

* Carpenter's cubit, two feet three inches.

welli-saye lies the broken statue of the King Bátiyatissa, who reigned from B.C. 19 until A.D. 9, and appears to have been one of those persevering zealots who "hope to merit heaven by making earth a hell:" the marks of his knees worn in the granite pavement are pointed out as memorials of superior piety, and certainly, if authentic, bear lasting testimony to the importunity of his prayers or the sincerity of his devotions. It is recorded of this king that by supplication he obtained Divine assistance to enable him to open the underground entrance into the interior cell of this temple; and that he succeeded in entering and worshipping the many relics of Buddha which it contained. In the thirteenth century, Mága, a foreign invader, instead of faith, employed force: he broke into the sanctum, plundered its treasures, pulled down the temples around Ruwanwelli, and ruined its dágoba, which was originally 270 feet in height, but is now a conical mass of bricks overgrown with brushwood, and 189 feet high. Sanghatissa placed a pinnacle of glass on the spire of Ruwanwelli, as the author of the Mahawanso says, "to serve as a protection against lightning." Sanghatissa reigned four years, and was poisoned in A.D. 246. The Mahawanso was written between A.D. 459 and 477, and shows that the non-conducting property of glass with regard to the electric fluid had been remarked previous to that period.

At a considerable distance from the outer enclosure of the dágoba the priest pointed out to me a stone slab twelve and a half feet long by nine and a half feet broad, which is supposed to cover the secret entrance by which the pious king, as well as the ruthless invader, gained admittance to the interior of the Ruwanwelli-saye. A few weeks previously to our visit, the late high-priest, an albino, had died at a very advanced age: he had been long known by the appellation of the White Priest of Anurádhapoora; and his senior pupil, who accompanied me in exploring the ruins, aspired to succeed his master. I was then along with the agent of the district, through whose recommendation he expected to be appointed; therefore no spot was so sacred, and no secret so precious, but that it might be communicated to me. The aspirant became high-priest, and ever after denied to European visitors all knowledge of the secret entrance to this monument, as well as several other places of peculiar sanctity; neither could it be brought to his unwilling remembrance that he had ever known them himself, or pointed them out to any one. The history of this building, its traditions, the list of offerings made to the relics enshrined within it, and the splendour of its external appearance, are recorded at length; but its chronicle contains so much exaggeration in regard to the number of the offerings, and so little variety of events, that the specimen already given may perhaps be considered more than sufficient, and will be my excuse for not dilating on the history of other buildings, of which only similar facts are written, and similar dull details have been preserved.

Toophárámaya, although inferior to many in size, yet far exceeds any dágoba in Ceylon, both in elegance and unity of design, and in the beauty of the minute sculptures on its tall, slender, and graceful columns; this dágoba is low, broad at the top, and surrounded by four lines of pillars, twenty-seven in each line, fixed in the elevated granite platform so as to form radii of a circle of which the monument is the centre. These pillars are twenty-four feet in height, with square bases, octagonal shafts, and circular capitals; the base and shafts, fourteen inches in thickness, and twenty-two feet in length, are each of one stone; the capitals are much broader than the base, and are highly ornamented. Toophárámaya was built over the collar-bone of Gautama, when it was brought from Maghada in the reign of Dewenepeatissa, B.C. 307; and the ruins of a building which adjoins it received the Dalada relic when it arrived in Ceylon, A.D. 309.

Lankarámaya was erected in the reign of Mahasen, between A.D. 276 and A.D. 302; it is in better preservation, but much inferior in effect to the Toophárámaya, from which the design of the building is copied.

The Abháyagiri dágoba, built by the King Walagam Bahoo, between the period of his restoration to the throne B.C. 88, and his death B.C, 76, was the largest ever erected in Ceylon: it was 405 feet* in height; and the platform on which it stands, as well as the fosse and surrounding wall, are proportionately extensive. The height of this

* 180 Cingalese carpenter's cubits.

ruin is now 230 feet, and the length of the outer wall one mile and three quarters; the whole of the building, except a few patches near the summit, is covered with thick jungle and high trees, even where the interstices of the pavement, composed of large granite slabs, were all that yielded nourishment to the trees or secured their roots.

The Jaitawanarámaya was commenced by the King Mahasen, and completed by his successor, Kitsiri Maiwan, A.D. 310: its height was originally 315 feet,* and its ruins are still 269 feet above the surrounding plain. A gentleman, who visited Anurádhapoora in 1832, calculated the cubic contents of this temple at 456,071 cubic yards; and remarked that a brick wall, twelve feet in height, two feet in breadth, and upwards of ninety-seven miles in length, might be constructed with the still remaining materials. Even to the highest pinnacle the Jaitawanarámaya is encompassed and overspread by trees and brushwood; these are the most active agents of ruin to the ancient buildings of Ceylon, as their increasing roots and towering stems, shaken by the wind, overturn and displace what has long resisted, and would have slowly yielded before time and the elements.

During our stay at Anurádhapoora, a Kandian lady presented a petition to the agent of Government, requesting his interference on behalf of her son, who was detained as a State prisoner for having been implicated in the rebellion of 1817–18. She stated that he was her only son, and that the large family estates were now ravaged and laid waste by wild animals; that in this remote district, for want of his superintendence, the tanks for irrigation were neglected, and cultivation was rapidly decreasing; moreover, that he was the hereditary guardian of the sacred edifices of this ancient capital, and that in his absence the buildings and temples were neither protected nor repaired, the revenues being either misapplied by the priests, or appropriated to their own use. The old lady also alluded to the antiquity of their family, whose ancestor, she said, had accompanied the branch of the sacred tree from Patalipoora,† B.C. 307. On inquiring, I found that the very remote antiquity of this family was acknow-

* 140 carpenter's cubits.

† The modern Patna.

ledged by the jealous chiefs of the mountain districts; and I could not help feeling an interest in the last scion of a race whose admitted ancestry reached far beyond the lineage of Courtenay, or the descent of Howard.

This chief soon afterwards obtained permission to visit his estates; and at a subsequent period, having assisted in securing the pretender to the Kandian throne (who had been secreted since 1818 in this part of the country), he was not only permitted to return to his estate, but was reinstated in office as chief of the district. Although not a clever man, his appearance and manners were dignified and gentlemanlike: he died in 1837, leaving a family to continue the race, and bear the dignified appellation of Surya Kumara Singha (descended from a prince of the solar and the lion race).

The system of adoption in the Kandian law, renders the continuation of a particular family much more probable than in any country where such a proceeding is unknown, or unsanctioned by fixed institutions or all-powerful custom. In Kandian law, a child adopted in infancy (and born to parents of equal rank with the person who adopted the infant) has the same right of inheritance both to titles and estates as if the actual child of the person who had become its guardian, and who, after a public adoption, was called and considered the father. In general, the children adopted were selected from the nearest relations of the person, who determined through this means to prevent all risk of being without children to watch his declining years, and inherit his family estates. Several of the highest rank of Kandian chiefs pretend to trace the descent of their families from those natives of Maghada who accompanied Mihindoo and the relics of Buddha from the continent in the fourth century before Christ. Two families claim descent from Upatissa, a minister of state, an *interim* king for one year, B.C. 505; and one of these, who maintained his right by inheritance to the name which he bore (Upatissa), produced to me a box containing a quantity of dust, and some minute frail shreds of tissue, which, he said, were the remains of a dress worn by his royal and somewhat remote ancestor. I have only seen a few written genealogies of Cingalese chiefs, and, in following them, found wider and more startling gaps than any I had been accustomed to leap over in a backward trace to the progenitor of some individuals who figure in the modern British peerage.

Amidst the ruins of the palace stand six square pillars supporting some remains of a cornice; each of these pillars is formed of a single stone, eighteen feet in length and three in breadth. There also is the stone canoe made by order of King Dootoogaimoonoo in the second century before Christ, to hold the liquid prepared for the refection of the priests; it measures sixty-three feet in length, three and a half feet in breadth, and two feet ten inches in depth. Within the precincts of the royal buildings, projecting from the mould, and half-covered by the roots of a tree, a stone trough, from which the State elephants drank, recalled to mind the history of King Elloona, and the busy, turbulent scenes enacted in bygone ages within those walls, where now the growl of the elephant, the startling rush of wild hog and deer, the harsh screams of peacock and toucan, increase the solemn but cheerless feelings inspired by a gloomy forest waving o'er a buried city.

Elloona having murdered his cousin, the Queen Singha Wallee, became King of Ceylon, A.D. 38, and was soon after imprisoned by his rebellious subjects: the queen, in despair, caused her infant son to be dressed in his most costly robes, and ordered the nurse to place him at the feet of the State elephant, that the child might be killed, and escape the indignities inflicted on the monarch. The nurse did as she was commanded; but the elêphant (without hurting the young prince) broke his chain, rushed through the guards, threw down the gates, and forced his way to the royal captive, who got on his back, and, rushing through the streets of the capital, escaped in safety to the sea-coast. From thence he embarked for the Malaya country: having raised an army there, he returned to Ceylon, and regained his kingdom after an absence of three years. Elloona recognized with affectionate joy the animal that had been the means of saving his life: and several villages were appointed to furnish food and attendants to the royal elephant during the remainder of his life.

The Isuramuni Wihare (a temple partly cut in the rock), the Saila Chytia (a small monument built on a spot where Buddha had rested himself), and the tomb of Elala, are amongst the ruins visited by the pious pilgrims. Elala was a successful invader who conquered Ceylon, B.C. 204, by means of an army which he led from Sellee (Tanjore). The Cingalese princes who possessed the southern and mountainous parts of the island as tributaries becoming powerful, Elala built thirty-two forts to protect the level country on the south against their incursions; these forts were taken in succession by the Prince Dootoogaimoonoo, who finally encountered his rival in single combat, and slew him with a javelin. They were each mounted on an elephant, and as the battle was preceded by a challenge, both the leaders fought under the insignia of royalty: on the spot where Elala fell, Dootoogaimoonoo erected a monument and pillar, on which there was inscribed a prohibition against any one passing this tomb in any conveyance, or with beating of drums. Elala is described, even by the Buddhist historians, as being a good ruler and valiant warrior; he must have been an old man when he encountered Dootoogaimoonoo, having reigned for forty-four years after completing the conquest of Ceylon: his death occurred B.C. 161. Time has hallowed the monument which it has failed to obscure, and the ruined tomb of an infidel is now looked upon by many Buddhist pilgrims as the remnant of a sacred edifice: although twenty centuries have elapsed since the death of Elala, I do not believe that the injunction of his conqueror has ever been disregarded by a native. In 1818, Pilamé Talawé, the head of the oldest Kandian family, when attempting to escape after the suppression of the rebellion in which he had been engaged, alighted from his litter, although weary and almost incapable of exertion; and not knowing the precise spot, walked on until assured that he had passed far beyond this ancient memorial.

Pilamé Talawé was apprehended in this district, and transported to the Isle of France; from whence he was allowed to return in 1830, and soon after died from the effects of intemperance. He had narrowly escaped death in 1812 for treason to the King of Kandy, as sentence had been passed, and his father and cousin had already suffered, before he was brought prisoner to the city. The commencement of a religious festival was the reason assigned at that time for sparing his life; although his slender abilities and slothful habits are supposed to have been more powerful arguments in favour of the king's granting mercy than the supplication of friends, or the intercession of the priests, to whom it was apparently conceded. Pilamé Talawé was the last of the direct branch of that family which exercised the privilege of girding on the royal sword at the inauguration of the Kandian monarchs.

Besides eight large tanks at Anurádhapoora, there are several of a smaller size built round with hewn stone; and in the side of one of these a priest pointed out apartments, cells which, he said, had been occupied by priests as places for contemplation when religion flourished and the tanks were full: one of these cells, which we examined, proved to be formed of five slabs, and its dimensions were twelve feet in length, eight feet in breadth, and five feet in height; the lowest stone, or floor of the cell, must have been nearly on a level with the water in the tank. We also saw many wells built round with stone; one very large one near the Ruwanwelli-saye is circular, and the size diminishes with each course of masonry, so as to form steps for descending to the bottom in any direction.

Near the footpath leading to the Jaitawanarámaya lies a vessel ornamented with pilasters cut in relievo; it is formed out of a single granite stone, and is ten feet long, six feet wide, and two feet deep. It was used to contain food for the priests.

The following is translated from an ancient native account of Anurádhapoora:—

"The magnificent city of Anurádhapoora is refulgent from the numerous temples and palaces whose golden pinnacles glitter in the sky. The sides of its streets are strewed with black sand, and the middle is sprinkled with white sand; they are spanned by arches * bearing flags of gold and silver; on either side are vessels of the same precious metals, containing flowers; and in niches are statues holding lamps of great value. In the streets are multitudes of people armed with bows and arrows; also men powerful as gods, who with their huge swords could cut in sunder a tusk elephant at one blow. Elephants, horses, carts, and myriads of people are constantly passing and repassing: there are jugglers, dancers, and musicians of various nations, whose chanque-shells and other musical

* Arches formed of areka-trees split and bent, or of some other pliable wood, were always used in decorating entrances and public buildings on days of ceremony or rejoicing; but I have never seen an arch of masonry in any Cingalese building of great antiquity.

instruments are ornamented with gold. The distance from the principal gate to the south gate is four gaws (sixteen miles); and from the north gate to the south gate four gaws: the principal streets are Chandrawakka-widiya, * Rajamaha-widiya, † Hinguruwak-widiya, and Mahawelli-widiya. ‡ In Chandrawakka-widiya are 11,000 houses, many of them being two storeys in height; the smaller streets are innumerable. The palace has immense ranges of building, some of two, others of three storeys in height; and its subterranean apartments are of great extent."

With the exception of the four principal streets, the others were built of perishable materials, and were named from the separate classes which inhabited them. The Chandalas (scavengers and corpse-bearers) resided beyond the limits of the city; yet it was a girl of this caste that Prince Sáli, only son of Dootoogaimoonoo, married, and chose rather to resign all chance of succession to the throne than to part from his beauteous bride. The detailed account of Prince Sáli's romantic attachment to Asoka Malla is probably less correct than a tradition preserved in Kotmalia, viz., that Sáli's mother was not of the royal race, but a woman of the Goyawanza (cultivator class), with whom Dootoogaimoonoo formed a connection at the time he was a fugitive in the mountainous district of Kotmalia, to which place he had fled to avoid the effects of his father's anger, and by which act he acquired the epithet of Dootoo, or the Disobedient, prefixed to his own name of Gaimoonoo. Dootoogaimoonoo forgave his son, and admired the bride; but appointed his brother, Saida-tissa, as successor to the throne, that the Mahawanzae (great solar dynasty) might be preserved in all its purity.

The great extent of Anurádhapoora, covering within its walls a space of 256 square miles, will not give any just grounds on which to estimate the extent of its population; as tanks, fields, and even forests are mentioned as being within its limits. The number and magnitude of the tanks and temples constructed by the Kings Dootoogaimoonoo, who reigned from B.C. 164 to B.C. 140, Walagam-bahoo, who reigned from B.C. 89 to B.C. 77, and Mahasen, who reigned from A.D. 275 to A.D. 302, are the best vouchers for the numerous population which at these periods existed

* Moon Street. † Great King Street.
‡ Great Sandy Street, or from the River Mahawelli-ganga.

in Ceylon; yet, as the tanks at least were formed by forced labour, we cannot rate the wealth of the nation by the extent of its monuments. The public works of Prakramabahoo the First, who reigned from A.D. 1153 to 1186, prove that even then Ceylon had a much more numerous population than it now possesses; and Cingalese accounts of that period state the number of males, exclusive of children, as amounting to 3,420,000. This number may be, and probably is, overrated; but let those who doubt that an immense population formerly existed in Ceylon compare the prodigious bulk of the ancient monuments of Anurádhapoora, Mágam, and Polannarrua, with those erected by later kings of the island; then let them compare singly the remains of the Kalaa tank,* the Kaudela tank,† or many others, with any or all the public works accomplished in Ceylon for the last 500 years. In constructing the immense embankments of these artificial lakes, labour has been profusely, often, from want of science, uselessly expended; as I believe many of these great tanks, which are now in ruins, would, if repaired, be found inapplicable to the purposes of irrigation for which they were designed: that is, the extent of plain which could be cultivated by means of these reservoirs would be of less value than the sums which it would be requisite to expend in repairing and maintaining the embankments.

In Anurádhapoora, the only sacred buildings of modern date are a few small temples erected on the foundations and from the materials of former structures; they are supported by wooden pillars, which, even in the same building, present a great variety of capitals, and perfect defiance of proportion. These mean temples, with their walls of clay and paltry supports, form a striking contrast to the granite columns, massive foundations, and stone pillars which still stand, or lie scattered in endless profusion amidst the ruined heaps and proud remains of former ages. They serve to prove that Buddhism only clings with loosening grasp where it once held sovereign sway over mind and matter.

In September, 1832, I again proceeded to Anurádhapoora,

* The Kalaa tank was completed before A.D. 477.

† The Kaudela tank is now an extensive plain between Minirie and Kandely.

through Dambool, Manawewa, Kágamma, near which are the ruins of the Nakha (finger-nail) dágoba, and Tirapan. In several places, when we approached within twenty miles of the city, we perceived great heaps of stones on the road-side: they were intended to commemorate events which are long since forgotten; but, nevertheless, every pilgrim adds a stone to these nameless cairns. About ten miles from Anurádhapoora, I sat down on the rocky bank of a very small pond in the Colon-oya forest: soon after, a native trader came up, and pointed to a spot near me, from whence, he said, his companion, only a few days before, had been dragged by a crocodile; the unfortunate man, while resting here during the heat of the day, had fallen asleep close to the water, and in this state was seized by the reptile. My informant, having procured assistance from a village some miles off, had attempted to recover the body of his companion; but was unsuccessful, as it was found that the pond communicated with an underground cavern. I emerged from this forest upon the plains around the Nuwarawewa (city lake), which at this time contained but a little water in detached pools; these were surrounded, almost covered, by a wondrous assemblage of creatures, from the elephant and buffalo, pelican, flamingo, and peacock, crocodile, and cobragoya, down through innumerable varieties of the animated creation: in the background, the crumbling spires of Anurádhapoora appeared over the wooded embankment of this artificial lake. I had supplied myself and my followers with abundance of pea-fowl, which were to be met with in numbers at every open space where water was to be found; and, on first entering one of these glades, I have seen twenty of them within a space of 100 yards in diameter. Pea-fowl are naturally wary; and if it is a place where they have been occasionally disturbed, it requires great caution to ensure getting near enough to shoot them. The morning is the best time for pea-fowl shooting, as in the evening they keep near the edge of the jungle, and in the forenoon they retire to some thick dark copse, generally overhanging water, and there rest during the heat of the day; it is at this time that the natives, who never throw away a shot, usually kill them at roost.

Since my former visit in 1828, all the dágobas had

suffered some diminution, in consequence of the heavy rains which had fallen in January, 1829; and the whole of the Abháyagiri had been cleared from jungle by a priest, whose zeal in the difficult and dangerous task had been nearly recompensed with martyrdom, a fragment of the spire having fallen on and severely injured this pious desecrater of the picturesque. The season had been particularly dry, and the foliage of those trees which grew on rocky ground presented all the variety of an English autumn; however, the change of the monsoon was approaching, and heavy rain fell during the night of my arrival. At daybreak next morning I ascended on the ruins of Mirisiwettiya, and found the forest-plains of this district shrouded by mist and rising clouds; but,—

> "Though the loitering vapour braved
> The gentle breeze, yet oft it waved
> Its mantle's dewy fold,"

and magnified forms of mount-like sepulchres were shadowed on the drear expanse. As the sun arose behind the rock of Mehintalai, the "silver-mist" was dissipated in small clouds, or fell in glittering drops: all was damp, vast, and silent, as if the waves of oblivion had only now rolled back from the tombs of antediluvian giants; and the half-formed rainbow, which glanced amid these monuments, was the first which had brightened the earth, or gladdened the remnants of a perished race.

---

[No. II.—CHAPTER XIII.]

## VISIT TO KANDY.*—MORAL LAWS OF GAUTAMA BUDDHA.

> The rifled urn, the violated mound.—BYRON.

> Abstain from all sin, acquire all virtue, repress thine own heart; this is Buddha's injunction.
>
> *Tenets of Buddhism*, by KITULGAMMA UNNANSE.

IN the month of May, 1828, I proceeded to Kandy, and witnessed that brilliant Buddhist festival, the exhibition

* For the latest account of Kandy *see* Burrows' "Guide," published by A. M. & J. Ferguson.

of the Dalada (tooth of Buddha); an expiring blaze of the ancient worship of Ceylon, whose beams even then gleamed flickering and unstable, and will suddenly sink in darkness, or surely and gradually fade before a brighter light. From one district, at least, I know the numbers who attended at this Dalada Puja were procured by compulsion more than attracted by devotion; and that it was the dread of present punishment, not the hope of spiritual benefit, by which they were collected. I anticipate that Buddhism, shorn of its splendour, unaided by authority, and torn by internal dissension, will not long have power to retain even its present slight control over the actions of its votaries by the mere excellence of its moral laws, and that it will fall into disuse before Christianity is prepared to step into its place, which for a time will be occupied by those vile superstitions and demon-worship to which the Cingalese are so prone.

Fifty-three years had elapsed since the King Kirti Sri had openly displayed the relic; and from the revolutions which had since taken place in the country, but few people remembered the ceremony, and still fewer had seen the Dalada, which they believed to be the most sacred thing on earth, and that only to see it proved their former merits by their present good fortune.

On the 29th of May, 1828, the three larger cases having previously been removed, the relic contained in the three inner caskets was placed on the back of an elephant richly caparisoned: over it was the Ransiwigé, a small octagonal cupola, the top of which was composed of alternate plain and gilt silver plates, supported by silver pillars. When the elephant appeared coming out of the temple-gate, two lines of magnificent elephants, forming a double line in front of the entrance, knelt down and thus remained; while the multitude of people, joining the points of their fingers, raised their arms above their heads, and then bent forward, at the same time uttering in full, deep tones the shout of "Sadhu:" this, joined and increased by those at a distance, swelled into a grand and solemn sound of adoration. The elephant bearing the relic, followed by the establishments of the temples with their elephants, also those of the chiefs, after proceeding through the principal streets of the town, returned to the great bungaloe: here the first Adikar removed the relic from the back of the elephant, and conveyed it to the temporary altar on which it was to be exhibited. The rich hangings were now closed around the altar, and the three inner cases opened in presence of Sir Edward Barnes, the Governor. The drapery being again thrown open, disclosed the tooth placed on a gold lotus-flower, which stood on a silver table: this was covered with the different cases of the relic, various gold articles and antique jewellery, the offerings of former devotees.

Whether prompted by their own feelings, or impelled by more weighty reasons to attend at this exhibition, still the relic was evidently an object of intense veneration to all the assembled Buddhists, and by those of the Kandian provinces it is considered the palladium of their country; they also believe the sovereign power of the island is attached to its possessors. It is a piece of discoloured ivory, slightly curved, nearly two inches in length, and one inch in diameter at the base; from thence to the other extremity, which is rounded and blunt, it considerably decreases in size. The Dalada, as we find in very ancient details of its adventures, was discoloured when it arrived in Ceylon: that a relic of Gautama should fade or decay was at the time urged as an argument against its authenticity; but a miracle settled the dispute, and silenced sceptics.

The sanctuary of this relic is a small chamber in the temple attached to the palace of the Kandian kings; and there the six cases in which it is enshrined are placed on a silver table hung round with rich brocades. The largest or outside cover of these carandus (caskets) is five feet in height, formed of silver gilt, and shaped in the form of a dágoba: * the same form is preserved in the five inner cases, which are of gold; two of them, moreover, being inlaid with rubies and other precious stones. The outer case is decorated with many gold ornaments and jewels, which have been offered to the relic, and serve to embellish its shrine. In front of the silver altar on which the tooth was exposed a plain table was placed; to this the people approached one at a time, and having seen the Dalada and deposited their gifts, they prostrated themselves, then passed on and made room for others. The

* The bell-shaped buildings raised over the relics of Buddha.

offerings consisted of things the most heterogeneous: gold chains and gold ornaments: gold, silver, and copper coins of all denominations; cloths, priest's vestments, flowers, sugar, areka-nuts, betel-leaves. The Dalada was exhibited and the offerings continued for three successive days. On the second day some wretched specimens of the science of defence were exhibited before the Governor, both with fists and also with wooden swords and targets: on the fourth night there was a display of native fire-works, well-made and skilfully managed. Night and day, without intermission, during the continuance of this festival, there was kept up a continual din of tom-toms, and sounding of Kandian pipes and chanque-shells. The Kandian pipe is a musical instrument in power and melody nearly resembling a penny whistle: but the chanque is a shell with a mouth-piece attached, and, under the influence of powerful lungs, is a most efficient instrument for producing a noise which was called music; its tones varying between the bellowings of a chained bull and the howling of a forsaken dog. I presume the natives consider these sounds peculiarly adapted for their sacred music, as such instruments are to be found in all temples, and may be heard at all hours, to the dire annoyance of any European who attempts to sleep in their neighbourhood.

The principal temporary building was 250 feet in length, of proportionate breadth, and supported by six lines of pillars. It was under this that the tooth was exhibited; and the whole was ornamented with palm-branches, plantain-trees, fruit, and flowers: so gracefully were these disposed, that the columns in the variety of their decorations, and some even in unity of effect, presented combinations which, if transferred to stone, would rival any specimen of elaborate Corinthian architecture. In the brilliant pageantry of this festival, the rich altar and resplendent ornaments of the relic, the great size and elegant decorations of the temporary buildings, the peculiar and picturesque dresses of the chiefs, the majestic elephants, and dense mass of people, threw an air of imposing grandeur over the spectacle, to which the old temples, sacred trees, and the wild and beautiful scenery around the Kandian capital formed an appropriate landscape. These combinations were rendered still more impressive by the disturbed state of the elements; for an extraordinary gloom and tempestuous weather continued during the whole time of the exhibition, and the torrents of rain which fell at that time caused the loss of many lives, and destroyed much property, in various parts of the island.

* * * * * *

The town of Kandy is judiciously planned, and the present regular arrangement of the streets was marked out by the Adikars under the direction of the king; the streets all run in straight lines, but do not cross at right angles. It is situated on an angular piece of ground, with the base resting on two lakes which were formed by the late king. The buildings remaining from the time of the native dynasty are several temples of Buddha and two colleges, at one of which every Kandian priest ought to be ordained: there are also temples to the gods Náta, Vishnu, Katragamma, and the goddess Patine; but there is nothing worthy of remark either in their architecture or decorations.

In the audience-hall, now used as a court-house, are some well-carved pillars of halmila wood: the trees from which they were formed were cut and squared near Nalande; from thence they were dragged over a hilly country, and up a steep mountain, the whole distance being upwards of thirty miles. The other remains of the palace and buildings inhabited by the royal establishment were, without exception, mean, and equally destitute of internal comfort and external beauty; the most striking object is a low octagonal tower with a peaked roof, from a balcony in which the king exhibited himself on occasions of public festivity.

Wikrama Bahoo the Third, who reigned from A.D. 1371 to A. D. 1378, was the first monarch who settled himself even temporarily at Kandy, then called, from a large rock which projects from the hill above the old palace, Sengadda-galla-nuvara; but it did not become the permanent capital of the interior until the reign of Wimala Dharma, which commenced A.D. 1592, and it continued the chief city until the native Government fell before the British power in 1815.

The burial-ground of the Kandian kings cannot be viewed without exciting reflections on the revolutions which alike occur to man's estate and the most ancient monarchies. Ere the last of one of the longest lines of kings which authentic history records had so far expiated his crimes, and received his measure of earthly retribution for the cruelties he had inflicted, by suffering a long imprisonment and an exile's death, the solid tombs of his predecessors were ransacked by the hands of avarice, or riven in sunder and ruined by the swelling roots of sacred trees. This hallowed spot, where the funeral piles were raised, the last grand solemn rites performed, and the last of earthly pomp and splendour was shown to the remains "of the race of the sun" and the rulers of the land, is now a wilderness, where decay revels and rushes rapidly on beneath dank vegetation and a gloomy shade. The tomb of Raja Singha, the tyrant who reigned during Knox's captivity in the seventeenth century, was nearly perfect, and preserved its shape in May, 1828; that of Kirti Sri was then entire. In 1837 the former was a heap of rubbish, from which the stones had been removed; and the beautiful proportions, even the general form of the latter, could no longer be traced. Hopes of plunder or unmeaning wantonness, at the time when Kandy was entered by the British, precipitated the fate of these monuments: neglected as they now are, there is nothing to retard it; and a few years will show, mingled in one common mould, the crumbling wreck of the tombs and the dust of their royal tenants.

During the continuance of the Dalada festival, the priests of Buddha, in different communities, headed by the seniors of their establishments, seemed to think it incumbent upon them to perambulate the town with their begging dishes, and to go through the ceremony of receiving alms. These parties moved on slowly with their fans before their faces, occasionally halting to receive whatever food was offered to them, but not asking for it. It appeared to me that this was evidently more of a temporary penance than a regular practice, although to live by alms is enjoined by the rules of their order. Their sleek faces and sly looks also spoke of better fare procured elsewhere with less trouble and more certainty than wandering in heavy rain through Kandy, and waiting for supplies from the more devout portion of those professing the Buddhist religion.

[No. III.—CHAPTER XIV.]

## KANDIAN FESTIVALS.

Besides the Dalada Puja, which, as I have already stated, was a rare occurrence, five annual festivals were celebrated by the king and chiefs in Kandy, with all the pomp and splendour that their circumstances could afford, or custom allow them to extort from those under their control. Although ordained for religion, and in honour of the gods, the festivals were also a source of profit to the native kings, and a cherished rule of their policy. As the chiefs were obliged to attend, their periodical visits enabled the king to levy exactions on the estate, or to secure the person of any influential or turbulent headman, who in his own district might have braved the power of the king and defied arrest. These five festivals are still kept up; and although they are now only tolerated, not encouraged, and without the show of regal state or compulsory attendance, still the Peraherra is an imposing spectacle.

The festival of the New Year is in April, and at that time the Cingalese indulge in the few amusements which they enjoy, and in such luxuries as they can afford. Before New Year's Day every individual procures from an astrologer a writing, fixing the fortunate hours of the approaching year on which to commence duties or ceremonies; and to the most minute points of these instructions he religiously adheres, believing that even an involuntary omission of any prescribed act at the appointed moment would render him liable to misfortunes. The following is an abridgment, omitting the astrological lore, of one of the annual documents, prepared for my benefit by the astrologer of Mátalé, who also took care to inform me of all eclipses, and to give me special instructions in writing how to avoid those misfortunes which they might occasion. "The emblem of the approaching year will be a red lion seated erect on a horse, and proceeding from an aperture resembling the mouth of a horse; this will be at the commencement of the year, nine hours and fifty-four minutes after sunset: at this fortunate moment milk should be boiled at each of the four sides of the house." Next day I was directed to look to the north while dimbul-leaves were suspended over my head, and with kolon-leaves placed under my feet; then, having anointed myself with different juices and aromatic drugs, I was to dress myself in perfumed clothes of red, white, and blue colours; then to look to the south, and cause fire to be lighted and cooking to begin. On the second day, at two hours and a half after sunrise, I was to commence eating victuals prepared with pounded salt and curdled milk. At twenty-seven hours,* while looking to the east, I was recommended to begin business by paying or receiving money. The whole concluded with a prediction, that, from the situation of the planets and other cogent reasons, I might expect both good and evil to happen during the year which was about to commence.

The second festival was held in the month of May, and was principally remarkable as being more essentially Buddhist than any of the others. During this festival such Samanairia priests as passed their examinations received upasampada (ordination).

The third festival, called by pre-eminence Peraherra (the procession), commenced with the new moon, and continued until the full moon in July; sometimes longer, if the procession was interrupted by meeting with a dead body of any animal, or any object considered unclean. The procession regularly increased in splendour every night until the last; at which time it was very imposing, from the multitude of people, rich dresses, brilliant lights, and large elephants. The arms and other relics of the gods were carried either on elephants or in palanquins; and, on the last night, the casket containg the Dalada, borne by an elephant, accompanied the procession to the limits of the town, and rested at the Gedigé wibare, near the tombs of the kings, whilst the remainder of the procession passed on to the Mahawelli-ganga at Ganorooa, three miles from Kandy. There the four Kapuralls of the temples of Vishnu, Nata, Katragamma, and Patine embarked on the river in ornamented canoes, and awaited the first dawn of day; then, drawing a circle in the water with their golden swords, they filled pitchers of holy water from within the magic ring, and the procession returned to the city. The different chiefs of districts and temples, with their elephants and followers, were then

† The Cingalese divide their day into sixty hours of sixty minutes each.

permitted to return to their provinces: and there, at some particular temples, the same procession on a limited scale took place.

The fourth festival, called the Festival of Lamps, was celebrated on the day before full moon in November: the whole town was illuminated on this occasion; and the immense number of niches alongside of the canal in front of the palace, as well as in the side of the lake, being filled with lamps, had a brilliant effect from the reflections in the water.

The fifth festival was called the Festival of New Rice. It was held in January, and appears to have been intended as a propitiatory offering at the commencement of the maha (great) harvest; for the Cingalese, judging from their own feelings, consider that an offering at the commencement is more likely to secure favour than an expected thanksgiving at the end of an undertaking.

The gods to whom these processions are principally dedicated are, Saman (Vishnu), Nata, Katragamma, and the goddess Patine. Wibhisaná, who is retained as a god at Kellania and in the vicinity of Colombo, is never heard of in Kandy. Vishnu is worshipped in his form of Ramachandra, and his statues are painted blue. Of Nata's history I could learn nothing with certainty; his statues are painted white. Katragamma is the same as Kartickya (Mars), and has received the name by which he is now worshipped in Ceylon from the place where his principal temple is situated, which is at the village of Katragamma, at the south-east of the island. He is more feared than the other gods; and many of his votaries lose their health, and even their lives, in a pilgrimage through the unhealthy country which surrounds his malignant shrine. His priests are Brahmins; and in the rebellion of 1818 they were the zealous assistants of the pretender who called himself king, and was the puppet of the rebel chief Kaepitapola.

The goddess Patine is, I believe, the same as Durga, and is invoked to protect her votaries from small-pox.

Wibhisaná was the brother of Rawana; and having assisted Rama in his invasion of the island, was, on the defeat and death of Rawana, placed on the throne of Ceylon, and reigned at Kellania.

To the list of gods the name of Mahasen (commonly

called Minneria-deyo) may be added, who, in the vicinity of Minneria, and in several parts of Mátalé, where temples have been reared to him, maintains his reputation as well as Vishnu or any of the more ancient and generally acknowledged deities. As Mahasen is a name of Katragamma as well as of the great Cingalese King, it is difficult to say whether these temples were originally dedicated to him; but I presume they were, and that King Mahasen has no legitimate claim to deification. However, in the temples of Mahasen the same warlike furniture may be found as in those of other gods; and the gigantic tanks and bridges formed under his superintendence give him a better claim to immortal gratitude than those who are only known by name as kings, heroes and gods, although they may have conferred similar benefits on earlier ages.

When Gautama Buddha visited Ceylon, Saman (Vishnu) appears to have been particularly worshipped, also Eiswara and Wibhisaná; and offerings were made to planets, ancestors, and demons.

The powers and attributes of the gods and demons of the Cingalese are not well defined; there are vices and crimes charged in the history of the gods, while the devils seem to respect the virtues which they do not practise, and their forbearance must be purchased by offerings and propitiatory ceremonies. The wild and wooded nature of the island, and the now thinly-scattered population, naturally tend to superstition; and it may be perceived by the native histories, that when the country was most prosperous and populous, the Buddhist religion was maintained in the greatest purity.

In the temples of the gods there is always some relic, generally connected with arms, such as bows, spears, or arrows; and if any person wished to erect a temple, he, by pretended inspiration, astrology, or other deception, proceeded to discover, with much ceremony and mystery, an arrow of the god, or some such relic, which had been hid in the spot selected for the building. The will of the god having been thus miraculously ascertained, the work was commenced; and, by permission of the king, land might be dedicated to the establishment, and have the same privileges as a Buddhist temple. The Kapuralls, or priests of a god's temple, require no other qualification than having sufficient cunning to dupe the superstitious, and bodily strength enough to enable them to go through the violent exertions and vile contortions which they exhibit, and denominate dancing and inspiration. The performance of all these ceremonies is accompanied by tom-toms, pipes, chanque-shells, halamba (hollow metal rings), and other noises, which they denominate musical. Over the principal temples are placed laymen of rank, who have charge of the revenues and are guardians of the relics; these chiefs do not take any part in the laborious exertions and insane excitement which, in this superstition, are supposed to propitiate the spirit that is invoked.

I discovered a temple in Mátalé to the Abudha Deiyo (unknown god), † and found he was patron of secret villainy (Mercury).

The images of the gods are only formed of plaster and brick, neither is their workmanship or design worthy of better materials; and if this worship and its idols were to disappear, the arts would have no cause to mourn, and morality might rejoice at the extinction of an impure superstition, which has much to debase and nothing to elevate its votaries.

*   *   *   *   *   *

† Acts xvii. 23.

# APPENDIX III.

## CHRISTIANITY IN CEYLON.

TENNENT says in his "History of Ceylon" that "the fanatical propagandism of the Portuguese reared for itself a monument in the abiding and expanding influence of the Roman Catholic faith. This flourished in every province and hamlet where it was implanted by the Franciscans, whilst the doctrines of the Reformed Church of Holland, never preached beyond the walls of the fortresses, are now extinct throughout the island, with the exception of an expiring community at Colombo." This latter statement is exaggerated; the Wolfendahl Dutch Reformed Church in Colombo is a flourishing community, albeit its services are in English, and its chaplain is Irish Presbyterian. The same may be said of the Galle Church, ministered to by a parson of the Church of Scotland, and there are also small bodies of adherents in Jaffna and Matara. What made the Franciscans so successful was their easy adaptation of the Roman Catholic faith as a companion to, instead of opponent of, Buddhism, and their giving long honorific Portuguese names to the natives in baptism, which the latter gladly added to their Sinhalese names, retaining them for three centuries to this day, though many of them now make no profession of any form of Christianity. When the Dutch seized the maritime provinces, many of the Portuguese with their Roman Catholic priests settled in villages within the territory of the Kandian king. Seven hundred of them in this way at Ruanwela. No doubt much mixture of races took place; for even Dutch soldiers were permitted to marry Sinhalese women, provided the latter professed

Christianity. Money was readily paid by the Sinhalese to both the Portuguese and Dutch for the privilege of prefixing Don to their names.

The Roman Catholic Missions have prospered under the tolerant British rule in Ceylon, and they number by far the largest body of Christians, the old Portuguese Mission being lately transferred from the care of the Archbishop of Goa to that of the newly-appointed Archbishop of Ceylon, who has three bishops under him at Colombo, Kandy, and Jaffna. There is a large number of priests and teachers; and educational establishments (notably St. Benedict's) are maintained at Colombo, as well as at Kandy and Jaffna.

The Anglican Church has had a bishop of Colombo since 1845, who has the oversight of the chaplains and clergymen settled over regular English congregations as well as of the agents of the Society for the Propagation of the Gospel, and in a less degree of the agents of the Church Missionary Society. The latter have a Conference of their own to settle the affairs and arrangements of their Mission. But all branches of the Anglican Church in the island have united through representatives to support a Synod necessitated by the disendowment and disestablishment of both the Episcopal and Presbyterian chaplains in Ceylon which was consummated between 1881 and 1886, the life claims of all incumbents in office before the earlier year being reserved. St. Thomas's College, Colombo, is a very notable and useful educational institution in connection with the Anglican Church.

Our estimate of the number of Christians in Ceylon is from 9 to 10 per cent of the total population, as follows:

Total population, viz., 2,900,000.

Total of Christians, about 290,000, distributed as follows:

| | |
|---|---|
| The Romanists with .. .. .. .. | 220,000 |
| The Episcopalians with .. .. .. | 25,000 |
| The Presbyterians and Congregationalists with | 14,000 |
| The Wesleyans with .. .. .. .. | 23,000 |
| The Baptists with ... .. .. .. | 8,000 |
| The whole Protestant community with ... | 70,000 |

We are, however, most interested in the history and

operations of Evangelical Missions at work in Ceylon. The Baptist Mission agents came first, arriving in 1812; the Wesleyans in 1814; the agents of the American Home and Foreign Mission in 1816; and the Church Mission in 1818; while a number of agents of General Booth's Salvation Army under "Major" Tucker (formerly Commissioner in the Indian Civil Service) arrived in 1885–6.

---

## PROGRESS OF MISSION WORK IN CEYLON.

I.—The work of the American Mission has been confined to stations in the densely-populated Jaffna Peninsula, where a succession of godly, devoted men and women have done an immense amount of good; more of the agents of this society, perhaps, than of any English Society have lived and died among the Tamil people whom they had come from the far West to instruct and evangelize. The work done in female education has been especially valuable; while Dr. Green's Medical Class of native students, and his compilations and translations of medical works into Tamil have been productive of great benefit to the whole island. A Christian College, and Industrial Technical Schools for the Jaffnese, are among the fruits of the Mission. Among the honoured names of the agents are Father and Mrs. Spaulding, Dr. Poor, Miss Agnew, Messrs. and Mesdames Saunders, Smith, Howlands, Hastings, &c. An interesting feature of this Mission is the succession of father and son in carrying on the work.

II.—The history of The Church Mission in Ceylon up to 1868 is recorded in a little Jubilee Memorial volume by Rev. J. I. Jones. The principal work of the Society has been in the vicinity of Colombo and Cotta, in Kandy, in the southern province at Baddegama, in Kurunegala, and itinerary work throughout the Central and parts of the North-Western, North-Central, and Western provinces. This refers to the Sinhalese Mission. The Tamil Mission has an agency in the Jaffna Peninsula. Churches and congregations with native pastors, boarding schools for girls as well as boys, vernacular and English schools, a

Christian college, and theological and normal classes, all form features of the Sinhalese and Tamil Missions as seen in the present day; and a large number of staunch Christian families at each station testify to the good work done through the Church Missionary Society. All the native pastors have their salaries provided through native Church Councils, which receive a grant-in-aid from the Home Committee of an annually diminishing amount, the saving being given to evangelistic work. The Rev. William Oakley, of this Mission, lived and worked in the island, without ever returning to England, for fifty-two years, until his death as a retired missionary in Nuwera Eliya in 1886. Much good literary and educational as well as evangelistic work has been done by Church missionaries, especially in connection with the language; the names of Lambrick, Ward, Selkirk, Trimnell, Marsh, Fenn, Jones, and Coles being familiar in this connection. An interesting branch is the Tamil Coolie Mission, which is under the ministerial charge of Church missionaries, with catechists and schoolmasters, assisted by a lay and undenominational committee from among the planters and merchants, who are responsible for the funds, all save the salaries of the missionaries, which are provided by the home committee. The coolies on the estates scattered all over the hill country are the objects of the Mission's teaching and care, and on many plantations schools are opened for the instruction of the children.

*Extracts from the Proceedings at the Annual Meetings, held in* 1881, *of the Baptist and Wesleyan Missionary Societies in Ceylon.*

III.—The Baptist Mission.—The Chairman (Mr. J. Ferguson) said they had now received the reports for the three divisions of the Baptist Mission in Ceylon. They were probably familiar with the districts to which those reports referred. Mr. Waldock's district had its centre in the neighbourhood of the Kelani river, while that of Mr. Carter was situated on the largest river in the island, and Mr. Pigott, apparently following up the inclination of the Baptist Mission to work along great rivers, had gone up to the headwaters of the Kelani and Kalu Gangas. The Sabaragamuwa district, as they knew, was part of the

Mission Extension work that some years ago excited so much interest. It was very satisfactory to feel now, that the three Evangelistic missions (the Wesleyan, Church, and Baptist) cover the whole ground, at least in nominal occupation, in South Ceylon, and supplement each other in the districts they occupy. The Baptist Mission in Sabaragamuwa and the Church Mission in Uva adjoin each other, while the Wesleyan Mission, having gone round the coast to Hambantota, has met with the work of its sister mission in Batticaloa, so that there is now no large district without at least being visited by a European missionary, and receiving attention from one or other of the three Evangelistic missions referred to.

In regard to the small accession of numbers reported, he would call attention to one fact which should be remembered, and which was stated on the authority of Sir Emerson Tennent, who was a very close observer. Sir Emerson, in giving evidence at home, stated that there were no missionaries in Ceylon so rigid in making up their returns of members as the Baptist missionaries. Therefore, although the figures were small, they indicated a much larger number of people under the influence of the mission. He had occasion lately, in the course of his daily work elsewhere, to look over some of the returns for forty years back of that and other missions, and he found that in South Ceylon there were probably 11,000 people under the influence of the Church, Wesleyan, and Baptist Missions about the year 1850. In 1860 that number had increased to 14,000; and in 1870 to 18,000; while now it could not be less than 25,000. About twenty years ago in making up the returns, before the first census was taken, it was estimated that the total Protestant population of Ceylon numbered 40,000. The census was taken in 1871, and the calculations then made went on to show that there were 54,000 Protestants, and there would be much reason for disappointment if the census that is shortly to be taken does not indicate that that number had increased to 70,000.* No doubt 70,000 Protestant Christians and 200,000 Roman Catholics would seem a small number out of 2,750,000—only ten per cent.,

* In the census of February, 1881, the Christian population is given at 268,000; of whom 200,000 were probably Roman Catholics and 68,000 Protestants.

but if we compare this result with what has been done in India—where the Christian population was not even one per cent.—we ought, not only to feel satisfied, but also most thankful for what has been accomplished. The people of this island needed Christianity now as much as in the time of Mr. Daniel, who said that the more he saw of the Sinhalese idolaters, the more he realized how correctly the 1st chapter of St. Paul's Epistle to the Romans described their condition. He was sure, from the reports that had been read, that the work of the Baptist Mission was one that would commend itself to the sympathies and support of all present.

IV.—The Wesleyan Mission.—The Chairman (Mr. J. Ferguson) said they had heard a clear and succinct report. For nearly twenty-one years now, he had watched the operations of the Wesleyan Mission in South Ceylon, and he had, during that time, been personally acquainted with all the Society's local European agents, and with a considerable number of the native agents, including among the former the revered Messrs. Gogerly and Spence Hardy. He had early formed a very high opinion of the admirable system under which this Mission in South Ceylon was organized and worked, and he had noted, year by year, the indefatigable labours of the missionaries for the good of the people and the furtherance of a knowledge of the gospel.

He would point out that the Mission in South Ceylon is singularly complete in embracing all classes of the population and every department of labour. The European and Eurasian adherents have the gospel preached to them in English, and those who speak Portuguese are not forgotten; while the great work is of course that among the Sinhalese and Tamils; so that the South Ceylon Wesleyan Mission was among the most extensive and complete in the island, or, perhaps, in any country where missions are found. The evangelistic labours of its agents—preaching the gospel direct to the people—had ever been one of the great objects of the Wesleyan Missionary Society, and he (the speaker) would never forget what he heard the Rev. Spence Hardy say on one occasion from that platform, that, in his experience, the most potent means, under God's guidance, of converting the

Sinhalese Buddhists was for the European missionary, possessed of a thorough command of the vernacular, to go right into the villages and to preach the gospel direct to the people. But the missionaries had not forgotten other departments of great importance—that of training the children, who would otherwise be left to grow up in ignorance, and be unable to read the gospel in their own language.

Then again, a distinguishing feature of the work of the agents of the Society had been found in the literature penned for the Sinhalese, and about their country and religions. He had only to mention a few names that would be familiar as the authors of most valuable and learned works, in Clough, Callaway, Gogerly, Spence Hardy, David de Silva, not to mention any of the present day. Hardy's "Jubilee Memorials" was one of the most charming books ever published with the Story of Missions, or, indeed, in connection with Ceylon. In that book Mr. Hardy gives the statistics of the Mission for the year 1863, and they had seen the report for 1881; so that there had elapsed an interval of eighteen years.

Very recently there appeared in the London *Times* a letter filling three or four columns in large type, attacking missions and missionaries. The writer made most sweeping statements. He seemed to regard it as an admitted fact that there were no conversions. Let us see the advance in eighteen years in South Ceylon in this Wesleyan Mission, which was as follows:—

| 1863. | | 1881. |
|---|---|---|
| 44 | Native Ministers and Catechists .. .. | 122 |
| 72 | Churches and other places of worship .. | 104 |
| 1,577 | Communicants .. .. .. .. | 2,609 |
| 3,789 | Adherents .. .. .. .. | 6,061 |
| 2,141 | Boys in Day Schools .. .. .. | 4,643 |
| 1,037 | Girls in Day Schools .. .. .. | 2,486 |
| — | Sunday Scholars .. .. .. | 4,820 |

He would like the anti-mission correspondent to consider what these figures for one limited section of the Eastern mission-field meant: but there was another rough-and-ready test which men of the world and business men, who believe in the practice of one—

> Who very wisely would lay forth
> No more upon it than 'twas worth,—

would recognize, namely, the contributions gathered in locally; and these, chiefly from natives, in 1863 were given by Mr. Hardy at Rs.4,520; while the total of local contributions in last year's report was Rs.39,325. The Sinhalese and Tamils, any more than other people, do not pay for what they do not value. Remembering that we are not yet in the seventieth year of the Mission, it might fairly be anticipated that ere long the people will be won to Christianity, not in an arithmetical, but in a geometrical progression in Ceylon as well as India. A very important step was taken some years ago in connexion with the extension of the work of the Wesleyan, the Church, and the Baptist Societies in South Ceylon, in which he (the Chairman) took some part. Nominally, the country was now covered by the three Evangelical bodies, but large districts and numerous villages had yet to have the gospel preached in them. Much remained to be done, and now that the schoolmaster was abroad in the land, it especially devolved on all Christians to follow up secular by moral and religious teaching. The Buddhists of China, Siam, and Burmah looked to Ceylon as the sacred home of their religion. The central position of the island added to its importance as a mission field; educated Ceylonese young men were going forth as medical assistants, surveyors, and in other capacities, to earn a livelihood in other parts of the world; while, again, the masses were about to follow, 500 Sinhalese now waiting to be transferred to Queensland. It behoved them to do all in their power to send forth good men and true, some, if not all, of whom might become teachers of the gospel in their turn. For this reason, among others, this Society deserved the hearty support of all who had the highest interests of the people at heart.

The following remarks are taken from an address by Mr. John Ferguson, at a Breakfast Meeting of the Wesleyan Missionary Society at Exeter Hall, in May, 1884:

"There are no more valuable Christian missions in the world than those which have settled in Ceylon. Geographically, Ceylon is the centre of the Eastern world. With reference to Asia, it has become very much what England has been so long in relation to Europe and the Western world. Christianity and education have made great progress in Ceylon, and there can be no question of the important bearing which the advance of Christianity, civilization, and education there will have upon the vast continent of India, upon Burmah, Siam, and Cambodia, and even upon China. In Ceylon ten per cent. of the children of a school-going age are being educated; in India the proportion is less than one per cent. From our island Sinhalese and Tamils are going out as teachers, also as magistrates and lawyers, to Madras, and some are even finding their way eastward to the Straits and on towards China. Most of these young men have been educated in mission-schools under the influence of Christianity, and wherever they go they carry with them and disseminate a civilizing and, I trust, Christian spirit; so that when you are working in Ceylon you are benefiting not only the people there, but the inhabitants of Southern India, and, directly or indirectly, the peoples of Indo-China, who, as Buddhists chiefly, are in such close relations to Lanka (Ceylon), the sacred land of Buddhism. While travelling in steamers and on railways, I have often heard disparaging remarks about mission work in Asia. Merchants and others who have been in the East often say they have never seen much good result from the work of missionaries. I asked them whether they had ever gone into the jungle, the country districts and villages, or even to the native churches in the bigger towns, and seen the missionary at work there. 'No,' they reply, 'they had never seen him at work in the jungle.' I have; I have again and again gone with the missionaries to their districts, and have seen for myself the good they are accomplishing. I have heard the testimony of the people themselves to the power of Christianity. I have astonished English and American friends by telling them of villages and districts in Ceylon, where Tamils and Sinhalese are as earnest and practical Christians as any in England or in America. In these days of scepticism you might fairly challenge men who deny the success of Christian missions and the good they are doing to send out a commission to Ceylon, to visit these Sinhalese and Tamil villages, where the people have their own pastors of their own race and locally supported, their Sunday-schools and day-schools, and where you might imagine yourself to be in the centre of England or in the most Christian part of America.

The time is coming when you may fairly look for reaping a great harvest in Ceylon, if you persevere with your missionary work in that island. I believe that the progress of Christianity and education there will be not only in an arithmetical, but a geometrical progression ere long, so that we may see Christianity permeate the whole island. One word with regard to the influence of laymen. I have often felt not only that inadequate support is given to mission work, but that missionaries themselves often meet with opposition from some of their countrymen, who go out into those regions on a mission which (as I heard described by Canon Westcott in Westminster Abbey on Sunday last) is more in the nature of selfishness than of self-sacrifice. I would impress upon the pastors assembled here to-day the great importance of seeing that the young men of their Churches destined for a Colonial or Indian life are true Christian laymen, because the influence of such upon their servants and others who observe their consistent life is immensely in favour of the spread of Christianity. When the natives observe that the civil servant, the layman — say the British merchant with whom they deal in business, is honest, truthful, and upright—they will say, 'He is a specimen of Christianity, we can trust him, and there must be something in his religion.'"

Wesley Christian College, Colombo, is the most notable educational institution in connection with this Mission. The South Ceylon Mission has now been divided into three districts: Colombo and the Western province; Galle and the Southern province; Kandy and the Negombo district, as well as the Central and Uva provinces.

The work of the North Ceylon Wesleyan Mission, with its important agencies, colleges and schools at Jaffna, Point Pedro, Batticaloa, and Trincomalee, deserves special mention.

## V.—A Sketch of Missionary Work in Ceylon.

The following account is from the pen of the late Dr. Macvicar, of Moffat (who was for many years chaplain of St. Andrew's Presbyterian Church, Colombo), and is given as illustrative of mission work in Ceylon:—

"About twelve miles from Colombo, the chief town of

Ceylon, on the high road to Galle, which is the second town, there is a belt or bar of land, lying between the sea on the one side, and an extensive lake, or rather lagoon, on the other. And as the sea in this quarter abounds in fish, and this lagoon has many arms leading from its ample basin into canals stretching along the coast, and into rivers flowing from the mountains, so as to form a great harbour, the surrounding country, which is very fertile, has become very populous. On the bank of land referred to, stands the thriving village of Morotto, remarkable for its fishermen and its carpenters. And here it was that the incident I am going to relate occurred.

"But, first, let me tell you of the peculiar beauty and interest which the lake of Morotto possesses. It is itself a very fine sheet of water; but the objects that surround it invest it with its peculiar beauty. Its bosom is everywhere fringed by various species of mangroves, their every branch steadied by roots falling right down from them, and dipping into the water, beneath which they fix themselves in the soil. Immediately behind, there is a belt of beautifully verdant copse or jungle, luxuriantly entangled, or hanging in rich festoons around noble trees, adorned now and then with magnificent blossoms. Then come extensive topes of coco-palms everywhere that the population extends; while beyond them, towards the interior, as far as the eye can reach, there is a forest—the trees, in their general appearance, not unlike those in a European forest, but on a grander scale. And all these vegetable riches, which adorn the spacious lake, like the sleeping waters of the lake itself, are seen reposing in a sunshine which for more than half the year never knows any shadows but those of the evening and morning, which bring such ample dews along with them that there is a perpetual verdure all the year. Add to this, that the horizon-line on the inland side is bounded by a lofty range of mountains, among which Adam's Peak rears its majestic summit, and it will be seen that the entire scenery is of dream-like beauty. The delight, however, with which the eye gazes is soon lost for feelings of quite another kind, when, ceasing to commune with Nature, we look to those monuments upon the banks of the lake, which claim man for their author. These remind us that, all-beautiful though nature be in this region, when viewed in herself, yet, viewed in reference to man, these are but dark places of the earth, full of the habitations of cruelty. There is one feature in nature, indeed, which seems to invite to the shores of this lake of Morotto as a fit place for the nurture of the darker superstitions. For up its waters, on some lonely and almost inaccessible islands, covered with lofty and seemingly leafless trees, there are seen hanging in the top branches, in ponderous masses, certain large, motionless objects, which remain black and without lustre in the brightest sunshine. They are many hundreds in number. Point to them, and ask the boatmen what they are, you will soon hear on the lips of every native in the boat the unearthly sound of 'woullá! woullá!' But what are they? Devote a long hour to the oar, in order to get nearer, and say that you are beneath them: they have left the trees, the air over your head is black with them—black with vampires or flying foxes, bats as large as eagles, in many hundreds, flapping their wings most sluggishly, and in most fitful silence, till one after another they have vanished from the air, and are only seen in distant trees, hanging again by their feet till nightfall. Whether it was the contrast between these unearthly creatures and all nature around, I know not; but I have never seen anything so like what one would fancy round the very mouth of hell, as these clouds of woullás.

"Let us turn our back upon them, then, and look down the beautiful sunny lake towards Morotto and the sea, whose distant roar is quite refreshing after the solemn silence of the forest, and the flights of the monster bats. The return to the place from which we set out will not be less agreeable for this, that the delicious sea-breeze will meet us in the face. But what is that dome, with its gilded pinnacle glittering in the sunbeams, on the top of the hill, surrounded by lofty bo-trees? It is a Buddhist temple, with its accompanying dágoba and pansala, where learned priests are thronging, each ordained by a chapter organized with profound policy, and venerating legitimacy of succession as much as any ecclesiastics in Rome—priests, but with this reservation, that man is the only god they acknowledge; while for man, alas! notwithstanding his possible godhead, when this life is over, they allow no heaven better than annihilation! The common people do perhaps worship Buddha, as if he were a real being, great and powerful, and consciously existing somewhere. But the sacred books adore his memory only; and the priesthood proclaim no god to the people but themselves. This is bad enough. Yes; what can be worse than atheism? And yet, let us hear what the boatman says of that headland on the other side of the lake, so remarkable for its hoary trees and dense impenetrable jungle. There is a treasure hidden there, he says. Then why not go and dig it up? 'Ah! it is guarded by a demon,' he answers; and reminds us of a custom practised in Ceylon, I am told, at no very remote period, the very thought of which makes the blood run cold. It was this: The owner of a treasure, when he apprehended from any cause that it was not safe at home, having selected some lonely spot in the jungle, dug two holes there, close beside each other; the one large enough to hold his treasure, the other much larger. He then returned to his home, and, having taken a large knife, and concealed it in his dress, called a trusty servant, showed him the bag of money, and required him to bear it along with him into the jungle. The faithful servant obeys; and when they have arrived at the secret spot, the treasure is deposited in its hole, and committed to the keeping of the servant, on which his throat is cut, and the body buried! And thereafter, he who receives this reward for his fidelity is believed to be a demon, and the treasure is safe in the keeping of the yakka! Such is a sample of those atrocities to which demon-worship prompts. Barbarities like these were indeed practised only in other times; but still, demon-worship forms the only positive religion of the heathen in Buddhistic countries. It prevails to a vast extent, not only in Ceylon, but in all Southern India; and this is truly lamentable, both in a religious point of view, and because it is so gloomy, unsocial, and inhuman. It is to a priest of this religion that the incident relates, to which we now proceed.

"He was an old man, and the temple where he ministered was his own. It presented its dismal front in a shady grove, almost fifty yards off a much-frequented by-road, which led from the highway to a populous village on the banks of the lake. And there had the old demon-priest remained for many a long year by his idols. And many orgies had he celebrated in every hamlet around, wherever there was any one sick who could afford to pay, or anything secret which was wanted to be known, or, haply, a new-married woman anxious about her first child, or a mother to whom child-birth was known to be a dangerous moment. Nay, I have been credibly informed of the daughters of Christian parents, who have stolen away to consult the kapurála. Such is the hold which demon-worship has upon the human mind. Is this much-frequented road, then, in one of the loveliest bypaths of the world, to be left with no retreat for the piously-disposed, but a demon-temple with its priest? No; the Wesleyan Missionary Society—that noble institution for the evangelization of the heathen, which secures the very best ministers of that communion for missionaries—has long had a station in Morotto; and it was resolved that a mission chapel should be erected opposite the demon-temple, on the other side of the road; each erection, however, out of the sight of the other. The chapel was accordingly built; and at the time to which this narrative refers, the missionary who ministered in it was a pure Sinhalese, Peter de Zylva by name, a man of great kindness of heart and energy of character. Mr. de Zylva's domiciliary visits were reaching every house and hamlet in Morotto, and his voice was ringing with the mysteries of redemption, musically, yet powerfully, from the desk in the Morotto chapel, Sabbath-day and week-day, while the passengers were arrested more and more, until his little flock became a large one, and the communicants numbered nearly a hundred.

"But how was it going with the old priest in his old demon-temple over the way? Was he plotting mischief and plying a bad tongue against the missionary who was thus turning the people from his temple into another, where his own religion was denounced as most sinful and unholy, and the cross of Christ proclaimed as the power of God unto salvation unto every one that believeth? This was nothing less than might have been expected from human nature under the circumstances. But not so here. While the people who used to frequent his temple were turning the opposite way, the old priest, sitting inside, listened day after day to the hymns and the prayers and the preaching of the Christian congregation and the Christian minister. This, happily, he could do with good effect in the silence which reigned around him, so near were both places of worship to each other; and such is the power of the Spirit of God, when an earnest Christian minister is His instrument, that, despite the hebetude of old age and the habits of a lifetime, despite the power of an hereditary faith and every suggestion of egotism, the old man felt that he could not help believing, and that he must go and unfold his mind to Peter de Zylva. He did so accordingly. And in answer to the always respectful and friendly question of the missionary—what brought him there?—he told him what had befallen his heart through listening to the preaching of the gospel; that he had done with his idols, and locked up his temple. 'And here is the key,' said he, 'which you must take, for the temple is my own; and I can do with it as I please. For me, henceforth, there remains nothing but to humble myself in penitence, and to believe in Christ.' 'A kapurála!' said Peter de Zylva, suspicious of his countryman; 'what can I do with yourself and your key? You must not throw yourself on us. We are poor people: we can do nothing for you that way.' 'Do not think so unworthily of me,' said the old man; 'I shall need but little, and that little not long.' 'And then as to this key,' rejoined Peter, 'suppose I take it, do you know what I shall do this very day?' 'No,' said the old man, 'nor do I care, if but the temple pass from my hands into yours.' 'Very well,' said the missionary, 'you see this stick of mine—(Peter usually walks with a heavy staff)—I tell you, I will take and smash every idol in your temple, this very day, and leave you nothing before night but chips and rubbish on the floor.' 'Do it,' said the old man: 'better you than I.' And it was done. Before acknowledging him as a Christian brother, the earnest but cautious missionary tried him on every point where a mistake or a cheat, on the part of the old man, seemed possible. But there was no mistake, no deceit. The conversion of the old demon-priest was one of those soul-delighting demonstrations of the power of the Spirit, where the best-defended strongholds of fallen nature are made to surrender unconditionally to the truth as it is in Jesus."

## APPENDIX IV.

### CASTE IN CEYLON.

Caste, though disavowed by Buddhism, has still some hold on the Sinhalese, and, as a matter of civil distinction, intermarriages of persons of different castes are almost unknown, except amongst the lowest of the population. The Tamils have all the Hindu castes, as essentials of their religion, from the Brahman downwards to the Koviya and Pariah. There are no Brahmans amongst the Sinhalese, and the Chaliyas (cinnamon peelers) strongly dispute the pre-eminence of the Vellalas or husbandmen. The fishermen are another great caste, and, curiously enough, they are the best and most enterprizing carpenters; then follow numerous divisions on to the dhoby (washermen) and jaggery castes, the members of which are employed to collect the juice from the flower sheaths of palms, to be fermented into "toddy" and yeast, distilled into arrack, or inspissated into coarse sugar called jaggery. Under the Kandyan dynasty, caste was strictly enforced—the son of a barber being inevitably and for life a barber. There is now no legal restriction, nor any social disability, save what the natives voluntarily choose to retain or submit to, and the anomaly of State-supported churches of Christians in Ceylon has also been removed, but officials, in some cases, foolishly encourage caste pretensions. The worse than waste of the temporalities (land, &c.) attached to Buddhist temples has, however, yet to be dealt with by Government. [See in further illustration the information in a later appendix, received as the sheets were passing through press.]

# APPENDIX V.

## 1.—A LIST OF THE BRITISH GOVERNORS OF CEYLON.*

1. Hon. FREDERICK NORTH (subsequently EARL OF GUILFORD), 12th October, 1798.
2. Lieut.-General the Right Hon. Sir THOMAS MAITLAND, G.C.B., 19th July, 1805.
   Major-General JOHN WILSON, Lieut.-Governor, 19th March, 1811.
3. General Sir ROBERT BROWNRIGG, Bart., G.C.B., 11th March, 1812.
   Major-General Sir EDWARD BARNES, K.C.B., Lieut.-Governor, 1st February, 1820.
4. Lieut.-General the Hon. Sir EDWARD PAGET, K.C.B., 2nd February, 1822.
   Major-General Sir JAMES CAMPBELL, K.C.B., Lieut.-Governor, 6th November, 1822.
5. Lieut.-General Sir EDWARD BARNES, K.C.B., 18th January, 1824.
   Major-General Sir JOHN WILSON, K.C.B., Lieut.-Governor, 13th October, 1831.
6. The Right Hon. Sir ROBERT WILMOT HORTON, Bart., G.C.B., 23rd October, 1831.
7. The Right Hon. JAMES ALEXANDER STEWART MACKENZIE, 7th November, 1837.
8. Lieut.-General Sir COLIN CAMPBELL, K.C.B., 5th April, 1841.
   Sir JAMES EMERSON TENNENT, K.C.S., Lieut.-Governor, 19th April, 1847.

* From 16th February, 1796, to 12th October, 1798, the colony was attached to the Madras Presidency.

9. The Right Hon. the VISCOUNT TORRINGTON, 29th May, 1847.
   The Hon. CHARLES JUSTIN MACCARTHY, Lieut-Governor, 18th October, 1850.
10. Sir GEORGE WILLIAM ANDERSON, K.C.B., 27th November, 1850.
   The Hon. CHARLES JUSTIN MACCARTHY, Lieut.-Governor, 18th January, 1855.
11. Sir HENRY GEORGE WARD, G.C.M.G., 11th May, 1855.
   Major-General HENRY FREDERICK LOCKYER, C.B., K.H., Lieut.-Governor, 30th June, 1860.
   Colonel CHARLES EDMUND WILKINSON, R.E., Lieut.-Governor, 30th July, 1860.
12. Sir CHARLES JUSTIN MACCARTHY, Kt., 22nd October, 1860.
   Major-General TERENCE O'BRIEN, Officer Administering the Government, 1st December, 1863.
13. Sir HERCULES GEORGE ROBERT ROBINSON, Kt., Lieut.-Governor, 31st March; Governor, 16th May, 1865.
   Lieut.-General STUDHOLME JOHN HODGSON, Officer Administering the Government, 2nd July, 1868, to 12th June, 1869, during Sir H. Robinson's leave of absence.
   The Hon. HENRY TURNER IRVING, Officer Administering the Government, 4th January, 1872.
14. The Right Hon. WILLIAM HENRY GREGORY (Sir W. H. Gregory, K.C.M.G., 1875), 4th March, 1872.
   The Hon. ARTHUR NORRIS BIRCH (C.M.G., 1875), Administrator of the Government, 17th April to 14th August, 1874, and 20th December, 1875, to 29th January, 1876; Lieut.-Governor, 15th January to 10th April, 1877 (during Sir W. H. Gregory's absences from the colony); Lieut.-Governor, 9th May to 3rd September, 1877.
15. Sir JAMES ROBERT LONGDEN, K.C.M.G. (G.C.M.G., 1883), 4th September, 1877.
   The Hon. JOHN DOUGLAS, C.M.G., Lieut.-Governor, 28th February to 16th September, 1881 (during Sir J. R. Longden's absence).
   Sir JOHN DOUGLAS, K.C.M.G., Lieut.-Governor, 14th July, 1883.

16. The Hon. Sir ARTHUR GORDON, G.C.M.G., gazetted Governor, August, 1883; assumed the Administration on December 3rd of that year.

Major-General Sir JOHN CHETHAM MCLEOD, K.C.B., Administered the Government during Sir A. Gordon's absence, June to November, 1885.

---

## 2.—CHIEF JUSTICES OF CEYLON.

Sir Edward Codrington Carrington, 1802.
The Hon. Alexander Johnston (provisional), 1806.
Right Hon. E. C. Lushington (provisional), 1807.
W. Coke, Esq. (provisional), 1809.
Sir Alexander Johnston (Chief Justice and President of the Council), 6th November, 1811.
Sir Hardinge Giffard, Kt., LL.D., 1820.
Sir Richard Ottley, Kt., 1827.
Sir Charles Marshall, Kt., 1833.
Sir William Norris, Kt., April, 1836.
Sergeant Sir W. Rough, Kt., April, 1837
Sir Anthony Oliphant, Kt., 1838.
Sir William Ogle Carr, Kt., 1854.
Sir W. Carpenter Rowe, Kt., 1856.
The Hon. P. I. Sterling (acting), 1859.
Sir Edward Creasy, Kt., 1860.
Sir R. F. Morgan, Kt. (acting), 1875.
The Hon. C. H. Stewart (acting), 1875.
Sir George Anderson, Kt. (acting), 1876.
Sir William Hackett, Kt., 1877.
Sir John Budd Phear, Kt., 1877.
Sir Richard Cayley, Kt., 1879.
Hon. L. B. Clarence (acting), 1882.
Hon. J. P. de Wet, Kt., and Sir George Anderson (acting), 1882–3.
The Hon. Sir Bruce Lockhart Burnside, 1883 (knighted in 1884).
Hon. F. Fleming (acting), 1885, during Sir Bruce Burnside's absence.

## 3.—BRITISH MAJOR-GENERALS COMMANDING THE TROOPS IN CEYLON.

(Previously to 1819 the Governors were not only officially but actively commanders of the troops.)

Sir Edward Barnes, K.C.B., 1819.—Afterwards Ceylon's great Governor, a remarkable man. He became Governor in 1824, and held the post until 1831. It was his mind that planned and executed the Kandy Road, and other main lines throughout the island. He likewise erected the Pavilion at Kandy; Barnes Hall, Nuwara Elliya; and Mount Lavinia House. A bronze statue in honour of him as Governor stands opposite the Queen's House, Colombo.

Sir James Campbell, K.C.B., 1822.

Sir Hudson Lowe, 1826. — Previously (1815–1821) Governor of St. Helena, and Custodian of Napoleon Bonaparte.

Sir John Wilson, K.C.B., 1831.

Sir R. Arbuthnot, K.C.B., 1838.

William Smelt, C.B., 1847.—The so-called Kandyan rebellion of 1848 occurred during Major-General Smelt's command, and there was an angry correspondence between Lord Torrington, Major-General Smelt, and General F. Braybrooke, relative to the officers of the Ceylon Rifle Regiment.

T. Reed, C.B., 1852.

P. Bainbrigge, C.B., 1854.

Henry F. Lockyer, C.B., K.H., 1857.—Major-General Lockyer, who had been Lieutenant-Governor after Sir H. Ward was transferred to Madras, left the island in ill-health, and died on board the S.S. *Ripon*, 16th October, 1861.

Terence O'Brien, 1860.—In the time of Major-General O'Brien, his son, Major O'Brien, was tried by court-martial for a letter published in the *Mofussilite*, reflecting on the civil authorities in Ceylon. The Major-General did not confirm the sentence, and the Horse Guards removed the censure of the local court.

Studholme John Hodgson, 1865.—It was during Major-General Hodgson's time that a commission was appointed to inquire into the military expenditure of Ceylon. There were food riots in Colombo, and the military were asked to assist the civil authorities in quelling them.

Henry Renny, C.S.I., 1869.
John Alfred Street, C.B., 1874.
William Wilby, C.B., 1879.
Sir John C. McLeod, K.C.B., 1882.
Sir Wilbraham Lennox, V.C., R.E., K.C.B., 1887.

Some of the Governors, such as General Brownrigg (1815) and Lieutenant-General Sir Colin Campbell (1841), held the two offices of Governor and Commander of the Forces. Major-Generals Sir John Wilson, Lockyer, O'Brien, Hodgson, and McLeod, acted respectively as Lieutenant-Governor, &c., during the absence or otherwise of the Governor from the island.

---

## 4. EXECUTIVE COUNCILLORS OF CEYLON.

*Colonial Secretaries.*—Hugh Cleghorn, 1799. R. Arbuthnot, 1803. Honourable J. Rodney, 1815. P. Anstruther ("the one-armed Rajah"), 1834. Sir J. Emerson Tennent, K.C.S., 1846. Charles Justin McCarthy, 1850. W. Chas. Gibson, 1861. H. T. Irving, 1869. Arthur N. Birch, C.M.G., 1873. John Douglas, C.M.G., 1878. C. C. Smith, 1885. Col. Walker, 1887.

*Queen's Advocates.*—William Coke, 1809. H. Giffard, LL.D., 1811. Henry Matthews, 1817. W. Norris, 1832. W. O. Carr, 1834. James Stark, 1841. Arthur Buller, 1842. H. C. Selby, 1848. H. B. Thomson, 1859. Sir R. F. Morgan, 1863. Richard Cayley, 1876. B. L. Burnside, 1880. C. L. Ferdinands (acting), 1882. Francis Fleming (Attorney-General), 1883. Samuel Grenier, 1887.

*Auditors-General.*—A. Bertolacci, 1809. John D'Oyly, 1815. E. Tolfrey, 1816. J. W. Carrington, 1817. H. A. Marshal, 1824. H. Wright, 1842. C. J. MacCarthy, 1848. W. C. Gibson, 1850. R. T. Pennefather, 1862. Robert John Callander, 1866. John Douglas, 1870. W. C. Barclay, 1876. W. H. Ravenscroft, 1877.

*Treasurers.*—Robert Boyd, 1809. J. W. Carrington, 1812.

Thomas Eden, 1816. John Drave, 1822. W. Granville, 1823. J. W. Carrington, 1824. F. J. Templer, 1843. J. Caulfeild, 1854. F. Saunders, 1861. G. Vane, C.M.G., 1865. W. D. Wright, 1882. G. T. M. O'Brien, 1886.

*Solicitor-General* (the first).—C. L. Ferdinands, Esq.

---

## 5.—A FEW PUBLIC (NON-OFFICIAL) BENEFACTORS IN BRITISH TIMES.

Geo. Bird, the late, who opened the first regular coffee plantation.

Robert Boyd Tytler, the late, who introduced the improved West Indian system of coffee planting, and also was the first to cultivate cocoa (cacao) in Ceylon.

David Wilson, the late, for his improvements in the preparation of coco-nut oil and coir manufactures; and the Messrs. Leechman, who succeeded him in Hultsdorf Mills.

Gabriel and Maurice Worms, the late, as pioneers who vested a large amount of capital in coffee and tea cultivation.

Christopher Elliott, M.D., the late, for his philanthropic labours among Burghers and Natives, and his independent attitude as a Journalist; also as the first head of the Civil Medical Department of the colony, and the projector of Hospitals, Colleges, &c.

A. M. Ferguson, C.M.G., M.R.A.S., for his labours in urging cultivation of new products, especially cinchona and tea; also as Journalist (*Ceylon Observer*) and Publisher (in conjunction with J. Ferguson) of *Tropical Agriculturist*, Manuals for Tropical Planters, Ceylon Handbooks and Directories, &c. Resident fifty years.

C. A. Lorenz, Barrister, the late, for disinterested work as Legislator and Publicist, more especially in aiding the advance of his own people, the Burghers.

John Capper, M.R.A.S. (Ceylon branch), Merchant and Journalist in Ceylon for over forty years, Author of several works on, or on subjects connected with, the colony.

The De Soyza Family (especially C. H. De Soyza, Esq., J.P.) and Mudaliyar Sampson Rajapakse, for enterprise in developing planting industry, constructing roads, endowing hospitals and schools, and numerous other public benefactions.

G. A. Crüwell, the late, as a Pioneer Planter who visited and reported, in *Ceylon Observer*, on Java, Southern and Northern India, West Coast of Africa (Liberia), Brazil, and Central America, for the benefit of his fellow planters in Ceylon; doing much to introduce the Liberian species of coffee and India-rubber trees.

James Alwis, the late, as Legislator and Author, in writing on the literature and history of his own people, the Sinhalese.

Sir M. Comara Swamy, Kt., the late, as Legislator and Author on subjects connected with his own people, the Tamils.

Hon. James Van Langenberg, M.L.C., Advocate, the late, for valuable work as legislator and lawyer.

George Wall, Planter and Merchant, some time Member of the Legislative Council, and Chairman of the Chamber of Commerce, and at present Chairman of the Planters' Association. Has, since his arrival in 1846, taken a leading part in discussing public affairs. Founded a Ceylon League to secure a reform of the Legislative Council.

Rev. Levi Spaulding, D.D. ("Father Spaulding"), the late, of the American Mission. He laboured uninterruptedly for over fifty years in the north of the island among the Tamils, educating and Christianizing a large number, aided by earnest, disinterested brethren and sisters, among whom Miss Agnew (who also never took furlough) died on the Mission-field after well-nigh fifty years' service.

Also Dr. Green, Medical Missionary of the same Mission, who translated and compiled standard medical works for his Tamil students; the same students proving of the greatest value to the Government and the people before a Colombo Medical College was established by Government, and Ceylon students were trained there.

The Rev. John Kilner, of the Wesleyan Mission, deserves to be remembered among the Jaffna Tamils, among whom he laboured.

Sir SAMUEL BAKER, for his experiments (agricultural, &c.) at Nuwara Eliya, extending over seven years, and his two books on the island: "Seven Years in Ceylon," and "The Rifle and the Hound in Ceylon."

REGINALD JOHN CORBET, the late, a leading Ceylon Planter of many years' standing, a Pioneer in Cinchona cultivation, ex-Member of the Legislative Council, and Chairman of the Planters' Association.

JOHN NIETNER, the late, Prussian-born, naturalized British subject, for his contributions to Natural History, especially "Entomology," and his little work, "Enemies of the Coffee-tree in Ceylon."

W. W. MITCHELL, Esq., H. BOIS, Esq., and J. J. GRINLINTON, Esq., C.E., F.R.G.S., for their active zeal in the public interests in a variety of ways.

G. H. D. ELPHINSTONE, Coffee Planter and Pioneer in the Dimbula District from 1868 onward, as well as Pioneer with Tea cultivation in several districts of the island; a most industrious, persevering colonist, under many difficulties; now Sir Graeme H. D. Elphinstone, Bart.

JOHN FERGUSON, M.R.A.S., Corresponding Secretary for Ceylon of the Royal Colonial Institute, Journalist and Author, for twenty-seven years a colonist; originated (in conjunction with the late R. V. Dunlop) Mission Extension to the Sabaragamuwa, Hambantota, and Uva districts; started agitation for railway extension beyond Nawalapitya to Uva.

Among a large body of Christian missionaries, authors, and true philanthropists, mention should be made of CLOUGH, LAMBRICK, HARVARD, DANIEL, GOGERLY, SPENCE HARDY, OAKLEY, CARTER, SCOTT, IRELAND JONES, and COLES.

Among *officials* whose names are not included in the lists given above, but whose special services to Ceylon deserve notice, are—

ANTHONY BERTOLACCI, who wrote a valuable work on the trade and revenue in Ceylon early in the century.

Major FORBES, late of 78th Regiment, for his interesting work "Eleven Years in Ceylon."

J. W. BENNETT, F.L.S., for his work "Ceylon and its Capabilities," and his contributions to the study of the Natural History of the Island.

Capt. James Stewart, Master Attendant of Colombo, for his investigation of the pearl fishery, and useful notes and papers on this and other practical subjects connected with the revenue and progress of the island.

Percival Acland Dyke, for the long period of forty years Government Agent of the Northern Province of Ceylon, to the development of which, and the welfare of the people, he gave the service of his life.

Sir Chas. Peter Layard, K.C.M.G., for a nearly equal period Government Agent of the Western Province, where he was in useful "labours more abundant."

Major Skinner, C.M.G., the great roadmaker of Ceylon, who began his work under Sir Edward Barnes, and closed his most useful career forty years later, under Sir Hercules Robinson.

Sir R. F. Morgan, Kt., included among the Chief Justices, did notable service to the Colony as its lawmaker for many years.

Guilford Lindsay Molesworth, C.I.E., as the successful Engineer of the Colombo and Kandy Railway, the discoverer of a route which had been overlooked by several predecessors.

Sir Charles Hutton Gregory, K.C.M.G., as Consulting Engineer for many years in connection with the development of its system of railways.

Sir John Coode, K.G., as Consulting Engineer, and Mr. John Kyle as Resident Engineer, for the Colombo Breakwater and Harbour Works, which have proved so successful.

G. H. K. Thwaites, F.R.S., Ph.D., for many years Director of the Royal Botanic Garden, and the compiler of the "Enumeratio Plantarum Zeylaniæ."

W. Ferguson, F.L.S., author of a "Monograph on the Palmyra Palm," pamphlets on "Ceylon Timber Trees," "Ferns," "Snakes," &c., and for his contributions to the Natural History of the island.

Henry Trimen, M.B., F.L.S., the gifted successor to Dr. Thwaites, who, as botanist and practical observer, has already laid the Colony under special obligations.

Hon. George Turnour, for his translation of the "Mahawanso" and other invaluable work connected with the ancient history of Ceylon.

LOUIS ZOYZA, Mudliyar, Chief Translator to Government, for his useful work as an Orientalist.

SIMON CASI CHITTY, Mudliyar, for his "Ceylon Gazetteer," and numerous other writings.

Dr. BARCROFT BOAKE, Principal of the Royal College, Colombo, and for many years Hon. Secretary Friend-in-Need Society, and for his literary and Natural History writings.

Hon. P. D. ANTHONISZ, M.D., M.L.C., as a Ceylonese surgeon who has risen to the highest eminence in his profession, and in the esteem of his countrymen by his good works, "The Anthonisz Memorial" (Hospital Wards), and his nomination to the Legislative Council affording evidence.

C. L. FERDINANDS, Esq., Solicitor-General, as the unofficial leader of the Burghers after Mr. Lorenz's death, and in office as Legislator and Criminal Prosecutor, respected for his conscientious, honourable, zealous pursuit of duty. Mr. Ferdinands incurred the displeasure of Governor Gordon for no fault of his own, and was passed over in 1886 for the Attorney-Generalship in favour of his friend Mr. Grenier, much to the regret of those who knew best his long and useful labours, and his high sense of duty.

The name of Sir J. EMERSON TENNENT finds a place in the list of Lieut.-Governors and Colonial Secretaries, but it deserves special mention as that of the author of the most valuable and complete work published on Ceylon up to his day, 1857–61.

# APPENDIX VI.

## PRINCIPAL RESULTS OF THE CENSUS

TAKEN ON 17TH FEBRUARY, 1881.*

[*Compiled from the Registrar-General's (Mr. L. F. Lee's) Report and Statements.*]

## AREA—POPULATION.

### GENERAL STATEMENT OF THE AREA AND POPULATION

(Exclusive of the Military and the Shipping).

| | Area in square miles. | Persons. | Males. | Females. | No. of persons per square mile. |
|---|---|---|---|---|---|
| CEYLON | 25,865 | 2,759,788 | 1,469,558 | 1,290,185 | 109 |
| WESTERN PROVINCE | 8,456 | 897,829 | 475,897 | 421,982 | 260 |
| NORTH-WESTERN PROVINCE | 8,024 | 293,827 | 158,026 | 185,801 | 97 |
| CENTRAL PROVINCE | 6,029 | 639,361 | 361,528 | 277,888 | 106 |
| NORTH-CENTRAL PROVINCE | 4,047 | 66,146 | 35,580 | 30,566 | 16 |
| NORTHERN PROVINCE | 3,171 | 302.500 | 151,565 | 150,935 | 95 |
| EASTERN PROVINCE | 3,657 | 127,555 | 66,577 | 60,978 | 35 |
| SOUTHERN PROVINCE | 1,980 | 433,520 | 220,885 | 212,635 | , 219 |
| **WESTERN PROVINCE.** | | | | | |
| Colombo, Municipality of | $9\frac{8}{25}$ † | 110,502 | 62,225 | 48,277 | 11,693 |
| Colombo District (exclusive of the Municipality) | 532 | 279,286 | 143,775 | 135,511 | 525 |
| Negombo District | 248 | 116,691 | 61,360 | 55,331 | 471 |
| Kegalla District | 651 | 119,955 | 64,698 | 55,257 | 184 |
| Ratnapura District | 1,434 | 105,874 | 59,380 | 46,494 | 74 |
| Kalutara District | 581 | 165,021 | 83,959 | 81,062 | 284 |
| **NORTH-WESTERN PROVINCE.** | | | | | |
| Kurunegala District | 1,840 | 215,173 | 114,989 | 100,184 | 117 |
| Puttalam District | 1,184 | 78,154 | 43,037 | 35,117 | 66 |
| **CENTRAL PROVINCE.** | | | | | |
| Kandy District | 904 | 288,332 | 162,277 | 126,055 | 319 |
| Matale District | 982 | 86,655 | 48,470 | 38,185 | 88 |
| Badulla District | 3,790 | 165,692 | 92,627 | 73,065 | 44 |
| Nuwara Eliya District | 353 | 98,682 | 58,149 | 40,533 | 279 |
| **NORTH-CENTRAL PROVINCE.** | | | | | |
| Nuwarakalawiya District (including Tamankaduwa) | 4,047 | 66,146 | 35,580 | 30,566 | 16 |
| **NORTHERN PROVINCE.** | | | | | |
| Jaffna District | 875 | 265,583 | 131,483 | 134,100 | 304 |
| Mannar District | 432 | 21,848 | 11,820 | 10,028 | 49 |
| Mullaittivu District | 927 | 7,638 | 4,213 | 3,425 | 8 |
| Vavuniyan-Vilankulam District | 937 | 7,931 | 4,549 | 3,382 | 8 |
| **EASTERN PROVINCE.** | | | | | |
| Batticaloa District | 2,595 | 105,358 | 54,598 | 50,760 | 41 |
| Trincomalee District | 1,062 | 22,197 | 11,979 | 10,218 | 21 |
| **SOUTHERN PROVINCE.** | | | | | |
| Galle District | 537 | 209,680 | 105,808 | 103,872 | 390 |
| Matara District | 548 | 151,923 | 77,516 | 74,407 | 277 |
| Hambantota District | 895 | 71,917 | 37,561 | 34,356 | 80 |

* One per cent. per annum can be added to the results to bring the figures up to date.—AUTHOR. † Exclusive of the area of the Colombo Lake.

STATEMENT SHOWING THE DISTRIBUTION OF THE POPULATION BY PRINCIPAL NATIONALITIES.

| | Europeans. | | | Eurasians and Burghers. | | | Sinhalese. | | | Tamils. | | |
|---|---|---|---|---|---|---|---|---|---|---|---|---|
| | Persons. | Males. | Females. | Persons. | Males. | Females. | Persons. | Males. | Females. | Persons. | Males. | Females. |
| CEYLON | 4, 836 | 3,181 | 1,655 | 17,886 | 8,927 | 8,959 | 1,846,614 | 962,430 | 884,184 | 687,248 | 380,490 | 306,758 |
| Western Province | 1,538 | 988 | 550 | 10,406 | 5,122 | 5,284 | 769,749 | 399,004 | 370,745 | 60,033 | 37,888 | 22,145 |
| North-Western Province | 87 | 50 | 37 | 588 | 314 | 274 | 249,515 | 132,575 | 116,910 | 19,915 | 12,042 | 7,873 |
| Central Province | 2,626 | 1,790 | 836 | 2,945 | 1,580 | 1,365 | 357,190 | 190,889 | 166,301 | 233,892 | 140,788 | 93,104 |
| North-Central Province | 30 | 18 | 12 | 35 | 21 | 14 | 53,406 | 28,053 | 25,353 | 4,634 | 2,926 | 1,738 |
| Northern Province | 136 | 85 | 51 | 814 | 344 | 470 | 1,379 | 919 | 460 | 289,481 | 144,679 | 144,802 |
| Eastern Province | 139 | 74 | 65 | 1,119 | 577 | 542 | 5,947 | 3,347 | 2,600 | 75,408 | 39,447 | 35,961 |
| Southern Province | 280 | 176 | 104 | 1,979 | 969 | 1,010 | 409,428 | 207,643 | 201,785 | 3,855 | 2,720 | 1,135 |

| | Moormen. | | | Malays. | | | Veddahs. | | | Others. | | |
|---|---|---|---|---|---|---|---|---|---|---|---|---|
| | Persons. | Males. | Females. | Persons. | Males. | Females. | Persons. | Males. | Females. | Persons. | Males. | Females. |
| CEYLON | 184,542 | 103,804 | 80,738 | 8,895 | 4,739 | 4,156 | 2,228 | 1,177 | 1,051 | 7,489 | 4,805 | 2,684 |
| Western Province | 49,977 | 29,151 | 20,826 | 3,437 | 1,820 | 1,617 | .. | .. | .. | 2,189 | 1,424 | 765 |
| North-Western Province | 21,955 | 12,337 | 9,618 | 837 | 461 | 376 | .. | .. | .. | 430 | 247 | 183 |
| Central Province | 35,633 | 22,150 | 13,213 | 2,913 | 1,549 | 1,364 | 484 | 256 | 228 | 3,948 | 2,529 | 1,427 |
| North-Central Province | 7,412 | 4,223 | 3,189 | 17 | 6 | 11 | 425 | 236 | 189 | 157 | 97 | 60 |
| Northern Province | 10,416 | 5,386 | 5,030 | 92 | 45 | 47 | 3 | 1 | 2 | 179 | 106 | 73 |
| Eastern Province | 43,001 | 22,067 | 20,934 | 428 | 249 | 179 | 1,311 | 681 | 630 | 202 | 135 | 67 |
| Southern Province | 16,418 | 8,490 | 7,928 | 1,171 | 609 | 562 | 5 | 3 | 2 | 384 | 275 | 109 |

STATEMENT SHOWING THE DISTRIBUTION OF POPULATION ACCORDING TO RELIGION AND NATIONALITY.

(Exclusive of the Military and the Shipping.)

| CEYLON. | Christians. | | Buddhists. | | Hindus. | | Mohammedans. | | Others. | |
|---|---|---|---|---|---|---|---|---|---|---|
| | Males. | Females. | Males. | Females. | Males. | Females. | Males. | Females. | Males. | Females. |
| Europeans | 3,132 | 1,651 | .. | .. | .. | .. | 1 | .. | 48 | 4 |
| Eurasians and Burghers | 8,883 | 8,921 | 25 | 21 | .. | .. | 2 | 2 | 17 | 15 |
| Sinhalese | 82,998 | 79,272 | 879,237 | 804,764 | 32 | 40 | 36 | 35 | 127 | 73 |
| Tamils | 44,089 | 38,131 | 8,350 | 4,463 | 326,818 | 263,513 | 466 | 249 | 767 | 402 |
| Moormen | 2 | 1 | 2 | .. | .. | .. | 103,799 | 80,737 | 1 | .. |
| Malays | 21 | 11 | 3 | 3 | .. | .. | 4,715 | 4,142 | .. | .. |
| Veddahs | 1 | .. | 361 | 325 | 317 | 371 | .. | .. | 398 | 355 |
| Others | 532 | 332 | 379 | 137 | 1,512 | 927 | 2,320 | 1,271 | 62 | 17 |
| Total | 139,658 | 128,319 | 888,357 | 809,713 | 328,779 | 264,851 | 111,339 | 86,436 | 1,420 | 866 |

STATEMENT SHOWING THE DISTRIBUTION OF THE TOTAL POPULATION ACCORDING TO SEX AND CLASS OF OCCUPATION.

| PROVINCES—DISTRICTS. | TOTAL. | | CLASSES. | | | | | | | | | | | |
|---|---|---|---|---|---|---|---|---|---|---|---|---|---|---|
| | | | I. Professional. | | II. Domestic. | | III. Commercial. | | IV. Agricultural. | | V. Industrial. | | VI. Indefinite and Non-productive. | |
| | Males. | Females. | Males. | Females. | Males. | Females. | Males. | Females. | Males. | Females. | Males. | Females. | Males. | Females. |
| CEYLON | 1,469,553 | 1,290,185 | 31,836 | 1,466 | 29,388 | 627,329 | 54,566 | 8,766 | 579,336 | 64,948 | 94,850 | 63,961 | 679,577 | 523,715 |
| Western Province | 475,397 | 421,932 | 11,159 | 701 | 12,240 | 219,373 | 21,825 | 4,719 | 156,402 | 4,362 | 36,769 | 18,667 | 237,002 | 174,110 |
| North-Western Province | 158,026 | 135,301 | 2,884 | 56 | 1,488 | 77,294 | 4,402 | 616 | 75,008 | 1,183 | 5,054 | 2,718 | 69,190 | 53,439 |
| Central Province | 361,523 | 277,838 | 5,520 | 245 | 8,147 | 110,518 | 14,550 | 803 | 182,253 | 57,281 | 21,580 | 5,602 | 129,473 | 103,389 |
| North-Central Province | 35,580 | 30,566 | 750 | 26 | 284 | 17,842 | 793 | 48 | 17,110 | 94 | 774 | 115 | 15,899 | 12,441 |
| Northern Province | 151,565 | 150,935 | 4,144 | 223 | 2,429 | 76,634 | 2,973 | 883 | 60,219 | 682 | 9,089 | 7,397 | 72,711 | 65,116 |
| Eastern Province | 66,577 | 60,978 | 1,991 | 64 | 918 | 30,479 | 2,559 | 161 | 19,542 | 96 | 4,454 | 1,425 | 37,118 | 28,753 |
| Southern Province | 220,885 | 212,635 | 5,388 | 151 | 3,382 | 95,189 | 7,464 | 1,536 | 68,802 | 1,250 | 17,160 | 28,012 | 118,189 | 86,467 |

# ESTATE POPULATION; CHIEFLY TAMIL COOLIE IMMIGRANTS.

STATEMENT SHOWING THE DISTRIBUTION OF THE ESTATE POPULATION, WITH THE NUMBER OF ESTATES IN EACH REVENUE DISTRICT.

| Districts. | No. of Estates. | Population. | | |
|---|---|---|---|---|
| | | Persons. | Males. | Females. |
| Ceylon | 1,758 | 206,495 | 124,692 | 81,803 |
| **Western Province.** | | | | |
| Colombo District | 25 | 1,074 | 695 | 379 |
| Negombo District | 52 | 1,886 | 1,372 | 514 |
| Kegalla District | 44 | 3,268 | 2,051 | 1,217 |
| Ratnapura District | 102 | 6,925 | 4,248 | 2,677 |
| Kalutara District | 15 | 1,002 | 655 | 347 |
| **North-Western Province.** | | | | |
| Kurunegala District | 27 | 2,539 | 1,527 | 1,012 |
| Puttalam District | 17 | 796 | 531 | 265 |
| **Central Province.** | | | | |
| Kandy District | 671 | 75,229 | 44,951 | 30,278 |
| Matale District | 141 | 18,182 | 10,985 | 7,197 |
| Badulla District | 271 | 37,242 | 22,310 | 14,932 |
| Nuwara Eliya District | 325 | 56,225 | 33,954 | 22,271 |
| **Northern Province.** | | | | |
| Jaffna District | 32 | 528 | 332 | 196 |
| **Eastern Province.** | | | | |
| Batticaloa District | 2 | 78 | 62 | 16 |
| Trincomalee District | 6 | 277 | 208 | 69 |
| **Southern Province.** | | | | |
| Galle District | 17 | 595 | 414 | 181 |
| Matara District | 11 | 649 | 397 | 252 |

# OCCUPATIONS.

## STATEMENT OF THE PRINCIPAL OCCUPATIONS OF THE POPULATION OF CEYLON.

| Principal Occupations. | All Races. | | |
|---|---|---|---|
| | Persons. | Males. | Females. |
| Population of Ceylon according to Nationality | 2,759,738 | 1,469,553 | 1,290,185 |
| **I.—Professional Class.** | | | |
| In employ of General or Local Government | 12,948 | 12,536 | 412 |
| Missionary, Clergyman, Minister | 422 | 409 | 13 |
| Church, Chapel—Service | 110 | 108 | 2 |
| Buddhist Priest | 6,279 | 6,279 | .. |
| Vihara Service | 68 | 64 | 4 |
| Hindu Priest | 1,198 | 1,198 | .. |
| Temple Service | 134 | 111 | 23 |
| Mohammedan Priest | 521 | 521 | .. |
| Mosque Service | 95 | 95 | .. |
| Barrister, Advocate, Proctor | 280 | 280 | .. |
| Law Student | 76 | 76 | .. |
| Petition, Pleading—Drawer | 120 | 120 | .. |
| Notary Public | 411 | 411 | .. |
| Physician, Surgeon, Medical Practitioner | 8,349 | 8,321 | 28 |
| Medical Student | 60 | 60 | .. |
| Midwife | 260 | .. | 260 |
| Chemist, Druggist | 107 | 104 | 3 |
| Music Teacher, Musician | 168 | 164 | 4 |
| Drummer | 181 | 181 | .. |
| Tom-tom Beater | 1,208 | 1,208 | .. |
| Actor, Comedian, Dancer, Nautch Girl | 197 | 116 | 81 |
| Snake Charmer | 121 | 80 | 41 |
| Devil Dancer | 1,532 | 1,528 | 4 |
| Inspector of Schools, Schoolmaster, Teacher, Schoolmistress | 2,720 | 2,185 | 535 |
| Astrologer | 201 | 201 | .. |
| **II.—Domestic Class.** | | | |
| Hotel—Manager, Keeper; Boarding-house, Rest-house, Eating-house Keeper | 712 | 477 | 235 |
| Domestic Servant (General) | 42,175 | 24,255 | 17,920 |
| Groom (Horsekeeper) | 2,[illegible]57 | 2,657 | .. |
| Wash-house Service | 87 | 62 | 25 |
| Barber | 1,898 | 1,851 | 47 |
| **III.—Commercial Class.** | | | |
| Merchant | 255 | 254 | 1 |
| Commission Agent, Broker | 249 | 244 | 5 |
| Accountant, Book-keeper | 908 | 908 | .. |
| Clerk (so returned) | 2,498 | 2,498 | .. |
| Shopkeeper (branch undefined) | 582 | 581 | 1 |
| Boutique-keeper | 15,573 | 13,101 | 2,472 |

| Principal Occupations. | All Races. | | |
|---|---|---|---|
| | Persons. | Males. | Females. |
| **III.—Commercial Class** (*continued*). | | | |
| General Trader | 19,770 | 16,676 | 3,094 |
| Petty Trader | 5,642 | 4,984 | 658 |
| Basket Woman | 2,512 | .. | 2,512 |
| Toll Renter, Toll Collector | 205 | 205 | .. |
| Carter | 9,081 | 9,081 | .. |
| Tavalan Man | 927 | 926 | 1 |
| Pingo Bearer | 286 | 286 | .. |
| Boatman | 2,214 | 2,214 | .. |
| Seaman (ashore) | 719 | 719 | .. |
| Storekeeper | 271 | 271 | .. |
| Messenger, Porter, Errand Boy | 799 | 792 | 7 |
| **IV.—Agricultural Class.** | | | |
| Land Proprietor | 1,977 | 452 | 1,525 |
| Planter | 1,966 | 1,966 | .. |
| Coffee Planter | 174 | 174 | .. |
| Coco-nut Planter | 101 | 101 | .. |
| Tobacco Gardener | 475 | 475 | .. |
| Estate Superintendent | 171 | 171 | .. |
| Estate Conductor | 742 | 742 | .. |
| Cultivator | 480,189 | 480,189 | .. |
| Garden Cultivator | 9,197 | 9,197 | .. |
| Coffee Garden Cultivator | 755 | 755 | .. |
| Agricultural Labourer | 166,421 | 103,674 | 62,747 |
| Climber | 6,872 | 6,872 | .. |
| Cowherd, Shepherd | 2,687 | 2,459 | 228 |
| Land Surveyor | 118 | 118 | .. |
| Grass—Cutter, Seller | 779 | 427 | 352 |
| Hunter | 310 | 310 | .. |
| Farrier, Veterinary Surgeon | 199 | 199 | .. |
| Horse, Cattle—Trader | 942 | 941 | 1 |
| Fisherman | 20,020 | 19,930 | 90 |
| **V.—Industrial Class.** | | | |
| Bookbinder | 103 | 103 | .. |
| Printer, Compositor | 851 | 851 | .. |
| Watch Repairer | 75 | 75 | .. |
| Fitter | 202 | 202 | .. |
| Saddle, Harness, Whip—Maker | 88 | 88 | .. |
| Carpenter | 14,477 | 14,475 | 2 |
| Mason | 5,012 | 5,012 | .. |
| Painter, Plumber | 361 | 361 | .. |
| Dyer | 304 | 266 | 38 |
| Dye-root—Digger, Seller | 464 | 175 | 289 |
| Cotton Spinner, Thread Manufacturer | 1,588 | 22 | 1,566 |
| Cloth Weaver | 1,616 | 1,471 | 145 |
| Lace—Manufacturer, Seller | 563 | 4 | 559 |
| Weaver (not otherwise described) | 91 | 15 | 76 |
| Draper, Cloth Dealer | 3,042 | 3,035 | 7 |
| Tailor, Milliner, Seamstress | 5,300 | 1,405 | 3,895 |
| Shoe, Sandal—Maker | 644 | 644 | .. |
| Dhoby | 17,297 | 10,622 | 6,675 |
| Mat, Basket—Maker, Seller | 14,671 | 442 | 14,229 |
| Hemp Manufacturer | 940 | 15 | 925 |
| Coir—Manufacturer, Dealer | 15,672 | 1,168 | 14,504 |
| Milk, Butter—Seller | 359 | 255 | 104 |
| Butcher, Meat Salesman | 667 | 665 | 2 |

| Principal Occupations. | All Races. | | |
|---|---|---|---|
| | Persons. | Males. | Females. |
| **V.—Industrial Class (*continued*).** | | | |
| Poultry, Egg—Seller | 216 | 212 | 4 |
| Fishmonger | 3,680 | 1,958 | 1,722 |
| Rice, Paddy, Grain—Seller | 4,712 | 2,023 | 2,689 |
| Gram Seller | 234 | 10 | 224 |
| Baker, Bread Seller, Rice-cake Seller, Coffee-boutique Keeper | 4,566 | 1,091 | 3,475 |
| Confectioner | 202 | 142 | 60 |
| Vegetable Dealer | 1,035 | 587 | 448 |
| Coco-nut, Koppara—Seller | 1,150 | 845 | 305 |
| Arrack Distiller | 99 | 98 | 1 |
| Liquor—Shopkeeper, Seller | 139 | 139 | .. |
| Arrack Renter, Tavern Keeper, Arrack Seller | 862 | 854 | 8 |
| Toddy Drawer | 3,280 | 3,280 | .. |
| Jaggery—Manufacturer, Seller | 416 | 233 | 183 |
| Coffee Seller | 590 | 548 | 42 |
| Coffee Picker | 2,719 | 5 | 2,714 |
| Tobacco Seller; Cigar, Snuff—Manufacturer, Dealer | 3,630 | 3,359 | 271 |
| Betel, Areca-nut—Seller | 2,810 | 1,530 | 1,280 |
| Cinnamon Seller | 214 | 214 | .. |
| Cinnamon Peeler | 1,857 | 1,777 | 80 |
| Tortoise-shell—Worker, Dealer | 336 | 334 | 2 |
| Oil—Miller, Monger | 2,305 | 1,706 | 599 |
| Timber Dealer | 801 | 801 | .. |
| Sawyer | 2,197 | 2,197 | .. |
| Cooper | 828 | 828 | .. |
| Timber Feller | 561 | 561 | .. |
| Firewood—Cutter, Seller | 463 | 175 | 288 |
| Cane—Worker, Dealer | 165 | 157 | 8 |
| Cadjan—Maker, Seller | 168 | 29 | 139 |
| Straw Seller | 153 | 149 | 4 |
| Plumbago Dealer | 90 | 90 | .. |
| Plumbago—Digger, Picker | 1,419 | 1,323 | 96 |
| Charcoal Burner | 102 | 81 | 21 |
| Stone—Cutter, Breaker, Seller | 1,034 | 909 | 125 |
| Brick, Tile—Maker, Seller | 481 | 477 | 4 |
| Lime—Burner, Seller | 944 | 677 | 267 |
| Road Labourer | 4,136 | 2,886 | 1,250 |
| Railway Labourer | 6,769 | 4,599 | 2,170 |
| Potter, Earthenware Dealer | 5,887 | 3,593 | 2,294 |
| Salt Dealer | 419 | 335 | 84 |
| Water—Carrier, Dealer | 147 | 132 | 15 |
| Goldsmith, Silversmith, Jeweller | 6,273 | 6,252 | 21 |
| Gem Digger | 1,135 | 1,135 | .. |
| Lapidary | 199 | 199 | .. |
| Tinker | 176 | 176 | .. |
| Brazier | 745 | 745 | .. |
| Blacksmith | 4,302 | 4,302 | .. |
| Ironmonger, Hardware Dealer | 60 | 60 | .. |
| Chanks—Fisher, Dealer | 94 | 94 | .. |
| **VI.—Indefinite and non-Productive Class.** | | | |
| General Labourer | 85,138 | 64,985 | 20,153 |
| Artizan (branch undefined) | 1,526 | 715 | 811 |
| Contractor do. | 565 | 565 | .. |
| Renter do. | 272 | 272 | .. |

# APPENDIX VII.

## STAPLE IMPORTS OF CEYLON FROM 1837 TO 1886.

### Cotton Manufactures; Rice; Fish (dried and salted); Cattle.

| Year. | Cotton Goods. | Rice. | | Fish. | | | Cattle. | |
|---|---|---|---|---|---|---|---|---|
| | Value. | Quantity. | Value. | Quantity. | | Value. | No. | Declared Value. |
| | £ | Bushels. | £ | Cwts. | Pieces. | £ | | £ |
| 1837 | 220,878 | 650,042 | 149,503 | 5,980 | 29,528 | 6,719 | | 1,801 |
| 1838 | 187,981 | 860,012 | 168,972 | 9.527 | 227,542 | 7,801 | Described as Live Stock, quantity not specified in Customs Returns. | 820 |
| 1839 | 128,607 | 884,628 | 182,800 | 8,581 | 107 | 5,674 | | 1,156 |
| 1840 | 158,326 | 1,043,064 | 202,838 | 6,949 | 72,000 | 8,946 | | 1,270 |
| 1841 | 184,691 | 1,106,152 | 188,483 | 9,996 | .. | 4,709 | | 1,727 |
| 1842 | 173,838 | 1,102,192 | 191,958 | 9,050 | .. | 6,913 | | 5,131 |
| 1843 | 160,865 | 1,594,114 | 279,128 | 7,981 | .. | 6,179 | | 7,596 |
| 1844 | 192,986 | 1,700,136 | 296,948 | 16,950 | .. | 14,670 | | 22,885 |
| 1845 | 288,554 | 2,167,884 | 879,885 | 28,028 | .. | 16,297 | | 25,557 |
| 1846 | 185,590 | 2,162,206 | 872,940 | 84,038 | .. | 17,479 | 47,287 | 28,745 |
| 1847 | 178,064 | 2,121,0?2 | 872,109 | 29,852 | .. | 16,480 | 61,594 | 28,914 |
| 1848 | 182,767 | 1,910,585 | 829,420 | 86,291 | .. | 86,848 | 47,265 | 26,425 |
| 1849 | 190,911 | 1,985,752 | 847,502 | 24,457 | .. | 24,457 | 8,895 | 17,884 |
| 1850 | 187.567 | 2,355,768 | 412,261 | 85.705 | .. | 85,705 | 8,507 | 17,120 |
| 1851 | 216,274 | 2,221,466 | 888,777 | 29,026 | .. | 29,026 | 8,994 | 17,698 |
| 1852 | 189.078 | 2,331,796 | 408,065 | 80,670 | .. | 80,670 | 7,951 | 16,368 |
| 1853 | 228,226 | 2,574,580 | 462,870 | 81,000 | .. | 81,000 | 9,295 | 18,886 |
| 1854 | 262,082 | 2,161,706 | 879,994 | 42,118 | .. | 42,118 | 12,524 | 25,268 |
| 1855 | 286.621 | 2,852,178 | 499,137 | 84,788 | .. | 84,788 | 16,584 | 83,280 |
| 1856 | 814.596 | 8,157.885 | 552,548 | 56.800 | .. | 56,800 | 11,317 | 28,515 |
| 1857 | 855,429 | 8,254,628 | 650,924 | 58,296 | .. | 53,396 | 10,575 | 21,685 |
| 1858 | 466,962 | 2,856,124 | 571,224 | 48,984 | .. | 48,984 | 11,228 | 25,119 |
| 1859 | ?80,936 | 8,511,768 | 702,854 | 58,275 | .. | 58.275 | 10,776 | 26,608 |
| 1860 | 540,284 | 8,182,204 | 636,423 | 55,989 | .. | 55,989 | 10,514 | 24,471 |
| 1861 | 567,464 | 4,181,096 | 886,219 | 61,882 | .. | 61,882 | 9,758 | 28,780 |
| 1862 | 505,844 | 4,218,601 | 1,265,581 | 61,042 | .. | 61,042 | 4,490 | 12,095 |
| 1863 | 790,408 | 4,415,821 | 1,324,745 | 60,905 | .. | 60,905 | 14,085 | 46,888 |
| 1864 | 997,272 | 8.948,896 | 1,183,019 | 75,248 | .. | 75,248 | 7,607 | 28,509 |
| 1865 | 545,044 | 4,851,414 | 1,455,424 | 66,970 | .. | 66,970 | 8,326 | 22,785 |
| 1866 | 860,310 | 8,777,820 | 1,188,196 | 70,190 | .. | 70,190 | 9,059 | 48,079 |
| 1867 | 891,776 | 4,518,827 | 1.862,998 | 71,709 | .. | 71,709 | 8,912 | 50,190 |
| 1868 | 642,802 | 4,455,315 | 1,836,594 | 78,294 | .. | 78,294 | 7,892 | 89,469 |
| 1869 | 784,921 | 4,406,216 | 1,824,418 | 75,189 | .. | 75,189 | 6,799 | 40,938 |
| 1870 | 976,987 | 4,785,892 | 1.539,145 | 76,968 | .. | 76,968 | 7,605 | 58,018 |
| 1871 | 840,917 | 4,278.708 | 1,890,580 | 78,575 | .. | 78,575 | 10,058 | 64,897 |
| 1872 | 838,400 | 5,867.302 | 1,744,878 | 88,962 | .. | 88,962 | 14,198 | 84,596 |
| 1873 | 865,060 | 5,708,142 | 1,855,146 | 108,169 | .. | 108,169 | 14,749 | 82,550 |
| 1874 | 889,851 | 5,717,775 | 1,858,277 | 98,648 | .. | 98,648 | 12,541 | 70,148 |
| 1875 | 780,903 | 5,527,620 | 1,714,762 | 86,999 | .. | 86,999 | 15,892 | 84,628 |
| 1876 | 952,510 | 5,855,645 | 1,908,084 | 87,598 | .. | 87,598 | 17,881 | 91,661 |
| 1877 | 718,289 | 6,938,160 | 2,254,902 | 98.250 | .. | 98,250 | 28,958 | 102,522 |
| 1878 | 494,210 | 6,668,969 | 2,167,414 | 84,429 | .. | 84,429 | 17,492 | 55,929 |
| 1879 | 561,552 | 5,954,934 | 1,985,854 | 74,822 | .. | 74,822 | 27,488 | 108,796 |
| 1880 | 704,889 | 6,094,999 | 1,980,875 | 90,396 | .. | 90,396 | 11,872 | 78,948 |
| 1881 | 512,878 | 6,030,820 | 1,960,017 | 91,426 | .. | 91,426 | 8,688 | 38,776 |
| 1882 | 452,112 | 5,757,025 | 1,871,088 | 92,841 | .. | 92,841 | 9,587 | 86,100 |
| 1883 | 491,799 | 5,746,184 | 1,867,510 | 120,378 | .. | 120,378 | 11,980 | 60,698 |
| 1884 | 557,382 | 5,490,768 | 1,784,500 | 101,619 | .. | 101,619 | 13,461 | 68,517 |
| 1885 | 847,212 | 5,784,129 | 1,868,592 | 127,134 | .. | 127,134 | 10,081 | 50,288 |
| 1886 | 457,292 | 5,567,100 | 1,809,307 | 118,050 | .. | 118,050 | 47,108 | 87,796 |

*Cotton Goods.*—All from England; up to the last four years, Colombo had a large trade supplying Southern India with cotton goods, but railway extension from Madras, and, above all, the abolition of customs duties on cotton in India, have taken away all this trade.

*Rice.*—All from India (mainly to feed immigrant population from India, and populations of large towns).

*Fish.*—All from India, for curries of same population.

*Cattle.*—All from India, for transport purposes and food for Europeans and Burghers.

## APPENDIX VIII.

### CEYLON: "THE EDEN OF THE EASTERN WAVE."

*The Land of Cinnamon, Palms, Tea, Coffee, Cinchona, the Chocolate Plant; Pearls, Rubies, and Sapphires; of ancient ruins second only to those of Egypt; of Tropical Scenery the finest in the world.*

[STATISTICS Arranged and Compiled by J. FERGUSON, of *Ceylon Observer* and *Tropical Agriculturist*, at the request of SIR A. N. BIRCH, K.C.M.G., Commissioner for Ceylon to the Indian and Colonial Exhibition of 1886; for exhibition in the CEYLON COURT.]*

Area in square miles ... 25,000
Population in 1887 ... 2,900,000

Divided into 8 provinces, administered by Governor and about 80 covenated Civil Servants.

*Races*:—Sinhalese, 1,930,000; Tamils, 725,000; Moormen (Arab descendants), 200,000; Eurasians, 19,000; Malays, 9,000; Europeans, 5,500; Veddahs, 2,500; others, 8,000.

*Religions*:—Buddhists, 1,760,000; Sivaites (Hindus), 600,000; Mohammedans, 200,000; Roman Catholics, 210,000; Protestants, 65,000; others, 65,000.

*Longest River*:—Mahaweliganga—150 miles (Ganges of Ptolemy).

*Highest Mountains*:—Pidurutalagala, 8,296 feet; Adam's Peak, 7,353; 150 mountain peaks from 3,000 to 7,000 feet.

* A few later results have been embodied in this page.—J. F.

*Towns*:—Capital, COLOMBO, 120,000 people, with splendid Breakwater, great steamer coaling and calling port of the East; Kandy (ancient capital), 24,000; Point-de-Galle, 35,000; Trincomalee (with grand harbour), 11,000.

*Wild Animals*:—Elephants, Cheetah, Black Bear, Buffaloe, Boar, Elk and Small Deer; Eagle; Crocodile; Shark.

*Revenue* ... ... ... ... ... £1,300,000

*Trade*:—Total Annual Trade ... ... £8,000,000

Total Imports from United Kingdom £1,250,000

Total Exports to do. ... £2,250,000

Total of Shipping entered and cleared annually, about 4,000,000 tons.

*Roads*:—2,500 miles, metalled and gravelled, among the best in the world.

*Railways*:—185 miles—first class Railway—5½ feet gauge.

*Canals*:—170 miles.

*Education*:—Total of Scholars, 120,000, or about 25 per cent. of children of school-going age; 1,200 miles of Telegraph wire; 135 Post Offices.

| | | Acres. |
|---|---|---|
| *Area Cultivated*:— ... ... ... ... | | 3,130,000 |
| Probable Extension of Cultivation within 10 years to ... ... ... ... | | 4,600,000 |
| Details of Cultivation:— | | |
| Under | Palm trees (Coco, Palmyra, Areka, Kitul, &c.) ... ... ... | 650,000 |
| Do. | Other Fruit-trees (Orange, Mango, Bread and Jak Fruit, &c.) ... | 50,000 |
| Do. | Rice ... ... ... ... | 660,000 |
| Do. | Other Grain ... ... ... | 150,000 |
| Do. | Garden vegetables, (Cassava, Yams, &c. ... ... ... | 100,000 |
| Do. | Coffee, Arabian and Liberian ... | 130,000 |
| Do. | Tea ... ... ... ... | 150,000 |
| | (to rise shortly to | 200,000) |
| Do. | Cinnamon, Cardamom, and other Spices ... ... ... ... | 60,000 |
| Do. | Chocolate plants (Cacao) ... ... | 15,000 |
| Do. | Cinchona Bark (Quinine) trees ... | 40,000 |
| Do. | Tobacco ... ... ... ... | 25,000 |
| Do. | Rubber and Gum trees ... ... | 5,000 |
| Do. | Fibre-yielding plants ... ... | 10,000 |
| Do. | Essential oil-grass (Citronella) ... | 20,000 |

*Exports* of Tea have risen from 25,000lb. in 1878 to 4,873,000lb. in 1885, and to 7,850,000lb. in 1886; expected to reach 24,000,000lb. in 1888; and 40,000,000lb. in 1890.

Do. of Cinchona Bark have risen from 200,000lb. in 1878 to 14,700,000lb. in 1886.

Do. of Cocoa (from Cacao plant) from 10 cwt. in 1878 to 13,056 cwt. in 1886.

Do. of Cardamoms (Spice) from 14,000lb. in 1878 to 239,000lb. in 1886.

Do. of Cinnamon from 650,000lb. in 1850 to 2¼ million lb. of late years.

Do. of Coconut Oil has risen to 400,000 cwt. from 35,000 cwt. in 1850.

Total crop of Coconuts in one year is equal to 700,000,000 nuts.

200,000 Tamil Coolies find work on plantations; likely to require 300,000 ere long with tea.

---

## SUMMARY OF INFORMATION REGARDING CEYLON.

ITS NATURAL FEATURES, CLIMATE, PROGRESS, AGRICULTURE, COMMERCE, INDUSTRIES, PUBLIC WORKS, RELIGIONS, SIGHTS, &c.

[Compiled and corrected up to March, 1887, by A. M. & J. Ferguson.]

CEYLON [part, as many believe, of the region known to the Hebrews as Ophir and Tarshish]:—Taprobanê of the Greeks and Romans (from Tâmraparni, *Sanskrit*, and Tambapani, *Pali*); Serendib of the Arab voyagers; Lankâ of the Continental Hindus and the Sinhalese; Ilangei of the Tamils; Lankâpura of the Malays; Tewalanká of the Siamese; Seho or Teho of the Burmese; Ceilao of the Portuguese, &c. Pearliform Island ("pearl-drop on the brow of Ind"), bounded by the Indian Ocean, Bay of Bengal, and Gulf of Mannar; greatest length and breadth 267 by 140 miles; circumference, 760 miles. Lat. 5° 53' to 9° 51" N.; Long. 79° 41' 4" to 81° 54' 50" E. Sun rises 5½ hours before he shines on Britain. Light from 6 to 6 nearly all the year round; but the sun sets about 42 minutes later in July than in November, indeed twilight in June occasionally exists till after 7 p.m.

### AREA.

About 24,702 square miles; or 15,809,280 acres, of which about one-sixth comprises hilly and mountainous zones, lying in the centre of the southern half of the island. Maritime districts generally level, and northern end of island broken up into flat narrow peninsula and small islets.

### DISTANCES

(approximate): from nearest point of Southern India, *via* "Adam's Bridge" and Ramisseram to Tallaimanaar, 60 miles; from Madras to Point Pedro, 250; to Galle, 545.—To Colombo: from Tuticorin, 450; Madras, 615; Calcutta, 1,385; Bombay, 900; Aden, 2,400; Suez, 3,800; Port Said, 3,950; Malta, 4,550; Gibraltar, 1,950; Brindisi, 4,500; Marseilles, 5,750; Cape, 5,000; England by Cape, 15,000; by Suez Canal to Southampton, 6,500; from Mauritius *via* Aden, 4,500; direct, about 2,500; Singapore, 1,600; Hong Kong, 3,000; Yokohama, Japan, 4,700; Freemantle, Western Australia, 3,000; King George's Sound or Albany, 3,400; Adelaide, 4,400; Melbourne, 4,900; Sydney, 5,450 (*via* Torres Straits, 6,500); Brisbane, *via* Torres Straits, 5,900; New Zealand (Auckland) 7,000 miles. The distances generally are counted from Colombo.

### HIGHEST MOUNTAINS.

Pidurutalagala (rising over the Sanatarium of Ceylon, Nuwara Eliya) 8,296 feet, or nearly 1,000 feet higher than Adam's Peak (7,353), usually described as the highest, because it is to voyagers the most conspicuous mountain in Ceylon. This latter is really the fifth in altitude, being inferior to Kirigalpotta (7,832), Totapola (7,746), and Kuduhugala (7,607), as well as to Pidurutalagala. Fully 150 mountains, ranging from 3,000 to 7,000 feet. (245 recorded trigonometrical altitudes over 1,000 feet, 145 over 3,000 feet, 118 over 4,000 feet, 53 over 5,000 feet, 28 over 6,000 feet, and 10 over 7,000 feet.) Most of the mountain ranges on which tea and cinchona or coffee is cultivated are wooded to their summits; but vast prairie tracts of hill region, chiefly on the eastern side, bear little beyond coarse lemon-grass. Mountain scenery generally rich and grand.

### GREATEST RIVERS AND WATERFALLS.

The Mahaweliganga (Ganges of Ptolemy), nearly 150 miles from its source, in its longest feeder the Agra-oya under Kirigalpotta (the "milk-stone-book" mountain) close to Horton's Plains, to its double debouchure near the great harbour of Trincomalee on the east coast. This river drains nearly one-sizth of the area of the island. Rivers not naturally favourable for navigation, except near the sea, where they expand into backwaters. Steam navigation by means of small vessels introduced on Colombo lake, between Colombo and Negombo on canal, and shortly expected on Kaluganga, and on Kelani river to Awisawella. The Kelani entering sea near Colombo; Kaluganga at Kalutara; Mahaoya, near Negombo; the Ginganga, near Galle; Walawe-oya near Matara, are some of the other numerous rivers. Rivers in mountain regions frequently fall over precipices, forming beautiful waterfalls. One in Dimbula and another in lower Maskeliya, both between 200 and 300 feet high; in Eastern Haputale one said to be 535 feet; and the foot of Ramboda Pass, celebrated for a series of beautiful falls. No proper surveys available; but a series of cascade-falls on Kurunduoya in Maturata measured from top to bottom, when nearly full of water, about 920 feet. In the arid regions of the north of the island some of the river beds which run full of water in the rainy months of the north-east monsoon (middle of October to middle of January) show only expanses of sand with a few pools in the dry or south-west monsoon season, during which the north-east of the island is almost rainless, while torrents are deluging the south-west coast.

### LAKES.

None inland, but ruins of magnificent tanks (Sea of Prakkrama, Minneriya, Kanthalai, Giant's Tank, &c.) in north and east of island; and fine, extensive backwaters on the sea-coast, such as the Negombo Lake, the Lakes of Bolgoda, Mullaittivu, Batticaloa, &c. The freshwater lakes, which add so much to the beauty of Colombo, Kandy, and Nuwara Eliya are artificial or partly so. The Labugama Reservoir for the Colombo Water Supply, covering 176 acres, among hills, 30 miles from Colombo, forms a beautiful lake.

### TIDES.

Generally almost imperceptible (at Colombo the rise and fall never exceed 3 feet, more generally 2 feet to 2 feet 6 inches on the springs, and 6 to 9 inches on the neaps), but in the debouchures of some backwaters and rivers the tide is more noticeable: at Panadure the tidal current runs in at the rate of 4 miles an hour. Powerful currents also sweep round the coasts, some of them owing their origin to the Indian Ocean.

### GEOLOGY AND MINERALOGY.

The geological formations met with in Ceylon are of the Palæozoic, Mezozoic and recent age. The greatest portion of the island consists of ancient sedimentary beds, doubtful whether deposited sea or lake, as metamorphoses havè obliterated all traces of fossil remains. Mountain ranges formed of primary and metamorphic rock. Principal rock: gneiss, with beds of laterite (locally named "cabook") and dolomite, according to some authorities—described by others as crystalline marble or primary limestone. Plenty of iron, but no trace of coal. Manganese, gold and platinum, but in such small quantities not apparently worth gathering. Molybdenum, cobalt, nickel, tin, copper, and arsenic also occur. Plumbago the only mineral of commercial importance. Cretaceous beds of Jaffna of Mezozoic age. Nitre in caves. Salt forms naturally, and is also manufactured in sufficient quantity at Puttalam, Jaffna, and Hambantota, to supply the consumption of the island. Calcareous tufa met with at Bintenna deposited from warm springs. Hot springs at Trincomalee and other places, but no direct evidence of present volcanic action (unless in Kelebokka valley), and earthquakes seldom perceptible, save as the outer verge of disturbances in Java and Eastern Archipelago. Greenstone, however, underlies gneiss at Kadugannawa, and with vitrefactions is observed in fissures of rocks at Trincomalee. Springs of sulphuretted hydrogen similar to Harrogate water occur in Puttalam district. Large tracts of alluvium occur in the Nuwara Eliya and other districts. Process of slow upheaval believed to be in operation on western coast, with compensating disintegration of mountain ranges. Recent formation: a breccia formed of particles of disintegrated rock held together by calcareous and ferruginous matter near Negombo and along coast. Gems abundant, especially about Ratnapura ("city of gems"), but, with exception of blue sapphire and red ruby, of slight value. A flawless sapphire is rare, and good rubies are excessively scarce. Zircon or "Matara Diamond," and amethyst, common. Chrysoberyl (or "cat's-eye") not uncommon, curious, and of late years prized in Britain. Moonstones (very beautiful form of "adularia") and "cinnamon stones" (brown garnets) common. Spinel and tourmaline very abundant. Many rocks and river beds sparkle with red garnets, beautiful but intrinsically valueless. Ceylon celebrated for fine pearls, chiefly from oyster or mussel banks of north-west coast. Gemming license in Ceylon is R10 per annum, subject to certain published rules.

## CLIMATE.

Varies in different parts, from hot and arid plains of north and east, to warm and humid south-west coast, and cool and wet mountain regions; but, for the tropics, generally healthy. Fever zone extends below middle altitudes of mountain ranges, and banks of rivers frequently unhealthy. Fever seldom or never occurs above 3,000 feet altitude, and is rare within the influence of the sea breezes. The hot months at Colombo are February, March and April, and sometimes (when the monsoon is delayed) May; when all, who can, escape to the hill regions, Nuwara Eliya especially. The heat in Ceylon, however, seldom reaches 90° in the shade: 95½° in April being the maximum in Colombo—95·8° on 22nd February, 1885, actual highest—where the mean of the year nearly touches 81°, sea-breezes tempering the heat for a large portion of the year. At Trincomalee the maximum was 101·7° on 10th May, 1886. The rate of mortality in Ceylon towns ranges from 1·65 per cent. for Jaffna (Colombo 1·76) to 4·06 for Kurunegala. The military death-rate in Ceylon is down to 25 in 1,000; and this rate is capable of still further reduction by sanitary measures. The opening of the Suez Canal and the facilities offered by steam communication have led to abandonment of Nuwara Eliya as a military sanatarium, invalid soldiers being sent "home" instead. The perfection of climate in Ceylon is supposed to be found at and around Bandarawela (distant 118 miles from Colombo), on the plateau of the Uva principality, at 3,900 feet elevation, the average temperature being 68°, with an average annual rainfall of 78 inches falling on 126 days; but the climate of Lindula, Bogawantalawa, Udapussellawa and Nuwara Eliya is also very good.

### METEOROLOGY.

Exposed to both monsoons (S.W. from April to September, N.E. from November to February), but storms seldom violent. Ceylon is most fortunate in being outside the region of the cyclones peculiar at certain seasons to the Bay of Bengal; also the hurricanes of the Mauritius seas, and the volcanic disturbances of Java and the Eastern Archipelago. Rainfall: 35 at Hambantota; 38 inches at Mannar; 48 inches at Jaffna; 53 at Anurádhapura; 52½ at Batticaloa; 61½ at Trincomalee; 78½ at Bandarawella in Uva; 81½ at Kandy; 85½ at Matale; 87½ at Colombo; 93½ at Kurunegala; 100 inches Nuwara Eliya; 106½ at Kalutara; 127 Ramboda; and from 117 to 150 on the Dimbula, Dikoya and Maskeliya ranges, outside the tablelands of Nuwara Eliya at 6,000 feet, and Horton Plains 7,000 feet altitude; 150½ at Ratnapura; 152½ at Nawalapitiya; 159 at Awisawella; and 200 at Templestowe, Ambagamuwa; and the maximum 228 at Padupola, northeast of Adam's Peak. In parts of Yakdessa the annual rainfall is often over 200 inches, as much as 50 inches of which have been known to fall in one month, and a dozen inches in as many hours. Temperature varies from a mean of 58° F. at the mountain sanatarium of Nuwara Eliya; 65 to 66 at Langdale, Dimbula, and at Bogawantalawa, Dikoya; a mean of 72 at Badulla, 75½ Kandy, and 81 at Colombo, 80 Galle, Ratnapura, Puttalam, Hambantota, and Anurádhapura; about 82 at Batticaloa, Jaffna, Mannar, and a fraction higher at Trincomalee. The extremes in the shade range from below freezing point at

Nuwara Eliya to 95·8 at Colombo and 101·7 at Trincomalee. Except in the north and east, climate moist as well as hot. Fertility due more to this circumstance than to richness of soil generally. Fruits of temperate regions fail from continuous warm moisture, but long-continued and extreme heat, acting as a wintering (the roots being laid bare), favours grape cultivation at Jaffna: successful growth also in Dumbera valley and near Nuwara Eliya. Snow is unknown. Hail not unfrequent in hill districts in very hot weather. Ice forms occasionally at Nuwara Eliya under clear radiating sky during the rainless months, December to February. Electrical phenomena—thunder, lightning, waterspouts, &c.—frequent and sometimes grand, and lightning occasionally destructive to life, especially to natives who climb trees or take refuge from rain under them. Coconut palms, papaya, plantain, and other pithy or sappy trees and shrubs are peculiarly fitted as lightning conductors. Lightning so frequently seen without thunder being heard, that Arabs compare a liar to Ceylon lightning. Optical phenomena, such as rainbows, Buddha rays, anthelia, mirage, occasionally very striking. Sunsets frequently beautiful, and zodiacal light sometimes seen. Moonlight and starry nights often splendid, and, when perfectly cloudless, peculiarly cool.

## BOTANY.

Ceylon, while presenting most points of resemblance in its fauna and flora to the neighbouring continent of India, differs in some respects, and assimilates to the Malayan Archipelago. There can be little or no doubt that cinnamon, for which Ceylon has always been famous, is really indigenous to this island. So doubtless, with rice. On the other hand, its best-known productions, coffee and coconuts, are introductions (the first certainly, the second also in the judgment of botanists), also tea, cacao, and cinchona. Most South American plants readily adapt themselves to the island, as is proved by the recent success of the cinchonas, cacao, and rubber trees. Tea is also growing luxuriantly in a climate peculiarly favourable to leafage. Ceylon is peculiarly noted for ferns and balsams; while orchids abound. Ebony, satin wood, and other fine cabinet woods, with serviceable timber, are plentiful in the forests. Calamander, the most beautiful of the cabinet woods, is becoming very scarce, only a few trees being reported as left. In the higher mountain regions, familiar European forms mingle with the richest tropical vegetation. Palms and bamboos are specially beautiful and luxuriant: few objects in nature being more magnificent than a talipot palm in flower, and few more elegant than the slender areka palm, or the tall bending green bamboo of the mountain forests below Nuwara Eliya. The coconut palm luxuriates along the western and south-western coasts, and indeed far inland up the river valleys, just as the palmyra, with its 500 different uses to the natives, abounds in the Jaffna peninsula. Many of the forest trees, such as the lagerstrœmia regina, red rhododendron, and scarlet-blossomed cotton tree, bear beautiful flowers; while the vari-coloured foliage of the jungle cinnamon, ironwood, &c., relieve the deep green of the forest, looking at a distance like rich floral masses. There are few parts of the world so rich in fungi as Ceylon, and one, new to science, has within the past generation, almost annihilated the great coffee enterprise of the island. Backwaters are rich in mangroves. Some of the seaweeds are also very beautiful. The indigenous species of plants enumerated by Dr. Trimen, of the Royal Botanic Gardens, Peradeniya, include:—Dicotyledons, 2,019; Monocotyledons, 710; Filices, Lycopodiaceæ, and Marsileaceæ, 260—total 2,989: double the flora of Britain, and about one-thirtieth of all species in the world yet described.

### ANIMALS.

Monkeys are numerous, five species of wanderoo (langurs), of which no less than four are recognized as peculiar to the island. The capped-monkey (macacus) famous for its grimaces, and capacity for learning tricks; the loris, a queer creature, the eyes much valued as medicine by the natives! Bats are very numerous in genera and species, flying foxes (pteropus) vampires, leaf-nosed, horse-shoe, and the beautiful painted bat, and others; musk and other shrews plentiful, a hill species peculiar to the island; the sloth-bear common in the low country; jackals everywhere; otters common in suitable places, from the shores to the highest hills; no tigers or lions (though the native name of the people signifies the "lion descended"); the panther or leopard (erroneously called cheetah locally) is the largest feline, and is common in most places; the tiger and red-spotted cats generally distributed; lesser civet numerous, its presence being often betrayed by its powerful scent; a paradoxurus, peculiar to the island, and palm cat common; mongooses numerous of five species, a very distinct one (onychogale Maccarthia of Gray) peculiar to the island; squirrels abound, two species of the remarkable flying squirrel, several small and pretty ground squirrels (equally at home on trees as well) can be seen and heard on all sides, and are amusing to watch; rats and mice only too numerous, the jeeboa or jumping rats, bandicoot and bush or coffee rat may be mentioned, a rat and a mouse also peculiar to the island; the porcupine generally found through hill and lowlands, as is also the black-necked hare; that strange mail-covered but toothless creature, the pangolin, is found up to a considerable elevation, as well as in the low country. Elephants, the lords of the forest, specially famous, are found from the sea-coast to the highest points of the island, are said to be decreasing in some districts, but still numerous in others. [Large numbers formerly killed by sportsmen; 1,600 (captured by being snared, or enclosed in kraals) exported to India from Northern Province in five years ended 1862. A license now required to shoot elephants, and the number killed or captured has much decreased: only 1,685 exported in eighteen years, from 1862 to 1880, valued at R452,000, a royalty of R200 for every elephant exported having no doubt checked the trade. Royalty reduced to R100 in 1882; exports in six years, 1880 to 1885, equalled 182 elephants, R96,885.] The wild boar common everywhere; buffaloes common in the wilder parts still, but their numbers much reduced during the last decade or two from disease and the rifle. Of deer, the fine sambur (locally elk), the spotted, the paddy-field, the red (rumtjae) and little mouse-deer (miminna) still common, and afford good sport to the hunter. Whales, dugongs, porpoises, and dolphins represent the marine carnivora which sport around the coast, where also the screaming cries of sea-eagles and the osprey may be heard, which find their "echo" in the distant hills from the large beautiful crested eagle peculiar to Ceylon, and others of the family; peregrine falcons have their stations here and there; kestrels, harriers, and many species of hawks numerous; owls of many species, from the fine forest-eagle owl to the little scops, not forgetting the renowned devil-bird, all fairly numerous; the sportsman is attracted by the numerous pea-fowls, jungle, and spur-fowl (these two peculiar to Ceylon), and quails, which are common in many places. The frog-mouth and several goatsuckers, swifts, including the species remarkable for making edible nests, swallows common, rollers, kingfishers, bee-eaters, the scarlet-breasted trogan, several species of sun bird (called humming birds locally), represent the feathered beauties of the Island; tailor and weaver birds, the wonderful nest builders, wagtails, and warblers in winter only (so they sing not here), but remind Europeans of sweet home; many varieties of thrushes, bablers, orioles, bulbuls, flycatchers, chats, and drongos everywhere; the splendid mountain jay and its sober-coloured friend the grey starling are peculiar to the island; grakles, munias (locally ortolans), larks, and pipits numerous; parakeets, hornbills, barbets, and gaudy woodpeckers, each having representatives peculiar to the island, and many other species so common as to be a marked feature in woodland retreats of hill and dale; a beautiful woodpigeon, paraquets, peculiar to Ceylon, the rock-pigeon, many species of fruit pigeons and doves, a titmouse, a lovely nuthatch, crows and shrikes, the ubiquitous magpie robin, the long-tailed jungle robin, and blackbird are fine songsters, the jungle robin inferior only to the nightingale itself; many others have songs, like Annie Laurie's, low and sweet, so are not noticed by casual observers. Not less interesting and extensive is the list of marsh and sea birds: the famous Marabon and other storks, the gigantic and other herons, beautiful egrets and bitterns of several species, the painted and other snipes, sandpipers, plover, dotterel, the cock of the reeds, the purple and other gallimules, and rails numerous in suitable places. The singular jacanus or water-pheasant, the scarlet flamingo, ducks of many kinds, the dab-chick, gulls, terns, snake-birds (darter), cormorants, and pelicans common round the coast and tanks; frigate-birds and petrels occasionally, altogether making up a wonderfully diversified list of fur and feathers for so small an area, over 360 species of birds having been recognized to date, of which no less than 45 are believed to be peculiar to the island.

The following reptiles are found in Ceylon:—Land tortoise, one; fresh water, one; fresh water turtle, one; marine turtles, four; crocodiles, two; water lizards, two; skinks, five; acontiads, four; geckos, sixteen; agames (or bloodsuckers), fifteen; chameleon, one; snakes of fifteen different groups, about sixty, eight of which are venemous and three deadly, whilst about twenty-three sea snakes are found on the coast, all said to be deadly. Of ground and tree frogs, forty; and one burrowing batrachian.

River fish, chiefly carp, are few in number and of inferior quality. Better kinds might be introduced: perches introduced Nuwera Eliya lake, and experiment with trout about to be made. There are from 500 to 700 different kinds of sea fish, mainly species of mackerel, to which the salmon-like seer-fish belongs, with sharks and rays. No cod, but sword and saw fish, mullet, perches, lobsters, crabs, prawns, "bêche de mer," chanks, edible and pearl oysters. Sea and land shells numerous and beautiful. The floor of the sea in certain parts is studded with richly-coloured corallines and the softer zoophytes, while the waters swarm with star and jelly fish and infusoria, so that frequently the waves, in breaking, display a line of phosphorescence, chiefly caused by the noctiluca miliaris.

Perhaps there is no sea-coast in the world richer in fishes and shells, and some of the fishes described have a right to the title "odd." Mr. Edgar Layard has described perches which "walk across country" (allied to those which Dr. John, of Tranquebar, found climbing palmyra trees); and the late Rev. B. Boake made acquaintance with air-breathing species which flourish in mud, but drown in pure water, and others which, disdaining the marsupial pouch possessed by the "sea-horses," carry their young in their mouths. Fishes actually live in the hot wells near Trincomalee in a temperature of 115°. The natives of Ceylon are great consumers of fish, the Buddhists salving their consciences by the subterfuge that they do not kill the fish, they only take them out of the water.

Myriads of insects, including butterflies, beetles, bees,

wasps, mosquitoes; white, black and red ants; ticks, scorpions, centipedes, tarantulas, multitudes of curious spiders, &c., are found in Ceylon, and the periodical swarms of butterflies, which proceed in the teeth of the prevailing winds, are peculiarly interesting. Many of the butterflies, moths (including atlas moth, cinnamon moth, and the variety which yields the *tusser* silk), beetles, and dragon-flies, are exceedingly beautiful. Efforts to domesticate bees have not been very successful hitherto: two or three wild varieties. Leaf-insects and "praying mantis" curious, and whole regions resound to the incessant noise of the cicada or "knife-grinder." Coconut beetles, cockchafers and their grubs, and coccus, known as coffee bug, very injurious. Grasshoppers and locusts occasionally destructive over limited areas. A species of wasp builds pendant nests (chiefly on coconut trees) six feet long. Spiders' webs sometimes so numerous, large and strong as almost to check the progress of travellers through forests. Land leeches excessively troublesome in the damp forests of the lower hills; Indian medicinal leech common.

## HISTORICAL NOTES.

From conquest by Wijaya, Prince from Northern India, about B.C. 543, to deposition of Sri Wikrama Raja Sinha, last King of Kandy, in 1815, Sinhalese annals record one hundred and sixty sovereigns. Portuguese first visited Ceylon 1505, erected fort at Colombo 1518. Dutch first visited Ceylon 1602, landed forces in 1640, and ousted the Portuguese in 1658, so that Portuguese occupation lasted 140 years. Dating from their landing in 1640 to the capitulation of Colombo in 1796, the Dutch occupation lasted 156 years; or 138, if the 18 years of warfare with the Portuguese are excluded. Acquired by England: Maritime Provinces, 1796 (separated from Madras Presidency and made Crown Colony 1798); Kandyan Kingdom, 1815. Torture, compulsory labour, and slavery, successively abolished 1803, 1832, and 1844. Trial by jury introduced 1811. Kandyan polyandry and polygamy (prematurely) prohibited 1856; law relaxed 1869. There was a formidable rebellion in 1817–18 in the Kandyan Provinces, and again a feeble rising, also of Kandyans, in 1848. The Kandyans, equally with the rest of the population of

Ceylon, are now loyal, contented, and pacific, so that the small military force (about 1,000 infantry and artillery) which the colony supports is scarcely required, since about 760 volunteers (Ceylon Light Infantry) and a strong body (1,500) of police are more than sufficient for the repression of any possible internal disturbance (religious or rice riots the only public form experienced), and it is believed for repelling (with the artillery), what we may deem impossible, sudden piratical attack. Ceylon, out of her small force, yielded valuable aid to India in repressing the mutiny of 1857, and Colombo has been found a convenient depôt for the dispatch of troops with reference to wars in China, New Zealand, Egypt, and South Africa, for which parts regiments have been taken from Ceylon.

### ANTIQUITIES.

Besides tanks, important and ancient Hindu and Buddhist temples and other ruins at Dondra, Anuradhapura, Polonnaruwa, Mihintalle, Segiri, &c., the Jetawanarama Dagoba at Anuradhapura, originally 316, is still 269 feet high, or more than half the altitude of the great Egyptian Pyramid, diameter at base 396 feet, side of square 779 feet. The sacred bo-tree (*ficus religiosa*) at this place is believed to be one of the oldest historical trees in the world, perhaps over 2,100 years. The Maligawa at Kandy is famous as containing the so-called tooth of Buddha—a piece of discoloured ivory. At Dambulla is a vast rock temple; while the small Aluwihara, near Matale, is interesting as the place where the Buddhist doctrines are said to have been reduced to writing about a century B.C. [*See* Burrow's "Buried Cities of Ceylon."]

### POPULATION.

(*Results of Census of* 1881: 1 per cent. can be added for each year since.)

2,759,738 (over 2,900,000 probably in 1887): 112 to square mile, ranging from 16 in North-Central Province to 216 in Western. *Races* (estimated): Sinhalese (Kandyan and maritime), 1,846,000; Tamils, 687,240; Moormen, 184,600; Malays, 18,895; Javanese, Kafirs or Negroes, Afghans, Arabs, Persians, Parsees, &c., 7,849; Veddahs, 2,228; European descendants, 17,886; Europeans, 4,836.

[About 200,000 of the Tamils are *immigrants*, balance of nearly 3 millions who came from Southern India (chiefly to labour temporarily on coffee estates) in 45 years ending 1885, and who have settled down here; besides which there is a floating Tamil population of nearly 200,000 more. Nearly one-fourth of the Europeans are *military* and families. Effective *military* number about 1,000. *Native soldiery* (since the disbandment of the Ceylon Rifle Regiment) consist of 88 Hindu gun lascars. *Total Military* (volunteers: European and native), with women and children, say 1,800. Constituents of *European* population, wives and families included: Military, 1,250; planters, 4,000; colonial service (civil servants proper number only 75, with 15 writers) 900; merchants and their employés, clergymen, physicians, storekeepers, railway employés, &c., 1,200. There are of all classes about 3,400 lawyers, advocates, and proctors in Ceylon, with 600 notaries; 300 clergymen and missionaries (450 in census); 155 physicians and surgeons (besides 3,000 native vederales); 200 justices of the peace and unofficial magistrates.]

### POLITICAL DIVISIONS.

[The latest regular Census was that of 1881.]

Eight provinces, viz.: Western, 3,456 miles; 897,329 population; 260 to square mile. North-Western, 3,024 miles; 293,327 population; 97 to square mile. Southern, 1,980 miles; 433,520 population; 219 to square mile. Eastern, 367 miles; 127,555 population; 35 to square mile. Northern, 3,171 miles; 302,500 population; 95 to square mile. Central (as reduced), 2,003 miles; 310,000 population. North-Central, 4,067 miles; 66,146 population; 16 to square mile. At the beginning of 1886, the Uva Principality was separated from the Central Province and made an eighth province, of 165,672 population and 4,026 square miles in area. Provinces sub-divided into korales or counties, and minor divisions, such as pattus, &c. [Besides municipalities and local boards in the chief towns, and "gansabawas" or rural village councils, there are also judicial divisions and circuits, liable to change, the enumeration of which would convey little definite information.]

### CHIEF TOWNS.

Colombo, according to census of 1881, with military and shipping added, 111,942 in area of 9½ square miles; Galle, 33,000; Kandy, 22,000; Jaffna, 40,000; Batticaloa, 6,700; Kurunegala, 4,222; Anuradhapura, 1,300; Badulla, 4,746. [The above are the capitals of the provinces. Negombo, Ratnapura, Kalutara, Panadure, and Moratuwa in the Western Province; Gampola, Matale, Nawalapitiya, Nuwara Eliya, and Hatton in the Central; Kalpitiya, Chilaw, and Puttalam in the North-Western; Point Pedro in the Northern; Matara, Ambalangoda and Baddegama in the Southern Province; Haldumulla and Lunugalla in the Uva Province are, some of them, of more importance as regards population than the provincial capitals, while Trincomalee (population 10,180), though no longer the chief seat of civil government in the Eastern Province, continues to be of importance as the naval head-quarters of the East Indian fleet, although now that Colombo, with convenient harbour works, has been made the mail-steamer port, it is expected the naval station will ere long be transferred to it, especially if a graving dock is constructed.]

### RELIGIONS.

Estimated: *Romanists*, about 218,000. *Protestants:* Episcopalians, 22,000; Wesleyans, 20,000; Scotch and Dutch Presbyterians, and Congregationalists (latter converts of American mission), 13,000; Baptists, 5,000. *Total Protestants*, 60,000. *Total Christians*, 278,000. Buddhists and demon-worshippers, 1,700,000; Gentoos (worshippers of Siva, Vishnu, Pulleiyar, and other gods of the Hindu pantheon), 595,000; Muhammadans, 198,000. So that we get 278,000 Christians against 198,000 Muhammadens, and no less than 2,300,000 idolators and demon-worshippers. [We rank as Christians 170,000 Sinhalese, 85,000 Tamils, 17,800 European descendants, 4,800 Europeans, and a few Kafirs, Veddas, and Rodiyas.] The proportion of Christians to whole population (nearly 10 per cent.) is far higher in Ceylon than in India, where those professing Christianity do not much exceed half-a-million out of the whole 250 millions or more. Ceylon is the classic land of Buddhism, and its fall here would influence a vast proportion of the human race (in Burmah, Siam, and China).

The King of Siam frequently sends offerings to the "Temple of the Sacred Tooth," in Kandy; also the Kings of Burmah, up till Thebaw's dethronement, and so interested in Ceylon was a late King of Burmah, that he had copies of the *Observer* newspaper translated for his benefit into Burmese. There were 6,300 Buddhist, 1,200 Hindu, and 521 Muhammedan priests returned in last census; besides 300 of temple servants, 140 tom-tom beaters, 1,532 devil dancers, 200 astrologers, 200 actors and nautch dancers, 120 snake charmers, 168 musicians. The total for church and chapel "service" was 110, besides 422 missionaries, clergymen, and ministers, including natives.

### LANGUAGES AND LITERATURE.

*Sinhalese*, founded on the Sanskrit, with a considerable infusion of Pali, and therefore belonging to the Indo-European family; but peculiar, except in its Sanskrit roots, to Ceylon. A Dravidian origin has been claimed for the language, but, as Spence Hardy shrewdly pointed out, all the names of places, mountains, and rivers are Sanskrit. *Tamil*, the leading branch of the Dravidian family, common to about 16 millions of people in Southern India and Ceylon. Spoken by the Moormen as well as the Tamils proper. A Portuguese patois still retains its hold amongst the European descendants, but Dutch has gone entirely out. Knowledge of English rapidly advancing in towns and villages. Historical and Buddhistical literature generally in Pali, with Sinhalese translations, commentaries, and glosses. Translation of *Mahâvansa* by Turnour (now being continued by Mudaliyar Wijesinghe) throws a flood of light on the history of Ceylon and India, while researches of Gogerly and writings of Spence Hardy and others have done equal service in revealing the true nature of the atheistical system of philosophy called Buddhism. Goldschmidt and Müller have more recently, by examining and interpreting rock inscriptions, illustrated the history of the Sinhalese language, though not much new matter has been added by their researches to the history of the country and people. Works on medicine and science, generally in Sanskrit, and almost wholly derived from India. Three daily English newspapers [the daily and weekly (foreign and local) *Observer* having by far the largest circulation], with weekly editions, published in Colombo, meet with fair and increasing support; also a bi-weekly English journal in Colombo, and the weekly *Government Gazette;* a Jaffna weekly paper; and several periodicals in English, organs of churches, missions, &c.; and a native press, Sinhalese and Tamil, with a few representatives in newspapers and periodicals. Among English periodicals the *Tropical Agriculturist* (monthly), begun in June, 1881, has an extending circulation throughout the tropics, and is regarded even among London publishers as a credit to Ceylon; a weekly Ceylon *Literary Register* was begun as supplement to *Observer* in August, 1886. An interesting collection of palm-leaf MSS. exists in the library of the Colombo museum.

### EDUCATION.

Through the agency of a Government Department of Public Instruction and a grant-in-aid system, chiefly availed of by the various missionary societies, about 120,000 children, or 1 in 24 of the population, are receiving instruction in English and the vernaculars. Private schools not connected with missionaries or religious bodies, are few and ill-supported. A knowledge of vernacular reading and writing, generally very imperfect, is communicated in some of the Buddhist temple "pansalas" and private native schools. A large proportion of the population can sign their names who can do little more. Education in missionary schools is, of course, strictly Christian. In Government schools the custom is, where no objection is offered, to read the Bible during the first hour. Attendance during that hour not compulsory, but pupils seldom or never absent themselves. Cost of Government Educational Department (educating some 28,000 pupils), R300,000 per annum (besides grants-in-aid, which amount to R200,000 for 60,000 pupils), of which R28,000 is returned in the shape of fees, sales of books, &c. Total outlay on education, public and private, is about R700,000 (£70,000), against R7,000,000 (£700,000) supposed to be spent by the population on intoxicating drinks. Science is now practically taught in the principal educational establishments in the chief towns, and technical training in agriculture and useful trades is gradually being added. Government grants, aggregating R8,000 per annum, are distributed among eighteen public libraries. The census gives about 3,000 teachers, &c., male and female, in Ceylon.

### OCCUPATIONS.

Vast majority of inhabitants engaged in agriculture: 650,000 in census. Settled inhabitants (Sinhalese and Tamil) cultivate chiefly rice and other grain, with coconuts, palmyras, arecas, other palms, fruit trees and vegetables; while 250,000 Tamil coolies (native born and immigrants), superintended by Europeans, grow on plantations, chiefly tea, with the old staple coffee, to which have, of late years, been added cinchona, Liberian coffee, cacao, rubber, cardamoms, croton-oil seeds, pepper, and other new products. Rice too, and tea, bark, and coffee from plantations, are conveyed mainly by Sinhalese "bullock bandy men" or carters, where railway communication does not serve. [There are about 14,000 licensed carts, mainly employed in plantation traffic, against half that number in 1850; this is exclusive of unlicensed carts employed not only by natives but by estate owners now in very considerable numbers. Bullocks in size and strength, and carts in capacity, greatly improved.] Fisheries (12,000 boats and canoes) and small class of shipping (vessels belonging to Ceylon, number 600; tonnage 25,000) employ a good many; 25,000 fishermen and boatmen in census—below the mark. The timber trade gives employment in felling, sawing, rafting, or carting, to very many. Local manufacturing industry, advancing: carpentry, weaving, coir-matting, oil-making, &c. There were 40,000 boutique-keepers and traders returned in census; 14,000 carpenters; 5,000 masons; 18,000 dhobies; 16,000 coir-workers; 15,000 mat and basket makers; 6,000 tailors and seamstresses; 3,500 cotton and cloth spinners and weavers; 600 lacemakers; 500 printers and bookbinders; 5,000 bakers; 3,300 toddy drawers; 2,200 sawyers; 1,500 plumbago diggers; 6,500 jewellers; 1,200 gem diggers; 4,500 blacksmiths; 2,000 barbers; 3,000 horsekeepers; 43,000 domestic servants. [There are about 1,000 small looms, and 2,000 wooden or stone oil presses, or "chekkus," scattered over Ceylon; while steam and other machinery is extensively in use for preparing tea, coffee, and coir, expressing oil, sawing timber, &c.; with perhaps

200 engines, aggregating fully 3,000 h. p., and 25,000 employés. About 100,000 coffee, oil, and plumbago casks, and now many thousands of tea boxes made, besides those imported and exported each year; and many thousands of women and children, chiefly Sinhalese, find remunerative employment in "coffee picking," and preparing cinnamon and cinchona bark, coir, and coconut oil, and plumbago, and to some extent bulking and packing tea, at Colombo stores.] The planting enterprize gives employment to large numbers of mechanics, native carpenters, and masons, who also find occupation on roads and bridges, water, harbour, irrigation, and railway extension works. Very serviceable bricks and tiles made in the island; and 5,000 Moormen (Arab descendants off North-west coast) have special aptitude as masons. Potteries for common earthenware utensils, common. Numerous distilleries, with simple apparatus for manufacture of arrack, and a few to obtain essential oils of cinnamon, citronella, and lemon-grass. Plumbago mining is increasing, giving employment in digging, carting, preparation and shipment to several thousands; and gem-searching (250 gem and 25 iron mines) employs a number (1,200) of not over-peaceable persons. Pearl fisheries uncertain—foreign divers (from coast off India) chiefly employed: good fisheries expected off North-west coast next few years. Chank fishery steady, but not very profitable.

## CULTIVATION.

*Grain*:—Rice, 660,000 acres. Kurakkan, varieties of millet (known locally as "dry grain"), Indian corn, &c., with kollu and other legumes, 150,000. *Total Grain* 810,000. *Palms*:—Coconuts: native "topes," 450,000; European plantations, 50,000;=500,000 total coconuts. Palmyras, arecanuts, kitul, &c., 150,000. *Total Palms*, 650,000. *Coffee*, *Tea*, *Cinchona*, *Cocoa* (properly *Cacao*):—European plantations (2,000 properties with 1,500 separate estates cultivated, or over 1,600, if divisions of large estates counted, cleared and in all stages of cultivation, excluding abandoned fields and making allowance for area covered by new products), coffee, 120,000 acres; native holdings, 10,000. *Total coffee*, 130,000. Cinchona, 35,000 acres; cocoa or cacao, 12,500 acres; tea, 175,000 acres;

Liberian coffee (European or native), 2,000 acres; cardamoms (European and native), 7,000 acres; African palm nuts, rubber, &c., 500; grand total of plantation culture, tea, coffee, and new products, 360,000 acres. Tea is cultivated from nearly sea-level to over 6,000 feet. [Coffee (Aribica) was cultivated from elevation of 1,500 to 5,000 feet: medium, best. Reserve of forest and chena in connection with plantations, 300,000; Government hill forest, suitable for coffee, tea, cinchona, &c., perhaps quarter of a million acres, and at least four times that extent of low lands suited for tea and cacao, and for coconut, grain, and garden cultivation.] Tobácco, 25,000 acres; cotton, 400 acres; sugar, aromatic grasses, aloes, &c., 5,500; garden vegetables: onions, chillies, brinjals, potatoes, and yams, cabbages, greens, pineapples, pumpins, cucumbers, &c., 100,000 acres. Plantain, jak, mango, breadfruit, orange, lime, guava, cadju, lovi-lovi, goraka, bilimbi, and other orchard cultivation, 120,000. Cinnamon, 30,000. Other spices—nutmeg, pepper, &c., 10,000 acres. Cultivated grass land, 15,000. Introduced timber trees, 500. Total cultivation, about 1,900,000 acres; or at most 2 millions—or about 1-6th of area. Sugar cultivation a failure, probably from excessive moisture of climate, in western, southern, and central provinces; a little still grown and manufactured at Baddegama, near Galle. Plantain (or banana) cultivation for fibre tried unsuccessfully near Matara. Natural pasturage—including patanas—1,000,000 in and around mountain zone; in island generally, 2 or 3 million acres probably; that on hills coarse and indifferent, and (up to 4,000 feet) infested by land leeches; in low country better, but great proportion in unhealthy parts.

[Note.—Arabian coffee used to grow around native huts, and bore scattered berries at the sea-level; and there were two or three plantations so low down as only 600 feet above the level of the sea, with a good many at an elevation of 1,000. There are also plantations at an altitude of 5,000 feet and higher. These, if situated on detached hills, on sunny slopes, or on ranges, such as the Uva, facing a hot, low country, do well. But the coffee leaf fungus has put a stop to all interest in coffee extension, or even in its cultivation, save in such favourite districts as those of Uva, parts of Dikoya and Dimbula, and detached plantations in other districts. The coconut flourishes chiefly at the sea-level and on the coast; also up river valleys with a few gardens in central province. Rice runs up to where Arabian coffee used to begin, at 2,000 feet altitude. We have now tea cultivation from sea-level to over 6,000 feet, so covering all elevations, with cinchonas flourishing from 1,700 to over 7,000 feet elevation, and cacao or chocolate plant in sheltered rich valleys and districts up to about 2,000 feet.]

### VALUE OF PLANTATION PROPERTY, AND EFFECTS OF EUROPEAN CAPITAL AND ENTERPRIZE.

The value of cultivated coffee (£2,000,000), tea (£4,250,000), cinchona (£1,400,000), cacao (£300,000), cardamoms, other products (£600,000), &c., grass land on plantations all round, may be taken at about 10 millions sterling. Add £500,000 for 100,000 acres reserve forest at £5 an acre, and 200,000 acres more of reserve belonging to plantations in private hands, in grass (natural), chena, or abandoned land, part of which may be utilized for new products by degrees, worth £1 per acre; and we get about 11 millions for old and new products plantation-land, chiefly in the hands of Europeans. Including buildings, machinery, carts, cattle, &c., the value is certainly not under the 12 millions. The value of coconut palm cultivation in the island we put at about the same sum, or 12½ millions sterling. Of other palms and fruit trees, at nearly 6 millions. Of cinnamon, £760,000. Other spices, £500,000. Cotton, tobacco, vegetables, and other garden produce, at 1¼ million. Of rice and other grain nearly 6 millions. Making a total value of cultivated land of about 35 million pounds sterling.

The value of forest-land, chena, and pasturage, in the hands of low-country natives, will make a considerable addition. The amount of British capital diffused by the planting enterprize since 1837 has been enormous, and the Sinhalese carpenters and other artizans, cart contractors, and cattle owners, with the Tamil rice dealers and coolie labourers, have profited largely by it—a profit in which the European capitalists and planters have only in a scanty measure participated. It is calculated that, reckoning the pioneers, not more than 10 per cent. of the European planters during the fifty years can be said to have bettered themselves in Ceylon. 43,000 deeds were registered and 27 million rupees secured on mortgages in 1878, at the height of coffee planting prosperity. Splendid roads have been opened and fine bridges erected over impassable rivers, and populous and thriving towns and villages have sprung up in the planting districts, where 40 to 50 years ago all was interminable jungle. The natives in the towns are rapidly adopting European habits, and many send their children to England for education or to take rank as barristers, physicians, and clergymen. The improvement has spread to the urban masses too: witness the declaration of the Rev. R. S. Hardy, a missionary of 40 years' experience:—"The contrast between one of their homes now and in the times I can remember is nearly as great as between a grimed native chatty (earthern pot) and a bright English tea kettle." Crime has, however, kept pace with the spread of wealth, and what is usually termed "civilization." Although the Sinhalese, on the authority of one of their own number (the late Mr. James Alwis), possess "not even a tincture of soldiership," they are prone to crimes of revenge and violence. In this respect the "low country Sinhalese," although most of them profess a religion which absolutely forbids the taking of life, hold a "bad pre-eminence;" the Tamils ranking second, and the Kandyan Sinhalese third.

RETURNS OF CROP,

from rice and grain lands, generally range from 5 to 30 bushels per acre, the average for rice being about 20 bushels in the husks, or 10 bushels clean. [The Government returns give averages of under 10 bushels for rice, and a fraction over 7 bushels for "dry grain;" in both cases unhusked grain. But these low averages arise from the defective mode in which the accounts are made up. An acre is about "2½ bushels sowing extent"—the average return 20 bushels; in favourable positions twice that quantity.] Coconuts, 1,500 to 3,200 nuts per acre, per annum, at 80 trees to acre. Tea in Ceylon has yielded on Mariawatte and one or two other favoured plantations over 1,000lb. made tea per acre for several years; on some more favoured plots over 800lb; the average so far is about 400lb.; on old poor land not more than 300lb. can be expected. Cinchona trees have given as much as 12lb. marketable bark at six years old in Ceylon, an acre of red bark trees (1578) gave 12,000lb. after five years. Coffee on plantations ranges from 1 cwt. to 3 cwt.; the average (previous to the appearance of a coffee leaf fungus, *Hemileia vastatrix*, in 1869) a little over 6 cwt.; for native gardens, 5: in both cases *clean* coffee. Of recent years, the average has been reduced to less than 2 or 3 cwt. Cinnamon gives on an average about 80lb. per acre. Lands fully planted and cultivated yield up to 125 and 150lb.; neglected and swampy lands not more than 40. A good deal of "jungle spice," cut from the forests, enters into the exports. Coffee (*coffea aribica*) until the last few years was regarded as almost the only really paying cultivation in which Europeans could engage, but the persistent attacks of leaf fungus forced attention to other articles, and the prospects of "new products," chiefly of tea (now regarded as the planter's staple), cinchona, and cacao now seem good. There are a few remunerative coconut estates belonging to Europeans, but Europeans cannot successfully compete with natives in this pursuit. The tree is said to love the sound of the human voice, the obvious meaning of which is that it flourishes best where best supplied with fertilizing matter and otherwise tended; this cultivation has vastly extended through the wealth acquired by natives from introduced European capital during the last twenty to thirty years. The once famous cinnamon of Ceylon, though still the finest grown, seldom yields more than a minimum of profit to the cultivator. Grain cultivation cannot, even at the occasional high prices which prevail, offer any inducement to European enterprize, and the natives persevere in the pursuit mainly for the reasons thus stated by the experienced and intelligent servant of Government who so long administered the Western Province, Sir C. P. Layard:—"You are right in your conclusion that the cultivation of paddy is the least profitable pursuit to which a native can apply himself. It is persevered in from habit, and because the value of time and labour never enters into his calculation. Besides this, agriculture is, in the opinion of a Sinhalese, the most honourable of callings. I do not think that the average yield of our fields is as low as 5½ bushels to the acre—twenty is nearer the mark; but all arable lands are not cultivated at once, or even in the same year, and the estimates of a season's sowing often include crops abandoned immediately after the seed has been sown, either on account of drought or flood. The uncertain climate of the maritime districts and a poor soil are both causes of the comparative smallness of our returns. In India, *i.e.*, both in Bengal and the grain-producing districts of the Madras Presidency, they have extensive tracts of alluvial lands on the banks of their rivers, the like of which, even on a small scale, cannot be found here." This has lately been disputed by Mr. Elliot, C.C.S., but he has only proved that rice growing is largely profitable in such favoured districts as Matara, Batticaloa, and some parts of the other provinces with good soil and special irrigational advantages; there are large areas where fruit, leaf, and bark-growing is and will be much more profitable than rice to the natives. Of course *all* the grain grown in the island is consumed within its limits, besides very large imports for the urban and coolie population. Of the produce of the coconut tree, by far the larger proportion is also consumed in the island. Taking the annual value of the oil, nuts, arrack, toddy, coir, &c., at 2½ millions sterling, nearly *one-third* is exported; the people consuming the remaining *two-thirds*, chiefly in the shape of nuts for food, with a good deal of arrack, toddy, oil, coir, &c. Of the produce of other palms the exports amount to about £120,000. Practically, the whole of the cinnamon grown is exported. Of the tea and coffee produced, the local consumption may be taken at 2½ per cent., or about 300,000lb. and 5,000 cwt., representing a value of about half a million of rupees against 20 to 30 millions of rupees' worth exported. Of the produce of the areca and palmyra palms (arecanuts, used for the almost universal Indian and Ceylon masticatory, with palmyra timber and coarse sugar), while much is consumed in the island, a good proportion is exported. But for the one important mineral plumbago (of which 212,000 cwt. were sent away in 1884, valued at over a million of rupees) the whole export trade of Ceylon might still be described as the produce mainly of the tea and coffee and cinchona shrubs, with the products of three palms, and in a subsidiary degree of the cinnamon, and now of cacao and a little Liberian coffee. The statement that Ceylon at one time grew grain enough to feed a population of 5 (much more 12) millions is very doubtful. Some of the great tanks appear never to have been completed, having been commenced by particular monarchs chiefly for their own glorification. Much more is to be hoped for from the irrigation works recently constructed or restored by the Ceylon Government. At present Ceylon grows TEA and COCONUTS mainly (with coffee, cinchonas, cacao, cardamoms, and other secondary products, besides its grain and fruit culture), and gets much grain, cattle, cloth, specie, and nearly all she wants in exchange.

### CROWN LAND GRANTED AND SOLD,

since 1833, about 1,300,000 acres, yielding a revenue of about £2,100,000. Average price, 1833 to 1844, 10s. 8d.; 1844 to 1883, 37s. 9d. Upset price, now £1; highest price realized nearly 250 rupees (£25) for hill forest land,—generally ranges £1 to £5 for forest land, and £400 per acre occasionally for building lots near Colombo. Half of lands sold, hill forest suited for coffee, cinchona, tea, &c.; half for grain, coconuts, Liberian coffee, cacao, tea, plantains, &c. Full title—no land-tax (only 5 per cent. on lands and houses *within limits of towns* for police purposes; in Colombo 3 per cent. for lighting and 2 per cent. just being levied for water); tithes (rent), levied on grain only, 10 per cent. of produce (a few cases of 20 to 25) against 50 per cent. tax often in India. There are insuperable objections, on the part of the natives mainly, to a land-tax, which would fall on coconut, fruit, and root culture, now free, but a liberal commutation system is being applied to the grain tithes, which were exacted by the native rulers in addition to other taxes, all of which, except the rice-tax, the British Government abandoned. Those who cry out against food and salt taxes in oriental countries may as well be reminded that, except through grain, salt, and cotton cloth, the vast majority of the natives of Ceylon would almost entirely escape contributing to the expenditure necessary for the support of civil government, military and police protection, and means of communication.

### STOCK.

Returns very defective. Perhaps there are 6,000

horses, 1,100,000 cattle (including buffaloes), 70,000 sheep, 100,000 goats, and 50,000 swine in Ceylon, with 1,000 asses and 200 mules. Ceylon imports (chiefly from India, with some from Australia) nearly all its horses, most of its draught cattle, and much cattle, sheep, goats, and poultry for food, to a total value of over a million rupees per annum. Two-fifths of the grain consumed (about 13 millions of bushels in all) is also imported. Prices, always high in Ceylon, have risen steadily, and the tendency is upwards, though a little checked by the planting depression in 1880–6. So with the wages of servants and labourers. Butcher-meat, especially up country, is likely to become scarcer and dearer in consequence of cattle establishments having been abolished on a large proportion of estates as not profitable. Artificial manures are found to cost less, generally, than the dung of cattle fed on cultivated grasses and expensive grain and oil-cakes.

## COMMERCE.

*Imports*, 50 millions of rupees. *Exports*, 40 millions: total value of commerce, 90 millions, nominally 9 million pounds sterling; or, excluding specie, 80 millions. [The *coasting* trade is also considerable.] Staple imports:—Rice, &c., 5½ million bushels, 1¼ million sterling; cotton goods, about £600,000; live stock, £100,000; salt fish, 100,000; other food requisites, £200,000; wearing apparel, &c., £110,000; machinery, £80,000; liquors, £120,000; manures, £50,000; coal, 200,000 tons. Staple exports:—Coffee, 200,000 to 250,000 cwt.; 1 to 1½ million sterling; tea, 10 million lb., £600,000 (likely to rise rapidly); cacao, 20,000 cwt., £80,000; cardamoms, 250,000 lb., £30,000; coconut oil, 4½ million gallons, £450,000; cinnamon, 2½ million lb., £120,000; coir, 100,000 cwts., £60,000; plumbago, 250,000 cwt., £260,000; ebony, 10,000 cwt, £7,000; other kinds of timber, £20,000; cinchona bark, 15 million lb., £500,000. Total exports from tea, coffee, cinchona, and cacao plantations, £3,000,000; from coconut palm, £800,000; other palms, £100,000; cinnamon and all spices, £200,000; tobacco, £100,000; timber, £25,000; plumbago, £100,000. In 1837 Ceylon exported only 34,000 cwt. of coffee, valued at £106,000; total value of trade, including the then valuable article of cinnamon, only £900,000 against 9 millions now. In 1833 the value of Ceylon exports was only £130,000; imports, £320,000; total £450,000. So that the increase of trade in little more than fifty years has been nearly 20-fold. Tonnage outwards and inwards nearly 4 millions now, against less than 100,000 tons in 1825.

### REVENUE.

Average, R13,000,000 per annum (R8,000,000 from taxes and R5,000,000 land sales, railway, and other receipts). This includes R1,000,000 direct taxation on all males (save Governor, military, and Buddhist priest) between 18 and 55, for thoroughfares; persons paying direct taxes number 515,000. Add R1,500,000 raised by road committees, municipalities, local boards, and village councils, and R100,000 under coolie medical ordinance from planters, making the total of about R15,000,000. Customs and railways yield nearly one-half of the regular revenue; excise on toddy (fermented juice of coconut tree) and arrack (spirit distilled from it) one-eighth. Grain tithes, land sales, salt monopoly, tolls, and stamps are the other great sources of revenue. Pearl fishery occasionally productive, but very uncertain; yielded altogether over 1 million sterling to British; greatest amount, £140,000 in 1798. Taxation not heavy—less than R3 (6s.) per head; but mass of people poor, and, under ancient village regulations, bestow labour on upkeep of irrigation tanks and channels. The revenue has doubled in 25 years, trebled in 30 years, and nearly quadrupled in 40 years, although cinnamon monopoly, fish-tax, &c., abandoned, and customs duties equalized and moderated. The maximum of revenue owing to heavy land sales and planting prosperity was attained in 1877, at £1,700,000; it fell in 1882 with planting depression to £1,206,000; but has since risen steadily, and is expected ere long to average £1,400,000.

### EXPENDITURE.

Civil, judicial, public instruction, medical, police, prisons establishments, and services, R6,600,000; pensions, R650,000; military contribution, R600,000; roads and buildings, R2,000,000. Railway services, with interest on loans (against large income), R2,100,000. Interest on breakwater and waterworks loans, R600,000. Irrigation works, R400,000, besides special advances. Minor items, such as conveyance of mails, immigration, &c. What the colony mainly requires is a liberal and judicious expenditure on

#### MEANS OF COMMUNICATION.

A line of railway 74½ miles long between Colombo (chief shipping port) and Kandy (capital of the central or planting province) was opened in August, 1867; an extension to Nawalapitiya from Peradeniya, 17 miles, in December, 1874: an extension from Kandy to Matale, 17½ miles, opened on 4th October, 1880. Besides the above, a seaside line has been constructed from Colombo to Kalutara, 27½ miles, opened in September, 1879; and a few miles of line to serve the breakwater. And on 3rd August, 1880, the first sod was turned of an extension from Nawalapitiya for 41¼ miles to Nanuoya, within 4 miles of the Sanatarium, Nuwara Eliya, and opened on 20th May, 1885. [From Nanuoya the line is intended to be carried 25¼ miles farther to Haputale, and thence to Badulla.] Altogether, about 183 miles of railway, all on the 5½ feet gauge, have now been opened. The railway at Kadugannawa reaches 1,700 feet sea-level; at Kandy, 1,600 feet; Peradeniya, 1,512; Matale, 1,200 feet; Nawalapitiya, 1,913; Hatton, 4,168; Nanuoya, 5,292 feet; the Moragalla tunnel at Kadugannawa is 365 yards long; the Poolbank tunnel, 614 yards; Talawakelle tunnel is 265 yards; sharpest curve 5 chains; ruling gradient, Kadugannawa incline, 1 to 45 (12 miles long), on Nanuoya extension, heaviest gradient 1 to 44. Other lines are contemplated to connect the main line with Kurunegala and Negombo and even Chilaw, and to extend from Kalutara to Galle; from Kalutara to Rakawana; and from Kurunegala or Matale with Jaffna; from Colombo to Kotte; and a city line in Colombo for the northern suburb of Mattakuliya, unless city tramways are adopted. A line taking in Kotte and other suburbs of Colombo would, it is believed, pay well. At present, two coaches run daily from Kalutara to Galle, and *vice versâ*; a coach runs tri-weekly (shortly to become daily) between Colombo and

Ratnapura, also from Colombo to Yatiyantota, and from Ratnapura to Pelmadulla; and mail-carts or coaches exist between Colombo and Negombo; Galle and Matara; also a coach or mail-cart from Nanuoya to Nuwara Eliya; from Matale to Dambula, and thence a bullock coach to Jaffna. In three days, a visitor to Colombo might easily run up *via* Kandy to Nuwara Eliya, passing through the finest of mountain scenery, and return; two days would suffice to pay a visit from Colombo to Nuwara Eliya and the middle planting region; while a run to Kandy and back, with a sight of the beautiful and grand scenery in view on and from the RAILWAY INCLINE, can be accomplished in one day. ROADS:—Metalled, 1,350 miles; gravelled, 790; ungravelled, 740=total miles of road, 2,900, or one mile of road for every nine square miles of extent in the island; upkeep of roads, canals, public buildings, and irrigation works, total expenditure of Public Works Department, £200,000; road pioneer corps number 500, with several trained working elephants. Canals navigable for boats, 180 miles, besides portions of rivers and backwaters. [In addition to expenditure from general revenue, roads and canals are made and kept up by thoroughfares' tax, equivalent of six days' labour per annum from each adult male. Groups of estates not intersected by thoroughfares can get cart-roads on paying half the cost, Government giving other moiety. In 1807 there were no carriage roads beyond the limits of the principal town in the maritime provinces; and none in the Kandyan country until 1820, the era in which Sir Edward Barnes' great road-making operations commenced, opening up the pacified Kandyan country to enterprize, and so rendering railways necessary and possible.] Besides the P. & O. Company's and Messageries steamers connecting Colombo, the mail-port, with India, China, Australia, &c., there are the Austro-Hungarian Lloyds and the Norddeutscher Lloyds steamers; also the British India Steam Navigation Company maintain a regular communication (weekly) between Colombo, Bombay, Calcutta, and intermediate ports. This company has also a fortnightly line between London, Colombo, Madras, and Calcutta, *via* the Suez Canal; and other similar lines, *via* the Suez Canal, are worked by the Star, the Clan, Holt's, the Glen, Anchor, the Ducal, the City, Bird, and other steam companies.

### PUBLIC DEBT OF CEYLON.

The cost of the Colombo and Kandy Railway (£1,740,000) was provided for by a special tax on coffee, and partly out of general revenue, and afterwards out of the receipts and profits of the line, amounting to from 8 to 10 per cent. on capital. The Kandy, Nawalapitiya and Seaside railways are now the free property of the colony. It may be said that, besides the network of splendid roads, "coffee" has given the colony 118 miles of first-class railway, worth 2½ millions sterling, and yielding about £120,000 per annum clear income. For the Matale railway a debt of £275,000 has been increased, and another of one million sterling in debentures for the first 41½ miles of the Dimbula-Uva railway extension, and another half million will be required to complete to Haputale. For the Colombo Harbour Works about £600,000 in all have been expended, of which £226,000 are to be given by the Public Loan Commissioners at 3½ per cent. for 35 years, and the balance, £350,000, at 4 or 5 per cent. for interest and sinking fund. £350,000 is also now estimated for the Colombo Waterworks. So that, when the works in hand are complete, the debt of the colony for general and municipal purposes will be about 2¼ million pounds sterling, with an annual charge for interest and sinking fund of about £135,000. The annual railway, harbour, and water supply receipts will then, however, not be less than £360,000 per annum, and, deducting working expenses, should yield sufficient profit to cover more than the annual claims, only the Dimbula Railway extensions will not pay properly until the new Uva traffic is brought on the existing lines.

### FORM OF ADMINISTRATION: CENTRAL AND MUNICIPAL.

Governor, aided by Executive and Legislative Councils; the power of making laws being vested in the latter concurrently (as is the case with Crown Colonies generally) with the legislative power of the Crown, which exercises that power by Orders in Council. Executive Council consists of five of the principal officers of Government, presided over by the Governor, who being personally responsible to the Home Government, can consult, but is not bound to follow the advice of, the Executive Councillors. All appointments to, or promotions in, the Civil Service with salaries over R2,000 per annum, vest in the Secretary of State, but practically all appointments, except to the higher offices, are left to the Governor. For writerships in the Civil Service four gentlemen are named for each vacancy by the Secretary of State or the Governor, and the candidate who receives the greatest number of marks is appointed. With salaries much more moderate in Ceylon than in India, we have a covenanted Civil Service numbering about 80 members for about three millions of inhabitants, instead of less than a dozen civilians with native assistants for a similar population in India. The Legislative Council is composed of the members of the Executive, four other principal officers of the Government, and six unofficial members selected by the Governor with reference to as fair a representation as possible of the various classes and interests—(at present representatives include Sinhalese, Tamil, and Burgher members; one European for planters, one for merchants, and one for general European interests)—sixteen in all, six, however, forming a quorum: and an Order of the Queen in Council declared the proceedings of the Legislature valid, though all unofficial seats be vacant. The Governor can command the votes of all official members except on points where religious principles are affected. Governor presides, with casting vote and ultimate power of veto. All ordinances are sent for the final approval of her Majesty, but only in rare cases is the operation of a law suspended pending that approval. Unofficial members can, after permission obtained, introduce drafts of ordinances where votes of money are not concerned. Eight Provinces, administered by Government Agents and their Assistants (with native revenue and police headmen, such as Ratemahatmayas, Mudaliyars, Muhandirams, Koralas, Vidanas, &c.), all under strict supervision of Government; centralization being the ruling principle, perhaps to an injurious extent. By means of Native Village Councils, Municipalities in the three chief towns (Colombo, Galle, and Kandy), and Local Boards in nine towns of secondary importance (ranging from 1,800 to 10,000 in population), the principles of self-government are being of recent years to a considerable extent diffused. As yet, however, the bulk of the natives appreciate the incidence of municipal taxation more than the benefits conferred by sanitary and other improvements. The Colombo Municipality has introduced gas, and (by order of Government) are spending over R3,500,000 on a water supply, the works for which are almost completed; Kandy and Galle have already made provision for water supply.

### LAWS.

The Roman-Dutch law is the common law of the land, and applicable in all cases not otherwise specially provided for by local enactments.* It obtains in cases of marriage, inheritance, succession, or contracts. The law as to matrimonial rights has been modified by Ordinance 15 of 1876, by abolishing community of goods as a consequence of marriage, and by prescribing the order of succession in cases of intestacy. The law of England, however, is of force (by virtue of the Ordinance No. 5 of 1852) in all maritime matters, and in respect of bills of exchange, promissory notes, and cheques. The law of England was further introduced by Ordinance 22 of 1866, in respect of Partnerships, Joint Stock Companies, Corporations, Banks and Banking, Principals and Agents, Carriers by Land, and Life and Fire Insurances. Roman-Dutch law, however, absurdly enough, prevails as to Contracts and Torts (damages). Property can be willed away, but intestate estates are divided according to the principles of Roman-Dutch law, controlled by Ordinance 15 of 1876. Local ordinances are subject to approval of sovereign, but may be brought into force at once. They cease to be operative, however, if not confirmed within three years. The Kandyans are subject to their own laws, and when these are silent the Roman-Dutch law governs them. In 1859 their marriage laws were greatly altered, and polyandry and polygamy, formerly sanctioned, were then expressly prohibited; but this salutary prohibition had afterwards to be in some degree relaxed, the legislation being in advance of the intelligence and condition of the people. Europeans and European descendants are now exempted from the operation of the Kandyan law as respects inheritance, and made subject to the Roman-Dutch law, by which a widow gets a just moiety of her husband's estate (excepting when a different provision is made by ante-

* A Civil Code is in course of preparation.

nuptial contract or by joint will, and the children the other moiety in equal shares. The Muhammadans have a code of their own in matters of marriage and inheritance. The Tamils of the north and east have their code also—the Tesavallami. The criminal law of the island, known as the Roman-Dutch law, was repealed by a Penal Code, which came into operation on 1st January, 1885, whereby the punitive jurisdiction of District Courts as regards imprisonment was raised to two years, and of Police Courts to six months. This has relieved the Supreme Court of a number of cases that used to be sent there for trial. The number of jurymen has been reduced to nine, and is to be further reduced to seven. The procedure in the courts is regulated by the Criminal Procedure Code, which came into operation at the same time as the Penal Code. These codes are largely transcripts and adaptations of the Indian Penal and Procedure Codes. The English law of evidence prevails in all the courts; and a special ordinance provides that substantial justice shall not fail through want of adherence to legal technicalities. Further codification of laws, so as to secure settlement of principles and avoidance of conflict and occasional uncertainty, desiderated (and is likely ere long to be carried), as well as a law of libel, which would recognize the functions and privileges of a free press better than do the antiquated provisions of Roman-Dutch laws. It is now proposed to substitute the English law of contracts and torts, and a civil code is in course of preparation, a criminal code having already been introduced.

### ADMINISTRATION OF JUSTICE: CRIME.

The ordinary courts are Supreme Court (Chief Justice and two Puisne Judges), District Courts, Courts of Requests, and Police Courts. The last have jurisdiction in all minor cases not punishable with more than £5 fine, six months' imprisonment, and twenty lashes. Courts of Requests have jurisdiction in all civil suits where the matter in dispute—land or money—does not exceed £10 in value. District Courts have unlimited civil jurisdiction in civil, matrimonial, testamentary, and insolvent cases (about 10,000 suits decided annually), and criminal jurisdiction in all cases not punishable with more than

£20 fine, two years' imprisonment, and twenty-five lashes. The Supreme Court has only an appellate jurisdiction in civil cases and over the criminal decisions of the District and Police Courts, and an unlimited jurisdiction in criminal cases. The latter is exercised by a judge and nine jurymen, the verdict of the majority prevailing, except in murder cases, when two-thirds are necessary. The appointment, temporarily, of a Commissioner of Assize, to assist the Supreme Court judges in criminal sessions work, has been sanctioned. The Supreme Court and the District Courts of Colombo and Kandy are generally filled by professional men. Occasionally these and all the other judicial offices are open to members of the civil service, or others appointed by the Governor or Secretary of State. There is no grand jury, its powers being exercised by the Attorney-General—assisted by the Solicitor-General (both being the recognized law officers of the Crown—who has a seat in the Executive Council, and is a member of the Government. All local ordinances are prepared by him—he advises the Government in all legal matters, and has the charge of Crown suits throughout the island, being assisted in his work by the Solicitor-General and local deputies ("Crown Counsel") for each circuit. An appeal lies of right to the Privy Council from all decisions of the Supreme Court in cases above £500: it may be allowed by grace in other cases. There are only two classes of lawyers in Ceylon—advocates and proctors admitted on examination. English and Irish barristers and Scotch advocates are entitled to plead as advocates. Notaries, who draw deeds but do not practise in the courts, are numerous (about 600), being appointed by the Governor with reference to the wants of districts. Many proctors hold warrants and act as notaries. The proportion of lawyers (about 340 advocates and proctors) to population is high, the people of Ceylon being excessively litigious, fractions of fruit-trees being sometimes the subjects of action. In crime, about 60,000 offences reported, and 90,000 persons apprehended annually; two-thirds usually acquitted: great proportion false cases. Summary convictions, 13,000; committals to gaol about 20,000, but one-third tax defaulters. About 2,500 convicts. About 100 murders and manslaughters reported annually. Total cost of crime to colony estimated at

R800,000 per annum. A Penal Code was (1883) passed embodying all the criminal law.

### POLICE.

Whether regularly organized and paid, as in towns, or rural system of unpaid headman called Vidanas, by no means perfect, the material to work on being far from good. Reforms in the regular police have, however, been carried out, the total number under an Inspector-General, with five Provincial Superintendents, being now over 1,500, costing R600,000 per annum for the department altogether. Some fifty of the constables are Europeans, besides all the superintending officers. The regular police is taught rifle drill, and in furnishing guards for prisons, escorts for treasure, &c., largely performs duties which previously fell to the military, mainly to the late Ceylon Rifles Corps.

### CURRENCY AND FINANCE.

Rupees and cents of a rupee; the copper or bronze subsidiary coinage, including a five cent piece, cents, half cents, and quarter cents. The latter have now superseded the old Dutch coins—fanams, pice, challies, &c.—as well as English pence and their parts. The silver half rupee is taken at 50 cents, the quarter at 25 cents, and the eighth (two anna piece of India) at 12½ cents. The rupee for some time has averaged 1s. 6d. sterling in value; but during 1886 fell temporarily to 1s. 4d. Gold coins are sold by the banks at about current rates of exchange. The note issue in Ceylon is now, since 1st January, 1886, a Government issue, and paper money to an average value of 4½ millions of rupees is in circulation. There are in the island agencies of the New Oriental Bank Corporation; Chartered Mercantile Bank of India, London, and China; the Bank of Madras; of the Chartered Bank of India, Australia, and China; of the National Bank of India; of the Comptoir d'Escompte de Paris, and through mercantile houses of others. The clearing-house returns for Colombo show about R55,000,000 of cheques per annum. Besides these private banking institutions, and some agencies of loan companies, there are the Government Savings Bank (with deposits equal to about R1,750,000, lodged by over

13,000 depositors) and the Loan Board, each of which lends money on good house security at comparatively moderate interest.

### WEIGHTS AND MEASURES.

British standard, to which local candies, leaguers, &c., are reduced. Coffee, our old staple produce, is usually sold locally by the bushel, from 4½ to 5 bushels "parchment" going to 1 cwt. clean coffee. Tea and bark by lb.; coconut oil by gallon or cwt., 12½ gallons going to cwt. For freight purposes, 10 chests tea usual size make 50 cubic feet, which go to ton; 16 cwt. coffee in casks, 18 in bags, go to a ton; 17 cwt. coconut oil, 12 cwt. coir and cardamoms, 14 cwt. hides, 16 cwt. horns and pepper, 17 poonac or oil cakes, 800 lbs. cinnamon or cinchona; measurement goods, 50 cubic feet to the ton. A maund of tea seed or leaf about 84 lbs.; bushel of rice, 68 lbs.; candy of copperah, 500 lb.

### CUSTOMS DUTIES,

port dues, pilotage, &c., are moderate, the leading principle in the customs tariff being 5 to 6½ per cent. on the value of imports, and the only export duties being R100 for every elephant, and R5 per ton on plumbago in lieu of Government royalty; with moderate charges on tonnage, which now has the benefit of safe and commodious harbour accommodation at Colombo, by means of the fine breakwater. Export levies of a fractional amount are also imposed on certain plantation products, for coolie medical aid purposes, 10 cents per cwt. on tea, coffee, and cocoa; 20 cents on cinchona bark; with 6 cents per chest of tea for harbour dues.

### COLOMBO HARBOUR WORKS.

Begun in 1875; foundation laid by H.R.H. the Prince of Wales, 8th Dec.; Sir John Coode, Kt., Consulting Engineer; John Kyle, M.I.C.E., Resident Executive Engineer: over £700,000 expended in all, and 4,211 feet of breakwater arm completed from starting point at shore end to pier-head with lighthouse, besides extensive reclamation work, forming safe, commodious harbour (with jetties), covering 250 acres, with from 26 to 40 feet of water. An expenditure of £400,000 more would provide a northern arm, jetties, and harbour reclamation, at Mutwal. The harbour revenue already exceeds R450,000 per annum, and it could be made R600,000 for the complete works. A graving dock for imperial-naval as well as commercial purposes is the first great necessity

### TRAMWAYS IN COLOMBO

are an anticipated city improvement, several lines being projected and tendered for to the municipality by a responsible agency.

### COLOMBO WATERWORKS

were commenced in 1881–2, to supply the city (covering 9½ square miles) with two million gallons of water daily, from a reservoir in the Labugama hills, thirty miles away. The contract for the hill and city (Maligahakanda) reservoirs, and for laying pipes, was given in from 1882 for R1,415,500), the work to be done in three years by Messrs. Mitchell and Izard; the consulting engineer being Mr. Bateman, of Westminster; Mr. A. W. Burnett being chief resident engineer. The Labugama reservoir (of 176 acres, 59 feet maximum depth of water, to contain 1,373,000,000 gallons, 360 feet top water above sea level), and pipes thence, have been laid; also about 144,000 yards of pipes in the city; but the Muligahakanda reservoir (to hold 9 million gallons) 100 feet top water above sea, proved a failure at its first and second trials. [Third and, doubtless, final trial.] The water supply is, however, being utilized independently from Labugama.

### POSTAGE.

Ceylon enjoys rather better than the boon of a "penny postage" for letters, the rate being 5 cents of a rupee, equal, at present, to about ⅘d., on each half ounce; two cents postage for newspapers, besides post-cards; but a fairly moderate rate for book, commercial packets, and parcel postage is a desideratum. External postage to many parts of the world moderate, although uniformity is much required, the letter rate being 30 cents to the Australian colonies, and 28 cents to the United Kingdom, while only 25 cents to the Continent of Europe. To India by Dak or B.I. steamers same as local rates. 123 post offices in Ceylon. Total of letters through Ceylon post offices, over 15 millions per annum, or between five and six per head. Postal revenue, R265,000; Telegraph, R65,000; total, R330,000. Total expenditure, R445,000, for which the large correspondence, including heavy parcels, of the Government Departments is carried, and official telegrams delivered free. If all officials paid postage and telegrams, the Postal-Telegraph Department would show a clear profit.

### TELEGRAPH RATES.

The telegraph stations now open in Ceylon (24 in all) are:—Anuradhapura, 3rd class; Badulla, 3rd; Batticaloa, 3rd; Colombo, 1st; Dikoya, 3rd; Galle, 2nd; Gampola, 3rd; Hatton, 3rd; Jaffna, 2nd; Kalutara, 3rd; Kandy, 2nd; Kurunegala, 3rd; Lunugala, 3rd; Mannar, 3rd; Matale, 3rd; Nawalapitiya, 3rd; Nuwara Eliya, 2nd (during season, January to June) and 3rd; Polgahawela, 3rd; Trincomalee, 3rd; Talawakele, 3rd; Mount Lavinia, 3rd; Moratuwa, 3rd; Nanuoya, 3rd.

On and from the 1st February, 1887, the following new scale of charges was levied on inland telegrams:—

1.—There are three classes of telegrams—Urgent, Ordinary, and Deferred, and the following are the rates of charge for State and private telegrams between any two offices in Ceylon:—

| Class. | First eight words or groups of three figures. R. | Cts. | Each additional word or group of three figures. R. | Cts. |
|---|---|---|---|---|
| Deferred | 0 | 40 | 0 | 5 |
| Ordinary | 0 | 80 | 0 | 10 |
| Urgent | 1 | 60 | 0 | 20 |

### EVERY-DAY TABLE OF TELEGRAPH RATES FOR ORDINARY FOREIGN MESSAGES.

*From any Ceylon Station.*

| | R.C. |
|---|---|
| To all countries in Europe, including Great Britain, except those named below, *via* Suez | 2·94 |
| „ „ „ „ Teheran | 2·94 |
| „ „ „ „ Turkey | 2·69 |

| | R.C. |
|---|---|
| To Russia, *via* Suez | 2·94 |
| ,, ,, ,, Teheran | 2·69 |
| ,, ,, ,, Turkey and Odessa | 2·69 |
| ,, Turkey ,, Suez | 2·94 |
| ,, ,, ,, Turkey or Fao | 2·12½ |
| ,, ,, ,, Teheran-Batoum | 2·94 |
| ,, Aden and Perim, *via* Bombay | 2·06 |
| ,, Zanzibar, *via* Bombay-Aden* | 4·87½ |
| ,, Durban (Natal), *via* Bombay-Aden | 5·56 |
| ,, C. Colony, all places, *via* Bombay-Aden | 5·69 |
| ,, Suez, *via* Suez | 2·56 |
| ,, Hongkong, *via* Madras | 4·00 |
| ,, Japan, *via* Madras† | 6·75 |
| ,, Amoy, Saddle Island, Shanghai, and Foochow, *via* Madras | 5·12½ |
| ,, Penang, *via* Madras | 2·00 |
| ,, Malacca ,, | 2·44 |
| ,, Singapore ,, | 2·56 |
| ,, Java ,, | 2·87½ |
| ,, Port Darwin, S. and W. Australia, and Victoria, *via* Madras | 5·44 |
| ,, New South Wales, *via* Madras | 5·50 |
| ,, Queensland ,, | 5·94 |
| ,, New Zealand ,, | 6·25 |
| ,, Tasmania ,, | 5·81 |
| ,, New York, *via* Suez | 8·50 |
| ,, Canada ,, | 8·50 |
| ,, Cuba (Cienferegos and Havana) *via* Suez | 5·81 |
| ,, Jamaica, *via* Suez | 7·56 |
| ,, Rio de Janeiro, *via* Suez-Lisbon | 8·12½ |

Code words of more than ten letters are absolutely inadmissible in private foreign messages. A foreign message may consist of only two chargeable words, viz., office of destination and addressee's name.

CEYLON POST OFFICE TELEGRAPHS—consist of 677 miles of line and 1,178 miles of wire. Manaar Gulf Cable 30 miles. Telephone lines, for departmental use only, 7·45 miles. Total number of messages despatched in 1885—65,227, and total receipts for messages for the same period was R221,822.

* In the case of State messages the charge is R3·50 per word, *via* Bombay.

† Special rate to Tsushima, *via* Madras, R7·87½ per word.

### DISEASES.

The most formidable diseases of Ceylon are malarious fevers, malignant dysentery, and wasting diarrhœa, with "sore mouth." These are varied forms of "FEVER" which occupies here the place of lung disease in England. Elephantiasis or "Cochin leg" is fever caused by inflammation of the absorbent vessels and glands; the remote cause of the inflammation is supposed to be a blood worm in the circulation. "Parangi," a loathsome congenital disease, aggravated by scarcity of nutritious food, prevails in some of the more remote portions of the island. It is said to resemble the "yaws" of the West Indies. Ceylon boils, signs (generally) of debility, are sometimes very trying, but rapidly disappear on a "change" to the cool mountain regions, or *vice versâ* to seaside. Liver disease is often troublesome, but is far less prevalent than on the continent of India, and sunstroke exceedingly rare. Cholera and smallpox become occasionally epidemic, but Europeans very seldom fall victims to either. With facilities for occasional change, and the exercise of care and temperance, the chances for European life here are scarcely, if at all, inferior to what they are in England. The large majority of the planters enjoy robust health. Surveyors, road officers, and railway engineers, when compelled to traverse feverish regions and endure exposure to sun and rain, incur much greater risk, as also planting pioneers in new districts. With all its moisture, the climate is favourable to the extension of consumptive lives. Here, as elsewhere in the tropics, life is practically passed in the open air, so that vitiated air in dwellings is seldom a source of disease. Children of European parents can generally remain in Ceylon till eight or nine years, and in the hill-country even longer, especially at Nuwera Eliya, with its average temperature of 58 degrees. Colombo is a specially healthy town, and its sanitation will be still more improved when the hill Water Supply is fully provided. Government Civil Medical Department and Hospitals cost over R700,000 per annum: about 200,000 cases treated in hospitals and dispensaries annually; in hospitals alone, 24,000 cases with 3,000 deaths, rest cured or relieved; there are 350 lunatics and 200 lepers in asylums. About 2,000 paupers noted by Government; no Poor Laws;

relief expended in town by Friend-in-need Societies voluntarily managed and supported, with some aid from General Revenue.

## OBJECTS OF SPECIAL INTEREST TO STRANGERS IN CEYLON.

Colombo and Western Province.—The Fort, Government offices, Sir Edward Barnes's statue, The Grand Oriental Hotel. The Military Buildings, Galle Face Esplanade and drive. The Lake; the Law Courts at Hulftsdorp, with busts of the late C. A. Lorenz and Sir R. F. Morgan, Kt., (by a Ceylonese, R. G. Andriesz). Town Hall, with pictures of H.R.H. the Duke of Edinburgh, Sir Hercules Robinson, Sir William Gregory, the late C. A. Lorenz, M.L.C., and Sir C. P. Layard, K.C.M.G. Cinnamon Gardens; Circular Walk Gardens, near which is situated the Colombo Museum, with statue of Sir William Gregory, K.C.M.G. Hulftsdorp Mills, and other establishments for preparing coffee, cinchona bark, coconut oil, and coir. Cinnamon culture, peeling and baling at Maradana, or at Ekela and Kadirana, near Negombo. Plumbago stores in Brownrigg street, Cinnamon Gardens. Welikada Jail, Lunatic and Leper Asylums. Koch Memorial Tower, Government Civil Hospital. Banyan tree, Hunupitiya. Railway and Breakwater Works. Government Factory and Elephant Shed. Colombo Ironworks. Gasworks. Malikaganda Waterworks Reservoir. Alfred Model Farm towards Kotte. General Cemetery and Galle Face Cemetery, for memorial stones. Wolvendal Dutch Church, with memorials of Dutch Governors on walls and floors. St. Peter's Episcopal Church, with some interesting monuments on the walls. Roman Catholic Cathedral at Kotahena. Colombo Royal College. St. Thomas' and Wesley College and other schools. Moor (Muhammadan) boys' school; Mission Schools, Borella and Kollupitiya. Ancient tortoise at Tanque Salgado, and large kumbuk tree near mouth of river, at Mutwal. Crow Island in mouth of river. Quasi peat and breccia formations north side of mouth of river and canals. Bridge of Boats and Railway Bridge across Kelani river. View of Adam's Peak from Colombo in early morning during N.E. monsoon. Boat trip on river to Kelani Buddhist Temple. Buddhist

Temples at Kelani and Kotte. Rich palm, bambu and general vegetation on banks of river. Mission station and schools at Kotte, Gonawala, or Moratuwa. Tea, Liberian coffee, and cacao cultivation, at Kalutara, Hanwella or Polgahawela. Henaratgoda Government Experimental Gardens. Trip to Ratnapura and scenes of Gem digging *via* side of Kelani river.

Galle and Colombo Road.—Groves of coconut palms, with jak, breadfruit, and other trees along the whole route. Bentota resthouse with river and oyster fishing and sea-bathing. View of interior with mountain range from the road at Beruwala near the 32nd milestone. Kalutara river (Kaluganga or black river), bridge, and town. Railway along seashore from Kalutara to Colombo. Panadure outlet for extensive backwaters. Moratuwa, a prosperous village of carpenters. Mount Lavinia Boarding House.

Galle and Southern Province.—All Saints' Church, Galle. Native bazaars and shops of jewellers and dealers in tortoiseshell and carved work; Wakwella and Cinnamon Gardens near Galle; drives and view alongside Ginganga of the Haycock and Adam's Peak mountains; Baddegama Mission Station; Richmond Hill Mission Station, and view. Cultivation of sugar and lemon grass, by Messrs. Winter & Sons, and others. View from Buona Vista, near Galle, and Mission Station. Tanks in Matara district. Temple ruins and salt formations, Hambantota. Temple ruins at Dewundara ("Dondra Head") near Matara. Weligama Bay. Urubokka dam, Weligama, and rock figure of Kusta Raja or the leper king. View of the Fort and Harbour of Galle from the site of the Roman Catholic Chapel at Kaluwella.

Colombo to Kandy, Gampola, Nawalapitiya, Hatton, and Nanuoya; also to Matale.—Ricefields at Mahara and along line. Mahaoya (river) and vegetation. Kadugannawa pass, Dekanda valley, Allagala mountain and railway incline with Miyangala gallery, "Sensation Rock" and tunnels. View of Dekanda valley from Incline. View looking back from Sensation Rock. Dawson's Monument at Kadugannawa. Peradeniva satinwood bridge, and railway iron lattice bridge. View from railway of the Mahaweliganga and of Pussellawa mountains, beyond Gampola. View of Mahaweliganga and Kotmale on railway and at Pasbage, and of Adam's Peak, Dolosbage, and Ambagamuwa onwards to Nawalapitiya. View towards sea over Yakdesse and low country from Ambagamuwa; waterfalls and rocky glen before Hogs' back tunnels; the Wattawella valley; Dikoya valley and Adam's Peak; Great Western mountain from Kottagalla valley; view over Pussellawa and distant mountains from St. Andrews; St. Clair falls; Devon falls; the *coup d'oeil* of upland and mountain forest and river scenery from side of Great Western and Nanuoya. The Matale railway bridge over the Mahaweliganga, view of Hunasgirikanda and Etapola, views of the Matale valley, Aluwihara, Balakaduwa pass. Tea on Mariawatte; coffee in Dikoya or Agrapatana: cinchona in Dimbula; cacao cultivation on Palakele and Wariyapola.

Kandy, Central Province, Uva, &c.—Sir Henry Ward's statue in Kandy. Dalada temple at Kandy. Audience Hall and Octagon. Prince of Wales' Fountain. New Jail Police Station and Kachcheri. Messrs. Walker & Co.'s factory for coffee and tea-preparing machinery, &c. Matale railway. Hantane Peak or Matana Patana for view, Gregory road, and Lady Horton's Walk. The Pavilion. Peradeniya Botanic Gardens, Gampola Bridge. Uva, Dimbula and Matale, for coffee, tea, cacao and cinchona cultivation. Ramboda falls and pass. Kadiyanlena, Kotmale; and Devon and St. Clair falls, Dimbula. Huluganga falls in the Knuckles. View of Adam's Peak from Ambagamuwa road. Waterfalls in the Horseshoe Valley, Maskeliya, and at the Balangoda end. Adam's Peak, the climb up and view from. Trip to Anuradhapura, *via* Matale and Dambulla (where rock temple); ruins at Polonnaruwa; the great tank region, &c. Elk hunting, elephant shooting, gemming, &c. The trip to Badulla and Haputale. Ella pass and the highest waterfall in Ceylon. Badulla temple and fort, and hot springs.

Nuwara Eliya.—The drive from the Nanuoya station upwards; the Blackpool and variegated forest tints. The "Longden Road" along the side of the Nanuoya; the drive round the Lake and Moon Plains; on the new Udapussellawa road, with beautiful alternation of forest and grass land ("patanas"), magnificent gorges, ferncovered gullies and waterfalls; the waterfall and "grotto" on Portswood estate; the view of the lake, bund and river from Lady Horton's Walk above the bund; "The Lady's Waterfall" below the patanas leading from the bund (Elliewatte Gorge), and Lady Horton's Walk; the view of Adam's Peak, Dimbula, &c., from One Tree Hill; also of the whole circle of mountains, Adam's Peak, Kirigalpotta, Kuduhugala, Totapola, Hakgala, Haputale, Namunakulakanda, Udapussellawa, Lover's Leap, Pidurutalagala, Kiklimana, and of the town, plains and lakes, from Naseby Hill, 6,400 feet; of Uva from Hakgala Gardens, with the gardens themselves, fernery, &c., and the delightful drive down. The climb to Pidurutalagala summit. The old graveyard.

JAFFNA.—The Fort and Batteries, the Dutch Church, the Batticotta Seminary, "the bottomless well," the F. N. Society's Hospital, the market, salt lewayas, and pearl banks off Arippu. Tobacco cultivation and the coral wells at Jaffna, &c. Giant's Tank ruins in Mannar district.

BATTICALOA.—Fort and Batteries, beautiful Bay of Vendeloos. Extensive rice and coconut cultivation.

TRINCOMALEE.—One of the finest harbours in the world. Fort Ostenburg, Fort Frederick. Nillavelli salt pans. Hot springs at Kanniya.

DAMBULLA, ANURADHAPURA, POLLONARUWA, &c.—See for full particulars of sights and way to make journey:—"Buried Cities of Ceylon."

SHOOTING TRIPS.—For snipe, hares, and small deer in Western, Southern, and other provinces. For Elephant, to Hambantota and Bintenne. For elk, cheetah, &c., in higher hill regions. For crocodiles, bears, &c., in Northern Tank regions.

## WRITERS ON CEYLON. AND AUTHORITIES TO BE CONSULTED FOR MORE DETAILED INFORMATION.

De Barros, De Couto, Ribeiro (Lee's translation, with valuable appendices), Valentyn, Baldæus, Knox (edited by Philalethes), Percival, Cordiner, Lord Valentia, Bertolacci, Marshall, Davy, Forbes, Bennett, Knighton, Pridham, Emerson Tennent; Fergusons. Casie Chitty's Gazetteer; Parliamentary papers; Ceylon Blue Books; Governors' Speeches; Sir H. Ward's collected Minutes and Speeches;

Ceylon Almanacks, Civil Lists, Manuals, Directories, &c. For *Natural History*:—Moon, Gardner, Thwaites, Kelaart, Hooker and Thomson, Templeton, Nietner, E. A. Layard, W. Ferguson, Boake, Steuart, Tennent (monograph on Elephant and on Pearl Oysters, Natural History of Ceylon), Legge, Moore, &c. On *Oriental and Buddhistical Literature*: —Turnour, Casie Chitty, Gogerly, Hardy, James Alwis, Fox, Callaway, Tolfrey, Upham, Childers, Rhys Davids; with transactions of Asiatic Societies of Britain, Bengal, Bombay, Ceylon, and Paris, American and German Oriental Societies, "Indian Antiquary," "Orientalist," "Literary Register," &c. On *Antiquities*,—besides above, Burrows' "Buried Cities of Ceylon." On *Elephant and Elk Shooting*:—Baker. For *Laws and Principles of Justice*, see "Thomson's Institutes," collected volumes of proclamations, ordinances, &c., with index, and reports of cases by Marshall, Murray, Morgan, Lorenz, Beling and Vanderstraaten, Beven and Mills, &c., and Supreme Court Circular volumes. On *Kandyan Law*:—Sawers, Armour, &c. *Tamil* and *Muhammadan Law*:—Muttukistna. On *Coffee Planting*:—Sabonadière's Coffee Planter of Ceylon; A. Brown's Manual; R. E. Lewis, Aliquis (description of coffee planting in rhyme, by the late Captain Jolly), pamphlets by Dr. Elliott, George Wall, P. Moir, Ballardie, Cross, Owen, &c. *New Products*:—On Tea, Liberian Coffee, Cinchona, Cacao, Cardamoms, Coconut and Cinnamon planting, see Manuals published at *Ceylon Observer* Office. *Poetry*:—Captain Anderson's "Ceylon" and other poems. On *Missionary Operations*:—Harvard, Selkirk, Emerson's Tennent's "Christianity in Ceylon," Life of the "Apostolic" Daniel, Hardy's Jubilee Memorials of Wesleyan Mission, Jones's Jubilee Memorials of Church Mission, Memoir of Mrs. Winslow and other American works, with reports of Baptist, American, Wesleyan, Church, and Romish Missions. On *Sinhalese Language*:—Clough, Lambrick, Chater, Carter, James Alwis, Jones, Nicholson, C. Alwis, &c. On *Tamil Language*:—Winslow, Percival, Rev. W. Clark, A. Joseph, A. M. Ferguson, jun., &c. For the most complete repertory of General and Statistical Information affecting the Colony, more especially of its Planting Enterprise, see successive editions of the "Ceylon Directory and Handbook of Information," by A. M. & J. Ferguson. For local Guides:—See Ferguson's

"Ceylon Railway and Sanitarium"; Burrows' "Kandy and Central Province"; Skeen's "Colombo and Environs"; Maitland's "Colombo and the Railway Service." For information bearing on every branch of Tropical Agriculture, see the *Tropical Agriculturist* published monthly at the *Ceylon Observer* Office.

# APPENDIX IX.

## CEYLON AND ITS PLANTING INDUSTRIES.

(*From the London "Times," August* 24, 1884.)

TO THE EDITOR OF "THE TIMES."

ROYAL COLONIAL INSTITUTE, 15, STRAND,

*August* 23, 1884.

SIR,—Ceylon and its planters have been several times referred to in the discussion in *The Times* on the prospects of sugar cultivation in the West Indies, and perhaps a brief *résumé* of the experience gained in the Eastern colony during a series of trying years may be of some interest and of service to planters elsewhere.

It is pretty well known how in the course of forty years, from 1837 onwards, Ceylon rose from being a mere military dependency (involving a considerable annual burden to the mother country) to the position of the first and wealthiest of British Crown Colonies. During that period its population, revenue, and trade so steadily advanced that they well-nigh excelled those of all the West Indian colonies put together. The change was due almost entirely to the development of coffee-planting, which sent in the heyday of prosperity in Ceylon as much in one year as £5,000,000 sterling worth of the fragrant bean into the markets of the world, chiefly through London. Other branches of agriculture prospered and advanced during those forty years, such as palm tree, cinnamon, and rice cultivation in the low country—coffee being grown on the hills—in the hands of the Sinhalese and Tamils. But it was through the capital introduced and the revenue created by coffee that the natives were enabled to extend their groves of coconut and palmyra palms, and that the Government could devote large sums to the restoration and construction of irrigation works, more particularly in supplying village sluices and tanks where the people were ready to make use of them.

So far as European colonists were concerned, coffee-planting almost exclusively claimed their attention, and many of the Sinhalese also embarked in this enterprize. While coffee continued profitable, the counsels of those who advocated the cultivation of other products was treated as so much idle breath. Theoretically it was shown many years ago that the climate and much of the soil of Ceylon were better suited for tea than coffee; but still the felling and clearing of the most beautiful and varied tropical forests in the world went on, until from 400 to 500 square miles of country were covered with the one shrub, *Coffea Arabica*, carefully planted, and scientifically pruned—topped at the height of an average gooseberry bush. Nature was, however, preparing the punishment of a gross violation of her laws—a violation paralleled by the would-be dependence of the Irish forty years ago on potatoes, or by the cultivation in other countries of too wide and unbroken an area of wheat, or of the vine. The penalty in Ceylon was first manifested in 1869, through a minute fungus on the leaf, very similar to the *oïdium* in the vine, rust in wheat, and the potato disease. For some seven or eight years not much was thought of it, save as an inducement to more liberal, careful cultivation; but the scientists called in to investigate, showed that little or no practical check could be offered, and within fifteen years,—to make a long story short—the minute, despised fungus had swept 100,000 acres of coffee cultivation out of existence—the poorly cultivated native gardens and neglected plantations being naturally the first to be abandoned. At the same time the export of the coffee bean fell last year to one-fourth the *maximum* of 1,000,000 cwt.

Here was certainly a grave misfortune overtaking a body of industrious men who had been the mainstay of a country's prosperity, and, moreover, their difficulties were aggravated by an extraordinary development of coffee production in Brazil. This was due to the interior of that South American Empire being rapidly opened up by railways made out of borrowed money; the labour, at the same time, used in cultivating fresh coffee plantations being slave. Such competition might be deemed unfair—more particularly as it has taken ten years' agitation in Ceylon to secure an extension of less than 70 miles of railway from the Colonial Office; but, in place of looking to the Government for factitious aid, the Ceylon planters ten years ago turned their attention to new products with all the energy and intelligence for which they are famous beyond any other tropical cultivators.

In many cases, of course, the new products, such as cinchona, tea, cacao (chocolate), and rubber, were experimented with as supplementary to the 175,000 acres of select coffee still maintained in cultivation; and let it be noted that in interspersing his coffee fields with cinchona and rubber trees, in planting belts or boundaries of such or areas of reserve in tea, the Ceylon planter was using one of the best means of checking the free dissemination of the fungus (*hemileia vastatrix*). As a consequence, possibly, or perhaps because the virulence of this pest is abating, during the current season Ceylon is giving an improved crop of coffee, and the export will be in excess of last year's.*

At the same time, the plantings of tea and cinchona bark have become established and important industries. The export of the latter this year will probably be equal to 10,000,000 lb.* against a beginning in 1869 with only 28 oz. Nor is it expected that South America can ever again compete with the East—Ceylon, India, and Java—in the production of the invaluable febrifuge.

Again, it is acknowledged on all hands now that Ceylon is better adapted to become a great tea-producing country than ever it was to lead with coffee. Situated in the pathway of the two monsoons, with an ample and well-distributed rainfall, in a most forcing climate, Ceylon is a perfect paradise for leaf crops. Fruit is more uncertain, and even in the best days of coffee great uncertainty often prevailed during the six weeks or two months of blossom-

* It was 324,000 cwt. against 260,000 cwt. the previous year.

† It was 11,492,000 lb.

ing season, when too much or too little rain often destroyed the chance of a due return for a whole year's labour. Coffee, too, could only be cultivated within a certain limited belt, from 2,500 up to 5,000 feet above sea level, whereas tea flourishes almost from sea-level to 6,000 feet and over. The tea shrub, in fact, is one of the hardiest of plants, growing in the open-air at Washington, United States, in New Zealand, &c. But the great advantage possessed by Ceylon and India for tea planting, is in cheap, suitable labour for the work of cultivation, leaf plucking, and preparing. The little island of Ceylon, as now opened up by railways and splendid roads, offers great advantages over most Indian districts for tea production. From both countries the tea supplied is of a pure, high quality. China teas have, in many cases, deteriorated of recent years, while the Japanese "greens," chiefly sent to America, are nearly all adulterated. I may, in passing, say that should the war now begun between France and China interrupt the tea trade or production in the Far East, there is no place whence a return can be so expeditiously got for the investment of capital in tea as from Ceylon. There is a wide extent of land available for tea, at an upset price of 10 rupees (16s.) per acre freehold, and a good crop of leaf can be had within three years of the planting. Assam planters who visit Ceylon are loud in their praise of what they see in the growth of our tea, our fine climate, unequalled roads, good supply of labour, &c. The progress already made in the tea industry may be seen from the figures appended.

The cacao, or chocolate-yielding fruit tree, is another new article of cultivation which has been successfully established in several districts in the island; the Ceylon product from this plant being pronounced in Mincing-lane to be equal to the very finest received from Trinidad or South America.

Indiarubber-yielding trees of various descriptions have, during the past few years, been extensively planted in Ceylon; but the industry is still purely experimental although good samples have been seen in the London market.

In fibres there ought, by and by, to be a great development of industry and trade in Ceylon, and, indeed, "capital" is the only element wanted to secure rapid progress in all the branches referred to. The fall of the Oriental Bank has reacted disastrously, rendering money very scarce for the poor but industrious planter, while, again, the credit of the colony has been damaged in many places through the non-success for many years and the final collapse of the Ceylon (but more properly Mauritius) Company, Limited. It is at this time, and in view of the absolute scarcity of capital and depression of credit, that many planters in Ceylon think their industries in "new products" should receive some official support; but they have no idea of interfering with the great principles of free trade or of making a grievance out of the advantage possessed by the slave-owning planters of Brazil.

It is a matter for congratulation that from the very beginning, the Ceylon planting enterprize has been based on a system of free labour, and that its products are so universally appreciated and beneficial as coffee, tea, quinine, chocolate, cinnamon, palm oils, &c. There is every reason to feel assured of a profitable return for money judiciously invested in these "new products" in Ceylon, and the much-tried sugar-planters of the West Indies cannot do better than make experiments in the same direction, although I am free to admit that the comparative scarcity and dearness of their labour places them at a heavy disadvantage.

J. FERGUSON,

Of the *Ceylon Observer* and *Tropical Agriculturist.*

---

The following are Statistics of some of the Planting Industries in Ceylon:—

*Coffee.*—1837:—2,500 acres cultivated; exported about 10,000 cwt. 1847:—45,000 acres cultivated; exported about 200,000 cwt. 1857:—85,000 acres cultivated; exported about 450,000 cwt. 1867:—168,000 acres cultivated: exported about 868,000 cwt. 1877:—272,000 acres cultivated; exported about 976,000 cwt. 1883:—174,000 acres cultivated; exported about 265,000 cwt., while 1884 is expected to show an export of over 350,000 cwt. of coffee—a welcome revival.*

* The actual export of coffee for season 1883–4 was 324,000. cwt.

*Tea.*—The export began with 482 lb. in season 1875-6: the export rose to 81,595 lb. in season 1878-9; and the export rose to 1,522,882 lb. in season 1882-3. The current season will probably show an export in excess of two million pounds,* and when the 35,000 acres of tea planted are in full bearing, in 1887-8, the season's shipments ought to be equal to 10 million pounds. Eventually it is estimated Ceylon should have 200,000 acres under tea, and an annual export of 60 million pounds and upwards. It depends on home capitalists very much how soon this result may be realized.

*Cacao.*—The export of cacao (or cocoa, as it is called in the market) began with 10 cwt. in 1878, and last year it was 4,000 cwt., while for the current year it is likely to reach 10,000 cwt.†

*Cinchona bark* began with an export of 28 ounces in 1869; rose to 507,000 lb. in 1879; and was last season equal to seven million pounds; while for 1883-4 the return will exceed 10 millions.‡

*Palm Trees and Cinnamon.*—Of the products of palm trees and cinnamon bushes, cultivated chiefly by native owners, Ceylon now sends an annual value of from £800,000 to a million sterling into the markets of the world, against less than one-fifth of this value thirty years ago.

[For later statistics of exports see table on page 272.]

---

## CEYLON AND ITS PLANTING INDUSTRIES.

THE EDITOR OF *The Economist.*

COLOMBO, *October* 26, 1886.

SIR,—The Ceylon commercial season closes on the 30th September each year, and the Colombo Chamber of Commerce Tables are made up as soon after as possible.

The actual results arrived at for our staple export trade cannot fail to be of much interest to those who have watched the gradual development of other planting

* The actual export of tea for season 1883–4 was 2,263,000 lbs.

† The actual export of cocoa was 9,863 cwt.

‡ The export of bark equalled 11½ million lb.

industries since the appearance of the leaf fungus which so woefully affected our coffee. Having drawn the attention of West Indian planters through the columns of the London press in August, 1884, to the way in which Ceylon planters had developed "new products" to make up for the failure in coffee, I would again put forward a few figures in support and illustration of the position I then took up.

Tea is rapidly becoming the main staple of the planters of Ceylon, and everything points to our export of this important new product rivalling that of India in about ten years' time. So far, it is comparatively the day of small things, but the following figures show the beginning of an important enterprise. It will be observed that the export progresses more nearly in a geometrical than an arithmetical ratio. The Ceylon exports of Tea have developed as follows:—

| | Tea. lb. |
|---|---|
| Total Exports from 1st Oct. 1885 to 30th Sept. 1886 | 7,170,829 |
| Do. do. 1884 do. 1885 | 3,796,684 |
| Do. do. 1883 do. 1884 | 2,262,589 |
| Do. do. 1882 do. 1883 | 1,522,882 |
| Do. do. 1881 do. 1882 | 623,292 |
| Do. do. 1880 do. 1881 | 277,590 |
| Do. do. 1879 do. 1880 | 103,624 |
| Do. do. 1878 do. 1879 | 81,595 |
| Do. do. 1877 do. 1878 | 8.515 |
| Do. do. 1876 do. 1877 | 1,775 |

Cinchona Bark shows the next chief development among new products, as the following figures will show:—

| | Cinchona. Branch & Trunk. lb. |
|---|---|
| Total Exports from 1st Oct. 1885 to 30th Sept. 1886 | 15,364,912 |
| Do. do. 1884 do. 1885 | 11,678,860 |
| Do. do. 1883 do. 1884 | 11,492,947 |
| Do. do. 1882 do. 1883 | 6,925,595 |
| Do. do. 1881 do. 1882 | 3,099,895 |
| Do. do. 1880 do. 1881 | 1,207,720 |
| Do. do. 1879 do. 1880 | 1,208,518 |
| Do. do. 1878 do. 1879 | 878,611 |
| Do. do. 1877 do. 1878 | 178,497 |
| Do. do. 1876 do. 1877 | 56,589 |

For a medicinal bark, and the preparations therefrom, there is no such scope for demand and consumption as in the case of tea. But to a fairly remunerative market, it is believed that Ceylon can supply 7 to 10 million lb. of cinchona bark annually without any difficulty; while if there were only the market, the export of the past season could probably be maintained for some years to come.

CACAO, or the cocoa or chocolate yielding plant, has not succeeded quite so widely as was expected in Ceylon, but there are certain districts in which the cultivation has now proved very successful. Some mistakes were made at first in the mode of planting, but these are now generally rectified, and there is the fair promise of increasing returns. This is especially the case during the present year, the weather having been very favourable to cacao. The annual exports have been as follows :—

| | | | | | | | | | | Cocoa. cwt. |
|---|---|---|---|---|---|---|---|---|---|---|
| Total | Exports | from | 1st | Oct. | 1885 | to | 30th | Sept. | 18-6 | 18,347 |
| | Do. | | do. | | 1884 | | do. | | 1885 | 6,758 |
| | Do. | | do. | | 1883 | | do. | | 1884 | 9,863 |
| | Do. | | do. | | 1882 | | do. | | 1883 | 8,588 |
| | Do. | | do. | | 1881 | | do. | | 1882 | 1,018 |
| | Do. | | do. | | 1880 | | do. | | 1881 | 479 |
| | Do. | | do. | | 1879 | | do. | | 1880 | 122 |

CARDAMOMS have been, for many years, quite a minor article among our products, but since the European planter has given his attention to this spice, the colony has taken the foremost rank for its exports, Ceylon, in fact, now ruling the European market for cardamoms as well as for cinchona bark. The exports of this spice have risen as follows :—

| | | | | | | | | | | Cardamoms. lb. |
|---|---|---|---|---|---|---|---|---|---|---|
| Total | Exports | from | 1st | Oct. | 1885 | to | 30th | Sept. | 1886 | 286,056 |
| | Do. | | do. | | 1884 | | do. | | 1885 | 152,405 |
| | Do. | | do. | | 1883 | | do. | | 1884 | 66,319 |
| | Do. | | do. | | 1882 | | do. | | 1883 | 21,655 |
| | Do. | | do. | | 1881 | | do. | | 1882 | 23,127 |
| | Do. | | do. | | 1880 | | do. | | 1881 | 16,069 |

In contrast with these instances of steady, continuous progress with what may be called "new products," I have to place the return for our staple coffee, showing an equally steady decline, consequent on the weakening

**effects of the fatal leaf fungus. The export figures are as follows:—**

| | Coffee, cwt. | | |
|---|---|---|---|
| | Plantation. | Native. | Total. |
| Total Exports from 1st Oct. 1885 to 30th Sept. 1886 | 215,576 | 8,117 | 223,693 |
| Do. do. 1884 do. 1885 | 294,506 | 20,305 | 314,811 |
| Do. do. 1883 do. 1884 | 312,458 | 11,483 | 323,941 |
| Do. do. 1882 do. 1883 | 245,631 | 14,422 | 260,053 |
| Do. do. 1881 do. 1882 | 522,949 | 41,897 | 564,846 |
| Do. do. 1880 do. 1881 | 415,456 | 38,302 | 453,758 |
| Do. do. 1879 do. 1880 | 622,306 | 47,308 | 669,614 |
| Do. do. 1878 do. 1879 | 767,293 | 57,216 | 824,509 |
| Do. do. 1877 do. 1878 | 551,046 | 69,246 | 620,292 |
| Do. do. 1876 do. 1877 | 851,201 | 91,846 | 943,047 |

It is satisfactory to know that Tea is so fully taking the place of coffee, over 130,000 * acres being now planted with this product, which grows well, not only within the limits of climate suited to coffee—namely, from 1,500 to 5,000 feet above sea-level—but from a few score of feet above, or almost sea-level, to nearly 7,000 feet altitude. The tea-plant is, in fact, one of the hardiest on the long list of the tropical planter, and nowhere has it found a more congenial home than in moist, hot Ceylon. The cry of over-production has, indeed, of late, been raised in reference to tea; but if English-speaking folks in America take to drinking tea in place of their favourite coffee, now likely, year by year, to decrease in supply, there will be a wide demand added to the present one. Moreover, so far as Ceylon is concerned, it has been shown that, through the great advantages possessed by the colony, that of a superior quality can be produced more cheaply here than in its great rival India, so that the remoter districts of the latter country must first suffer. The exports in which the Ceylonese people are chiefly interested, *i.e.*, cinnamon, plumbago (our only commercial mineral), essential grass oils, and the products of the coconut palm, *i.e.*, oil, copra, and coir fibres, keep well up, although the crop of coconuts is liable to alternate, according to the season. In a favourable season, the number of nuts gathered in

* Over 150,000 acres now, in 1887.

Ceylon is now estimated at a thousand millions—the greater portion, however being utilized locally for the food of the people.

Briefly, the total value of our staple exports for the past season may be put at £2,400,000 sterling; while for the current commercial year, October, 1886, to September, 1887, the following estimates prepared for the *Ceylon Observer* from district returns, indicate a very considerable advance :—

*Season* 1886–7.—*Probable Shipment of Staple Exports.*

| | Quantity. | Value. |
|---|---|---|
| Coffee ... ... ... ... | 185,000 cwt. at 75/ | £693,750 |
| Tea... ... ... ... ... | 14,000,000 lb. at 1/1½ | 787,500 |
| Cinchona bark ... ... ... | 12,000,000 lb. at 8d. | 400,000 |
| Cocoa ... ... ... ... | 22,000 cwt. at 80/ | 88,000 |
| Cardamoms ... ... ... | 300,000 lb. at 2/ | 30,000 |
| Coconut oil ... ... ... | 280,000 cwt. at 27/6 | 385,000 |
| Copra ... ... ... ... | 150,000 cwt. at 14/0 | 105,000 |
| Coconut Poonac ... ... ... | 50,000 cwt. at 7/ | 17,500 |
| Cinnamon ... ... ... | 1,500,000 lb. at 1/3 | 93,750 |
| Do. chips ... ... ... | 500,000 lb. at 5d. | 10,416 |
| Plumbago ... ... ... | 200,000 cwt. at 8/ | 80,000 |
| Coir of all kinds ... ... ... | 110,000 cwt. at 15/0 | 84,000 |
| Ebony ... ... ... ... | 7,500 tons at 100/ | 37,500 |
| Deer Horns ... ... ... | 2,000 cwt. at 50/ | 5,000 |
| Sapan Wood ... ... ... | 2,500 cwt. at 40/ | 5,000 |
| Kitul Fibre ... ... ... | 1,800 cwt. at 50/ | 4,500 |
| Essential Oils ... ... ... | 6,500,000 oz. at 1d | 27,000 |
| | Total... | £2,853,916 |

J. FERGUSON,

Of the *Ceylon Observer* and *Tropical Agriculturist.*

# APPENDIX X.

## THE PROSPECTS OF ENGLAND'S CHIEF TROPICAL COLONY.

### AN INTERVIEW WITH A CEYLON JOURNALIST (MR. JOHN FERGUSON).

(*From "The Pall Mall Gazette," August 29th; and "Budget," Sept.* 5, 1884.)

"We have not now 'all our eggs in one basket.' At present the city will not look at Ceylon as a field for investment. Money is scarce owing to the fall of the Oriental Bank, and our credit has been greatly damaged by the collapse of the Ceylon (more properly the Mauritius) Company. It should be known, however, that in our climate, roads, railways, cheap free labour, we have every encouragement for tropical agriculture in Ceylon. Our natives are being so rapidly educated that by 1900 A.D. English will practically be the language of the majority of the people. Colombo is the shipping centre of the Eastern world, thanks to Sir John Coode's new harbour; and capital judiciously invested in tea and cacao culture especially, is as likely to bring a good return as any agricultural enterprize I know of anywhere." Such is Mr. Ferguson's summing-up of England's principal tropical colony. He is inclined, it will be seen, to take an optimistic view of Ceylon and its future, but he speaks with the accumulated experiences of twenty-three years' residence in the colony. Then he has the numerous correspondents of his papers, the *Ceylon Observer* and the *Tropical Agriculturist*, scattered all over the tropical world where English planters are at work; some reporting on tea in Assam; on planting prospects in Java and Fiji; on the Liberian coffee in West Africa; and on planting in Brazil; while he himself has just been making the all-round-the-world trip, visiting California and Florida *en route*. "Nowhere is tropical agriculture so thoroughly studied and experimented on as in Ceylon."

Young Men Wanted.—"We now ask for young fellows of the right sort—even public schoolmen, university men—any one with pluck and energy who comes determined to fight his way against all odds. Do not mistake me. We do not want to be flooded out by thriftless never-do-weels, who have failed at everything they have turned their hands to, but resolute chaps with a little capital to invest, though they must first serve an arduous apprenticeship, for there is no royal road to tea-planting. No young fellow should come out without some money and letters of introduction to planters or merchants. A tropical country is very different in its conditions from Australia and New Zealand, where a man can turn to at once. Let us suppose our model young man landed at Colombo and dispatched to a station to serve his novitiate. In some cases he might have to pay from £50 to £100 a year for his board and training, but if he shows any aptitude for his work and is a willing horse, he would well repay his cost for food and shelter."

The Fungus Scourge.—"The story of the coffee blight is soon told. A few years ago, coffee alone was seen over hundreds of square miles of hillside and valley, eastward, south, and north of Adam's Peak. Then in 1869 the fungus appeared, and year after year it did its deadly work, and half ruined us. Here are some figures which put the matter in a nutshell. Take the coffee production from 1847 to 1883 now. You have in 1847 an acreage of 45,000, with an export of 200,000 hundredweight; in 1857—85,000 acres, and 450,000 hundredweight; in 1867—168,000 acres and 868,000 hundredweight; in 1877—272,000 acres, and 926,000 hundredweight; in 1883—174,000 acres, and 265,000 hundredweight; whilst 1884 is expected to give from 300,000 to 350,000 hundredweight. I think we may fairly say that the point of depression has been turned, if the estimate proves anything like correct."

Tea will Save us.—"What happened after the coffee blight became serious?" "Why, naturally enough, many of the plantations were deserted, the capitalists took fright, superintendents were thrown out of employment, and set off to other countries. There was a regular migration to Northern Australia, Fiji, Borneo, the Straits, California, Florida, Burmah, and elsewhere. I should say that out of our 1,700 planters we lost at least 400 in this way. In Northern Australia, at Port Darwin, three or four of our Ceylon planters have planted coffee and cinchona; in California some are busy with vines and oranges. Some have gone to Florida among the orange groves; but a Florida orange grove requires twenty years to come to full maturity, though the trees begin to bear long before that, say in six years. There is a ready market in America for the fruit, but a man requires to work hard there and to know his business before his speculation is likely to prove remunerative. But in Ceylon our indomitable planters, who stuck to their posts, began to turn their attention to other products—tea, cinchona, rubber, cacao; some 175,000 acres of coffee being still under cultivation. Many of the coffee planters ran belts of rubber trees and cinchona between his coffee bushes, thus helping to check the spread of the dread coffee fungus. I think the statistics show that the scourge is abating; but whatever comes of coffee, Ceylon will become a great tea-growing country within the next few years. When the 35,000 acres of land now under tea come into full bearing, in three or four years we expect to export ten million pounds. Some day Ceylon will have 150,000 acres under tea, and an annual export of sixty million pounds and upwards. Home capitalists have only to say the word. From 482 pounds of tea exported in 1875-6, the amount in 1882-3 reached a million and a half pounds. The yield of cacao for this year is likely to reach 10,000 cwt. Last season we exported 7,000,000 pounds of cinchona bark, this year it will be 11,000,000; while of cinnamon and palm tree products (grown chiefly by natives) we ship nearly a million sterling's worth. The Sinhalese and Tamils are quite ready to follow the European planters in reference to the new products of late years being introduced into Ceylon. They have planted the cinchona, cacao, and rubber trees; but specially are the Sinhalese likely to become extensive growers of the tea plant."

The Land and the Climate.—" Now is the time to buy

land, for we are on the turn after years of depression, and such land as you can now buy for 16s. an acre, may in a year or two be doubled or trebled in price. Just as was the case in the years between 1868 and 1875, when every one was 'going into coffee,' and forest land sold for £20 an acre in some districts. Since 1833 some 1,300,000 acres of Crown lands have been sold (to Europeans and natives), at an average price from 1833 to 1844 of 10s. 8d.; from 1844 to 1883 the average has been 35s.; and the upset price now is 16s. There is no land tax, except within the areas of the towns." "And what about the climate?" "Delightful—for the tropics most healthy, and not much hotter than it has been in London during the past few weeks, even at our hottest on the hills. Most of the planters and their assistants enjoy the best of health, though of course pioneers and those who have to work through new forest and in the low country, often suffer from malarious fevers. But then have you not the cool mountain station to fly to as a restorer? There is Nuwara Eliya and Bandarawela, on the plateau of Uva Principality, where you get coolness, with health-laden breezes—and I have even broken the ice in my water jug, in a Nuwara Eliya cottage. Given a change now and then, good food, care, and temperance—a European is as well off as regards climate (some might say better) than at home here."

Free Labour.—"One of our greatest advantages is 'Free labour.' Close at our shores are the twelve million coolies of Southern India, whose average earnings are between £3 and £4 a year each. Yes, and he is able to live on it, too, and to support a wife and family. From this vast source we draw our supply of labourers, and fine well-trained, diligent fellows they become. They come over with perhaps a wife and three or four children; they are engaged for a period, a month's notice sufficing to terminate the contract on either side. There is a hut ready for them, with a bit of ground for a garden, in which they grow vegetables and so on; the planter gives them a blanket and food until they are able to repay him out of their earnings. Their wages average from ninepence to a shilling a day for a man; a woman can make about 7d., and a child 5d., so they are well off; they save money, and when they go back to their own village in a year or two's time, they have probably some five or six pounds in their pouch.

This the careful coolie invests in a piece of land, which, on his return to the Ceylon plantations, he leaves in charge of a relative or a friend until he goes home again. Our Kandyans, or highlanders, are splendid axemen, and it is they who do the felling of our forests and the clearing of the land ready for planting. Then the South Indian coolies do the digging and planting. The land, by the way, lies generally on timbered slopes. The axemen begin at the bottom, cut each tree half through, and work up to the top. The highest fringe is cut clean through, and with its weight brings down the rest of the slope in the fall. The Sinhalese themselves refuse to do any agricultural work for Europeans. It is beneath them. They are our carters, employed in taking the tea and coffee, and so on, from the stations to the coast. If I remember rightly there were some 13,000 licensed carts a year or two ago. The Sinhalese are also our boatmen and artisans and domestic servants. Now many of our Sinhalese and Tamils are wealthy. One, indeed, is the richest man on the island, with an income of some £20,000 a year or more. Some of the coolies, I must confess, are sad thieves. You may of a Sunday meet a man and his wife on the road, one of them carrying a cock, the other a hen. The birds are all their portable property, which they are compelled to take with them while visiting some friends, lest they should be stolen."

Ceylon Railways.—"The cost of the Colombo and Kandy Railway, of 74 miles, was £1,740,000. Then an extension to Nawalapitiya from Peradeniya, 17 miles, was opened in 1874; and an extension from Kandy to Matale, 17½ miles, in 1880. Besides these, a seaside line has been constructed from Colombo to Kalutara, 27½ miles. In August, 1880, the first sod was turned of an extension from Nawalapitiya for 42 miles to Upper Dimbula, whence it was intended to be carried 25 miles farther to Haputale. Altogether about 180 miles of railway, all on the 5½ ft. gauge, have been opened, or are under construction. But there is one grievance which I should like to point out concerning these railways. The length of forty-two miles from Nawalapitiya to Upper Dimbula will probably be opened in May, having cost £900,000 of money. But then they are going to stop short instead of pushing on as was proposed to Haputale, the real terminus, with new traffic, which is only 24 miles farther, and would cost £400,000, and open up a vast amount of splendid country, which at present is compelled to send its produce round by road, a distance of 200 miles—a road which is subjected to floods, too, to say nothing of the delay and cost."

The Tea Planter at Work.—"Let us suppose that a young man has learned his business, and has a thousand or two of capital. He buys 200 acres at 16s. an acre. He would begin by opening up, say, twenty-five acres his first year, clearing, draining, and planting. Then, in his second year, he would prepare another twenty-five acres. Up to and including the third year his outlay would be about £20 to £25 an acre. In his third year there would be a crop of tea-leaf—a small one. In the fourth and fifth year he might expect, supposing that he is lucky, to have a crop of tea of 400 lb., to the acre, which he would lay down in England at 9d. a pound., which would produce in the market from 1s. 3d. to 1s. 6d. a lb., thus leaving a margin of 6d. profit. Then he would advance, not laying out too much capital to start with, but gradually feeling his way. All the year round tea requires one man per acre, in crop time a fuller force. It is hard physical work, though there may be no absolute manual labour. At five in the morning the bugle sounds for all hands, the planter comes down to the muster, the coolies go off to their work, the master has his coffee and follows them, going on foot of course, from point to point, supervising and directing, and at 11 a.m. he returns to his breakfast. Until 3 p.m. he remains indoors, attending to business matters, then going out again for another spell of work and inspection. And so the days pass." "Snakes?" "Boots and clothing are a great protection against snakes, and during the last sixty years I don't think there has been one case of death among the whites. The natives, of course, have no protection from clothing, and are more careless. In Ceylon our coffee machinery for pulping, for skinning, for drying, has been brought to a state of perfection, and the machines manufactured at Colombo are known throughout the tropics. It is this attention to improvements that has helped us so materially. Our planters are men with ideas, which they are quick to put into force. So it is with the new industries—tea, cinchona, cacao—the machinery for their preparation is being improved every day. You see Ceylon is a comparatively small country, and the planters are able to compare notes. A hears how B is doing this, he tells it to C, they have a talk about it, and so the matter grows. Each district has its little centre (not to mention the health resorts on the hills), where there is a club and other facilities for the intercommunication of ideas."

The Ways of the Heathen Chinee.—"On my way from Singapore to China I fell in with a Sumatran tobacco planter who had imported Chinese coolies at a cost of £7 to £10 a head, on an engagement of a number of years. Smallpox broke out among them. Now a Chinaman prefers death to disfigurement; he has no notion of revolving through endless cycles with a pitted face, so they took to suicide, and every morning the overseer came in with his report:—'Another ten to thirty pounds gone, sir. One to three more of 'em found hanging to a tree just now.' This was a serious difficulty. So at last the planter issued a proclamation to the effect that the body of the next hung Chinaman, instead of being carefully coffined, would be cut into pieces. This device stopped suicide. Another curious fact respecting the peculiarities of the Chinese is worth mentioning. When a Chinaman signs articles on board ship one of them is that if he dies on the passage his body shall be embalmed and sent back to China. In the steamer between Yokohama and San Francisco, one of our stokers met with an accident. The doctor said the only chance for him was to cut off his leg. 'No, no,' said the stoker, and 'No, no,' chorused his comrades. But in a day or two mortification set in, and the leg was sacrificed. The man died, and his friends were horribly savage at the desecration wrought by the doctor's knife and saw. But they made the best of it and embalmed the mortified leg with the dead body of poor John. The Chinese in the Straits earn, if they are good workmen, about 4s. a day. Perhaps, we have three Chinamen all told in Ceylon, but it is curious to notice that after four days' steaming from Colombo to Singapore you are virtually in China, for the Chinamen are gradually filling the Straits up. Of course there is much to be said on both sides—but the Californians, so far as I saw, miss their Chinese servants sadly—in fact, a Chinaman is at a premium. In my opinion the time had not come in Western America to stop Chinese immigration. At present only traders are allowed to enter the country, though for every Chinese coolie who dies one is allowed to take his place. A big business is done in certificates from all I can hear. Why, I heard that one of the most violent of the anti-Chinese agitators still kept to his Chinese servants. He is not a true patriot, like the Englishman who refused to eat slave-grown sugar. Some two or three years ago a Queensland planter engaged 500 of our Sinhalese to go to his sugar plantations. They went, much to our surprise, for such a thing as Sinhalese emigration was unknown. They proved a bad bargain, for they were nearly all selected from gaol-birds of the worst type. Few of them ever found their way to the plantations, many were absorbed in the towns, whilst a few found their way back home."

An Opening for English Girls.—"There is just one word of advice I should like to give to fathers and brothers. To the latter, if you go to Ceylon or India—or to any other colony, for the matter of that—arrange after you have a house of your own to get your sister out with you. England is overstocked with women, who are clamouring for work and votes and husbands, too. Now England is sending out some of her best blood to its distant possessions. Why should the young men go and not the young women? I am convinced that the presence of his sister would have saved many a young fellow, in the pioneering days in the tropics, from drink and ruin, if she had been there to look after his bungalow and minister to his wants. Fellows used to come in from a hard day's work on the mountain slopes, fagged and weary, to their bungalow. There was food for them prepared by native servants, but it was often not fit to eat. So some went to the beer or brandy for consolation. Things are better now, and ladies more numerous; but still, in colonizing, whether to tropical or temperate climes, sister and brother may well go out together. But there is no need for me to expatiate on the advantages of my proposal."

"What do you think of the prospects of the North Borneo Company?" I asked Mr. Ferguson, as he rose to go. "I cannot say from actual experience, but we have one or two correspondents there from whom we hear now and then. It took Ceylon seventeen hard years of pioneering before we began to think that success would be permanent, and North Borneo is yet a very young country. There are at present a few plantations of tea, coffee, and cinchona scattered along the coast, while collectors are at work in the interior gathering ivory and minerals. It is like other new colonies—it needs capital and men."

KEW GARDENS.—"I cannot, by the way, over-estimate the value of the work which Sir Joseph Hooker and Kew Gardens do for us, not only for Ceylon, but for all the tropical countries wherein fresh products are being tried. The Kew authorities have correspondents and collectors in all parts, and if any one wishes to try experiments he has only to write to Kew for advice and specimens, which are forwarded to him from the gardens. You might think that it would be easier for us to send to the country where the plant or fruit was indigenous rather than to England, but the difficulties would often prove too great. Kew is of vast service to the planters in many respects." "The military force," said Mr. Ferguson, in conclusion, "situated in Ceylon, costs us £120,000 a year, or 10 per cent. of our revenue.* Now why should we be compelled to expend this sum on British troops we don't want. It is a serious grievance. You use Ceylon as a convenient centre, from which you may draw in case of any little war in India, in China, in New Zealand, in South Africa, or Egypt. I do not think it fair to impose this burden upon us."

* This burden has since been greatly reduced, very much through the influence of Governor Sir Arthur Gordon. In some other parts of *The Pall Mall* report of this interview I have made corrections where my remarks were slightly misunderstood.—J.F.

# APPENDIX X.

## "THE SHADOW OF THE PEAK."

(*Inserted by permission from "The Philosophical Magazine" for January*, 1887).

### THE PECULIAR SUNRISE-SHADOWS OF ADAM'S PEAK IN CEYLON. BY THE HON. RALPH ABERCROMBY, F.R. MET. SOC.*

THERE are certain peculiarities about the shadows of Adam's Peak which have long attracted the attention of travellers; a good deal has been written about them, and several theories have been proposed to explain the observed phenomena. In the course of a meteorological tour round the world the author stopped in Ceylon for the express purpose of visiting the Peak, and was fortunate enough to see the shadow under circumstances which could leave no doubt as to the true explanation, and which also entirely disproved certain theories which have been propounded on the subject.

The following account is taken from a paper by the Rev. R. Abbay, many years resident in the island, entitled, "Remarkable Atmospheric Phenomena in Ceylon," which was read before the Physical Society of London, May 27th, 1876, and published in *The Philosophical Magazine* for July, 1876. Writing from descriptions, for he himself had never witnessed the appearance, Mr. Abbay says:— "At sunrise apparently an enormous elongated shadow of the mountain is projected to the westward, not only over the land but over the sea, to a distance of seventy or eighty miles. As the sun rises higher, the shadow rapidly ap-

* Read before the Physical Society on November 13th, 1886.

proaches the mountain, and appears at the same time to rise before the spectator in the form of a gigantic pyramid. Distant objects—a hill or a river (or even Colombo itself, at a distance of forty-five miles)—may be distinctly seen through it; so that the shadow is not really a shadow on the land, but a veil of darkness suspended between the observer and the low country. All this time it is rapidly rising and approaching, and each instant becoming more distinct, until suddenly it seems to fall back on the spectator, like a ladder that has been reared beyond the vertical; and the next instant the appearance is gone. For this the following explanation is proposed:—The average temperature at night in the low country during the dry season is between 70° and 80° F., whilst that on the summit of the Peak is from 30° to 40°. Consequently the lower strata of air are much less dense than the upper; and an almost horizontal ray of light passing over the summit must of necessity be refracted upwards and suffer total internal reflection as in the case of an ordinary mirage."

It will be remarked that Mr. Abbay does not allow for the difference of elevation, and the sequel will show that this theory cannot be maintained.

Adam's Peak is a mountain that rises in an abrupt cone, more than 1,000 feet above the irregular chain to which it belongs; the summit reaches to 7,352 feet above the sea. On the south side the mountain falls suddenly down to Ratnapura, very little above the sea-level; while on the north it slopes irregularly to the high valley of the Maskeliya district. The peak also lies near an elbow in the main chain of mountains, as shown in the diagram of the topography of the Peak (fig. 1), while a gorge runs up from the north-east just to the west of the mountain. When, then, the north-east monsoon blows morning mist up the valley, light wreaths of condensed vapour will pass to the west of the Peak and catch the shadow at sunrise only, if other things are suitable. The importance of this will appear later on.

The only difficulty in getting to Adam's Peak is the want of a rest-house within reasonable distance of the summit. Fortunately the kindness and hospitality of T. N. Christie, Esq., of St. Andrew's plantation, Maskeliya, enabled the author, in company with Mr. G. Christie and

Professor Bower, of the University of Glasgow, to make the ascent with great comfort and with a few necessary instruments. Our party reached the summit on the night of the 21st February, 1886, amid rain, mist, and wind. Towards morning the latter subsided, but at 5·30 a.m. the sky was covered with a confused mass of nearly every variety of cloud. Below and around us cumulus and mist; at a higher level, pure stratus; above that, wild cirro-stratus and fleecy cirro-cumulus.

Soon the foreglow began to brighten the under surface of the stratus-cloud with orange; lightning flickered to the right of the rising sun over a dense mass of cloud; opposite, a light pink-purple illumined an irregular layer of condensed vapour; while above, a pale moon, with a large ill-defined *corona* round her, struggled to break through a softish mass of fleecy cloud. Below lay the island of Ceylon, the hills and valleys presenting the appearance of a raised relief-map; patches of white mist fill the hollows; true cloud drove at intervals across the country, and sometimes masses of mist coming up from the valley enveloped us with condensed vapour.

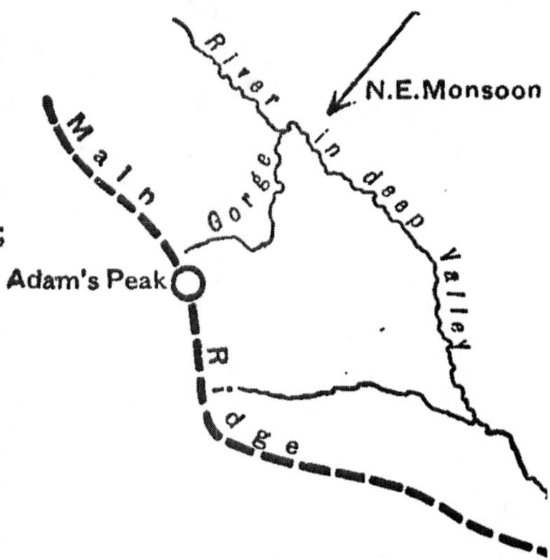


FIG. 1.—DIAGRAM OF THE TOPOGRAPHY OF ADAM'S PEAK.

At 6 a.m. the thermometer marked 52° F.; we had been told that the phenomenon of the shadow depended on the temperature at the summit falling to 30° or 40° F.; and when, shortly after, the sun rose behind a cloud, we had almost lost all hope of seeing anything; but suddenly at 6.30 a.m. the sun peeped through a chink in the clouds, and we saw the pointed shadow of the peak lying on the misty land. Driving condensed vapour was floating about, and a fragment of rainbow-tinted mist appeared near the top of the shadow. Soon this fragment grew into a complete prismatic circle of about 8° diameter by estimation, with the red outside formed round the summit of the Peak as a centre. The author instantly saw that with this bow there ought to be spectral figures, so he waved his arms about and immediately found shadowy arms moving in the centre of the rainbow. Two dark rays shot upwards and outwards on either side of the centre, as shown in the Diagram, fig. 2, and appeared to be nearly in a prolongation of the lines of the slope of the Peak below. The centre of the bow appeared to be just below the point of the shadow, not on it; because we were standing on a platform below a pointed shrine, and the subjective bow centred from our own eyes. If we did not stand fairly out in the sun, only a portion of the bow could be seen. Three times, within a quarter of an hour, this appearance was repeated as mist drove up in proper quantities, and fitful glimpses of the sun gave a sufficient light to throw a shadow and form a bow. In every case the shadow and bow were seen in front of land and never against the sky. The last time, when the sun was pretty high, we saw the characteristic peculiarity of the shadow. As a thin wreath of condensed vapour came up from the valley at a proper height a bow formed round the shadow, while both seemed to stand up in front of us, and then the shadow fell down on to the land, and the bow vanished as the mist passed on.

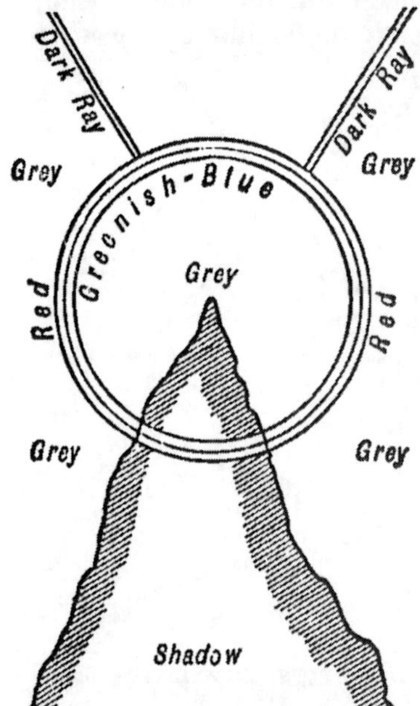


FIG. 2.—DIAGRAM OF RAINBOW ROUND THE SHADOW.

Here, then, was an unequivocal explanation of the whole phenomenon. The apparent upstanding of the shadow was simply the effect of passing mist which caught the darkness of the Peak at a higher level than the earth, for when the condensed vapour moved on the characteristic bow disappeared, and the shadow fell to its natural plane on the ground. When the mist was low, as on the two first occasions, the shadow fell on the top as it were, and there was no appearance of lifting, only the formation of a bow.

The well-known theory of the bow is that light diffracted in its passage between small water-globules forms a series of bows according to the size of the globules, their closeness, and the intensity of the illumination. Had the mist been so fine and thin as merely to catch and raise the shadow, but not to form a bow, there might have been some doubt as to the origin of the appearance. Our fortune was in the unsettled weather which made the mist so coarse and close that the unequivocal bow left no doubt as to the true nature of the cause.

About an hour later the sun again shone out, but much higher and stronger than before, and then we saw a brighter and sharper shadow of the Peak, this time encircled by a double bow. Our own spectral arms were again visible, but the shadow was now so much nearer the base of the Peak, and we had to look so much down on it that there was no illusion of standing up, and there were no dark diverging rays. The inner bow was the one we had seen before; the outer and fainter one was due to stronger light.

The bows were all so feeble and the time so short that the author did not succeed in obtaining any sextant measurements of the diameters of the bows; but his thermometric observations conclusively disprove any idea of mirage. At 6 a.m. the thermometer on the Peak marked 52° F., while at Colombo the temperature stood at 74°·85. The difference of 22°·85 is just about the normal difference in temperature due to a height of 7,352 feet.

The Colombo figures were procured through the courtesy of the Surveyor-General for Ceylon. They are got as follows:—Colombo observations only give the *minimum* that morning as 73°·6 F. and the 7 a.m. reading as 75°·5. The mean curve of diurnal temperature for the month of February, as determined by the Office, gives a difference of 0°·65 between the 6 a.m. and 7 a.m. observations; and by subtracting that correction from 75°·5 we get 74°·85 as the 6 a.m. reading.

The questions have been frequently asked—Why this lifted shadow should be peculiar to Adam's Peak? why a similar appearance is not observed from any other mountain top? and why the shadow is rarely seen at sunset? There are not many mountains which are habitually visited that are either over 7,000 feet, or that rise in an isolated, well-defined pyramid. Still fewer can there be where a steady wind, for months together, blows up a valley so as to project the rising morning mist at a suitable height and distance on the western side to catch the shadow of the peak at sunrise. The shadow is not seen during the south-west monsoon, for then the mountain is covered with cloud and deserted. Nowhere either do we find at sunset those light mists lying near the ground which are so characteristic of sunrise, and whose presence is necessary to lift the shadow.

The combination of a high isolated pyramid, a prevailing wind, and a valley to direct suitable mist at a proper height on the western side of the mountain, is probably only rarely met with; and at present nothing yet has been described that exactly resembles this sunrise shadow of Adam's Peak in the green island of Ceylon.

But there is another totally different shadow which is sometimes seen from Adam's Peak, just before and at the moment of sunrise, that has been mixed up in some accounts with the shadow we have just described. The shadow of the base of the Peak stretches along the land to the horizon, and then the shadow of the summit appears to rise up and stand against the distant sky. The first part seems to be the natural shadow lying on the ground; and the sky part to be simply the ordinary earth shadow of twilight projected so clearly against the sky as to show mountainous irregularities of the earth's surface. As the sun rises the shadow of the summit against the sky gradually sinks to the horizon, and then the ordinary shadow grows steadily shorter as the sun gets higher in the usual manner. This can only be seen at sunrise from Adam's Peak, because the ground to the east is too high and mountainous to allow the shadow of the summit to fall on the sky before the sun is too far down.

The author found a similar effect, only at sunset, on

Pike's Peak, Colorado, 14,147 feet above the sea, and nearly double the height of Adam's Peak. There, towards sunset, the shadow of the mountain creeps along the level prairie to the horizon, and there begins to rise up in the sky till the sun has just gone down, and the anticrepuscular shadow rises too high to catch the outline of the Peak. The author only witnessed a portion of this sequence, for just about the time that the shadow stretched to the horizon clouds obscured the sun, and the rise of the shadow could not be observed; but from all the descriptions he heard there can be no doubt that the character of the shadow is identical with that of Adam's Peak, only that, as the order of sequence is reversed, it is more easy to follow the origin of the shadows.

Since the above was written the author's attention has been called to the sketch of the shadow exhibited by the well-known traveller, Miss C. F. Gordon Cumming, in the Colonial Exhibition. This picture represents the shadow lying down, but not raised, on an irregular surface of white mist and mountain tops. The most interesting thing is a prismatic fringe of colour along the straight outside edges of the shadow; but there is no trace of a bow round its point.

When we consider how much the appearance of the shadow depends on the height, size, and aggregation of the mist we need not be surprised at the numerous phases of reflection and refraction that have been described by travellers; but the general principles which have been laid down in this paper appear to govern all.

---

[Since the above was written, the Rev. R. Abbay has come forward to dispute some of the conclusions arrived at by Mr. Abercromby, and, indeed, to controvert his main contention.—J. F.]

# APPENDIX XII.

## TEA IN CEYLON.

*The following useful information was prepared by* THE PLANTERS' ASSOCIATION OF CEYLON, *and circulated at the late Indian and Colonial Exhibition at South Kensington in* 1886.

IN the minds of the British public the name of Ceylon has been chiefly associated with the production of coffee and spices: the latter in poetry, but in poetry only, imparting their fragrance to the very air.

While Ceylon coffee and Ceylon spices are of superior quality and remain most important articles of trade, it is Ceylon tea that is rapidly becoming the staple product, and the one for which the island will soon be most celebrated.

Seldom or never has an industry made such progress, or a new article of consumption overcome by its intrinsic merit the opposition of vested trade interests as has Ceylon tea.

In 1873 the exports of tea from Ceylon were 23lbs.; in 1885, they have been 4½ million lbs.; in 1886 they will be about 10 million lbs.; and in the near future 40 million lbs. will be exported.

The area under tea in the island is rapidly extending, and already about 120,000 acres have been planted. Over 700 European planters and 150,000 Indian and Sinhalese labourers are engaged in the cultivation. Some of the plantations are but little above sea level, while others run up to an elevation of 6,000 feet. The average altitude of the larger districts is about 4,000 feet above sea level, an elevation at which the climate is pleasant and most healthy. A railway runs up into the hills and a good system of cart roads exists, so that most of the estates are already within a day's journey from Colombo—the capital and shipping port.

At a time when dietetics has almost become a science, when purity and cleanliness in food and beverages are so

COOLIE GIRL PICKING TEA-LEAVES.

strongly insisted on, it is strange that greater attention has not been called to the more than doubtful nature of much of that which is consumed as tea.

It has been said that, if to be an Englishman is to eat beef, to be an Englishwoman is to drink tea. True it is that the article which in the sixteenth century was a luxury, costing ten guineas a pound and consumed by a hundred people, has in the nineteenth century become a necessity, costing two shillings a pound and consumed by millions.

Did the people of Britain thoroughly understand the difference between British-grown tea—such as Ceylon's—and that of China or Japan, it is certain that those who could get the pure, clean, machine-prepared leaf which is turned out from the planter's factory, would never touch the far from pure article prepared by the hands and feet of the unwashed Mongolian.

In China and Japan tea is mostly cultivated in small patches by the peasantry, who gather the leaves and prepare the tea in their huts in a very unfastidious manner. The tea, either in a half-manufactured or finished state, is sold to petty dealers, who in turn sell to larger dealers.

The large dealer mixes and manipulates teas, packs and sells them to the European merchants for shipment to England, Australia, or America. The manipulation of tea is an art in which the Chinaman excels, and in many of the inferior kinds the quality is infinitely deteriorated—thus, "the dust of the leaf is mixed with clay and manipulated into the form of the ordinary leaf"—this is with appropriate philological coincidence termed "lie" tea. "Tea leaves which have been already used are again manipulated and rolled into shape and sold as genuine tea."

The teas of Japan, which are almost entirely consumed by our American cousins, are frequently and admittedly "faced" with a mixture of Prussian blue and soapstone.

The Ceylon estate cultivation and manufacture is very different, and it may not be uninteresting to give a brief account of how *pure tea* is made. Visitors to the Ceylon Court in the Colonial and Indian Exhibition will find an interesting series of photographs from life, attached to the exhibits of tea, illustrating the various operations.

The tea bushes are planted in lines at regular distances over hundreds of acres of carefully roaded and drained land, which is regularly weeded every month. Once a year the bushes are pruned down to a height of about two feet; and eight weeks after the pruning the first "flush" of young shoots is ready to be plucked, and during the height of the season the flushes re-occur every ten days. Coolies, having a small basket attached to their girdle, then go round and pluck the bud and a couple of the tender half-developed leaves. At mid-day, and again in the evening,

WEIGHING-IN GREEN TEA-LEAF ON A TEA ESTATE.

the leaf is weighed and taken into the factory. The leaf

is at once spread very thinly on trays or shelves to wither. The time which the leaf takes to wither—to become soft and pliable without drying up—varies with the weather, but as a rule the leaf gathered one day will be sufficiently withered the following day.

The withered leaf is then placed in the rolling-machine, an ingenious and effective machine which is driven by water or steam power. The rolling lasts for nearly half-an-hour, at the end of that time the leaf has become a moist mass of twisted and bruised leaves, out of which the expressed juice freely comes, technically called "the roll." The roll is then placed in trays to ferment or oxidise; during this process it changes from a green to a copper colour. The subsequent strength and flavour of the tea depend, to a great extent, upon the fermentation—a chemical process, the success of which is not entirely within the control of the planter, but depends greatly on the weather, and takes a time varying from two to six hours.

The next process is that of firing. The roll is thinly spread on trays, and placed either over charcoal stoves or in large iron drying-machines, and at the end of half-an-hour it is thoroughly crisp and dried, and has become tea. The tea is then sorted or sized, by being passed through sieves of different meshes (see working model of a tea-sifter in the Ceylon Court) giving the varieties of broken-pekoe, pekoe, souchong, congou, and dust. The broken-pekoe, which consists chiefly of the opening bud of the leaf, gives the strongest tea, perhaps too strong a tea to be infused by itself; and a mixture of pekoe and souchong makes the most pleasant drinking tea.

The final process is that of weighing and packing. When a sufficient quantity has been manfactured the tea is again slightly fired, to drive off any suspicion of moisture, and packed while warm in lead-lined boxes carefully soldered down to exclude air.

Such is the mode of careful, cleanly preparation in the specially erected factory of the Ceylon planter; and every drinker of genuine Ceylon tea may be certain that it is *absolutely pure.*

Ceylon tea stands unrivalled for its combination of strength and flavour; and the pure tea gives a beverage pleasant and beneficial to those who drink it. One cannot doubt that, were the well-meaning evangelists in the cause of temperance to realize the difference between pleasantly-strong well-flavoured stimulating tea and the "wishy-washy" decoction infused from the cheaper China teas, their efforts to substitute "the cup which does not inebriate" for that which does might be made much more successful.

In addition to the other good qualities, Ceylon tea possesses that of being economical; for it is generally admitted that two pounds of Ceylon will go as far as three pounds of China.

The tea you drink should be—

1.—Pure.
2.—Wholesome.
3.—Pleasant.
4.—Economical.

And Ceylon tea justly claims pre-eminence on these grounds.

Would-be purchasers of Ceylon tea must be warned that there is danger (just as there is with everything which has earned a good name and become popular) of a spurious or admixed article being sold instead of what is genuine.

# APPENDIX XIII.

## WORKS OF PUBLIC INTEREST EXECUTED, AND ENDOWMENTS MADE, BY THE DE SOYSA FAMILY, AND CHIEFLY BY C. H. DE SOYSA, Esq.

ROADS.—Cart road from Haragama to Len Oya. Good cart road at a point near eleventh mile post on Galle road. Good cart road farther north on same road. Good cart road tenth mile post at village Angulana. Several roads in the Chilaw district. Good cart road in populous villages terminating at Mampe. Excellent cart road from Polgas Owitte in Salpity Korale crossing village Mattegodde, terminating at Delgaha Manatte. The widening and repairing of many roads in and about Moratuwa.

FIELDS AND TANKS.—The building of the Malluwawawe at Gonagama. Irrigating a large field at Kandevalle, with a view to giving employment to the neighbouring destitute villagers.

AMBALAMS, &c.—A comfortable rest-house for the use of the foot passengers at Haragama. An extensive and well-kept cemetery at Moratuwa for both strangers and members of the congregation. Rest-house at Moratuwa with separate compartments for both sexes.

CHURCHES.—The church at Hanguranketta. A fine church at Maravilla. St. John's, Panadura. Holy Emmanuel's, Moratuwa. Contributions towards building the churches at Negombo and Kurunegala. The Panadura burial ground, which was liable to inundations, was raised at a large cost.

HOSPITALS.—Building of the Hospital at Maravilla.

The De Soysa Museum and the Lying-in Home at Colombo. Panadura Hospital.

SCHOOLS.—Schools at Koralawelle ; Prince and Princess of Wales' Colleges, costing Rs.150,000. Donation, Rs.80,000 to St. Thomas' College ; donation to the Jaffna College.

PUBLIC RECEPTIONS.—Reception to the Duke of Edinburgh, costing £10,000. Establishment of "Alfred Model Farm," £10,000.

SOCIETIES.—The establishment of the Moratuwa Co-operative Society for the improvement of people. Establishment by Jeronis De Soysa, Mudaliyar, of the Society called Satarana Sarana Samagama—the Gansabawa being the outcome.

IMPROVEMENTS TO TOWN.—By building Fort Offices, Cottages, Slave Island Buildings.

RELIEF FUNDS.—Subscription to Relief Funds.

TRANSLATION OF BOOKS.—Undertook cost of translating Hithopadesa into Sinhalese.

HOUSES.—Building two cottages at Mount Lavinia, the income of which goes towards the expenses of Emmanuel Church.

LIBRARIES.—Establishment of Library at Moratuwa. Besides various other acts in Ceylon, too numerous to mention.

Add to these the £1,000 which Mr. de Soysa handed to Sir Arthur Birch, Commissioner for Ceylon at the Indian and Colonial Exhibition in September, 1886, for the purchase of the fittings of the Ceylon Court as a contribution to the Imperial Institute, and £500 in cash for these Institutions; and £1,000 given to the London Hospitals as a memento of his first visit to England, in November, 1886.

# APPENDIX XIV.

## BENEFACTIONS BY S. D. A. RAJEPAKSE, Esq.

Entertainment.—To the sailors of the men-of-war which brought His Royal Highness the Prince of Wales to Ceylon: R3,000.

Contribution to the Colombo "Friend-in-Need Society."—In commemoration of the visit to Ceylon of their Royal Highnesses, Albert Victor and George, the sons of the Prince of Wales: R1,000.

Contribution to the Colombo "Friend-in-Need Society."—To help the Society when it was in want of funds: R1,000.

Rajepakse Prize.—Annual value, R100. In connection with the Royal College, Colombo.

Rajepakse Prize.—For midwifery, in connection with the Medical College, Colombo. Annual value, R100.

Weeresinghe Prize.—To perpetuate the memory of A. W. M. Weeresinghe, in connection with St. Thomas's College, Colombo. Annual value, R100.

Endowed "Duke of Edinburgh's Scholarship."—In commemoration of the visits of His Royal Highness the Duke of Edinburgh to Ceylon; Principal R8,000; in connection with St. Thomas's College, Colombo.

Endowed "Gregory Scholarship."—In commemoration of the eminent services of Sir W. H. Gregory, K.C.M.G., as Governor of Ceylon; Principal, R8,000; in connection with St. Thomas's College, Colombo.

Endowed "Prince of Wales' Exhibitions."—In commemoration of the visit of His Royal Highness the Prince of Wales; Principal, R10,000; in connection with St. Thomas's College, Colombo.

Contribution to the "Gregory Statue."—In commemoration of the administration of the Government in Ceylon by Sir W. H. Gregory, K.C.M.G.: R5,000.

Contribution to the "Galle Clock Tower."—Erected in commemoration of the eminent services of P. D. Anthonisz, Esq., M.D.: R3,500.

Contribution.—To the relief of the villagers distressed by the flood of 1872: R2,000.

# APPENDIX XV.

[As a curiosity and of special interest to English readers, we give the following "Genealogical Tree" of one of Ceylon's worthiest sons and most generous philanthropists.]

## GENEALOGICAL TABLE,

SHOWING THE DESCENT OF S. D. A. RAJEPAKSE, MUDALIYAR OF HIS EXCELLENCY'S GATE, AND J.P. FOR THE ISLAND.

B. D. A. Rajepakse, Mudaliyar of the Grand Ronda.

A. D. A. Rajepakse, Maha Vidane, Mudaliyar of Welitara District. ⚭ Daughter of Lewis Mendis Wickremanaike, Attapatoo Mudaliyar of Maha Badda.

A. D. A. Rajepakse, Mudliyar of Mutwal and Welisara Districts. ⚭ Caroline de Soyza Wijeysirriwardena.

S. D. A. Rajepakse, Mudaliyar of His Excellency's Gate, and J.P. for the Island.

FURTHER PARTICULARS.

| | S. D. A. Rajepakse's |
|---|---|
| Carlo de Miranda, First Interpreter and Chief Mudaliyar of the Maha Badda. | Maternal Grandmother's Grandfather. |
| Solomon de Miranda, First Interpreter and Chief Mudaliyar of the Maha Badda. | Maternal Grandmother's Father. |
| R. de Zoysa Rajepakse, Maha Vidane Mudaliyar of Maha Badda. | Maternal Great-grandfather. |
| S. de Zoysa Rajepakse, Cappina Mudaliyar, and Mudaliyar of Calna Modera District. | Maternal Grandfather. |

## GENEALOGICAL TABLE,

TRACING THE DESCENT OF S. D. A. RAJEPAKSE (THROUGH HIS MOTHER) TO CARLO DE MIRANDA, FIRST INTERPRETER AND CHIEF MUDALIYAR OF THE MAHA BADDA.

Carlo de Miranda, First Interpreter and Chief Mudaliyar of the Maha Badda. ╤

Solomon de Miranda—First Interpreter and Chief Mudaliyar of the Maha Badda. ╤

Susana de Miranda ╤ Solomon de Sosa Rajepakse, Kappina Mudaliyar.

Caroline ╤ A. D. A. Rajepakse, Mudaliyar of Mutwal and Welisara Districts.

S. D. A. Rajepakse, Mudaliyar of His Excellency's Gate, and J.P. for the Island.

FURTHER PARTICULARS.

S. D. A. Rajepakse's (Mudaliyar) Mother's Father.—S. de Zoysa Rajepakse, Kappina Mudaliyar and Mudaliyar of Kalna Modera District.

S. D. A. Rajapakse's Mother's Grandfather (father's father).—R. de Zoysa Rajepakse, Maha Vidane Mudaliyar of Maha Badda.

S. D. A. Rajepakse's Father.—A. D. A. Rajepakse, Mudaliyar of Mutwal and Welisara Districts.

S. D. A. Rajepakse's Grandfather.—A. D. A. Rajepakse, Maha Vidane Mudaliyar of Welitara District.

S. D. A. Rajepakse's Great-grandfather.—B. D. A. Rajepakse, Mudaliyar of Grand Ronda.

S. D. A. Rajepakse's Paternal Grandmother.—The daughter of Lewis Mendis Wickremanaike, Attapatoo Mudaliyar of Maha Badda.

S. D. A. Rajepakse's Maternal Great-grandfather.—R. de Zoysa Rajepakse, Maha Vidane Mudaliyar of Maha Badda.

S. D. A. Rajepakse's Maternal Grandfather.—S. de Zoysa Rajepakse, Cappina Mudaliyar, and Mudaliyar of Calna Modera Districts.

S. D. A. Rajepakse's Maternal Grandmother's Father.—

Solomon de Miranda, First Interpreter and Chief Mudaliyer of the Maha Badda.

S. D. A. Rajepakse's Maternal Grandmother's Grandfather.—Carlo de Miranda, First Interpreter and Chief Mudaliyar of the Maha Badda.

# APPENDIX XVI.

## COLOMBO AND THE BUDDHIST TEMPLE AT KELANIYA.

THE following lively description by Julian Thomas ("The Vagabond" of the *Melbourne Argus*), of his two days' visit to Colombo, will be read with interest:—

"The eleventh morning out from Albany, at daylight, Point de Galle or Matara is visible. Low shores, then rolling foothills, then a high mountain chain towering into the clouds; over all, the peculiar soft olive-blue haze which denotes the presence of dense tropical vegetation. White mist lies in the valleys, giving the appearance of lakes overshadowed by the mountains. I am reminded of the Gulf of Darien as I first saw it twenty years ago at early morn. Tennent well says that this island, from whatever direction it may be approached, 'unfolds a scene of loveliness and grandeur unsurpassed, if it be rivalled, by any land in the universe.'

"From the sea, Ceylon appears like the mountain region of Otago, New Zealand, planted in the midst of a tropical garden. Verily 'every prospect pleases' here. Now and then in the dense coconut grove one sees glimpses of colour in a red-tiled roof or brown thatch. There is a heavy population—nearly three millions—in a country one-sixth less than the area of Ireland, and a large portion of which is covered by mountain ranges. A large number live, if not entirely on the water, at least by the products of the sea. Fishing catamarans are sailing up and down the coast, and we pass many of them lying-to and drawing in their nets. The style of boat is known to every schoolboy. It is nearly the same as the *woga* canoe of the South

Seas. The sixty miles coasting voyage between Galle and Colombo is altogether one of the most beautiful in the world. We see Kalutara at the mouth of a large river. A charming settlement this, twenty-seven miles south of Colombo, with which it is connected by railway, being known as the Richmond of Ceylon. Twenty miles farther on is Mount Lavinia, another popular seaside resort, where a monster hotel bids for custom. And now the shore becomes dotted with bungalows, there is a break in the palm grove, and Colombo is ahead. A city of high buildings, towers, cupolas, red-tiled roofs, open spaces, flowering trees, green lawns—a magnificent capital of 120,000 inhabitants, a mixture of Shanghai and Old Panama and Honolulu. Verdure everywhere, colour everywhere, life everywhere. We round Sir John Coode's Breakwater, and in the harbour are ships of many nations —British, French, Italian, and German steamers, an English gunboat, and native sailing craft of an infinite variety. A brigantine well-sailed passes us. She is of English build, but is manned entirely by blacks. Bound this to the Eastern Maldives or the coast of India. But it is strange to see the children of Ham 'running' a vessel of their own. The Australian is here brought face to face with the fact that there is a civilization other and older than his own. Catamarans of all sorts and sizes crowd around the vessel. Every variety of Oriental race and costume is represented. The light-brown native Sinhalese, with their long black hair secured by huge tortoiseshell combs, have an effeminate appearance which makes new chums mistake all the males for women. The conquering Tamils, from Southern India, are darker and more manly. There are Hindus of every cast and style of undress— 'Moormen,' *tambies*, tall muscular Afghans, Parsees and Chinese, swarthy Malays, and Eurasians (fat and oily) of Dutch and Portuguese descent. All from the magnificently attired dealer in the precious stones of Birmingham to the scantily-clad boatmen, appear to have been waiting from their creation for the arrival of the *Rome* to screech at us in a babel of tongues; to rush up the gangway and storm us with applications to buy; to be filled with an overpowering desire to take away our washing, or to carry us off to the Grand Oriental Hotel or the Galle Face Hotel. And as they fight and yell on one side of the ship, there comes a chorus from the other, 'Habbadibe! Habbadibe!' which, being interpreted, means, 'Have a dive,' signifying that the hundreds of little rascals, nearly naked, who are floating about on pieces of wood, or paddling frog-like in the water, are willing to dive for our amusement and their own profit after any silver coins we may throw overboard. 'Good-day, Sahib; Habbadibe! Habbadibe!' they shout, keeping a sing-song time. A sixpence or a shilling dropped into the water sends fifty pairs of legs into the air; for a second the white soles of their feet are seen, another second, and arms and heads flash up again, and one of the lads shows the coin before pouching it like a monkey. Sometimes a fight takes place, but it is of a bloodless character.

"Colour is the prevailing feature; a red waist cloth or a rag bound round the head, contrasting with the dusky skins, has an effect which, *en masse*, pleases the eye. Nothing can make our Australian larrikins beautiful, but the meanest Oriental here is picturesque. To our colonial-born youth these natives suggest so much. Visions of the Arabian Nights are conjured up. Those of us who have read the Thousand and One Tales, think of Aladdin and Sinbad, of the Old Man of the Sea, and the Hunch back of Bagdad, as celebrated in literature as he of Notre Dame. Many of us make up our minds to do the Haroun al Raschid's trick here, and see what adventure may happen to the adventurous. But first to get ashore. I let a Moorman, 'Abdallah' by name, a runner for the Grand Oriental Hotel, take possession of me, and form one of a party in a steam launch which for sixpence a head lands us on the quay. Two minutes' walk to the hotel. I engage a room, and then a carriage, and with Abdallah, who professes he knows all the city, I drive around Colombo. I have first three well-known men to see and interview—Arabi Pasha, Mr. John Ferguson, and Colonel Olcott. Ahmad Arabi, Egyptian exile, lives at Elizabeth House, Mackenzie Place, in the Cinnamon Gardens. The residence is an ordinary bungalow, with no particular style about it. The Malay policeman who receives my card expresses his doubts as to whether the 'Badger,' as he pronounces 'Pasha,' will see me. But Arabi and myself have mutual friends, and I soon have the pleasure of shaking hands with him and Yacoob Samy, another exile. We have cigarettes and coffee, and Arabi, who now speaks English fairly well, expresses his pleasure at hearing that Colonel J. M. Morgan is United States Consul at Melbourne. We do not talk politics, and in truth our conversation is limited. It is very strange to think that this quiet-looking gentleman in the fez was five years ago master of Egypt. A son of the soil, a *fellah*, whose kindred are bare-footed tillers of earth, Ahmad Arabi is the most remarkable man in his country since the days of Mahomet Ali. 'The Wallace of Egypt,' I once styled him to an enthusiastic Scotchman in the 'Far North' of South Australia.

"I do not think there is a city in the world so beautiful in the luxuriant verdure which clothes it as this. As one drives about Colombo the botanist has great pleasure in noting the trees, the flowers, and the shrubs. One admires the graceful waving coconut palms (*cocas nucifera*), the plumes of the betel palm (*areca catechu*), of which Dr. Hooker wrote—'The cultivated areca raises its graceful head and feathery crown like an arrow shot from heaven in luxuriance and beauty above the verdant slopes;' and the fan beauty of the Travellers' tree (*reevenela Madagascarensis*). You pass along avenues where Suriya trees (*thespesia populnea*) cast their shade, with their poplar-like foliage and large yellow flowers; you notice the heart-shaped leaves and yellow-pink flowers of the tulip tree, often used to line a garden wall or rail. Great specimens of the *pterocarpus indicus* spread their shady boughs overhead. Now you see your familiar friend, the silky oak (*Grevillea robusta*) lining the roadway with yellow flower-heads hiding among the fringe-like leaves. Beside the bungalows are Australian she-oaks (*casuarina equisitifolia*), their height and vigour of growth here being remarkable. Banyans with hanging aerial roots stand beside that beautiful sight, the Flamboyante, or flame tree (*poinciana regia*), with its large feathery, twice-pinnate leaves and bunches of scarlet flowers. There, too, is the sacred Bo tree (*ficus religiosa*) of the Buddhists, whose aspen leaves have the midribs prolonged into a tail-like extremity. As you listen to the rattling, rustling noise of the leaves shaken by the wind, you think of the superstition of the Hindus that connects this with the spirits of their departed Brahmins. The green foliage is exquisite, and the shade most inviting. Here is the coral tree (*erythrina indica*), bearing triangular leaves and curled combs of scarlet flowers on the topmost boughs. You notice the palmate foliage and warty bark of the *eriodendron anfructuosum.* The *bauhinia purpurea* and *variegata* add their share of shade and colour. Among the leaves, shaped into two rounded halves, long pods hang at this season. There is an airiness and lightness about the great tamarinds (*tamarindus indicus*); from the at present bare boughs of the silk cotton tree (*bombax malabaricum*) hang round pointed pods just bursting to shower flakes of white down over their neighbours. This cotton is used for stuffing pillows and mattresses here. A grand tree is the Ceylon oak (*scherchera trijuga*), so like in general appearance to the British oak. Beside it grows the large-leaved *carrega arborea*, and overspreading the roadway is the rain tree or *inga saman* (*calliandra fuaman*), having foliage somewhat like the false acacia, and crown-shaped flower heads of pink colour. The air is perfumed with the fragrance emitted from the white flowers of the frangipanni, that with long leaves cluster at the end of the thick naked shoots.

"Besides all these, cultivated for their beauty and their shade, one sees great groves of fruit trees, the jak trees (*artocarpus integrifolia*), so much grown by the natives, whose huge fruit, hanging from the boughs and trunk, varies in weight when ripe between 30lb and 50lb. The pulp containing the albuminous seeds tastes very like a banana. Bread-fruit trees (*artocarpus incisa*), closely allied to the above, you notice in the groves, also the plantain and bananas raise their broad light-green leaves among them with clusters of fruit. Many are the mango trees (*manganifera indica*) planted about. A noble tree is the wild bread-fruit (*artocarpus nobilis*), its large vein-furrowed leaves casting a delightful shade. Most beautiful are the gardens—a wealth of colouring, a luxuriance of vegetation. There are hedges of *aclypha tricolor*, whose leaves are variegated, yellow, red and brown; and also of *aclypha bicolor*, tinted green and yellow, with the peacock flower (*poinciana pulcherrima*), and borderings to the pathways of feathery *aralia Guilfoylii*, called after our own botanist. In the shade of the great trees and palms around the bungalows grow innumerable species of crotons, mingling their many-tinted leaves, showing all shades between brown, purple, yellow, red and green. There, too, flourishes the hibiscus, whose bright, scarlet flowers catch your eye. One variety is called the "shoe-flower," because you can blacken and polish your boots with its crushed petals. You see these plants in the hedge-rows mingling with an arborescent sunflower (*stifflia crysantha*). Here, again, are the *poinsettia pulcherrima*, with its bright scarlet, calycine leaf-like bracts, and the ever-flowering oleander (*nerium oleander*). A curious specimen is the potatoe tree (*solanum macrantha*), resembling a great over-grown potatoe plant. The exquisite purple of the *bougainvillea spectabilis* overspreads verandahs and arbours, and *alamandas* add their yellow blossoms. Now and then you see a *spathodea*—large-leaved, and bearing great red flowers. Often you notice the orange vermilion blossoms of the West Indian coast bramble (*lantana mixta*), introduced by Lady Ward from Australia, and now fast over-spreading the waste land of the island. At intervals, great clumps of bamboo add their feathery beauty, and you even see the castor oil tree (*ricinus communis*) grown in gardens, with occasionally the nutmeg (*myristica officinalis*). Add to these the cinnamon, and there is such a wealth of botany and floral beauty in Colombo as you will find nowhere else in the world; and the most extraordinary thing is, that all this beautiful and useful vegetation has been imported, none of the trees and plants I have mentioned being indigenous to Ceylon. But Ceylon is still essentially a Buddhist country, the nominal followers of this form of faith forming nearly 62 per cent, of the population. The Buddhists are divided into two sections, the Siamese and Burmese, and I believe they quarrel as much as the High and Low Church factions in England. It is the former who have possession of Vidyalankara College and Temple at Peliyagoda, near Kelani, whither I am driving to-day. There are two very eminent Buddhist priests here, a printing press is in operation, and an Oriental library is being built. But it is to see the people at their festival that I drive out to Kelani. Certainly I am satisfied, for I never expect again to witness such a picturesque throng. All Ceylon and Colombo seem to be *en route* to Grand Pass, three miles from the city, where Governor Sir Edward Barnes, in 1825, built a bridge of boats across the Kelani river. Young and old, male and female, singly or in families, on foot or in bullock 'hackeries,' the natives—Sinhalese and Tamils—are trooping into the country, all clad in new and striking coloured garments, all bearing flowers, all picturesque, making up *en masse* a picture of laughing life seldom to be met with. Men and women wear two garments, the skirt, *sulu* or kilt, and the upper jacket or scarf. The brighest hues of Manchester are displayed in the prints. The men sport great tortoise-shell combs in the hair, whilst the women adorn theirs with pins. Sometimes the hair hangs straight and sleek down the back. All have umbrellas to protect themselves from the sun, and all are alike in the outward resemblance of the sexes. The dress and combs and hair confuse a stranger, and he knows not Eve from Adam.

"A bullock 'hackery' is a vehicle only known in the East. Small, humped cattle, the size of Shetland ponies, are harnessed roughly to carts without springs, which, covered with thatch, often contain two floors, on which the passengers, however, have to lie down. Sometimes one comes across a bullock drawing a light buggy, and trotting along briskly. By Brahmin and Buddhist alike the cow is held to be a sacred animal. They must not eat its flesh. But they ill-treat these poor little bullocks in a manner which arouses my indignation. The patient beasts are especially suffering on this day when the faithful are hurrying to the shrine of him, who, of all men, most enjoined humanity to the brute creation. Two little animals are drawing, perhaps, a family of a dozen. Blows and oaths are showered on them without ceasing, and my soul is wroth within me; otherwise this is a perfect afternoon. After crossing the bridge of boats at Grand Pass you drive along a narrow road bordered by coco-palms and bananas and tamarinds. But there is never any distance without habitations. Some of mud, red tiled, are permanent abodes; others of thatch, seem erected by the roadside just for these days of festival. Food and flowers are for sale everywhere. Never save in the city of Mexico have I seen so many flowers as here. The whole country seems full of them. There is an overpowering fecundity of nature in Ceylon—all around, in still life, in the animals, in the human race, you see it—everything is increased and multiplied abnormally. This might well be the birthplace of our race; a man need not be a patriarch here to be surrounded by troops of grandchildren. And so laughingly exchanging greetings with the pilgrims, whom my Muhammadan driver, I daresay, curses a good deal, the time passes till, two miles from Kelani railway station, we enter Petiyagoda. The throng by this time is immense. There have been special trains from Colombo in the afternoon, and thousands are trudging along the road, on foot or riding in hackeries. Unhappily for them the rain has commenced to fall heavily.

"There is a regular bazaar around the entrance to the temple. Everything, it seems, can be bought here. This is the great harvest of the stall-holders. On this, their New Year's Day, the Sinhalese 'indulge in the few amusements they enjoy, and in such luxuries as they can afford.' One of these luxuries consists in having their fortunes told by astrologers, who predict the propitious hours in the approaching year on which to commence duties, pleasures or journeys. I wonder if the astrologers foresaw or fortold the abominable weather on this *fête* day. However, I am here, and must see it through. At the bottom of the steps I am taken possession of by an emasculate-looking individual, who informs me that he is the temple guide. He is a full-blooded Sinhalese and acknowledges to the name of Perera. This, with Fernando and De Silva, is as common in Ceylon as Smith, Jones and Brown are in England. There are no end of 'Des' and 'Dons,' too, in the Directory. This is the remnant of the Portuguese occupation. Many of these high-sounding names belong to full-blooded 'niggers,' whose ancestors were baptized by the Roman Catholic missionaries, but who relapsed into Buddhism on the first chance. I tell Perera I shall call him 'Peter,' to which he cheerfully assents. And I inform Peter that I am a Buddhist, 'higher up' than his priests, as he can plainly see. He treats me with an accession of respect, whether real or fictitious I know not, and we walk off to see the relics. There are a number of curious, silver statuettes, which may be idols dug up on this spot where, before the advent of Buddhism, Vishnu and other male and female deities were worshipped. One god, Wibhisana, is still held in repute here, having a local reputation among the ignorant, although the educated Buddhist despises such superstitions. Then I am taken to the great show. In a pavilion there is a placard in English. 'The bones of Buddha may now be seen.' 'The bones of Buddha' at this temple on a silver dish under a glass case are not much of a show. They appear like a very decayed tooth smashed up, and do not impress me, although, naturally, I give my contribution towards building the library for which the plate is held out here. My rupee inspires more respect and faith in my Buddhism.

"Architecturally, all Buddhist temples are alike. The *Dagoba* is the principal feature in all. Derived from *dhatu-garba*, the matrix or receptacle of a relic, a dagoba is a mere bell-shaped tomb of brick or stone, covered often with a preparation of lime, forming a sort of *chunam*, which receives a high polish. The Dagoba is surmounted by a spire and enclosed by a row of pillars. The Dagoba—the imitation of the tomb of Buddha—is a useless piece of work, as for that matter church spires are, unless when used as landmarks. The shrines around, where the praying takes place, are ordinary buildings. Peter leads me through the crowd to the sacred altar, behind which is a gigantic painted wooden figure of Buddha, and of several gods or saints. Peter is anxious to explain to me that the Great God Almighty is not here, but that He will come some day, incarnated in a new Buddha. I marvel that all over the world there should be the same belief in an earth god—that we should ever make Him in our own image. Buddha's injunction was, 'Abstain from all sin, acquire all virtue, repress thine own heart.'"

# APPENDIX XVII.

## STATISTICS OF CEYLON RAILWAYS.

(PREPARED BY J. FERGUSON.)

See *The Railway Map* inserted at end of the Volume.

Gauge, 5 feet 6 inches, same as Indian Lines.

| Lines. | Miles. | Total Cost. Rs. | Per Mile. Rs. | Speed Miles Per hr | Traffic Receipts in 1885. Rs. |
|---|---|---|---|---|---|
| Colombo and Kandy .......... | 74½ | 17,384,830* | 233,353* | 25 | 1,648,940 |
| Peradeniya and Nawalapitiya .. | 17 | 2,674,627 | 157,331 | 20 | 249,869 |
| Colombo and Kalutara ........ | 27¾ | 2,192,214 | 84,823 | 25 | 248,673 |
| Branch line Mahara Junction and Mahara Quarry ........ | 2½ | 220,790 | 88,336 | 15 | 19,867 |
| *Free property of the Colony* .. | 121¾ | 22,472,461 | 184,000 (Average) | 22 (Av.) | 2,167,349 |
| Kandy and Matale (with debt of £275,000 .................. | 17½ | 3,391,952 | 193,966 | 20 | 73,044 |
| Nawalapitiya and Nanuoya (with debt of £900,000) .......... | 41¾ | 10,778,000 | 256,500 | 12 | 366,927 |
| Railways complete and working | 181 | 36,637,413 | 202,417 (Average) | 18 (Av.) | 2,607,320 |
| | Already Surveyed and Estimated. | | | | |
| Dimbula-Uva (Haputale Section) | 25½ | 6,500,000† | 254,902 | 12 | |
| Kalutara and Bentota Section | 9 | 550,000 | 61,000 | 25 | |

Total Miles 215½.

| | |
|---|---|
| Traffic Receipts in 1885 as above .................... | Rs. 2,607,320 |
| Working Expenses and Improvements to Lines ...... | 1,467,699 |
| Profit...... | Rs. 1,139,621 |

Or nearly four per cent. on total capital cost, although the full benefit of the expenditure on Nanuoya Line can only be realized when the extension reaches Haputale, where the new Uva traffic is tapped.

---

* This includes large amount wasted by Limited Company, afterwards paid off.

† This is the Consulting Engineer's estimate, but with the experience of rock and earth work gained on the Nanuoya Section, it is believed that Rs. 5,000,000 or Rs. 200,000 per mile will suffice for the Haputale Section if constructed by the P. W. Department.

# RAILWAY MAP OF CEYLON.

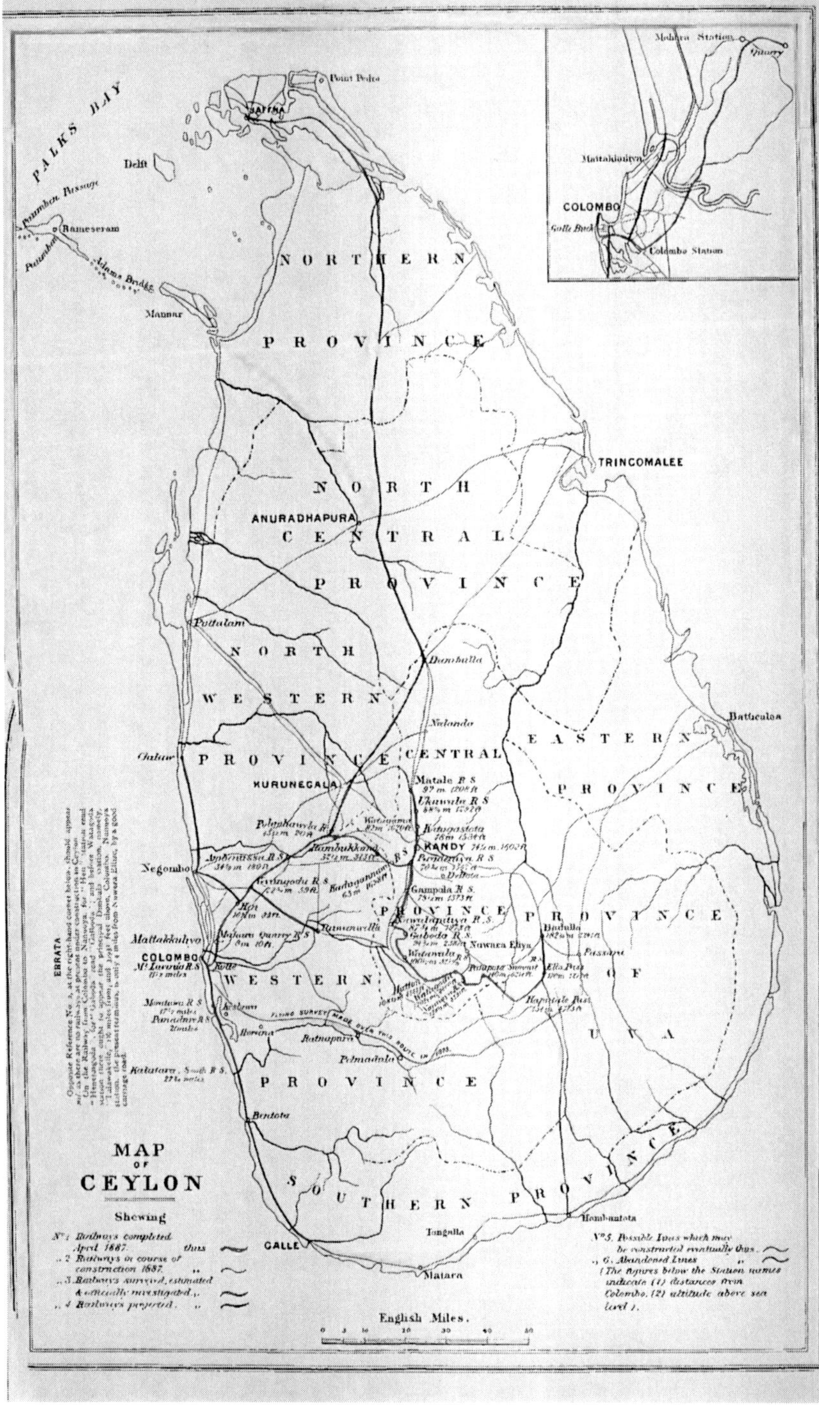

# APPENDIX XVIII.

## CASTE IN CEYLON.

In illustration of the remarks on pages 39–40, and 251, we may refer here to evidences of a very unfortunate revival of caste feeling in the rural districts of Ceylon. This is attributable, in the opinion of many observers—among the natives more particularly—to an influence emanating from the present Governor, Sir Arthur Gordon, who has, most unfortunately, in public utterances, official documents, and ceremonies, made much of "natives of birth," and led the agents of Government and native headmen, and through them, minor officials, to believe that caste distinctions may well be revived. As a consequence, there have been many quarrels, assaults, and even minor riots in native villages owing to caste animosities and jealousies which were supposed so have died out. The people who consider themselves of the higher castes are now on the *qui vive* in many places to resent those of alleged lower castes dressing themselves above the waist, or on more than one shoulder, using jackets or combs for their hair, which, under the benign and civilizing influence of past Governments, had become an almost universal practice among the people. Governor Sir William Gregory in his tours through the island, especially the remoter parts where caste distinctions lingered longest, specially discouraged any caste or dress distinctions, and even censured Government officers for allowing people of so-called "lower castes" to appear with their bodies (women as well as men) not properly covered from the waist upwards. This did much to encourage dressing, self-respect, and even a mild ambition among the industrious classes, and provoked no jealousy, because even a Governor's word, or even nod, is law to the Sinhalese of all ranks. About 1880, however, in a translation of Kandyan laws made in manual form, partly under official auspices, entitled "Niti-Niganduwa," an attempt was made to classify different castes, and within the past three years, it is said, rightly or wrongly, this classification—(effected so as to exalt one caste)—has been as good as recognized at all Government offices. This has provoked much angry feeling, and amidst a great deal of discussion in the native press and much pamphleteering, two productions especially have come under our notice. The writer of these in a private note thus expresses himself in answer to our inquiries as to the reasons which led him to publish :—

"*June* 9, 1887.

"SIR,—Though I cannot say that I wrote the review of 'Niti-Niganduwa' with an unruffled mind, yet I can assure you that I wrote the 'Chaturvarnaya' with the best of feelings. I have been a constant reader of the *Observer* for the last thirty or forty years, and I have the happiness of being personally known to you, therefore I say it with all sincerity that it is neither from the Government nor from our countrymen that we can expect to get some relief from the grievances under which we now labour, but from you.

Ten or twelve years ago there was a Muhandiram of the tom-tom beater caste. He was not only using his crooked comb and the high comb, but on State occasions he was using his sword and belt, and nobody ever thought of molesting him; but now there is a feeling abroad that Government now recognizes caste—hence the late tragedy at Attidiya. A registrar of marriages in the Southern Province lately objected to a marriage party coming to his premises in carriages, and did not give a chair even for the bride or bridegroom, though they were a respectable class of people.—Yours obediently, ——."

From the pamphlets themselves we quote as follows :—

From "A Review of Niti-Niganduwa and the Caste-System in Ceylon." By W. W. Colombo, 1885.—"While wealth, science, and general knowledge have been advancing with astonishing rapidity, bigotry, pride, and prejudice in a section of our community have made still more gigantic strides, and threaten to outrun all the efforts hitherto made to arrest their progress. Without in the least degree trying to help their countrymen in their onward course, they are always trying to aggrandize themselves and to secure a monopoly of Government high posts and ranks showing that they are entitled to them by birth. . . .

"It might, perhaps, be asked, was not the late Louis De Zoysa Maha-Mudaliyar, that well-known oriental scholar, a man of the Salagama caste, and yet was he not promoted to the highest rank which a native can aspire to? Yes: every man is in some degree the mirror of his age. . . .

"Mr. De Zoysa's age was an age attempting, with a strong, unrelaxed, endeavour to be earnest, persevering, and ambitious. Compulsory labour having been abolished, and amalgamation of classes having taken place, the peasant had been shown how he might rise to be noble; the horny-handed craftsman how he could tread the paths which lead to the highest places of national distinction; and the humble scholar how he could advance into the saloons of greatness. . . .

"Mr. De Zoysa was allowed to climb up to the summit of the hill of official promotion; but his followers, like the Jews of old, are obliged to wander about in the wilderness. The Government since then, forsaking the liberal and enlightened policy of the former Governors, and instead of making an outward progress in the right direction, is now pursuing a downward course. . . .

"A paragraph in the issue of the *Ceylon Observer* of the 27th July, 1885,* having given us occasion for alarm we traced out its origin to the existence of a book printed at the Government Press so far back as the year 1880; since then it has been in circulation through the hands of Government officials. That work, though entitled 'Niti-Niganduwa, or the Vocabulary of Law,' has in it, headed 'Historical,' a chapter embodying a distinctive classification of castes with the assertion that the 'Gowiya is considered the chief caste in this kingdom.' What induced the compiler in getting up a Vocabulary of Law to insert therein a classification of castes, and to state the superiority of the caste to which he belongs, is a problem which has to be solved. A man of ordinary intellect and common sense will easily divine the mystery and the object of the compiler to be to secure for himself as an author a prominent post under Government, whilst his showing will induce the Government to hold such others of his community in such estimation as to obtain for them a monopoly of the most honourable and lucrative offices to which natives are eligible. That book, though printed in the year 1880, it is strange

---

"* The paragraph referred to is as follows:—'CASTE RE-ESTABLISHED IN CEYLON.—This may be news to *some* readers of the *Observer*. Others have already known and felt this. The Portuguese and Dutch with all their old-world ideas and crude notion of things never stooped to the meanness of upholding the senseless, absurd system of caste. But it has been left to the British Government and to enlightened statesmen of the Liberal school to re-establish caste in Ceylon. It is said that a *brochure* on caste, as it existed amongst the Sinhalese, was got up under well-known local auspices, printed in England, and distributed amongst influential members of the Civil Service. But the absurd part of the story is that Sir Arthur Gordon regards it in the light of the Englishman's Bible, an authority beyond question like Dod or Debrett. According to this authority appointments, as well as preferments to honorary rank and title, are to be confined to a few families; the rest are to be discarded. The Clerical Examination Scheme is to be done away with. Go on, brave Sir Arthur! Go on in the same style, and we shall have cause to thank you as one of Ceylon's benefactors!—*Com.*'

to observe, made its way through Government Departments in such a manner that either none (excepting those of the community who expected to be benefited) or very few of the other classes were aware of its existence and the havoc it was playing, till the appearance of the paragraph referred to. . . .

"The reason why most of the Gowiyas have succeeded so far in securing to themselves lucrative and responsible offices under the Government is attributable to the fact (which is now evinced) that it has been for a series of years past their object, if not the motto, to impress upon new officials and heads of Departments, as far as possible, that they are the leading members of the native community and that to them exclusively belonged posts of responsibility and honour under the Government. . . .

"But justice compels us to say that caste has no claim on any right-thinking mind; for, as a system, 'it is founded on a lie,' 'it puffs up certain classes with pride,' 'it keeps many of our people in social degradation,' 'it divides man from man,' it concentrates all religion in outward ceremony,' and 'it is a great obstacle to progress.' . . .

"What is the object of introducing a list of castes into the Niti-Niganduwa? Are we to understand from it that caste is to be *Anglicized,* and receive the sanction of the Legislature, that different occupations, professions, and trades may be made hereditary and preserved in an unbroken line? If Tikiri Appu, the son of an ordinary peasant whose father, grandfather, or great-grandfather had never held any office under the late Kandyan Government or under the present British rule, has pushed his way into a prominent situation, and into power and influence, we ask, what evil has he done? Whom has he injured? Has Tikiri Appu by his success robbed another of industry, talent, application, or energy? Does not Tikiri Appu deserve the signal honour and emolument won by hard study and patient perseverance? Has Loku Appuhami, the grandson of Unambuwe Dissawa, a reckless young man who has squandered away his patrimonial estate in profligacy, a just ground of complaint against the success of Tikiri Appu? Are we to understand that every native is to toddle, in unbroken generations, in the foot-prints of his father and grandfather? Why? that would hurt the feelings of most of the up-country Ratemahatmeyas and low-country Mudaliyars and reduce them from their hard-won eminence into the degradation of sluggish cultivators and drowsy cow-herds. If such be the views of Messrs. Panabokke and Co., one thing is pretty certain, viz:—others will not gratify them by thinking as they think. 'No, no,' says honest, true humanity, 'Let those who have won a position by fair means enjoy it.' 'Yes,' murmur the objectors, 'let the past be past, but keep down others.' Why? Where is the reason of this, or the justice? If some might struggle honourably for eminence, why not others also? If some have attained eminence, and hold it as legitimate standing ground, why wonder at, much less complain of, aspirants for like success by similar means? . . .

"The great difficulty of arriving at a fair and reasonable conclusion as to the number and order of castes in Ceylon, arises from the suppression of truth, suggestion of falsehood, and the alteration of historical records. So that no two natives will give the same order and classification to all the castes. Such being the case, all the prominent classes of natives have a hobby of their own. The Gowiya caste assert *now* for the first time, as we learn from Niti-Niganduwa, that they are a mixed race of Kshestriyas, Brahmins, and Vaisyas; the people called Karawe, that they are of a Kshestriya descent; and the people called Salagama, that they are Brahmins. I shall not enter into a disquisition of that subject now. There are no Kshestriyas, Brahmins, or Vaisyas, properly so called, amongst us, at present; for all the Sinhalese people are now either Buddhists or Christians. And no sooner had we forsaken the Vedas and the Shastras, than, according to the law of caste, we had become Chandalas or out-castes. Christianity asserts that God made all mankind of one blood, which is a physical fact as easy of demonstration as any truth in natural science; whilst Buddhism repudiates caste, Buddha declares that 'a man becomes a Brahmin by what he does, and a Wasalaya (an outcast) by what he does.' . . .

"It is very much to be regretted that the Government now appears to be under the delusion that the aristocratic class among the Sinhalese is the higher grade of the Gowiya caste, which is indeed a very great mistake; for there is no aristocratic class among the Sinhalese; whilst descendents of high Government officials and others to whom various accidents have contributed to give an importance among all castes, consider themselves as entitled to lead in their respective spheres. Nor does the Government seem to know that landed proprietors and professional gentry are to be found among all the prominent castes as well as among the Gowiya caste. There is, therefore, a wide-spread effort among some of the most bigoted of the Gowiya caste, to make the most of the present opportunity; and hence the work in question is a genuine production of by-gone days, though it existed only in the imagination of those who desired it, realizing the words of Sir Walter Scott:—

> "'Oh what a tangled web we weave
> When first we practise to deceive!'

"True it is that the claims of caste are ignored in the administration of the law; but yet in certain departments they are *now* guarded with some anxiety, which seems both inconsistent and unnecessary, as it is sometimes construed by the caste men as an authoritative recognition of caste. There is no necessity at all to interfere with any lawful usage. The Government need not insist on a renunciation of caste as the condition of public employ; nor should the feelings of any public servants be wounded by an unnecessary intrusion on their prejudices. The question is one of private opinion and feeling, on which every man may be left to his own judgment, provided that Government extend no advantage to one which is unfair to another. Natives can observe what rules they choose among themselves; but the public service ought to be ordered exclusively on public considerations. I know a Mudaliyar of a certain Kachcheri, an illegitimate son of a very low grade of Gowiya, who puts the question, 'What is your caste?' to every native candidate for any post in that Kachcheri; and if the man is not one of the Gowiya caste, throws every obstacle in his way, as if being born in that caste were a sure passport for public service in Ceylon. In the public service, it requires clerks, accountants, interpreters, and Mudaliyars of Korales; and not Kshestriyas, Brahmins, Vaisyas, and Gowiyas who are the servants of the above three castes. Candidates, therefore, have a right to encouragement according to official qualifications alone, without inquiries made regarding their parentage or connections. All castes should be equally and impartially admitted, and the most qualified will always receive the preference. What is needed, therefore, is to place the test of superiority in the better discharge of duties, and not in the curiosities of a pedigree. Then no distinction shall be known among individuals but those which arise from talent, ability, and integrity of conduct.

"A community can make progress only when every member of it has the reward of merit laid open to him; and capacity and talent for the discharge of duties required in the social state are diffused pretty equally among the different orders of the community. It is, therefore, a very bad policy, if the officials of a country, instead of encouraging mutual good will and reciprocal kind attentions, say to the great bulk of the people: 'Neither talents nor exertions shall avail you: you are born in a degraded caste: you cannot therefore be eligible for Government posts!' A large part of this evil is to be laid to the account of some of the high officials, who, though not openly, yet tacitly, encourage caste distinctions in the distribution of prizes left at their disposal, according to their own whims and caprices, irrespectively of claims and qualifications. It is, therefore, the duty of a paternal Government to arrest this evil alone by disowning all respect for a folly which is so detrimental to the well-being of a large community such as the Sinhalese, as those in authority in former days did, who are still remembered with the deepest gratitude, as the greatest benefactors of our country. . . .

"According to the present state of our country the union of all classes in one corporate body is what is most desirable. But can we realize such a consummation so long as there is no peace among all classes? There is in our community a section that has always some complaint, some cause to grumble, something to be dissatisfied with. They complain that in public schools their children are obliged to sit on the same form with the children of other castes. They grumble that in the railway carriages they have to sit side by side with other castes of people enjoying the comforts and conveniences of the new mode of travelling, like themselves. They are dissatisfied that the Christian women of Talanpitiya, a village of the Paduwas, who, having acquired habits of decency, had left off their old fashion of going half-naked, as if the privilege of covering the bosom were their own peculiar prerogative. . . .

"The Oriental mind regards the State as pre-eminently the fountain of honour; and its service is the most coveted, as well as the most profitable profession. The ambition to enter it has, therefore, in this country, always outweighed every objection of caste, rank, and religion itself. . . .

"The Portuguese Government freely employed all castes of men in their service, so that one Don Cosmo, a man of the Salagama caste, became a general. And the Dutch Government never refused the services of men of any caste for posts of honour. Under the British Government also the same indiscriminate admission to offices, as of old, has been tolerated. . . .

"A great number of men are now employed in the public service. The introduction of railways and the electric telegraph has provided places for many more. But though the passion for public employ continues unabated and insatiable, yet is there a single man of the so-called higher order of the Gowiya caste men in the Railway, Postal, or Telegraph Department? . . .

"We believe it, therefore, to be the paramount duty of a parental Government towards those whom it has taken under its care and control, not to be predisposed towards one class to the disadvantage of another.

"Since of late natives have been admitted to high offices of trust with greatly augmented salaries in the Revenue Department. But was there a single Burgher or a native of another caste chosen for any of those places other than the Gowiyas, although there are natives of other castes, as well educated, if not better, who possess so mnch influence in their respective communities, as those that have been already selected possess in their own community.

"We trust therefore, that the present Government will continue to bear in mind that Magna Charta of the great body of the Sinhalese declaring that it be 'fully understood that it is the principle of this Government to recognize no distinction of caste or colour, the only ground of promotion being talents and qualifications' penned on the 3rd April, 1841, by no less a personage than the Right Honourable J. A. Stewart-Mackenzie, one of the most distinguished and enlightened British rulers that ever administered the affairs of this island.

"After all this controversy, one thing remains now indisputably clear—that there are in the world only two castes—the 'good' and the 'bad.'"

---

"A Few Thoughts on Chaturvarnaya, or the Four-fold Social System of Castes." By W. W. Colombo, 1886.—"We sincerely hoped that under the pressure of steam, electricity, European influence, diffusion of knowledge and extension of Christianity, the pernicious caste system in Ceylon would have been, before long, entirely done away with. But we were sadly disappointed in our hopes; for, whilst these powerful influences are in full operation, a reaction in favour of caste has taken place of late; and those who are benefited thereby have taken advantage of this reaction. . . .

"The compilers of 'Niti-Niganduwa' endeavour to show that there are four principal and eighteen inferior castes, whereas there are only four great castes, some mixed castes and out-castes. . . .

"According to the strict rules of the caste system no sooner a man has forsaken Brahminism, than he is an out-caste; and loss of caste is equivalent to civil death. The out-caste is denied admission to his father's house; the nearest relations refuse to eat with him or speak with him. He is excluded from religious ceremonies and social meetings. His wife is released from the conjugal rights; his children belong to him no longer; his property is forfeited. Therefore, as we are no longer Brahmins in religion, we are no longer Brahmins, Kshestriyas, Vaisyas or Sudras. Christianity declares that God has made all men of one blood; and that God has no respect of persons. Buddhism repudiatescaste. Buddha is represented by European writers as a philosophical opponent of popular superstition and Brahminical caste. This sage having enumerated the qualities he would require in the woman who aspired to be his wife, the king Suddhodana, his father, directed his minister to go into the great city, Kapilawastu, and to enquire there in every house after a girl possessed of these good qualities, showing at the same time the prince's enumeration, and uttering two stanzas of the following meaning. 'Bring hither that maiden who has the required qualities, whether she be of the royal tribe or of the Brahmin caste; of the gentry or of the plebeian class; my son regardeth not tribe or family extraction; his delight is in good qualities, truth, and virtue alone.' In Nepaul, where Buddhism is professed, the original inhabitants were all of one caste, or had no caste; but their descendants, in the course of time, became divided into many castes according to the trades or professions which they followed; though even now we are told that in Nepaul caste is merely a popular usage, without the sanction of religion, and altogether a very different thing from caste properly so called. In Tibet and Burma, both Buddhistical countries, caste is unknown. In China there are clans, resembling those of the Scotch Highlanders, but this institution differs from caste, and is peculiar to this singular country. But in Ceylon there appears to have been a greater leaning toward caste than among any other Buddhistical people, which had arisen from their connection with the Tamils.

"Some writers assert that the people of this country are of Aryan descent. Yes; so they are to some extent. As Wijaya and his followers came from Wango (Bengal) they may be called Indo-Aryans. But as we learn from 'Maha Wanso' that he sent for wives for himself and his associates from amongst the Tamils of Southern India (Madura) in the Pandian kingdom, and that they were accompanied here by eighteen officers of state, together with seventy-five menial servants, we see that at the very outset of the Wijayan dynasty in Ceylon, there was a commingling of Aryan and Dravidian races.

"From that time Tamils from Southern India coming over to Ceylon, and joining themselves with those who arrived at first, a hybrid race called Goviyas arose, half Aryans and half Dravidians; whilst some of the aboriginal tribes kept themselves aloof from these adventurers. However, in course of time, all were incorporated in one common name, the Sinhalese; although some of the aboriginal races are no more Sinhalese because they had adopted the Sinhalese language, than the Cornish people are English because they speak the English language. . . .

"The Tamil word *Vellala* also, which the Goviyas have adopted by way of distinction as their caste name, as the word Goviya, means a cultivator.

"Mr. Panabokke being fully conscious, with these strong and incontrovertible evidence before us to the contrary, that he could not maintain the theory of some of his low-country brethren that the Goviyas are Vaisyas—that is, of the Welanda caste—started a new theory, by which as if trying to avoid Scylla, he struck on Charybdis, and made the Goviyas sink still deeper in the mire, in reducing them to a lower position instead of raising them to a higher one, and in making them a mixed caste. We see, therefore, that the pride of caste is a mere bosh. It is indeed a pity that as a Buddhist he did not take heed of Buddha's words:—

" 'A man does not become low-caste by birth.
Nor by birth does one become high-caste,
High-caste is the result of high actions,
And by actions does a man degrade himself to caste that is low.'

" 'Is there no caste feeling amongst the English?' is a question very often put to us by some of our countrymen; and our answer had been always 'certainly not.' On the contrary their religion teaches them the 'Fatherhood of God and the Brotherhood of Man,' that caste and class feelings ought to be laid aside, and that there is no respect of person with God. The social institutions of England neither prevent social union and interchange of ideas between the various classes of society, as those of Ceylon, nor operate to set class against class, to bar the lower rising to the upper, and to make the national union impossible. On the contrary, in England all ranks and orders so run into each other and blend imperceptibly together, that it becomes impossible to separate them into sharply defined strata, or to say where the upper end and the middle or the lower begin.

"My dear countrymen, we are either Buddhists or Christians. Therefore, those who now attempt to maintain unhallowed distinctions must be told that all such distinctions have been lost with the Vedas and the sacrifices.

Caste, in fact, originated like slavery, in a war of races, and breathes still the true spirit of slavery. It is true that during centuries of this slavery, the iron has entered the soul, that the hereditary bondsman now hugs his fetters. Popular prejudices will no doubt long resist the light of truth on this as on other subjects of education. The attempt to point out to the sticklers of caste that the distinctions which they consider inviolable have no sanction in their religious books, may be as useless as to argue with the devil-dancers that their ceremonies are unauthorized in the Bana-books. But what was the cause of the decline and fall of the Kandian kingdom? It is this pernicious system of castes. It had become one of the greatest clogs on the advancement of our people, thoroughly preventing improvement in our social and political status beyond a certain point. Such a system, elevating one class and depriving another, kept the ideas of the latter for ever subdued, and entirely snipped from them the aspiration after superiority and influence, which form the greatest incentive to active exertion. . . .

"Is caste, on the whole, advancing or retrograding in Ceylon? is a question which cannot but be highly interesting to every lover of his country and every admirer of the present Government. It must, however, be confessed that, considering all in all, it seems to be now putting on new life and vigour. Therefore, its votaries are now showing themselves more openly; its claims are now more broadly proclaimed; and every engine, likely and unlikely, is now being brought to action to maintain its sinking credit. But we sincerely hope that like the giant struggling to retain the breath which is fast leaving his body, its downfall would be equally rapid. For the precedent laid down by the Right Honourable J. A. Stewart Mackenzie, one of the ablest of our Governors by his Minute of April 3rd, 1841, the Magna Charta of the Sinhalese, declaring that it be '*fully understood that it is the principle of this Government to recognize no distinction of caste or colour, the only ground of promotion being talents and qualifications,*' should not be set at nought by his successors.

"To those who are at all acquainted with the natural workings of the human mind in general, and the tendency of the caste-system in particular, it can occasion no surprise that caste and irreligiousness should co-exist to a great extent in the same state of society. This is the case in Ceylon at this moment.

"It is a melancholy consideration that of these two mighty delusions, a certain portion of our countrymen are the willing subjects who profess to be Christians for public show, but from whose back doors would be seen men of yellow robes wend their way to their houses on poya and other Buddhistical days; and that to their influence a great part of the miseries of our country is owing.

"And it is a fact too palpable to escape observation, and too certain to admit of denial, that those who have no fixed religious principles amongst the better educated classes of our people are the greatest sticklers of caste.

"The purest portion of all moral theories and the highest ideas of all patriots have been gathered from, or will be found concentrated within, the Christian system. Its universal and living acceptance implies the prevalence in every mind of peace, and goodwill, and generosity. If the most accomplished 'thinker' in society set himself to frame rules for its reconstruction and transformation into a state of happiness, he would find all his labours concentrated within the short sentence, 'Whatever ye would that others do to you, do ye also to them.' If the most benevolent theorist commenced to form rules for the advancement of individual comfort, and of the comfort of all individuals, he would find his labour useless, because it would issue in the commandment given with greater power and in more solemnity than when the rocks were shaken, that 'ye love one another.' There are no more powerful injunctions of universal justice and goodness than these two gentle commandments; and if all who profess to obey them even understood what they profess, we should have no more grievances to make, while by-and-by caste with all its concomitant evils would be things unknown. They would destroy themselves by transmutation. . . .

"One of the greatest dangers to which Missionary schools in this country is now liable, is that of being secularized through Government influence, whereby the whole tenor of some schools, their masters, and their pupils, are brought down to the level of non-Christian schools. Is it then surprising that education given in such schools is more secular than religious? How can it be otherwise when the whole object of the masters and mistresses of such schools is to realize as large a grant as possible from Government? What plan can be more directly calculated to arouse religious hatred, and to give a sectarian direction to education, than to announce to religious bodies that the public purse is open to as many of them as choose to embark in the cause of public instruction, and that the grants to each will be proportioned to the amount of secular instruction they impart? By this scheme the Government literally renounces the idea that education is a matter of common and civil concern, resigns the functions of the state into the hands of the people, and gives full rein to the development of religious rivalries. The result is exactly what might be expected. A nondescript sort of education is imparted in such schools—neither a sound religious education, nor a substantial secular education. . .

"Christianity is the basis of all modern civilization. It is from it that we take our respect for morality, for chastity, for the ties of family; it is from it that we learn not to covet that which is not our own, and to respect the rights of others; from it we learn to love even our enemies. Christianity, setting aside its Divine origin, is the foundation-stone of all that is great, and good, and sublime in human society; all evils in civilization are departures from the noble tenets of this pure faith; every form of tyranny and oppression is anti-Christian, and hateful to God. Therefore, Christianity, education, and civilization should go hand in hand.

"Christianity, education, and civilization have within the last fifty years made a rapid progress in this country. Still they have much yet to do. They must penetrate not only into our institutions and theories, but they must become the guide and lamp of our actions.

"It is, therefore, a sound religious education that would enable our countrymen to strangle the Hydra with its four heads,* which coils around their necks. . . .

"On a calm and comprehensive review of the state of our country from the commencement of the British rule here, it is impossible to resist the conviction that, in spite of the best intentions and efforts of Government, in spite of railways and electric telegraphs, and in spite too of growing trade and extending commerce, caste feeling amongst the different sections of the community still threatens to be one of the most prolific sources of evils in our country, preventing as it does all mutual good understanding between each other, and making national union impossible. But so long as Government seems to permit one section of the community to say to the other, with respect to political privileges, '*Hitherto shalt thou come, and no further*,' this evil shall not cease. Therefore, whether it will increase or diminish will entirely depend upon the action of Government, which alone can with a firm hand, as in the renowned days of Governor Sir Colin Campbell, make each other shake hands and confess

> "'I have sinn'd; oh, grievously and often;
> Exaggerated ill, and good denied.'

And advise each—

> "'Be wiser, kindlier, better than thou art.' . . .

"Progress, we are told, characterizes the age. Progress has characterized every age. With us, however, progress *downward* is going on step by step with time. Progress upwards of which the age makes its boast, lags lazily. A large body of men are allowed to grow up without any kind of intercourse with those who are placed above them in point of wealth, perhaps intellect, and probably in worth. There are few ties binding together the various sections of the community. The circles of this great trunk scarcely touch. A hard rind of pride divides them. All are men with many common sorrows and many

"* Called Kshestriya, Brahmana, Vaisya, and Sudra; or, Raja, Bamuna, Welanda, Govi.

common objects, but they help not each other. What has been done to their less fortunate countrymen by those who are placed above them in point of wealth, intellect, and worth? How many of them have gone down amongst them with kindness in their manner and in their hearts, to help them onwards and upwards?

"It is, however, an encouraging feature of the times that notwithstanding all these discouragements there are such men amongst us as Messrs. Rajapakse and Soysa who do so much for the advancement of their countrymen. And if there are some more men like them, then can certainly progress characterize the age. . . .

"We know that within the last fifty years, Ceylon, from being an obscure country, has risen to the importance of a rising British Colony, and one of the greatest emporiums in the East, whose exports and imports are not much less in amount than in any other country in Asia. This is, therefore, no time to clog its advancement by caste and class agitations, legislative enactments, or internal commotions. We know also that the so-called Sinhalese aristocracy is not an aristocracy of birth. Under the Portuguese and the Dutch Governments, all public functions, civil and military, among the Sinhalese, were hereditary, and gave nobility to the second generation. Hence the son of a Mudaliyar or Muuhandiram was called an Appuhami, and the son of an Aratchy or Kankany, an Appu. They were exempt from direct taxation and compulsory labour. And there were Appuhamies and Appus amongst all the prominent castes of the Sinhalese. Therefore, we see that there is no aristocracy among the Sinhalese resembling the English aristocracy. In England the aristocracy consists of men of birth, wealth, and distinction, who have attained to eminence in honourable professions; but in Ceylon there were Gatteru, Sattambiyo, and Rateberawayo, as Ratémahatmayás and Kórálas; and men of questionable origin, as Mudaliyars and Muhandirams whose descendants now make the greatest noise about *birth* more than *education*. In making these remarks our object is to point out the danger into which our country is exposed by these designing men. Its peril does not arise from foreign enemies, but from a dozen crotchety men amongst us, who, adroitly seizing the present favourable opportunity, raise a 'hue and cry,' regarding '*birth and independent means*,' as if they were the only men entitled to offices of trust and emoluments among the Sinhalese.

"His Excellency the Governor, in his opening address to the Legislative Council, was pleased to remark that 'the time has arrived when greater facilities for the attainment of responsible posts in the Government service should be afforded to natives of birth and education.' We hail the introduction of such a scheme as a great boon to our country; but the term 'natives of birth,' is a vague and indefinite term * capable of different constructions. Therefore, nothing is more likely to frustrate the good intentions of Government than the bestowal of such preferments to a single section of the native community, as there are, according to the general acceptation of the phrase, men of 'birth and education' among all the prominent castes of people in Ceylon. However,

---

* It is a very wrong term, for which "worth" should be substituted.—J. F.

"'If past experience may attain
To something like prophetic strain,'

we are afraid that an attempt would be made by a certain section of our community to make this a prerogative of theirs, and to give no small irritation and alarm to others. In that case it would only be a means of creating strife and contention among the natives. We hope, therefore, that the scheme in contemplation would be a comprehensive and liberal one suited to the present advanced state of our country.

"A community can make progress only when every member of it has the rewards of merit laid open to him, and when capacity and talents for the discharge of the duties required by the State are pretty equally diffused among the different classes of the community. Besides it would be a most ungenerous principle of legislation if the Government of a country, instead of encouraging mutual good-will and reciprocal kind attentions, should create dissensions and commotions in a community, in bestowing preferments on one section of it, which are denied to another section of the same community who have equal claims for such preferments. Such a course would, moreover, not only wage war against every principle of our nature, but paralyze all social, moral, and intellectual improvement in that community. That such was the actual state of Ceylon when the English first landed in this country is well known to all who possess any information on the subject. All the good which the English Government has been hitherto endeavouring to do to the Sinhalese community, therefore, cannot be fully realized until the principles of eternal justice (the first principles of all rule and legislation) be applied to remove such unnatural distinctions among our people.

"The British Government has given the people of Ceylon a degree and kind of liberty which most of our countrymen had never enjoyed either under the despotic heathen Kandyan kings, or under the benign Christian Government of the Portuguese and the Dutch. We, therefore, only seek for the continuance of that liberty and the enjoyment of the essential rights of human nature; and it is in this that the *glory* and *prosperity* of a nation *properly* consist. This we can secure only by the *union* in all the parts of the State, *harmony* in them all, and *authority* over them all.

"But these are matters which some of the members of our Legislative Council think beneath their notice. It is enough for them if they can annoy or embarrass the Government, and obtain the reputation among the unreflecting of being active patriots. We have little taste for such patriotism, and little respect for those who profess it. We desire to see in Council men whose minds are large enough to comprehend all the interests of the country, and who will not suffer themselves to be turned aside by petty motives from doing justice to all classes alike.

"Ceylon has never before enjoyed such liberty as she does since the past few years. All classes have liberty to act and speak in accordance with their convictions. No man is, by reason of his wealth or of his rank, so high as to be above the reach of the law, and none, on the other hand, so poor and insignificant as to be beyond its protection. There is no longer any power in the State, under the influence of a gust of passion, to order a man to be trampled to death by elephants.

"Therefore, as the British Government has so well earned the gratitude and good wishes of all classes of our countrymen, by the unselfish and sincere desire which animates it to promote the welfare of the people committed to its charge, by the solicitude which it manifests to study the feelings and sentiments of the people in all important matters, and by the spirit of benevolence which underlies its actions, it is with great pain and remorse we say with respect to the present reaction in favour of caste, which some of its officials seem to foster, that they

> " 'See the right, approve it, too;
> Condemn the wrong, and yet the wrong pursue.'

"British equity has clearly seen that no ideas of religion or honour can be permitted to violate the rights of life, freedom, or property. It remains to give the full and legitimate effect to this principle, by protecting human nature at large against the injurious and irrational distinctions of caste. Public schools are not afraid of contradicting the native sciences of astronomy, astrology, geography and medicine, without hurting the feelings of the people. Why should caste be then entitled to greater tenderness, when it is attended by so much injury to the moral and social improvement of the country? On this account, caste is considered by missionaries a deadlier foe to the moral and religious progress of this country than idolatry itself. Resting as it does wholly upon opinion, repudiation of caste would be welcomed by thousands who have not the courage to effect such an emancipation. . . .

"If the strongest argument against slavery be, not the cruelties that are its common adjunct, but its essential injustice, its absolute infraction of a Divine ordinance, its contrariety to the whole providential economy; then are we led to conclude that there is needed only a candid examination of this kindred evil by the Christian public, and the abolition of caste will be decreed by a power which has already worked marvels that will excite the attention and admiration and gratitude of all future generations; for, wherever the love of Christ is felt in its power and purity, there will be an effort to raise every individual within the sphere of its influence to the highest pinnacle of moral and social dignity he can possibly attain."

# APPENDIX XIX.

## THE CEYLON PEARL FISHERIES IN 1887.

(*From Letters to the "Ceylon Observer," by A. M. Ferguson, C.M.G.*)

MANNAR, 4*th April*, 1887.

THE change of scene yesterday on the Pearl banks was from almost dead silence and solitude before dawn to the existence of active operations. Two thousand five hundred persons were cn the shore, or in boats and trading vessels. Last evening this number was quadrupled. It is likely to be largely increased, as but short notice could be given of the fishery.

The sight of boats starting shorewards at one o'clock yesterday would have delighted an artist's eye. The comparison suggested was that of doves flocking to their windows. Reaching the shore about four o'clock, the oysters had to be carried to the Government enclosures, counted, apportioned, and a third, belonging to the boatmen and divers, sold. The retail trade is going on down to single oysters.

Officers of the Highlanders seem determined to add pearl mussels to the enemies whose defences they have successfully carried—for their representative here was determined not to return empty-handed; but all were surpassed, however, by a great Madras native merchant, who last evening, at an auction held in the lamp-light in the timber and palm-leaf shed, purchased half a million oysters from the eight hundred and forty-two thousand of Government share. His first bid was R35 for a quarter of a million, but prices went ultimately down to R15. Several chetties complained of a breach of understanding that only R9 be bid. The auction scene was most amusing, the purchasers showing much human nature. Mr. Twynam showed admirable patience and tact.

We timed the so-called Arab diver, and got eighty-three seconds, or one over Sir Henry Ward's maximum; but Mr. Twynam once got ninety-three, or over one and a half minute. Mr. Twynam has seen two men perish from staying under too long. They gasped before reaching the surface, then sunk like lead. Death was caused by asphyxia, or paralysis of the nerves. The lives of the divers are generally good: the vast majority are meat-eating Muhammadans, closely related to the people of this place, who are really South India settlers. The heat, scenery and race are all Indian. Whether the Sinhalese, pure Aryan, or mixed, no trace of them at Silavaturai pearl fishery or port. The general portly, well-fed appearance of the Ceylon Indian Tamils is striking.

Masses of extraneous matter are taken up with the shells, but thrown away, which would be prized as precious by European naturalists. Fine corals, brilliant scarlet-striped star fishes, pearl shells, and covered growths, generally red coloured.

Concrete kottos, or auction booths, are abandoned for mats on ground, the allotted land being defined by coir strings. After the fisheries, the floor was sold and resold at good prices. Purchasers now take oysters to private kottos allotted them at safe distance from inhabited portion. This and other strict sanitary measures, and digging of wells for good water near the beach, make a vast improvement, and cholera has been practically banished. Much credit is due to Mr. Twynam, who is only happy when at work. He seems impervious to sun heat, which is awful. This, with the stench of the putrifying, is the reason why Europeans cannot flock to this wonderful romantic sight as to elephant kraals; it was perfectly sufficient to have one whiff last evening from the kotto where samples were washed.

Shells are rapidly opening to skates and old womanfish, but more destructive are small whelks, which, if they once effect an entrance, rapidly destroy. Over one hundred boats went off at ten last night. People sleep at the bank, and work from dawn to one o'clock.

The pearl fishery divers find it to be so cold at six to eight fathoms (thirty-six to forty-eight feet)— the depth at which the oysters are generally found to exist in greatest abundance and healthiness—that they (the divers) are glad to warm themselves in the sun for a while after coming up from the performance of their task. In my telegrams I have mentioned the cases of two divers whom Mr. Twynam saw die from remaining too long under water, and I have suggested as the cause the non-æration of the blood, or what has lately been noticed as a cause of drowning, the sudden collapse or paralysis of certain muscles and nerves. The so-called "Arab diver" who was timed by us to eighty-three seconds, differed from others in putting a compressor on his nose, and he was noticed to open his mouth widely and inhale air in large volume before going down with his stone and basket. He brought up—or rather, he collected in the rimmed net bag which he had round his neck until he filled it, and which, like the stone, was hauled up separately—forty-two oysters, which was considered a very good haul. All the divers when they come up seem glad to inhale a good gulp of air, but they do not, or only very rarely and temporarily, show signs of distress. Of the two fatal cases noticed by Mr. Twynam, one was a novice who, no doubt, miscalculated what he could bear, from want of experience. The other was a practised diver, but he may have had organic disease. Captain Donnan states that he has never known the divers take anything to help them except snuff! Mr. Twynam once induced a diver to go to the bottom in fifteen fathoms (twice the average depth on the pearl banks), but he was so alarmed at the prolonged period from the man's diving to his reappearance, that he has not and never will repeat the experiment. The great difficulty in artificially propagating the pearl-bearing mussels, and the reason why all experiments here and in Southern India have failed, is the depth, six to eight fathoms, at which alone this species of shell-fish flourish.

There are two divers to each stone, who are alternately up and down. We saw on board the guardship (one of the immigration vessels, a fine two hundred and fifty ton ship with three tall masts) a stone made of our common gneiss rock, and a specimen of some substitutes made of concrete at the breakwater. The weight seemed to be from thirty to forty pounds. The weight of the stone helps to carry the diver rapidly down, and as I have said, he has the net bag for the shells slung round his neck. On touching ground the diver detaches himself from the stone, which the force of hauling coolies on each fishing boat proceed at once to pull up. Others haul up the basket when the diver casts it off and gives the signal of a jerk to the rope. The diver himself has only to give play to his buoyancy to rise, but he is careful to avoid contact with the boat, and will often dash off horizontally outwards in coming to the surface, which he does almost simultaneously with the bag of oysters he has gathered. While he holds on by the side of the boat, the contents of his net bag are emptied into large ola baskets, foreign substances being thrown back into the sea, the net being soon again ready for use. In each boat we found a belted native "counter," who responded to the question "etena chippee?" but I noticed that Mr. Twynam always added a percentage to the number given. It seems as if the exact truth could not be stated: indeed, I fancy that a good deal of fairly correct estimation goes for counting in the division of the spoil finally. The people, however, divide the oysters into fairly equal heaps, because they know not which heap may be allotted as the boat's share. The boat now gets a third instead of the ancient fourth, which latterly was found not to be a sufficient inducement, and Mr. Twynam's calculation is that each man of some 2,300 employed in the boats yesterday made about R3 wages.

The boatmen and divers' share of oysters can at once, on division, be sold, so that the people employed have whatever advantage may accrue from being first in the market. At the Government auction last evening it was amusing to hear one man allege that he did not purchase, as Saturday was an unlucky day! Another said people would blame him if he bid; a man in the background said he did not want people to know what he was bidding; while a bidder up to R25 said emphatically, "I'll not bid higher." Some were at work all night carrying away their lots of oysters, but a walk I took early this morning over shells and fragments of shells everywhere, showed that the work of washing, except in the case of a few small retail purchasers, had not yet commenced. The demand here for ola mats and baskets, and for cadjans and palmyra leaves, is very large, hundreds of temporary abodes going up in all directions.

Climate and soil are against vegetation here; but the bay, bounded on one side by Kudramalle (well known to the Greek and Roman voyagers as *Hippouros*), is very spacious and pretty. But there are a good many rocks scattered about. The fleet of graceful-sailed boats sweeping along the horizon and making for the banks reminded me somewhat of the sardine fishing vessels I saw in the Mediterranean.

As to attaining anything like certainty or steadiness, or being able artificially to propagate the oysters, we seem as much in the dark as ever. On board the guardship yesterday (whence I saw another exciting scene of 114 boats crowding round the ship to announce their loads and to skim shorewards, the noise and confusion being wonderful) I had the advantage of going over the charts of the pearl banks with Mr. Twynam and Capt. Donnan, who readily answered all my questions. The general results were that an extensive area of bank, with from six to eight fathoms of water on it, extends from near Mannar to Chilaw. The apparent conditions of bottom coral existing nearly everywhere seems to be generally very similar: spat and young oysters appear periodically on all. But it is only on the limited spaces called the Modaragam and Cheval-pars that really good fisheries are ever realized; and even in regard to them, too often when all is most promising, millions and millions of oysters will suddenly disappear. If it can be any comfort to us our Indian neighbours have been much more unfortunate, a minute parasitic shell killing off holocausts of the oysters. And this reminds me of the theory which Capt. Phipps originated, which Mr. Thomas of the Madras Civil Service (the great fisherman) took up, and which the naturalists of the British Museum supported, that what had hitherto from all time been known as the spat of the pearl oyster, is the spat of quite a different shell! All that Mr. Twynam, Capt. Donnan, and other experienced persons, natives as well as European, can say is, "Then we should like to see the real spat of the pearl oyster. Destructive criticism is ingenious, but where is the substitute?" The disputed spat has always preceded oysters on the banks. Messrs. Twynam and Donnan have seen the spat changing into oysters on long tall sea-weeds, and as those long weeds have died down, the spat has gone down, adhered to the coral, and become growing oysters. If experience is to be set aside, a more than Darwinian evolution must be substituted, and at present the opinion in Ceylon is that all the old authorities were right, and that Capt. Phipps, Mr. Thomas, and even a British Museum naturalist, are mistaken. Shellfish which grow in millions of millions must have spat in proportion, and in that case it must be apparent. But where is it apart from the old spat?

I must acknowledge a most interesting communication which has reached me from Capt. Donnan. It is to the following effect, the date being the 13th April:—

"We are now working on the Cheval, having left the Matarakam on Saturday last, and if the weather keeps fine, of which there is every appearance at present, we shall do much better in the way of revenue than I expected when I recommended the fishery. I have been ashore only once since you left. You will remember that 'Arab' diver with the nose nipper. Well, I had him alongside this morning, and told him to let me see how long he could remain under water, and I carefully timed him, one minute and forty-nine seconds, which is the longest dive on record on these banks or beds. The other 'Arab,' with air-pump and dress, only worked one day with it, when he only sent up 1,500 oysters, and now, without the dress, he is sending up from 2,500 to 3,000 oysters per day; so that the helmet, dress, and air-pump are not calculated to succeed at pearl-diving. I found also in 1884, off Chilaw, with four of Mr. Kyle's divers, that the natives sent up more oysters per day, man for man, than they did; a result which very much surprised me at the time, and now it has been confirmed again."

It will be observed that the so-called "Arab" diver, really a Hindu, from the Bombay Presidency, remained under water for a period extending to 109 seconds. I suspect that if sceptical criticism were brought to bear on the stories which allege subaqueous existence by divers for periods up to six minutes, this latest feat would be found to take rank amongst the most remarkable in the annals of diving where the diver has not been artificially supplied with air. No doubt the organs of the human body are capable of being educated by continued practice to endurance of abnormal conditions and of adaptation to such conditions: to those of extreme heat for instance, if gradually applied. I could, therefore, understand a man who commenced a diver's life, "sound in wind and limb," obtaining gradually the power of remaining under water and repressing inspiration and respiration for two minutes, or at the very utmost two and a half. But those who know that the blood is the life, and that it must, as it circulates, be ærated, or lungs and heart will cease to act, will be slow to believe in a staying power under water of three minutes, far less of six. The other "Arab" alluded to by Capt. Donnan had an imperfect diving dress which, it will be observed, was rather an encumbrance than a help to him as a regular diver, in which capacity he was only thoroughly successful when he abandoned the adventitious aid. Much service to the pearl fisheries of Ceylon was naturally expected from the class of European divers who, by means of external air supplied to them, can remain not minutes but hours under water. But the hopes entertained have not been realized. For the ordinary operations of rapidly collecting and bringing shells to the surface, a regular diving dress is as much of an impediment as was Saul's armour to the shepherd lad who slew the giant with the simple weapons of a pebble from the brook projected by a sling. For exploring the banks and reporting on their condition, more might have reasonably been expected. But a thickly mailed and heavy-booted European diver, with seven to nine fathoms of water pressing on him, is no light entity to walk over and inevitably crush the colonies of molluscs.

The stay under water in the case recorded by Capt. Donnan was twenty-seven seconds in advance of Sir Henry Ward's timing, twenty-six beyond our own, and sixteen in excess of the longest dive ever observed by Mr. Twynam. I have Captain Donnan's authority for saying that the period under water now observed by him is the longest on record in the annals of the Ceylon Pearl Fishery. Captain James Steuart, so long the Inspector of the Pearl Banks, and who collected so much information regarding them, never knew a diver to remain at the bottom longer than eighty-seven seconds, or to attain a greater depth than thirteen fathoms. Six minutes is the period mentioned in the "Encyclopedia Britannica," latest edition, but as no authority is given I must remain sceptical. In the same article it is stated that, as the result of their trying vocation, the divers are short-lived. Here, also, I prefer the testimony of such largely-experienced and careful observers as Mr. Twynam and Capt. Donnan. The men, generally, make good earnings, live well, being nearly all meat-eaters, look well and have as good chances of prolonged life as those who follow less hazardous occupations. One reason, no doubt, is that instead of any attempt to remain under water for prolonged periods, their average stay below is somewhat under rather than over one minute. With prolonged intervals to recover breath, to rest and to sun themselves by the sides of the boats, (working as they do by relays) their labour hours, as far as diving is concerned, extend only to the seven or six and a half hours from daylight to one p.m.

# APPENDIX XX.

## ANURADHAPURA, THE ANCIENT CAPITAL OF CEYLON, AND ADJACENT RUINS AND TANKS, IN 1887.

(*From Letters to the " Ceylon Observer," by A. M. Ferguson, C.M.G.*)

ANURADHAPURA, *April* 11*th*, 1887.

HERE I am at length, in the greatest and most ancient of " the buried cities of Ceylon," which and the surrounding countries, away to the mountains of Matale and "the Knuckles," I have looked over from the summit of the Miriswatte Dagoba; the streets of which, including the "*via sacra*," I have traversed, and the temples, palaces and baths of which I have examined, with intense interest, feeling as I looked on

> " Those temples, monuments, and piles stupendous,
> Of which the very ruins are tremendous,"

that the half had not been told me. Yesterday I stood on the mound which tradition indicates as the site where one of the "decisive battles of the world" was fought; where the Tamil invader, Elala, fell to the sword of the Sinhalese monarch, Dutugemunu, and the tide of Damilo progress southwards was arrested—at least temporarily. For what power short of the ruin of European enterprise in Ceylon, can arrest the southward flow, peaceful, but determined and constant, of the successors of the old South of India invaders? The present Government of Ceylon, instead of resisting, has done and is doing all it can to welcome and encourage the influx of the Tamils who come to exchange their labour for silver coin. Who can calculate the final results of this ebb and flow, but more flow than ebb? Even now the strength of the Tamil element in Ceylon, including, as essentially Tamils, the industrious and enterprising Moormen, is exceedingly strong, and it is daily growing.

I have been six miles away to Mihintale, a dagoba-crowned rock, which we ascended by about two thousand steps, most of them separate blocks of stone, some cut in the rock. The ruins here are most interesting, and the views from the summit were beautiful. This was the favourite residence of Mahindo, who, about three centuries before Christ, introduced Buddhism to Ceylon. I lay on the stone bed on which he was wont to meditate and so secured great merit! Over Mahindo's pokuna or bath there is sculptured a very curious five-headed cobra. But see Burrow's book.*

KALAWEWA, *April 15th.*

This wonderful tank will be completed in October, and then send irrigation water down to Anuradhapura, fifty-four miles by the Yodiela (the giant's canal), and into the Kurunegala district. Mr. Wrightson walked with me this morning to see the enormous statue of Buddha, cut out of the solid rock, one of the largest things of its kind in the world. There is quite a town here, the people employed on the restoration being about six hundred, families and bazaars making up fully one thousand. The tank will be seven miles square, with twenty feet of water.

Entering Anuradhapura on a dark night, after rain, all I was able to notice was the rush of the classical Malwatte, with myriads of bright-glancing fireflies on the forest trees. Next morning, when I looked out as daylight brightened the scene, I had for the chief object in my view the grand mass of the Jetawanarama dagoba. In the foreground, close to a raised bund, was a strip of water. This was all the Basawakulam (curious interjection of a Tamil termination into a city so essentially Sinhalese) had to show as a tank, and most of it was the result of the exceptionally heavy showers which had fallen in the first week of

* "The Buried Cities of Ceylon," by S. M. Burrows, C.C.S. Published by A. M. & J. Ferguson, Colombo, 1886.

April. When the waters of the Yodiela reach Anuradhapura, as they will do within the next few days, I presume Basawakulam will receive the benefit of the supply, to the increased beauty and salubrity of the city, I should think. It is no use suggesting that the Tamil termination "kulam" should be changed to the Sinhalese equivalent "wewa," for, however much it may be regretted, the ancient capital of the Sinhalese monarchy in Ceylon is likely as development goes on to become more Tamil than Sinhalese.

When Kalawewa is completed and a lake of seven square miles stands above the forests and fields which stretch away to Anuradhapura, some readers may be surprised to learn that it will not only be the largest restored tank in Ceylon, but that it will rank with the largest in the world. Mr. Henry Parker in his elaborate Report on the Giant's Tank, written so far back as November, 1881, instituted a comparison which is now unjust to Kalawewa, inasmuch as its probable area was then taken at only 2,800 acres, or little more than half the real area of the tank as restored, which is 4,425 acres. Mr. Parker then under-estimated also the area of Padawiya, the largest tank in Ceylon, larger even than the Giant's Tank. If his revised estimate, after examination of the locality, could be accepted, this Padawiya tank with 20,000 acres area would closely approach in extent the great Madras tank of Viranam, with its 22,000 acres extent. But, taking Mr. Parker's more moderate estimate of 10,000 acres for Padawiya, then Kalawewa in October next will rival this, and, perhaps, equal it, if the spill is ultimately raised five feet. Meantime, the corrected comparison of areas alone (capacity in millions of cubic feet being in a good many cases doubtful or unascertainable), is as follows:—

| Country. | Reservoir. | Area in Acres. | Remarks. |
|---|---|---|---|
| Madras...... | Viranam .......... | 22,000 | Ancient. |
| Ceylon ...... | Padawiya.......... | 10,000 | Estimated. |
| Do. ...... | Giant's Tank ...... | 6,380 | As proposed. |
| Madras...... | Semprampakam.... | 6,000 | Estimated. |
| Ceylon ...... | Kalawewa ........ | 4,425 | Ascertained. |
| Do. ...... | Kanthalai ........ | 3,584 | As restored. |
| Do. ...... | Allai.............. | 3,000 | do. |
| Do. ...... | Rugam .......... | 3,000 | Original tank. |
| Bombay .... | Sholapur .......... | 3,000 | As enlarged. |
| Madras...... | Red Hill .......... | 1,600 | do. |
| Bombay .... | Vehar ............ | 1,394 | As constructed. |

Of the above tanks, Vehar, in the Bombay Presidency, and the Red Hill reservoir above Madras (the bursting of which latter some years ago produced so much alarm, some loss of life, and great inconvenience), are intended solely for the supply of water to the Presidency towns; Madras 400,000 population and Bombay twice that number. The reservoir at Labugama, a sub-range of the Adam's Peak system, whence our chief city, with its 120,000 inhabitants, is now supplied with water, covers 176 acres.

It is very curious to see how, in the course of ages, the south-west monsoon winds and rains have worn away the ends of the pinnacle platforms of the great Anuradhapura dagobas on which they have impinged, so that in some cases there is scarcely any projection on the western sides of the dagobas, the pinnacle appearing to rise from the western edge of a platform. The intention of Government at first, I believe, was merely to strengthen the top platform of the Abhayagiria dagoba so as to render it secure, but finally reconstruction, which is now considerably advanced, was resolved on, and but for the objection of the appearance of pandering to Buddhism, and the other that Ceylon has no money at present to spare on merely archæological purposes, no doubt the resolution would be commendable. For by means of a winding stone staircase which runs up through the interior of the platform, the summit can be attained, commanding a grand and varied view of the ruins of the ancient city, its tanks, its rice-fields, its forest surroundings, with many mountain ranges as backgrounds to the scenery. It was up this winding path, through the monkey-haunted jungle which now covers the ancient structure, that the prisoners employed had originally to carry the stone, lime, sand, and broken brick: all the materials and tools used in the restoration. It must have been hard work with a vengeance, as we can testify from merely walking up the steep path when the sun was shining hotly.

The extensiveness of the road system and its ramifications through the tank regions, involves a limit to the extent to which water can now be impounded and its level raised in such great tanks for instance as Kalawewa. An average of ten feet of water does not seem in proportion to a bund of sixty feet in height. But even so, an area of seven square miles will be permanently covered, and if the spills were raised much beyond the five feet additional for which provision has been made, the damage of submerging many miles of useful road would be real and great. Such considerations did not trouble Maha Sen, Waligambahu, Dhatu Sena, Prakramabahu and other great tank-builders, far less did they think of providing for the possibility of a railway line to connect the shipping port on the west of the island with the tank region of the north, its capital city. With reference to contingencies in the distant future our Government ought to get Mr. Wrightson to place on record his scheme of a railway line which would not be a continuation of the line that has already reached Matale in its northern course ; but which, springing from Veyangoda or Polgahawella, would reach Anuradhapura by a far easier and less costly course. A railway terminus in the shadow of our Ceylon pyramids, and in close contiguity to Elala's tomb and the thousand pillars of "Brazen Palaces," "Halls of Audience," "Baths" and "Pavilions," may seem wildly visionary ; but so at one time did the idea of a railway from the sea into the centre of the mountain region of Ceylon. So also was the restoration of Kalawewa once regarded ; but that is now, practically, an accomplished fact, and thus the visionary "castles in the air" of one generation become the substantial realities of succeeding periods. For the present, however, what Anuradhapura and the region around it want are irrigation water to facilitate—(to render possible, indeed)—the cultivation of rice, and good roads for the transport of surplus crops and the commodities received in exchange.

Of the thousands of buildings which once existed, at Anuradhapura, at least, nearly all are prone with the earth, or hopelessly ruined, except the grand dagobas and the splendid baths, to which latter is unhappily attached the very uneuphonious name of *pokuna*. Next to the pyramid-dagobas in interest, and far more perfect in structure (except in the case of the repaired, we may say reconstructed, Thuparama), are the numerous and really beautiful baths of Anuradhapura, one of which, or rather two-in-one, a twin-bath or pokuna, is certainly amongst the most striking sights, and makes one of the finest pictures, in the ancient capital. It is exceedingly picturesque in its semi-ruinous condition, the steps being displaced as by an earthquake shake, and lying in admired confusion, though none are broken, and few even chipped. This beautiful work could at slight expense be restored, and by means of Yodiela water from Tissawewa, be converted into what we suspect the Buddhist priest-worshipping kings never could or would have contemplated, a public swimming bath, to which others than members of the royal family and of the priesthood would be admitted. In the prominence of its baths, ancient Anuradhapura reminded me of ancient Rome, where the finest maidenhair ferns flourish in the Baths of Nero and Caracalla. But there is one great difference, and it scores in favour of the Buddhist kings. The insane and wicked ambition of the Cæsars was for each to use the bath or palace of his predecessor merely as the foundation on which to erect a structure after his own fancy and in honour of himself. In the Italian city, therefore, we have the superimposed remains of baths, doubly ruined; by the instincts of insensate ambition, originally, and then by the hands of time and vandalism. But no similar idea seems ever to have crossed the mind of Sinhalese monarchs. There was plenty of space, and each king in choosing a new site and constructing a new ablution-tank (we hope the word pokuna will be outlawed and driven to take refuge in the rock fastnesses of Sigiri), merely strove to excel in elegance of structure and capacity the bath of his predecessor. He who constructed the twin-bath ought to have his name, if it could be ascertained, associated with one of the finest remains in the ancient capital of Ceylon, and one of the most beautiful things of its kind in the world. Photographs give a fair idea of the twin-tanks of stone, their exquisitely-carved balustrades and their flights of steps, but it is worth taking a journey to Anuradhapura to see and stand in admiration beside the "Kuttam pokuna," the largest division of which is 132 feet long by 50 feet wide, the descent being, we should say, at least 30 feet. It is a truly noble and elegant structure, every stone of which is almost as perfect as the day it was hewn. The qualifying question arises, for whose use was this magnificent bath provided? It lies in suspicious proximity to the Jetawanarama dagoba, which is said to have been built by Maha Sen, about the close of the third century of our era, to commemorate his reconversion to orthodox Buddhism (whatever that was) from the Wytuliam heresy (whatever that may have been). Having built a shrine so enormous, it was only befitting that the repentant monarch should provide for the hordes of priests attached to it baths of proportionate size. We could scarcely restrain our burning indignation as we found that object after object of archæological interest resolved itself, on inquiry, into something for the honour, convenience, and pampering of one of the most utterly useless systems of priestcraft that ever cursed humanity. Amongst the wonders of Anuradhapura are some large stone canoes, and it is believed that even these were constructed to hold food for the priests. Similar care was taken to provide monolithic vessels for the dyeing of the priestly robes, and to quote Burrows:—"Wide districts, fertilized, perhaps, by the interception of a river and the formation of suitable canals, were appropriated to the use of the local priesthood; a tank, with the thousands of acres it watered, was sometimes assigned for the perpetual repairs of a dagoba." The depth of subserviency was reached when a monarch devoted himself and his family as slaves to the priesthood; but this was too much even for Sinhalese public opinion, Buddhists as the people were. To look for remains of residences of the common people amidst the ruins of Anuradhapura seems hopeless: they built with mud, and roofed with leaves. But surely the monarchs and nobles had their palaces and their baths? We certainly do hear of "the queen's palace," and "the king's palace," and of 'pavilions," but even regarding these, the qualifying remark has to be made that the buildings were probably "shrines;" and what is certain is that nine-tenths at least of the existing ruins of Anuradhapura, once a great city covering an area of 256 square miles (Colombo is spread over only 11), are identified as the remains of buildings devoted to the custody of doubtful relics of an arch-atheist and pessimist, and to the delectation of holy beggars who taught that there is no God, no soul, no immortality; only extinction of sentient existence by the practice of unnatural and impossible austerities, and by honouring a non-existent being called Buddha, and bestowing bounty on his very exigent "mendicant" priests.

The calculation which Tennent makes regarding the mass of materials in the Jetawanarama dagoba shows what might have been done for the people, or what the people might have been led to do for themselves, had fair play been extended to them by the kings and nobles and priests who lived only or mainly for their own aggrandizement. The Jetawanarama dagoba, built by Maha Sen about 275 A.D., was originally 316, and is still 249, feet high, so that the summit is nearly 600 feet above sea-level. Neither the priests nor the Government entertain any design of "restoring" this vast mass, but no doubt an easy path to the top will be added to the many fine drives and walks for which Anuradhapura is now distinguished, and which renders it so different a place to that into which Skinner and MacCaskill cut their way through dense jungle somewhat more than half a century ago. The diameter of the great Jetawanarama dagoba is 360 feet, and Tennent estimated the contents of the whole at 20 millions of cubic feet. He added: "Even with the facilities which modern invention supplies for economizing labour, the building of such a mass would at present occupy 500 bricklayers from 6 to 7 years, and would involve an expenditure of at least a million sterling. The materials are sufficient to raise 8,000 houses, each with 20 feet frontage, and these would form thirty streets half a mile in length. They would construct a town the size of Ipswich or Coventry; they would line an ordinary railway tunnel 20 miles long, or form a wall 1 foot thick and 10 feet high reaching from London to Edinburgh." When it is remembered that, apart from purely stone ruins, some five times the mass of materials (chiefly fine large flat bricks, tens of thousands of which have resisted outrage and time), when it is considered that materials multiplied at least by five times enter into similar structures at Anuradhapura, some idea can be formed of the fearful misapplication of materials and labour which took place in honour of a false faith and a parasite priesthood at the ancient city. As in the case of the Medici and St. Peter's at Rome (a grand building, but more a shrine of idolatry than Christianity), love of art, devotedness to æsthetic beauty, will be pleaded, and no doubt the ancient monarchs of Anuradhapura were some of them men of as good taste as Sir William Gregory described the last bloody and murderous tyrant of Kandy to be. He compelled Ehelapola's wife to pound the head of her own child in a mortar, but, as a set-off, he formed the beautiful Kandy lake and built its fine bund-wall. If the dates usually given can be accepted, it is curious that Thuparama dagoba (moderate in size when compared with the pyramids of Jetawanarama, Ruanwelli, Abhayagiria, and Mirisiawatte) is not only one of the most ancient buildings in India, but one of the most elegant in design. Ruskin may rant and rave against stucco and whitewash, but there can be no question that the restored Thuparama, with its snow-white, bell-shaped, pointed form, contrasted with the ancient monoliths and ruins, and the umbrageous trees and greensward amidst which it rises, is "a thing of beauty." In shape it is now a perfect contrast to the top-heavy mass shown in the works of Forbes and Fergusson; and the appearance of Thuparama as merely whitewashed, helps to a vivid realization of how beautiful the great pyramid dagobas must have looked when, covered with fine polished chunam, their vast masses gleamed white against the sky. But the glories and the gems of Thuparama and of Anuradhapura (although we do not forget our admiration of the baths) are the monolithic, capital-crowned pillars which stand upright or at various angles of inclination around. The Thuparama dagoba, built originally, so the Mahawanso asserts, in 307 B.C. (and if so, it is certainly the oldest building in all India), was damaged by the Malabars, and has been several times repaired, and lately restored. But the exquisitely proportioned monoliths are here intact, and if they were hewn and the capitals sculptured, as seems certain, nearly twenty-two centuries ago, then certainly the ancient founders of Anuradhapura had the principles of true art and the sense of true beauty developed in a remarkable degree. Nothing strikes a visitor to the quadrangle in which stands the sacred bo tree more than the complete but most pleasing contrast between the umbrageous expanses of the Indian figs and the tall, rounded, perfectly straight, cylindrical stems of the palmyra palms, each crowned with its capital of clustered leaves. As I looked on these classically beautiful trees I could not help the reflection that here were the natural models on which the long slender pillars around Thuparama were formed. The palm, so prevalent now, must have existed in those early ages; and even if artists from India formed the transcendently elegant pillars, we must remember that over large portions of India the palmyra palm (*borassus flabelliformis*) is a familiar object. The beauty and utility of the palmyra palm is scarcely appreciated as it ought to be. Those who have seen only dense groves of stiff-looking trees in the peninsula of Jaffna can scarcely imagine the tall growth and noble proportions of the single specimens in the rich soil of the bo tree quadrangle at Anuradhapura. As a timber tree for roofing purposes the palmyra is well known and valued for its extreme lasting powers. For cabinet-making purposes it is not much used, because, probably, of the difficulty of working it. But old wood rightly treated is scarcely, if at all, inferior to ebony. Mr. Alexander, the forester of the North Central Province, took a polished stem to the Edinburgh Forestry Exhibition, which was universally admired as "black marble." The pillars at Thuparama, as well as the thousands of others scattered, erect or prone, around the many and in some cases vast dagobas of Anuradhapura had for object the defining of processional circuits, round and round which hundreds of thousands of successive bands of pilgrims paced, all down the centuries, in order to obtain "merit," and of this surely the poor simple people, with their devout instincts, ought to have obtained a large store, seeing that Thuparama enclosed the veritable collarbone of Buddha, while close by, in another shrine, was the still more sacred canine tooth of the Bhodisat, the sage, in Gaelic Bodach, an old man, as Caielach (Tamil, *Kalevi*) means an old woman.

From the calculation that ancient Anuradhapura, with its area of 256 square miles (including gardens, tanks, and cultivated fields), had a population of a quarter of a million, the descent is extreme to Fergusson's statement, in the 1876 edition of his work, that the site of the city was then entirely deserted and its vicinity closed in with almost impenetrable jungle. Even when that sentence was written, the clearing, road-formation, tank and canal restoration, and general revival, which have now made such extensive progress, had been commenced, and were well forward. We have noticed that Anuradhapura is a perfect centre of highways, radiating away to the Northern, Eastern, North-Western, and Central Provinces, and so to the west and south of the island, while there are few out-station towns in Ceylon better supplied with local driving roads and paths. This advantage is, of course, largely due to the desire of the authorities to render access to the antiquities of the place facile to travellers and visitors. We believe we mentioned in a previous letter that, besides the Government principal and minor roads, a large mileage of what are called "green roads" has been cleared by the natives. These roads have to wait for bridges, culverts, and gravelling, but meantime they are traversable by carriages and carts in the dry season (seven or eight months out of the twelve), and by foot-passengers all the year round.

From houses in the town we heard as we entered after dark and on subsequent days, the notes of music and the sounds of song and hymn, such as are common to the civilization of a century later by 2,000 years than that in which the town named after the constellation Anuradha was founded, while rays of light from lamps filled with kerosene, imported from a western world then undreamt of, vied in brightness with the phosphorescence of myriads of fireflies hovering over the vegetation which clothes the sides of the Malwatte oya. The present population of revived Anuradhapura, including, it must be admitted, large proportions of active Tamils and enterprising Moormen, must be fully 2,000, the promising nucleus of an aggregation of humanity which in the ages to come may equal, and even surpass, the hundreds of thousands who lived and loved and fought the battle of life and died on its fields in the ages that have gone into the eternity of the past. If after October next, when the scheme of tanks, canals, sluices, and spills between the grand tank of Kalawewa and the town reservoirs of Tissa, Abhaya, and the supply channels which lead from them to houses and fields, are all complete and fully at work, then if the population of what is now Anuradhapura, and of the area over which it once extended, does not increase in almost geometrical ratio, all ordinary human calculations must be deemed valueless.

There is, I believe, some evidence amongst the ruins of Anuradhapura of colours having been used in designs and ornamentation, and it seems quite probable that the fine white lime stucco which at one time covered not only the brickwork of the dagobas, but rough stone-work, such as the pillars of the Brazen Temple, may have been elaborately frescoed. In such frescoes, had any survived the ravages of time and of ruthless human destructiveness, the author of tree and serpent worship might have hoped to find the tree which, in support of his theory, ought to have accompanied the serpents on the sculptures. Or he probably thought the nagas and trees, in due proximity, were painted on the "curtains," which he conjectures were hung between the processional pillars, successive circles of which surrounded Thuparama and the other dagobas. But if that was the case, it is surely curious that the conjunction was not perpetuated in the Rock Temple and ordinary wihara frescoes. As far as my observation has gone, representations of trees are not common on the walls of Ceylon wiharas, and I can recollect no case of tree and serpent, together or separately, represented as objects of worship. Amidst the elaborate frescoes of the rock cave temple of Dambulla I do not remember any picture of a tree, although the artist, in reproducing the marine landscape connected with a ship conveying the branch of the sacred bo to Ceylon, shows his sense of proportion by representing the fishes in the sea as considerably excelling in size the ships! But I must leave this question of the presence or absence of evidence in Ceylon of the former prevalence of tree and serpent worship to professed oriental scholars who have made the subject a special study. I am merely an outsider, scarcely entitled to "benefit of clergy," relating the impressions made on my mind by what I have seen and read. According to Fergusson, the beautifully sculptured moonstones, the design of which—elephant, lion, horse, bull, hanza, lotus, and frieze—remained unchanged for fifteen centuries, are peculiar to Ceylon! This certainly looks like indigenous art. What are called "pavilions" at Anuradhapura, a name given, I believe, by Mr. Dickson, Fergusson supposes were "preaching halls" connected with dagobas; so that the more we investigate, the more it becomes evident that *all* or *nearly all* the grand lithic remains of buildings at the ancient city, as well as the mainly brick pagodas, were devoted to the glorification of Buddhism and the convenience of its so-called "priests," who were bound by the laws of their order to spend their lives in meditation and self-denial. But we know how mediæval Christian monks interpreted their "vows of poverty." The Buddhist mendicants of our day who hold and misuse such large "temporalities" have certainly the merit of being true to the traditions of twenty centuries. The dagobas contained "bushels" of relics, but it is singular that the only relic ever publicly exhibited in the past or now is the so-called tooth. The saintly Tissa ("a sair saint to the croon") is said to have been privileged above all laymen by being admitted to see the relics contained in the inner sanctum of the holiest of the great dagobas, and he was doubtless correspondingly edified. We do not read that he worshipped the relics, however; for Buddhist idolatry was evidently long posterior to the early age in which he flourished. It was, however, in full force when the second ancient capital of Ceylon was founded. Fergusson, indeed, regards Polonaruwa as specially interesting from this fact, that it is full of the idolatry of Buddhism, having been founded after Buddhism had become extinct in India. Interest of another kind attaches to this city of Prakrama (which I was very sorry not to be able to visit), from the fact that the Sat Mahal Prasada, so conspicuous amongst its wonderfully perfect buildings, is the lineal descendant of Birs Nimroud of Assyria. There is indeed nothing more curious and interesting in the great work on Indian Architecture than the mode in which the influence, first of Babylonia and Nineveh, and then of Greece and Rome, is traced by the erudite author in much of the architecture of India and Ceylon; while at the same time there is a great deal that is quite original and indigenous. To Fergusson we are also indebted for the calculation that the Brazen Palace at Anuradhapura, when complete (according to the plan of gradually diminishing stories, which alone he believed to be possible), vied with the simple but majestic Anuradhapura dagobas in height, and was equal to the most elevated of the great English cathedrals. In noticing the surpassingly elegant pillars of Thuparama I ought to have mentioned their resemblance to the "lats" of India, on which the edict of Asoka and other monarchs are inscribed, and which again seem to have influenced the form of the minarets in Saracenic architecture. But I must no longer linger amidst the ruins of Anuradhapura further than to express my agreement with the conviction that the choice of the place as the capital of the Wijayan conquerors was largely influenced by the fact that Mihintale, with its rock caves and boulder plateaux, was already a scene of religious worship before the immigrants from northern India conquered the indigenous Yakho race, and before the apostles of the new philosophy of negation bound conquerors and conquered in the chains of their godless and cheerless, if plausible, creed. The same fact, probably, of the rock caves being sacred to demon or naga worship influenced Mahindo, son of the great Asoka, in choosing Mihintale as his residence when he came to introduce Buddhism in the second century B.C., his sister soon following with the branch of the sacred Bo.

I now proceed to notice some other rock temples beyond the precincts of Anuradhapura. Within those precincts are a good many curious examples, the most striking being that close to Tissawewa, Isurumaniya, to wit, which, existing as a shrine from 300 B.C., if we can accept the native dates, presents now a most incongruous combination of natural magnitude of rock, ancient sculpture, and exquisite stone carving, and the most tawdry modern ornamentation of glaring paint and toy-like shrines and begging boxes. As a whole, Isurumaniya, with its combination of Buddhism, Hinduism, and (there can be little doubt, of a cult which preceded both) demon-worship with the physical symbol of the serpent, presents one of the most curious problems of the mysterious ancient city of the "dead past."

From Kalawewa I was able to visit a rock temple, the Aukuna wihara, which, though not very ancient when compared with some of the monuments of Anuradhapura, is certainly very interesting. The sight of the solemn, colossal figure of Buddha carved from the solid rock, one of a series of huge vertical strata, was well worth the journey. Although the protecting porch which once covered the figure no longer exists, every well-executed detail is in as perfect preservation as when the statue was sculptured by order of Parakrama Bahu nearly 700 years ago. Purposely, no doubt, the figure—which is in good proportion and good taste, 40 feet high, with feet 72 inches in length—faces the great tank. Without a particle of sympathy with Buddhist idolatry, we can distinguish between that foul sin and the true art thrown into the pose and repose of this grand figure. When I said that every detail was complete, I ought to have added that the flame ornament (answering to the nimbus of Christian art*) which ought to be on the head of the figure, lies beside it. There is also the inevitable cobra carved on a slab, but no representation of a tree or any approach to it. It was the solitary priest of the wihara connected with the rock statue who insisted that the English engineer engaged in the restoration of Kalawewa was an incarnation of one of the ancient tank-building giants. Mr. Wrightson adds to his other accomplishments that of photographer, and amongst his collection was the likeness of another similar colossal rock statue of Buddha, but, he believes, of more ancient date. It stands 41 feet high, at Seperawa. Fergusson, however, in noticing photographs taken by Captain Hogg, R.E., remarks that these statues are extremely similar to one another, and, except in dimensions, to that at the Gal wihara in Polonaruwa. The few figures of Buddha unearthed at Anuradhapura looked poor and dilapidated when compared with the fresh-looking "ruins" of stone monuments, older than the statues by many centuries. The statues of monarchs there, at the Dambulla Rock Temple, and elsewhere, are, I suppose, as authentic likenesses as are the pictures at Holyrood of the long line of mythical or doubtful Scottish kings, from "Fergus the First" onwards.

On my way back from Kalawewa to the central road, Mr. Wrightson's kindness enabled me to visit the specially interesting ruins of Vigittapura, a city said to have been founded at an earlier date even than Anuradhapura by one of the six brothers of Wijayo's Indian Queen. There is the inevitable dagoba, which we ascended, admiring, as a bright contrast to the surrounding ruins of long past ages, the pretty wild flowers which brightened its sides. From the top we had a good view of the ruins of wiharas and fortress defences, which we could not, for want of time, examine in detail. It was certainly interesting to look on pillars and slabs hewn probably over twenty-three centuries ago; for the Mahawanso, quoted by Burrows, states that the settlement of Prince Vigitta was a city and fortress

* So close is the analogy between the architecture, images, and ritual of Buddhism with those of the Romish Church, that the Abbe Huc expressed the conviction that the devil had used Buddhism to cast discredit on "the Church."

"surrounded by a triple battlement and entered by a gate of iron!" when Anuradhapura was but a village. There are inscriptions here in the Nagara character, and besides the remains in the cleared space, the jungle around (specially pestiferous) is said to be "strewn with ruins." Somewhere near one of the four "altars" of the dagoba on which we stood and looked over the site of one of earth's most ancient cities and fortresses, Buddha's jawbone is said to be hidden. In hearing of such "bushels of relics" one is inclined to be irreverent enough to ask how many jawbones the sage ascetic was possessed of. Vigittapura is famous for the incidents of its siege more than 2,000 years ago. The city, founded by Gautama Buddha's cousin, B.C. 500, had, in B.C. 163, fallen into the possession of Mysorean invaders, and was held by a captain of Elala, the Damilo monarch or usurper.

Dhutugamunu conquered this fortress with others before his final and decisively successful battle and single combat with Ellala at Anuradhapura. Forbes, quoting from the Mahawanso, gives the following animated account of the siege:

"The assault having been determined on, Kadol, the famed war elephant of the Singalese prince, was directed against the eastern gate, up to which he rushed through a shower of weapons and weighty stones that were hurled at him on his near approach to the walls. On reaching the entrance, a party of the besieged who were stationed over the gate commenced pouring down molten lead, which, falling on the elephant, he became ungovernable, and fled to shelter himself in a small tank near the walls. Kadol's wounds having been dressed, and his body fortified against similar attacks by cloths thickly folded and shielded over with plates of copper, he was again brought to the assault, and succeeded in forcing the gate, at the same time that others of the assailants entered by a breach in the walls of the fortress."

On the morning after I had visited the romantic ruins of Vigittapura, apparently the most ancient in Ceylon, apart from the rock caves, I stood on the great gneiss rock of Dambulla, and enjoyed the extensive and varied view of successive mountain and vast forested plains, brightened by glimpses of streams and tanks and rice fields.

I do not wonder that Mr. Campbell, of Islay, was struck with the appearance of the gneiss of which the great rock of Dambulla is formed; for the crystallized strata, worn away and polished on the rounded sides of the rock, look as if Nature had tried her artist hand in adorning the mass with engraved serpentine designs and striations, beautiful in themselves and bearing the most curious resemblance to hieroglyphic inscriptions. Would that this natural alphabet could tell us somewhat of the date, or rather successive dates, of the metamorphic rock, and the mode of formation of its vast caverns. But while, with the utter absence of marine remains, we have in existence, potent as ever, agencies which sufficiently account for the production of the phenomena we are examining, I see no reason to suppose that these are ocean-caves formed by the beating of billows against the sides of the rock and eroding its softer portions away through countless geological ages. All through those ages, doubtless, existed and operated the same air-ocean of moisture waves driven by wind currents which exists and operates in our day. Apart from any tilting and dividing processes to which the strata may have been subjected, and which may have separated them widely, the effects of millions of monsoon storms on decomposing rock, aided finally by the agency of man with his splitting wedges and hewing hammers and chisels, sufficiently account for the series of yawning caves which have rendered the rock of Dambulla famous.

The stratified and contorted character of the rock accounts for the water which percolates down from the summit into one of the caves, to which, as of mysterious origin, the priests draw the attention of visitors, and which is treasured and considered as sacred as Ganges water is in India. I did not taste the heaven-born fluid, any more than I did the contents of a lakelet in a depression of the vast rock, a rock stated by Tennent to be 500 feet in height and about 2,000 feet in length.

As was natural to an accomplished enthusiast like Islay Campbell, it was not for his geological theories alone he sought support amidst the cave recesses in the great gneiss rock of Dambulla. In the elaborate and richly-coloured frescoes by which the stone roofs of the caves are covered and adorned he sought evidences of identity with the northern folklore which he had studied so deeply and illustrated so happily. He had heard of the giants as well as the demons of Sinhalese folklore, and, considering how many theories have been founded on the supposed identity in Indian literature of the Yavans with the Ionians, we cannot wonder that the accomplished savant of Islay saw more than a verbal similarity between the *Yodi* of the Sinhalese and the *Odin* of the Scandinavian pantheon of deified heroes.

# APPENDIX XXI.

## REFERENCE TO FRONTISPIECE.

The inscription on the statue to Governor Sir William Gregory tells its own story to some extent, but it may be added that a sum of about R25,000 was subscribed by all classes—chiefly by Ceylonese, and especially the Sinhalese section—for the erection of the statue. It was executed by F. Boehm, A.R.A. It is erected in the Cinnamon Gardens, in front of the Colombo Museum—the most interesting and most generally useful, as well as handsomest, public building erected in Ceylon during British times. The conception, arrangments, and carrying out of this museum were entirely due to Governor Gregory. He had for his architect Mr. J. G. Smither, F.R.I.B.A. The structure, laying out of grounds, and surrounding wall, cost about £12,000. The museum is occupied entirely with Ceylon exhibits, and presents a very adequate display in all departments, and especially interesting archæological exhibits refering to the early days of the Kandyan Kingdom. An oriental library occupies one part of the building, and the Ceylon branch of the Royal Asiatic Society holds its meetings in an adjoining room. The natives of all classes and races visit the museum in great numbers, and it is a centre of attraction to visitors —passengers landing at Colombo—from all quarters.

### THE COLOMBO MUSEUM.

(*By a Ceylon writer in* 1882.)

"If want of interest in local exhibitions was not so commonly observable amongst the residents of almost all the principal towns and cities of the civilized world, it might, perhaps, be considered remarkable that so few of the European residents of Colombo take any interest in the beautiful museum which stands so prominently amongst the buildings in the Cinnamon Gardens. It is merely another phase of the principle involved in the assertion that a prophet is not without honour, save in his own country and his own father's house. Our museum is by far the most beautiful building in Colombo: it is pleasantly situated, and surrounded by prettily cultivated grounds; it is, moreover, replete with objects of local interest, and entrance is free to all. And yet, with all these attractions, there is scarcely one in a hundred of us who has done himself the pleasure of paying a visit to the building, or, if he has, it was, in all probability, several years ago, or when the collection of specimens was of such a meagre and rudimentary nature as to scarcely merit the name of collection at all. In those days, possibly, visitors may have been justified in making use of such expressions as 'really, there is nothing worth seeing or worth the trouble of a visit'; but at the present day the visitor would indeed be hard to please who could not find many objects in which he takes an interest, or which are calculated to attract his attention. In spite of many difficulties, the lukewarmness of the authorities, the inefficiency, if not worse, of the assistants, the active opposition of the few, and the discouraging callousness of the many, and in spite of the disappointment which must necessarily arise from want of intelligent interest in the work by the greater number of the European community, the curator, with the aid of great industry and an affectionate interest in his work, has succeeded in getting together a very goodly show wherewith to minister to the amusement and instruction of those who make the museum a pleasurable resort.

"The collection—entirely of an insular character—already comprises such a number of interesting specimens, that the scanty half-hour of an afternoon, which is generally all that most residents can afford for the purpose before the doors are closed at six p.m., is all too short for even a casual glance at one-half of them, much less a careful examination; and we would advise any one who really wishes to see the museum thoroughly, and acquire a knowledge of what it contains, to take it in instalments at their leisure, as opportunity offers. Inspection of the contents of the lower room might well occupy the whole of the first visit, whilst there need be no waste of time if the gallery is to be got through in an hour and a half. In writing this we must not be understood to be addressing the passengers from the steamers in the harbour who want to see all Colombo in the afternoon, travel to Kandy during the night, drive round the town before the seven o'clock train leaves, and be on board ship again by noon, having learnt all about Ceylon, and a great deal more besides, in less than twenty-four hours; and yet we are assured that out of the 9,062 Europeans who during the past year have visited the museum, the greater number are visitors from the shipping. There can be but little doubt that the exhibition has been subjected to one very serious drawback during past years, and that is the constant state of change in detail and arrangement which have occupied the officials so incessantly.

"Complaints were rife of empty cases, and lack of specimens, and the justness of such complaints could not well be gainsaid; but it was an unfortunate state of affairs which has absolutely necessitated, as experience proved, the utility of change of position, or as the growth of the collection called for more accommodation. The extraordinary dilatoriness of the Public Works Department has, without doubt, done much to injure the good fame of the museum, and even now there are a very great number of specimens which are lying idle in the store-rooms for want of cases in which they could be exhibited; and with the transport vote cut down as it is to half the usual amount, and altogether inadequate to the necessities of the case, there seems to be little hope of progress in the immediate future. This transport vote, we may explain, provides for all the cost of collection by the curator and his assistants, taxidermists and peons, cart and coolie hire, tolls and canoes, and travelling expenses, purchase of specimens, &c., &c., and, when it is reduced as it has been to such an insignificant amount, the resources of the collector's establishment are entirely crippled, and progress most effectually stayed. There have been many critics from time to time who have not been backward in attributing blame to the curator, when, had they only been aware of the true state of the case, they would, without doubt, have been astonished that so much has been done with so little in the way of support. Lately, however, very considerable changes have taken place in the arrangement of the collection, many of them most advantageous, whilst some, we think, will have again to be altered. The entrance hall, once crowded with gigantic fishes, requires something to do away with the idea of emptiness which cannot fail to strike a visitor, whilst the two bare benches which are placed in it are by no means æsthetic in appearance. The west room on the ground floor, known as the Ceylon Products' room, has much that is new, and more is promised. Zoology has been relegated entirely to the upper story, save the new fish room, to which we shall further allude presently, and the minerals have been brought downstairs. These have been very cleverly placed in cases against the wall, and make a very interesting show, though necessarily there must in time be many more specimens collected, until eventually they will require a room entirely devoted to mineralogy. Perhaps the most interesting exhibit in this section is the series of fossil deposits showing the formation of the west coast of the island, from Dondra-Head on the south, to Karativo on the north-west coast. There are also many specimens of sea shells taken from the forests of the Northern Province, and a piece of fossil coral (if we may be allowed to make use of such an expression) from the summit of Tangala Hill, say, 150 feet above the sea level. This room, having now been rendered secure with iron bars, the gold Buddhas and jewellery, which had been placed in safety after the disappearance of a portion of them, as well as the collection of coins, are now exhibited again in central cases. The new arrangment of the coins is especially happy, and this part of the collection looks peculiarly neat and appropriate. The exhibition of Ceylon products is at present insignificant and altogether unworthy of the institution, but this want will happily be very shortly amended on the arrival of the two hundred samples which are to come from the Indian and Colonial Exhibition in London. These will all be shown in goblet-shaped bottles, and will, without doubt, look very well. They will be supplemented, it is hoped, by contributions supplied by the principal producers in the island. Perhaps the most interesting specimen at present on view is a sample of clean coffee, exhibited by the Messrs. G. & M. Worms at the London Exhibition of 1851. This may be regarded as a curious relic rather than an object of any special value. The Exhibition itself is seldom alluded to in the present day, except as the father of all the exhibitions which have been so numerous in all parts of the world of late years, and the memory of the Messrs. Worms is fast fading away, except in the recollections of a few of our older colonists.

"We must not omit to make mention of another innovation in the conduct of the museum, which has its first results in the Ceylon Products' Room. This is the admission of loan collections, which it has at length been decided to accept for exhibition when opportunity offers. The first to avail himself of the permission has been Mr. D. W. DeAbrew Rajapakse, who has sent a tortoise-shell box and Sinhalese gentleman's comb, several ancient native swords, and two Mudaliyar's caps of the Dutch period, say, about 1790. It is to be hoped that other disinterested individuals will follow suit, and let the public of Ceylon have a sight of the treasures of many kinds which are at present hidden away in ancient almirahs in the recesses of the native walawas. Before we pay a visit to the galleries, we must not forget to mention the newly-fitted room at the back of the museum, which has been opened to the public as a fish room, in which are shown nearly all the great stuffed fishes which at one time or other have been seen in the hall or the gallery. In fact, they are all here except the gigantic shark, which still remains in the east gallery, and of which we shall have more to say by and by. The fish room is the first practical illustration of the necessity which is beginning to be felt for more accommodation, and it will not be very long before an additional building on a considerable scale will be urgently called for. In the meantime, visitors wishing to see the fish room, should ask one of the attendants to show them the way, and they cannot fail to gain some knowledge of the monsters which people the Eastern waters. The smaller fishes and the crustaceans and other marine wonders will be met with upstairs."—Communicated to *Ceylon Times.*

---

## THE COLOMBO MUSEUM.

(*From the "Ceylon Directory and Hand-Book" for* 1876–78.)

This institution was founded by the late Governor, the Right Hon'ble Sir William H. Gregory, K.C.M.G., and the building has been erected at a cost of R120,500, from the designs of the Government Architect, Mr. James G. Smither, F.R.I.B.A.

The Museum grounds, which are about seven acres in extent, are bounded on the south and east by the public road, and on the remaining sides by cinnamon plantations. An ornamental balustrade runs along the roadside, and two pairs of iron gates, with massive piers surmounted by handsome gas lamps, give access to the carriage drives by which the building is approached.

The Museum occupies a central position on the ground at a distance of 70 yards from the high road, the principal front facing the south. The building is designed in the Italian style of architecture, and is two storeys in height, with a frontage of 171½ feet, and a total depth, including the offices and outbuildings in the rear, of 232½ feet. The principal façade consists of a wide central projection and side wings connected by arcades, behind which broad verandas form external means of communication between the several galleries, at the same time affording shade from the sun and shelter from the rain, as well as additional floor space for exhibitive purposes. The arches of these arcades (which are continued along the sides of the wings), are supported on square piers on the ground floor, and spring from light coupled columns with foliated capitals on the upper storey, the intervals between the piers and columns being filled in with open balustrades.

In the middle of the principal front is a commodious Carriage Portico, from which seven stone steps ascend to the ground floor level. At the head of the steps is a Loggia which is separated from the portico by three semicircular arches springing from coupled columns with polished shafts and enriched capitals, thus dividing the steps into three distinct flights. At either end of the Loggia is an open archway communicating with the arcades, and facing the steps are three large entrance doorways which give access to the interior of the building.

The Central Hall, which is first entered, is 29½ feet by 24¾ feet, and 19 feet high, the latter being the height of the lower storey throughout. Beyond the hall, and opposite the principal entrance, is the Grand Staircase, which is separated from the hall by a transverse open corridor communicating with the arcades on either side. The corridor is formed by a set of three semicircular arches, upon panelled square piers next the hall, and a parallel set of arches towards the staircase springing from round columns, the piers and columns being highly polished and embellished with ornamental capitals. The enclosure containing the staircase is carried up to the full height of both storeys, and is lighted by three large windows in the north wall. The Staircase is constructed of polished teak, with ornamental balustrades of metal, and rises, first in a single flight 9 feet broad up to a wide intermediate landing, and continues in two return flights, each 8 feet broad, to the level of the upper floor. At the head of the staircase is a wide open corridor similar to that below, communicating with the upper arcades right and left, and composed of semicircular arches in two rows springing from polished columns enriched with ornamental capitals.

Returning to the ground floor: to the right of the Central Hall is the Library (29½ feet by 24¾ feet), which is lighted by six wide and lofty doorways opening into the arcades in front and rear. This room is fitted up with handsome bookcases of polished teak placed against the end walls, and projecting from the spaces between the doorways on the buttress plan; and in the middle of the room is a large table press, including a desk for the Librarian. Beyond the Library is the Reading and Lecture Room (49 feet by 24¾ feet), to which light is admitted by a recessed window at either end, and five doorways opening into the east veranda. Against the west side are placed two ornamental cases for ancient *MSS.*, and the remaining wall spaces are hung with framed portraits of literary and scientific celebrities. The room is comfortably furnished and fitted up with seven starlight gas chandeliers. The front verandas, portico and hall are also lighted with gas.

To the left of the Central Hall is a gallery, the same size as the Library, and lighted in a similar manner by large doorways opening into the arcades. This room is intended for the exhibition of Ceylon products, and is fitted up with polished teak wall and buttress cases glazed with plate glass. Beyond the "Ceylon products" room is a large gallery for Antiquities, which corresponds in size with the reading room, and is lighted in the same manner with a window at either end, and large doorways opening into the west veranda. Adjoining the "Antiquities Gallery" is the Director's office, with private entrance, strong-room, and other accommodation, including the Director's private staircase of communication with the upper galleries. The whole of the rooms on the ground floor communicate with one another by means of large and lofty central doorways. The floors throughout are laid with Portland cement, and the ceilings are of teak.

In the rear of the Grand Staircase the necessary accommodation is provided for the public, and an open arched corridor leads to the Taxidermist's and "setting up" rooms, an extensive unpacking and store room, stabling, &c.

The upper storey of the building is occupied entirely by the "Natural History" Galleries, which consist of three large rooms 20 feet high, lighted as below with wide and lofty doorways in the side walls, opening into broad open verandas, and with recessed windows, in addition, in the end galleries. The Central Gallery runs east and west, and is 93 feet in length by 25½ feet in breadth, with an extra space or alcove on the south side opposite the Grand Staircase, 30 feet by 10½ feet. The end galleries, which are placed north and south, are each 49 feet long by 25½ feet wide, and are connected at either end with the Central Gallery by an open screen extending completely across the room, and consisting of three semicircular arches springing from single columns, with highly polished shafts and ornamental capitals. A similar triple arrangement of polished columns and arches connects the side walls of the Central Gallery across the opening leading to the Grand Staircase, and this is again repeated across the opposite alcove, the arrangement producing altogether an exceedingly light and elegant effect. The alcove is lighted by three large doorways, which also give access to the flat over the carriage portico. The internal walls on this, as well as the ground floor, are architecturally plastered, and embellished with ornamental strings, cornices, &c. The plain surfaces of the walls are painted the very palest green, all mouldings and ornaments being finished deadwhite or polished. The doors and windows throughout the building are of polished teak, with semicircular arched heads filled in with scrolls, of wrought iron on the lower floor, and of wood above. The floors of the upper galleries are laid with polished teak, and the ceilings are of the same material. The latter are flat, and are divided into panels which are diagonally boarded and ornamentally moulded.

The Central Gallery is entirely fitted up with handsome Spanish mahogany wall and table specimen cases glazed with plate glass and French polished. These cases are all dust-proof, and were manufactured in England especially for the Museum. The wall cases occupy the spaces between the doorways, and project into the room on the buttress system, which has been found to answer perfectly, all the specimens being lighted in the most satisfactory manner. The table cases are placed opposite the intervals between the above, and in a line down the middle of the gallery. All have plate glass sloping tops, and are successfully lighted from the doorways on either side, ample space being left between the cases for an inspection of their contents. Two of them have super-cases (in addition to the slopes) entirely of plate glass, and are fitted up below with drawers enclosed within plate glass doors. The other cases are open beneath, and are each furnished with a shelf at top on brass supports for specimens in bottles. In the alcove are two wall cases with plate glass fronts.

The East and West Galleries are fitted up with wall cases at either end, and in the East Gallery is a middle row of table cases in addition. The latter are open below and fitted with top shelves corresponding with those in the Central Gallery. The fittings in the two end galleries are all of polished teak glazed with plate glass.

Descending the Grand Staircase, a slab of white polished marble will be observed, inserted in the wall facing the principal entrance, bearing the following inscription in gold letters:—

"This Museum, completed A.D. 1876, was opened to the public, January 1, 1877. H.E. the Right Hon'ble Sir William H. Gregory, K.C.M.G., Governor; A. Haly, Esq., Director; J. G. Smither, Esq. F.R.I.B.A., Architect; F. Vine, Esq., M.S.E., Superintendent of Works; A. M. W. Marikar and S. Perera, Contractors."

A fine life-size portrait bust of H.R.H. the Prince of Wales adorns the Grand Staircase. This is the work of the eminent sculptor, Mr. Marshall Wood, who has presented the bust to the Museum.

Considering that the Museum has been open but a short time, a very satisfactory collection of objects has been brought together. The book shelves in the Library are filling rapidly; and the two cases in the Reading Room contain a most valuable collection of Buddhist manuscripts, many of them presented to the Ceylon Government by the King of Burma. A descriptive catalogue of these, prepared by Mr. L. de Zoyza, the learned Sinhalese Translator to Government, shows that the collection of *MSS.* consists of 188 volumes, in 209 distinct works, and are classified as follows: A.—Consists of texts of the Canonical Scriptures of Buddhism. Of these there are twenty-seven volumes in Burmese characters, presented by the King of Burma; and fourteen in Sinhalese characters, copied at the expense of Government, or presented by private individuals. B.—Consists of miscellaneous religious works. Of these there are seventy-one volumes. C.—Consists of historical works, legendary tales, &c., and contains twenty-five volumes. D.—Philological works. Under this head there are twenty-nine volumes. E.—Poetry, &c., sixteen volumes. F.—Miscellaneous works, scientific, medical, &c. Of these there are six volumes. The Library proper contains about 450 volumes, comprising: Works relating to Ceylon, publication of learned societies, natural history, languages, Oriental literature, periodical publications, archæology, history, chronology and ethnology, astronomy, geography and miscellaneous. In the "Ceylon products" room there is a fine collection of modern pottery, also a selection of the curious masks used in plays and devil dances. The collection of raw materials is as yet far from complete, and at present some of the cases contain fragments of statuary from Polonnaruwa, portions of bronze lamps from Kurunegala, and a few other antiquities; but this is a temporary arrangement. In the North Veranda are some fine specimens of bamboo, rattan, and Ehetu creeper. In the "Antiquities" room the most striking object is the great stone lion from Polonnaruwa, and facing it is the perforated stone window from the Palace at Yapahu. Round the room are sculptures from Anuradhapura, Tissamaharama and elsewhere, and in the west veranda are several inscribed monoliths from various parts of the Island: the oldest of these records the construction of Wiharas by King Gajabahu, A.D. 125–131, and is in a remarkably perfect state of preservation.

# APPENDIX XXII.

## REFERENCE TO MAP OF CEYLON.

*(In pocket of Cover.)*

While this Map affords a fairly approximate idea of the location of the chief agricultural industries of the island, and of the land suitable for extension, it must not be supposed that the areas are accurately laid down. Cacao, for instance, although confined to a few limited localities at present, will very likely be found to succeed in several additional districts. It is hard to say again where tea will not grow in Ceylon, at any rate in the moist zone—so that 250,000 acres may be a moderate estimate of the area when cultivation is fully extended. Where coffee is superseded in the central province, tea may be counted to take its place along with cinchona in nearly every district. So with palms; it is well-nigh impossible to show the precise areas covered with palm cultivation—especially with the areca and kitul, which extend far into the interior—while even coco-nut palms, mainly confined though they are to the sea-coast, form flourishing plantations up the banks of the Mahaoya, some forty miles inland, while at Mátalé 1,400 feet above the sea level, there are two or three considerable areas of very fine coco-palms. But the chief purpose of the map is to give a popular idea of the different planting industries of the island, and we feel sure it will be found to answer this end.

Corrections of the Map to September, 1887.

| | |
|---|---|
| Total population of the island .. | 2,900,000 inhabitants. |
| Length of railways .. .. .. | 181 miles. |
| Length of roads .. .. .. .. | 2,500 ,, |
| Total area cultivated .. .. .. | 3,130,000 acres. |
| Land of all kinds in private hands, about | 4,000,000 ,, |

The present cultivated area comprises:

Cardamoms, about 15,000, with a probable extension to 30,000, acres.
Jak and other fruits, about 150,000 acres.
Coffee, from 130,000 to 150,000 acres.
Tea, from 160,000, with a possible extension to 250,000, acres.
Cacao, 15,000 acres.
Cinchona, from 40,000 to 60,000 acres.
Rhea, &c., 5,000 acres.
Rubber trees, aloes, gums, &c., from 5,000, with a possible extension to 50,000, acres.

In the Map the figures for population should be altered as follows:—

| | | | | |
|---|---|---|---|---|
| Northern province to | | | 302,500 | inhabitants. |
| North-Central province to | | | 66,146 | ,, |
| Eastern | ,, | ,, | 127,555 | ,, |
| North-Western | ,, | ,, | 293,327 | ,, |
| Central | ,, | ,, | 310,000 | ,, |
| Uva | ,, | ,, | 165,672 | ,, |
| Western | ,, | ,, | 897,329 | ,, |
| Southern | ,, | ,, | 433,520 | ,, |

# GENERAL INDEX.

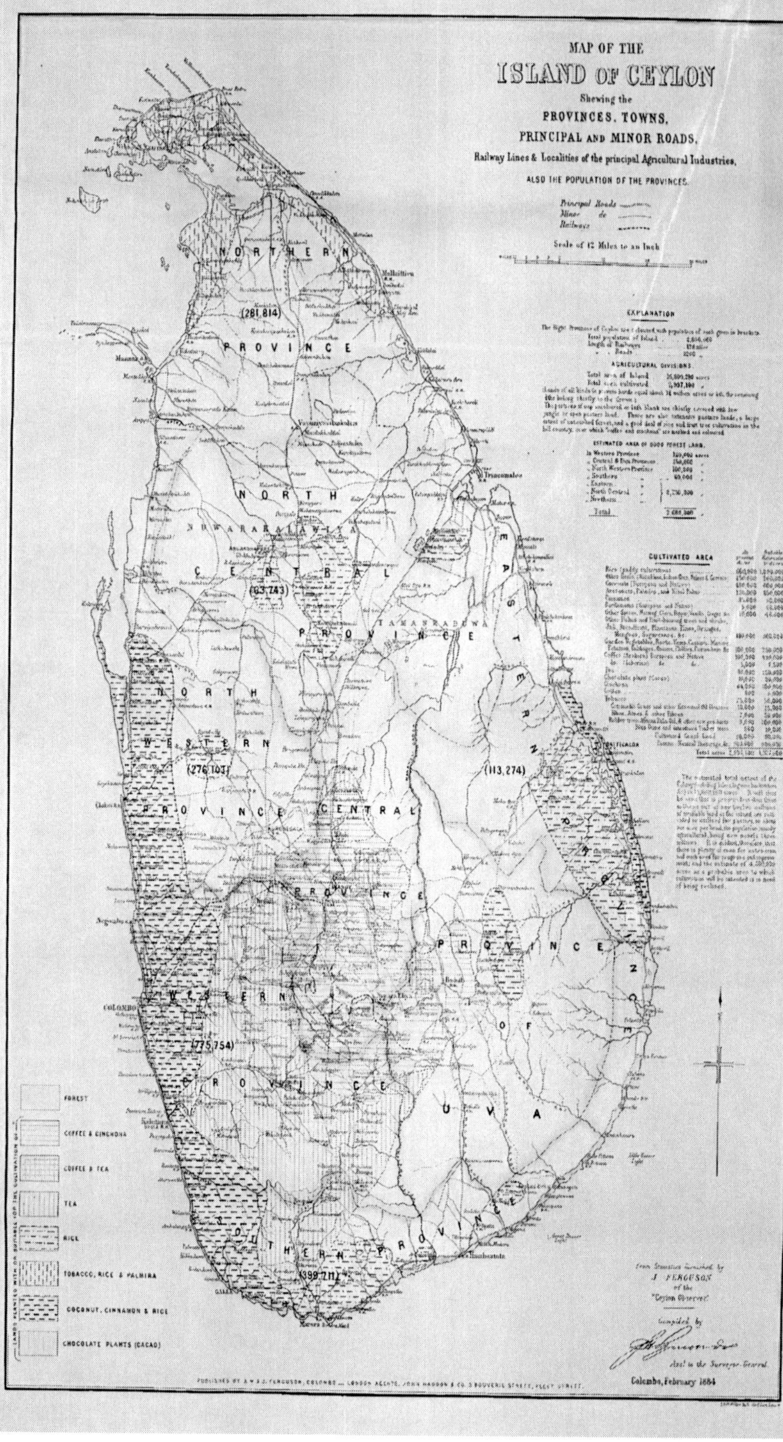
MAP OF THE
ISLAND OF CEYLON
Shewing the
PROVINCES, TOWNS,
PRINCIPAL AND MINOR ROADS,
Railway Lines & Localities of the principal Agricultural Industries,
ALSO THE POPULATION OF THE PROVINCES.
Principal Roads
Minor do
Railways
Scale of 12 Miles to an Inch
EXPLANATION
AGRICULTURAL DIVISIONS
ESTIMATED AREA OF GOOD FOREST LAND.
CULTIVATED AREA
NORTHERN PROVINCE
(281,814)
NORTH CENTRAL PROVINCE
(63,743)
NORTH WESTERN PROVINCE
(276,103)
CENTRAL PROVINCE
EASTERN PROVINCE
(113,274)
PROVINCE OF UVA
WESTERN PROVINCE
(775,754)
SOUTHERN PROVINCE
(399,711)
COLOMBO
Trincomalee
FOREST
COFFEE & CINCHONA
COFFEE & TEA
TEA
RICE
TOBACCO, RICE & PALMIRA
COCONUT, CINNAMON & RICE
CHOCOLATE PLANTS (CACAO)
J. FERGUSON
of the
"Ceylon Observer"
Compiled by
Asst to the Surveyor-General
Colombo, February 1884